AF426807

Makin' A Joyful Noise

Makin' A Joyful Noise

The Lives and Times of the
(*Slightly*) Fabulous
LIMELITERS

Richard S. Ginell

Pine Canyon Publications
Frazier Park, California

Published by Pine Canyon Publications
Frazier Park, California

ISBN: 979-8-218-28668-2

Cover design by Victoria Plumb

Book design and production by Lucky Valley Press
Pacific Grove, CA   www.luckyvalleypress.com

Printed in the USA on acid-free paper

Title page photo: publicity shot, early 1960s

CONTENTS

Acknowledgments

If you were at all conscious in the early 1960s, you couldn't avoid knowing about the Limeliters. They were all over the media; their live albums were staples at suburban parties, their performances and commercials constantly came at you on the tube or over the radio. As a child in Los Angeles, I remember seeing Lou Gottlieb, Alex Hassilev and Glenn Yarbrough on TV, standing in the middle of a new car lot with their instruments in hand, peddling the latest monster machines from Detroit, scurrying about in the madcap manner of a Marx Brothers film. I recall listening to Dodgers baseball games on my transistor radio, where, between innings of Vin Scully's poetic play-by-play, Glenn's sweet tenor would inform us about the wonders of mountain-grown coffee beans as Lou and Alex hummed mellifluously in the background. And I remember the day in 1963 when two friends of my parents, Ted and Claire Littman, brought copies of *The Slightly Fabulous Limeliters* and *Through Children's Eyes* over to our house, igniting an ongoing passion in our family for the Limeliters.

The foundation of this book is constructed from dozens of hours of recorded interviews with Lou, Alex and Glenn over a period spanning from February 1978 all the way to fall 2016. When I first interviewed Lou, Alex, and Glenn in 1978, my original purpose was for a projected magazine profile, one of those where-are-they-now, what-are-they-up-to essays that have become staples of late 20th century journalism. Yet so much fascinating information was piling up from these early interviews that the story could not be contained in a mere magazine article—and my thoughts eventually turned toward writing an entire book on the Limeliters' saga.

My first encounter with Lou on March 29, 1978, came about in a most capricious way. Learning through Alex that Lou was in town visiting his son Tony in Van Nuys, I rang him up, hoping to set an interview time for some future date. But Lou shocked me by spontaneously asking if I could come over in about an hour-and-a-half! In a panic, I hurriedly threw together a bunch of questions and sped out toward Fulton Avenue, where I arrived just in time to catch Lou and Tony striding across the street toward the apartment.

That was some interview. Still immersed in his hippie period, Lou would roll himself a joint about five minutes into our talk, take a few puffs and work himself into a wheezing, almost giggling state before coming down gradually into a placid mood. He was full of exuberant stories about the music business, about the philosophy of open land at Morningstar Ranch, about how he loved to play the piano. To prove one point, he even digressed for a while to lead himself, Tony and me in a three-voice chord that had him rhapsodizing in sheer ecstasy. It would be a jolt to try and reconcile the countercultural Lou of 1978 with an older, more sedate Lou seated before his Macintosh console in 1991, the old fires not quite banked but burning on a cooler flame.

I must thank Lou especially for permitting me to use many incidents and quotes from his unpublished autobiography, *Limelite and Wondersound*, a candid chronicle more believable as a wild novel than an account of a real life.

In addition, Lou supplied me with a find whose story also reads like something out of fiction. Lou was an indefatigable correspondent in the late 1950s; whenever he was away from home, he wrote to his wife Dolly every single day, regaling her with his latest observations, whims, diatribes, and always a professed desire to be back home in EI Cerrito, California.

As Lou recalled it, sometime in early 1991, a friend of his was rummaging through the Richmond city dump, and what did he find but a box of Lou's discarded letters, dating from 1958 to 1961. It seemed that Dolly, who had been separated from Lou since the late '60s, had thrown them out as she prepared to move to Maryland, using her son-in-law's dump truck. Lou's friend quickly dispatched the letters to their author—and when Lou complained to Dolly about her actions, she supposedly replied, "I am no longer curator of the Lou Gottlieb Archive." In any case, the letters revealed a wealth of information—the most valuable being exact dates, observations, and motivations from the period when the Limeliters first teamed up. A biographer could hardly ask for a closer first-hand view of such a critical time, in the absence of similar letters from Alex and Glenn.

In addition, Lou graciously made his computer facilities available to print out early drafts of the text—no small task in pre-Internet times. He also put in many hours of work paginating, editing, and correcting typos and misstatements of facts along the way, acts that spoke volumes for his patience and generosity. And in the last year of his life, we kept up a lively e-mail correspondence that of course was never enough but will always be a treasured memory.

Glenn proved to be a totally relaxed, tireless raconteur, despite his protests that he has "the world's worst memory." Glenn didn't have the easy elegance of speech of Alex, nor the photographic recall and sudden shafts of humor of Lou, but he had the instincts of a born storyteller, the theatrical ability to snare your attention and keep the thread going with his low-key delivery. Once, in Santa Barbara, Glenn and I went at it for over four-and-a-half hours without a break as recollections of his colorful youth tumbled from him like a waterfall.

Alex, too, would plead amnesia at times as we conversed in his handsome house in West Hollywood, blacking out completely on a number of incidents. Yet a little prodding and the right words would often pry some of those memories loose, delivered in a rich, resonant bass voice, always analyzing and placing things in perspective. With ingrained Russian pessimism, he would say that he was always aware that there was a clock ticking on the American experiment, that sooner or later, the clock must run out, that the waves are lapping at the foundation of our culture. Indeed, virtually every talk with Alex, from our first session back in 1978 all the way to the present, would evolve into a thoughtful meditation about the state of the world.

Rein Neggo, Jr., Glenn's manager from 1967 until his untimely death in May 1994, generously supplied me with several obscure recordings, lots of press clippings, a look at some rare videos, and hours of often unblinkingly candid recollections. Marilyn Child brought out some priceless amateur tapes of live performances by Alex, Glenn, Bob Gibson, and herself from Aspen in 1958-59, recordings that shed new light on the evolution of the Limeliters' sound. And ace guitarist Jimmy Stewart was astute enough to tape and preserve a portion of Lou's off-kilter solo comic act from 1965.

Brian Brick, one of the most dedicated Limeliters collectors on the planet, brought a lot of items and information to my attention that otherwise would have slipped right by—and I also ran the discography past him and Rediscover Music's Allan Shaw for anything I might have left out. Theater critic and playwright Rick Talcove was my walking encyclopedia of American musical theater and, also the one who helped me track down Marilyn Child.

Althea Smith, who ran West Knoll Records and put out the Limeliters' homespun annual catalogues, Glenn's former manager Doug Lyon, and Sheryl Ingber and Paula Batson of BMG Music in Hollywood graciously supplied me with review copies of recent recordings. I am indebted to Ramon Sender's The MOST (Morning Star-Open Land) newsletters of July and Autumn 1996 for their illuminating accounts of Lou's last days, drawing upon the voices of Nancy Collins, John "Cable Car" Nelson, Vivian Gotters, Judge Rex Sater, Stephen Fowler, Delia Moon, Pam Read Hanna, Sandi Stein and Rena Morningstar.

Bernadette Moore, the keeper of the holy grail at BMG Music in New York—a.k.a. RCA Victor's astonishingly thorough session files— couldn't have been more helpful and patient as she let me examine every scrap of paper in the file on the Limeliters. Alas, Elektra claimed that its files were thrown out long ago, and Warner Bros. allegedly destroyed its session files that dated from before 1970, so I had to make do with whatever I could glean from the original pressings, various record catalogues and memories.

The facilities of the Research, Powell, and Music Libraries at UCLA, Cal State Northridge's Oviatt Library, the Music Library at UC Berkeley, the Public Libraries of Beverly Hills and Los Angeles, the Brand Library in Glendale, and the Rodgers and Hammerstein Archive of Recorded Sound in the New York Public Library at Lincoln Center were all tremendously useful over the years.

Among record outlets past and present too numerous to mention, Village Music of Mill Valley, Asta's of Oakland, the Magic Flute and Amoeba Music of San Francisco, the Pasadena City College Swap Meet, Moby Disc of Sherman Oaks (where that long-sought copy of the Stax *Reunion* album finally turned up!), Jane Hill's House of Records in Santa Monica, and for my most recent finds, Games Exchange of Grover Beach and Freakbeat Records of Sherman Oaks.

My thanks also for the memories and comments of Chet Atkins, Jack Ballance, Lee Barker, Theodore Bikel, Ron Byers, Marilyn Child, Judy Collins, Robert Commanday, Andy Corwin, Bud Dashiell, Vikki Dougan, Rick Dougherty, Roger Gambill, Kathryn Goria, Anthony Gottlieb, Red Grammer, George Grove, Gladys Hassilev, Tamara Hassilev, Jan Holland, Jac Holzman, Ken Kragen, Miles Kreuger, Doug Lyon, William Malloch, Frank Modica, Jonathan Moore, Peter Nero, Milton Okun, Tom Paxton, Neely Plumb, Dick Rosmini, Henry Roth,

Grover Sales, John Sebastian, Bob Shane, Jimmy Stewart, Mary Travers, Mary Beth Treen, Ellyn Windsor, Anne and Holly Yarbrough and Bill Zorn.

Of course, I must thank Ted and Claire Littman, who were responsible for first putting the Limeliters in my ears, as well as Lewis Beale, Jim Benson, Ken Boros, Susan Brodie, Pamela Bryan, Gloria Cheng, Bruce Cook; Jim Farber; Harvey, Pearl, Lee, Janice, Sarah, Frona and Stanley DeCovnick; Adam, Brian, Margot, Stephan, and Wendy Sue Ginell; Joseph and Debbie Gold; Kevin Henry, Sarah House-Peters, Lisa Keefe, William and Joan Kraft, Amy Krupski, Mike Lang, Erika Ledin, Peter Levinson, Mark Leviton, Heidi Mauricio, Deborah Pearl, Bonnie Perkinson, Donna Perlmutter, Elizabeth Plumb Gessel, Rodney Punt, Joe and Bonnie Rosenblatt, Elise Rotchford, Buddy Sampson, Rick Schultz, Rick Sherwood, Salli Stevenson, Mark Swed, Adrienne Tien, Brooke Vigoda, Leslie Westbrook, Denise Willson, Scott and Dory Yanow, and Chloé Ziegler for their unflagging support.

Also, here's to my parents Dr. William and Sally Ginell for their everlasting love and making EVERYTHING possible. A very big thanks to my talented niece, Victoria Plumb, who made the sprightly designs of the front and back covers. Thanks are also due to my brother Cary Ginell, who gave me access to MCA's Decca files, his videotape of Lou's funeral, his own extensive record and book library, and knowledge of American country and folk music—and my sister Carolyn Plumb, who, as co-founder of Marshall Plumb Research Associates of Burbank, was able to give me both moral support and research help.

And a special heartfelt thanks to the wonderful Lisa Ledin, who first heard about this book on the day we met in 1993 and never gave up hope that it would someday be published, ultimately connecting me with David and Ginna Gordon of Lucky Valley Press. I couldn'-a done it without-cha!

Richard S. Ginell
Frazier Park, California

Introduction

A small, sorrowful throng gathered at the end of a cul-de-sac on a hillside overlooking Interstate 80 at the Rolling Hills Cemetery in Richmond, California Sunday July 14, 1996. It was a stunning afternoon—warm and breezy, with cotton candy fog shrouding the Marin County mountains way in the background across San Francisco Bay. Too stunning for a funeral, one thought.

Lou Gottlieb, the co-founder, comic laureate, and bass player of the Limeliters, the mastermind of their sound and the embodiment of their zany, intellectual spirit, had passed away suddenly three days before—with only the briefest of warnings to his family and friends. No one had any inkling he was mortally ill. His eldest son Tony—an artist manager and music industry figure in Nashville—said Lou told him only the previous Monday that he had been visited by an "angel of death" and that he was ready to move on, a message Tony pooh-poohed at the time. A frightening bit of email—Lou's favorite means of communication in his last years—described his symptoms in some detail and indicated that he was passively accepting his fate. But the end came so suddenly thereafter, especially in the light of the fact that he was still performing with the Limeliters as recently as July 1, it caught even his closest friends off guard. He was 72 years old, and a young 72 at that—physically and most of all, in mental outlook.

Lou's daughter, Judith Spector, up from Berkeley just a few miles to the south, introduced her brothers Tony and Bill from a portable wooden podium in the middle of the cul-de-sac. Over to the side near a grassy hill, stood Lou's founding partners in the Limeliters, Alex Hassilev—tall, dapper in a gray suit, rocking back and forth—and Glenn Yarbrough, portly, as always, clad in a typically casual denim jacket, composed, enigmatic.

Alex spoke first, offering a funny, touching, unsentimental memoir of his friend, partner and debating opponent of 37 years, reminiscing about the day at the Cosmo Alley in Hollywood when he and Glenn first met this professorial character with a big briefcase and high-flown vocabulary. "He was a man truly unique on this planet," Alex said in his rich, resonant way, "a truly sui generis individual, who could go from the heights to the depths, to every place in between in a single sentence—and frequently did—and kept us all in stitches...I was in a constant state of exasperation with Lou, constant, but you know why? I was exasperated with Lou because he was such a great person, with such great potential knowledge and abilities, so whenever he went off into his Lou-like strangeness, my desire was to say, Lou, no, no, stick to that high road!'"

And then the final ironic thrust. "He chose my birthday to expire, making sure I will never forget him. He played his last joke on me. I will miss him forever."

Glenn—who had left the Limeliters thrice, in 1963, 1977 and 1981, but continued to tour on the bill with them occasionally—remembered in his casually stage-savvy way that Lou had asked him to sing "Danny Boy" the second day they knew each other. With the congenital stubbornness that would mark and perhaps adversely affect his entire career, Glenn refused, saying he didn't want to sing anything that people knew. But more than two decades later, he relented, and he would do it again on this day, unaccompanied, in that unique, fluttering tenor Lou so loved.

Ed Labowitz—an attorney, folksinger and fan who had been donating legal services to the group for many years—then recited Kaddish, for throughout Lou's sometimes bizarre religious dabblings all over the spectrum, he always considered himself a Jew. And finally, the one-time-only trio of Alex, Glenn and Rick Dougherty, the third replacement for Glenn in the Limeliters' long history, sang the late Harry Chapin's "Circles" at a funereal tempo as aircraft streaked overhead. By now, there wasn't a dry eye in the audience. Some of us thought we were hearing the last performance of the Limeliters (not true, as events later proved), the poignant lyrics of meeting again someday hitting painfully home.

Standing on that hillside, on that splendid yet sad day, one's memories raced back to an idyllic afternoon in December of 1988 at Glenn's rented home in Santa Barbara. There, in a rare '80s get-together, the unique, erudite, incompatible personalities of Lou, Alex and Glenn fused together with an exciting explosion. In almost choreographed order, the reminiscences, mutual teasing, jokes, observations about life and the world, and the sheer joy of being together came rushing out in a spontaneous free-associative manner, with one anecdote by a Limeliter leading to another by the next. The eavesdropping author would float a leading question about the origins of the group, and then he could sit back and just take in a non-stop, always quotable oral history without having to say a word for as much as half an hour. One could also think back to the days when they were young and ambitious in the go-go 1960s, when these personalities and distinctly different voices must have clashed and blended with even greater force. It was precisely this clash that gave the Limeliters' sound its profile and power, two large, loud, weighty bass-baritones topped by a sweet fluttery tenor of matchless flexibility. It was not a homogenous blend like, say, that of the Kingston Trio—whose sound through several personnel changes had always been defined by the whiskey baritone of Bob Shane, or the relatively bland sound of the Brothers Four. One could feel the tension between the three voices on their records, and that clash—which Lou the musicologist inimitably called *spaltklang*—gave the Limeliters' sound an edge and a virility that none of the competition could ever even hope to match. Singer/songwriter Paul Simon once told Lou, "Art (Garfunkel) and I have been singing with each other since we were fourteen years old. The Limeliters sing against each other."

Many remember a time when folk music captured the imagination of a nation. It was a particularly hopeful period in our national history—when we were secure in our military might, with the McCarthy witch hunts behind us, where long-repressed injustices such as racial segregation were being addressed at last and the economy was going gangbusters. Young Americans and many of their elders were discovering a treasure trove of old and not-so-old music that lay right underneath their noses for too long.

The folk revival lasted roughly from October of 1958, when an obscure cut from the first Kingston Trio album, "Tom Dooley," rose steadily, implausibly, to the No. 1 position on the pop charts to November 1963, when President Kennedy was assassinated. Of course, there were important signposts prior to and after these dates, but this was the peak period, the boom years when America's folk music had become popular music. The existence of the original Limeliters fits compactly into these years, with a few months to spare on either end. And the Limeliters were arguably the folk revival's most vibrant group, revivifying the old songs and polishing new ones to a degree perhaps unmatched by any rivals before or since.

There were many Kingston Trio imitators in the late '50s and early 60s. Yet although the Limeliters themselves began life as imitators—an extension of the Weavers and Lou's previous group, the Gateway Singers—no one could imitate them in turn. While they had a following, they left no school, no literal disciples, although rock groups like the Association have acknowledged the influence of their harmonies. They were one of a kind, and Alex believes that may have been a compelling reason why they were not bigger than they were. "The Limeliters were a unique musical experience," Alex says. "They were not everybody's cup of tea, but they were very much what they were, very clearly defined as opposed to the Kingston Trio, which became enough of a mass phenomenon so that that image could be re-created successfully. The Limeliters never were like that."

There is another reason, too. The Limeliters never made a secret of the fact that they were intellectuals, eggheads if you will, and America has habitually distrusted eggheads. Alex feels there was always an invisible sense of distance between the group and their audience—an intellectual, not physical, distance—whereas the Kingston Trio played Everyman, frat boys whom you could have a beer with and sing along with on a more-or-less equal basis. Lou's ten-dollar words might have seemed hysterically funny to those in the know, but they would fly straight over the heads of many who did not have a university education or a daily newspaper habit. As *Time Magazine* put it so accurately in 1961, "if the Kingston Trio are the undergraduates of big-time U.S. folk singing, the Limeliters are the faculty..."

Yet the Limeliters' recordings also captured and transcended their time. Listen to those RCA Victor albums of the early '60s; most of them radiate a joyous, lusty vitality that cuts cleanly through the years and fashions. Just as the Beatles captured the ambience of the youth culture of the mid-late 1960s, the Limeliters' records evoked the hope, optimism and energy of the early 1960s, the Kennedy era, when anything seemed possible before the angst of the decade set in. What makes the Limeliters' saga so fascinating is not only their rise to the highest ranks of the folk pack, but also the buttoned-down '50s atmosphere from which they emerged, and the way the three Limeliters immersed themselves into the unbuttoned '60s and '70s after their first breakup. Lou's early jazz and academic leanings and tumultuous adventures on his Morningstar Ranch in the hippie era, Alex's experiences as a record producer and actor, and Glenn's lucrative solo flights down the middle of the road and an irrepressible desire to be a sailor cover a lot of musical and sociological territory. Obviously, there is far more to the Limeliters' story than just folk music.

And there are other themes that run through their saga—the ease in which they struck it rich, their willingness to walk away at the height of their fame (indeed, Glenn did so twice, with the group and on his own), the struggles they have had to try and win it back. In turning their backs on their revenue machine to find their own heads, the Limeliters put into practice the true anti-materialistic spirit of the '60s—and as a result, the '80s and '90s were not as kind to them.

Down the hillside just a little way the funeral party went until it arrived at the pinewood casket which contained Lou's remains. Right next to the gravesite was that of his father, Abraham Gottlieb, an emigre from the Old Country who lived to see the Limeliters' success. As the casket was lowered into the earth, Alex, until now a monument of stoicism, finally broke down as he murmured something in Russian to his departed partner. Glenn observed the heartbreaking scene from a distance, lost in thought.

All three men, oddly enough, were only children—and they were perhaps the only brothers to each other they ever had. Now one of them was gone and as one observer stared at the beautiful distant hills of Marin, he could almost hear the playful strains of "Jehosophat" from a treasured old LP, the words of Lou and longtime friend Gene Raskin never so pertinent and poignant.

"We'll go on singing day and night
We'll sing until we die
And after that, Jehosophat,
We'll sing up in the sky!"

A recording of a live performance of the
Gateway Singers at Stanford University in 1957,
discovered and finally issued in 2009.
*L to R - Travis Edmonson, Elmerlee Thomas,
Lou Gottlieb, Jerry Walter.*

Chapter One

Only a twisted novelist could have invented a character like Lou Gottlieb, for his life story was loaded with wildly swerving changes and zigzags. Unquenchable curiosity marked Lou's life from the start, and it led him into some very curious situations and lifestyles.

"Lou has always had this restless, searching mind," said his longtime friend, author and lecturer Grover Sales. "I talked to Dolly (Lou's wife) one time about it. He was going through a period where he was reading everything of Herman Melville and I said, 'God, he's really gone on this.' And she said, 'That's nothing. You should have seen him when he got hung up on Marx!'

"He will go through periods where he will get hooked on a language, a subject, or a certain author or a certain musician. Whenever I'm with Lou, I always ask him, who are you digging and who are you reading?"

In his long lifetime, Lou dove headfirst, recklessly, uninhibitedly into almost every progressive movement or trend of mid-and-late 20th century America. And along the way, with all the ups and downs, one senses that he must have had a great time.

Louis Edward Gottlieb was born on Oct. 10, 1923, in Los Angeles, the son of a Latvian Jewish immigrant Abraham Gottlieb and Rosa Giusti de Grandi, born of Italian Catholic parents in Guatemala City. Lou liked to say that he was the "sole issue of Abie's Italian Rose ... the hyphen in the phrase Judeo-Christian."

Tellingly, in light of the later adventures of his son, Abraham Gottlieb was a radical activist and a lifelong Zionist who knew

Bukharin (a leading Bolshevik figure and eventual victim of Stalin) when he was a student in Riga. According to Lou, his father was implicated in political activities against Czar Nicholas II in 1903 and had to flee the country. He spoke Latvian, Russian and could understand Yiddish, but he considered German—the then-common linguistic currency of Riga's cultural life—his native language. After visiting Palestine for a brief period, Abraham Gottlieb carne to the United States via Ellis Island in 1904. Originally intending to study mechanical engineering in Chicago, he instead found himself infatuated with New York City, then well into the process of absorbing the great turn-of-the-century wave of Slavic immigrants. Gottlieb studied medicine at Columbia University, working in a safety-deposit-box factory to support himself. When he got his degree, he moved to San Francisco where he started a medical practice that continued for nearly 60 years (specialty, orthopedic surgery).

Lou's mother had, if anything, an even more fascinating background. Rosa's mother, Maddalena Grandi de Giusti (nicknamed "Nonina"), born in Italy, was one of the first female college graduates in Europe and taught Italian to the sister and mother of Kaiser Wilhelm II of Germany. Nevertheless, as a woman of her time, Maddalena was eventually convinced that marriage and subsequent motherhood were more important than career—and she set sail for Buenos Aires in search of an arranged match. On board, she met Nicola Giusti, a deserter from the Italian artillery. They married in Buenos Aires, and the already pregnant Maddalena rode across the Andes on muleback rather than sail with Nicola around Cape Horn.

Nicola and Maddalena reunited in Lima, and eventually settled in Guatemala, where they produced six daughters, of which Rosa was the fourth. Nicola changed his name to Francisco "Don Pancho" Marcucci, eventually owned and managed seven sugar plantations—and with a libido unrestrained by marriage, proceeded to father anywhere from 19 to 35 children by other Guatemalan ladies. The knowledge of that was enough to drive Maddalena and her surviving four daughters to San Francisco in the early 1910s.

Lou estimated that his father met his mother sometime around 1915 and that they were married in Santa Cruz in 1920, moving to Los Angeles soon thereafter. He recalled that his first childhood memory occurred at the age of three when at a dinner party he was asked to tell the guests to "come to the table." Not having spoken any intelligible words prior to that, his words, "Turn to de taybo," were greeted with inevitably joyous approval by all in the room. "I am convinced the overwhelmingly favorable reaction evoked by my theatrical debut line was the cause of my becoming a performer," Lou wrote in his unpublished autobiography, adding with tongue locked in cheek, "I still enjoy stepping into a proscenium, so I've tried to upgrade the act perceptibly."

When Lou was four, his father invested his life's savings in a six-acre patch of chapparal-covered land in La Crescenta, a Los Angeles suburb northwest of Pasadena, with the intention of building the Sun Ray Sanitarium for crippled children. The land was covered with trees for a young, growing boy to climb, along with three houses and two stables that were the headquarters of the Flying A Riding Academy. The Academy was run by one Jitney Wright, a stunt man and rodeo performer who became an early hero for Lou and much later, the subject of an autobiographical song, "Jitney Wright."

At about the age of five, Lou's mother started him on piano lessons, requiring that he practice at least a half-hour daily. That was easier said than done, given the distractions of the Sanitarium with its riding academy, and the nearby Verdugo Woodlands swimming pool. However, the musical bug had paid a fruitful visit, for Lou was fascinated by a Victrola that his parents owned. He would listen over and over to one-sided, dark red-labeled Victrola operatic 78s, even singing along as best he could.

The stock market crash of 1929 ultimately had a devastating effect upon the Gottliebs. Abraham was spending less and less time at home, and in 1931, Rosa divorced him. Heavily invested in the stock market—he once lost $20,000 in a single day—Abraham eventually could not keep up payments on the six-acre property, and it was repossessed in 1931. When Rosa was served the eviction notice, she moved herself and Lou to Sparr Heights and began to teach Spanish evenings at Glendale High School while attending classes in downtown Los Angeles for a teaching credential.

Lou, his mother, grandmother (who died in 1935), Aunt Justine and her two sons ended up renting a house on 213 West Chestnut St. in Glendale in May 1933. Lou's father would come to pick him up every Sunday, when they would check in on some of his dad's patients, catch a movie downtown, visit friends, or just rent a boat and go sailing in Echo Park or Westlake (now MacArthur) Park. He would just honk the horn on his car, never saying a word to his ex-wife, and at the end of the day, would give Lou the weekly amount of ten dollars child support to give to his mom. All things considered, Lou insisted that he had a happy, almost idyllic childhood, obviously loved and encouraged by both parents, receiving attention as befitting an only child.

Lou's piano lessons, discontinued for a while after leaving La Crescenta, resumed in Glendale under the tutelage of one of his mother's Spanish students, James Drummond Reager, a pupil of Theodor Leschetizky in Vienna. By the time Lou started going to Theodore Roosevelt Junior High School, he first tasted the "rush" of performing successfully before a live audience. He started studying arranging in private with Virgil Ray, picked up the oboe and clarinet, and inspired by some Red Nichols 78s, formed a school jazz band that played all of two tunes—"St. Louis Blues" and "Milenberg Joys."

The Swing Era was starting to roll around this time; indeed, historians agree that it started not too far from Theodore Roosevelt Junior High School at the Palomar Ballroom at Third St. and Vermont Ave. where on Aug. 21, 1935, the struggling Benny Goodman orchestra suddenly set off pandemonium among the young. Over the objections of his mother, Lou and his friends would take the Pacific Electric Railway's Big Red Cars down to the Palomar in 1937, escorted by his Aunt Justine. When Benny played the Palomar, as many as 5,000 kids would crowd into the ballroom. "If anyone had fainted," Lou remembered, "they would have never hit the ground; that's how closely packed was the crowd standing in front of the bandstand." Lou especially loved Teddy Wilson's fleet, lithe, swinging solos, and Harry James' commanding trumpet. He would also troop down to the Palomar to see the Glen Gray Casa Loma Orchestra, Artie Shaw's innovative and conventional big bands, Red Norvo and his wife Mildred Bailey, Tommy and Jimmy Dorsey, Charlie Barnet.

The teenaged Lou would go to a ballroom downtown to see the unstoppably swinging Count Basie band, in a date sponsored by the Negro Musicians Union, Local 767 after the Palomar burned down in 1939. He discovered the intricately orchestrated riches of the Duke Ellington Orchestra in 1940 at the staid old Glendale Civic Auditorium, mesmerized by the Duke's charisma and the seemingly infinite number of ways he could manipulate the colors of a big band. He would buy jazz 78s from a jukebox-servicing firm that would sell discs worn out on one side (jukeboxes could only play one side of a record then) for a nickel apiece.

Lou was a hopelessly infatuated jazzer—way, way before Woody Guthrie, John Jacob Niles and Leadbelly became a part of his life. At the same time, Lou's mother would take him downtown to see the pianistic icons of the time—Sergei Rachmaninoff, Josef Hofmann, Ignace Jan Paderewski. All were not only great pianists, they were also great showmen, knowing how to please a crowd and create unique musical and personal profiles. Obviously, Lou's mom had the classical concert stage in mind for her only son—and to his dying day, he never quite abandoned the dream himself.

Once Lou started attending Glendale High School, he picked up the string bass, the instrument that would be his main axe and prop when he rose to fame. He never took a lesson on it; he just picked up on the instrument upon the encouragement from the school's band teacher, Harry Anderson.

Other aspects of Lou's adolescent growth—physical, hormonal, and otherwise—were taking place as well. He would eventually tower over his five-foot-seven father and, having skipped a couple of grades at school, he found himself behind his classmates in physical coordination. He was never one for sports, and he had what was to become a lifelong aversion to physical confrontations. No such aversion applied to women, however—and at the age of seventeen, admittedly "rarin' to go," he experienced his "first time" in a Tijuana whorehouse, an event later celebrated in the song "Hotel del Rio."

Just before he turned seventeen, in the fall of 1940, Lou enrolled at UCLA as a music major. Only the weekend before, in search of cheap thrills, Lou and a friend decided to visit San Bernardino's red-light district in a car borrowed from a mechanic. They returned to Hollywood, caught the King Cole Trio's last set at the Radio Room, and were headed home when they became involved in a fender-bender. Though the other driver did not press charges, Lou did not have a driver's license, nor was the car registered, so he was taken to Juvenile Hall and thrown in jail for a night. His mom's lawyer got him out quickly enough, and Lou was sentenced to four weeks of traffic school, but the experience of being incarcerated was seared into his memory.

While enduring the often stultifying theory classes at UCLA, Lou formed a jazz quartet called the Mad Bachelors (named after a horse at

Santa Anita). After Lou's freshman year was over, they would ride 120 miles south to San Diego to play matinees at the Show Boat Cafe. In the spring of 1942, Lou joined a combo headed by Jack Ross which eventually settled into the Casa Manana in Culver City. During one memorable stretch, the group opened for the inimitable Louis Armstrong and the great trombonist Jack Teagarden. At times, Pops' drummer Big Sid Catlett would sit in with the Jack Ross group's last number, sending Lou into musical orbit.

Four decades later, Lou could still marvel about a historic juxtaposition in his life then—studying counterpoint at UCLA with none other than the Viennese classical giant Arnold Schoenberg by day; watching Satchmo by night. Certainly, Lou's classes with Schoenberg made a tremendous impression upon the future Ph.D. candidate in musicology although he wasn't sure why, for Lou never took to Schoenberg's music and the old European lion was a stickler to the traditional rules of theory in the classroom. Nevertheless, Lou felt he was in the presence of a great man, and he wished that he had been more able to take advantage of what Schoenberg had to offer.

With Louis Armstrong, there wasn't any doubt, for Lou was both fascinated by the uninhibited trumpeter's physical presence and his triumphantly joyous music. Indeed, Lou thought his two great teachers had some physical characteristics in common—short stature, a tendency to pace "in a splay-footed stride with both hands clasped behind their back."

Once, Lou mustered up the courage to tell Armstrong, "One of my teachers at school reminds me a lot of you, Pops."

"What's his name?" queried Satch.

"Arnold Schoenberg."

"Must be a 'fay cat. No colored man's got that name."

If there was any other sign of mutual awareness between these two towering revolutionaries of classical and jazz music, history has not recorded it.

In the summer of 1942, Lou got a job playing piano at the Gay Nineties Club in San Diego in the sextet of Lyle Griffin, from whose prolific romantic exploits Lou learned the most. That fall, back at UCLA, Lou decided to spin off on his own as the leader of a piano-guitar-drums trio, (occasionally doubling on vibraphone), playing at a tough country-western joint called Lyle's Frontier on Pico Blvd.

However, Lou's days as a civilian/student/musician were about to be numbered. The Japanese had attacked Pearl Harbor the previous December, and the draft beckoned ominously, but Lou had heard some tales from a musician friend named Hal Smith who had volunteered to get into Fort Ord's Army band, a life considerably less taxing than basic training. Having heard that the bandleader at Fort Ord would be at the Musicians Union, Local 47, building in downtown L.A. for auditions, Lou felt that would be the easiest way to fulfill his military commitment.

Lou passed the audition, was inducted March 26, 1943—yet after a 24-day furlough, surprise!, Lou had to go to Camp Roberts near Paso Robles for 13 weeks of basic training, despite "assurances" that his transfer to Fort Ord was imminent. As it turned out, it was a partially lucky break, for eight weeks into Lou's basic training, the Fort Ord band was sent to the remote Aleutian Islands off Alaska. But it also meant that Lou was being trained for a possible one-way ticket to combat in the South Pacific.

Officers' Training was a possible alternate route, but Lou couldn't swing that deal. Then he tried to transfer from the infantry to the Air Corps band—no mean task—citing in his application the tall tale that he had arranged music for the Jack Teagarden and Louis Armstrong bands! The fabrication worked—and soon after basic training was over, Lou found himself on a troop train headed for the Army War College in Washington D.C. There for ten months, Lou would play six nights a week in a dance band at a large USO nightclub at Tenth and K Streets.

It was certainly a good time to be a young male with a large libido, for according to Lou, the ratio of women to men in wartime Washington was something like nine to one. At one gig, where Lou, his trumpeter Jimmy Salko and an 18-year-old drummer destined for glory named Louie Bellson were playing a trio date, Lou guessed that there were about 400 women on the dance floor and only three men. Midway through his hitch there, Lou and Salko were able to rent a room downtown that had twin beds, whereupon in Lou's inimitable words, "our production increased geometrically."

But Lou's Washington idyll ended when orders came down from on high that no men fit for combat duty could remain at the War College— and he was transferred to the Headquarters of the Second Army in Memphis. Lou would have probably been part of the expeditionary force poised to invade Japan were it not for the events of August 6, 1945.

That was, of course, the dropping of the atomic bomb on Hiroshima, followed a few days later by the second bomb on Nagasaki, which made invasion plans a moot point. Lou remembered how thrilled he was when the bombs were dropped, knowing that he was going to be headed home shortly. The real awful impact of those events, though, would burrow deeply into Lou's consciousness only in later years.

Back in Los Angeles, having been discharged February 10, 1946, Lou moved into the two-bedroom Miracle Mile apartment of his father, who had remarried during the war {his mother died of cancer while he was in the service). Lou's new stepmother was Miriam Solomon, a Jewish social worker from whom Lou learned his first smatterings of Jewish traditions. The young veteran promptly formed a new jazz combo, the Lou Edwards Trio, patterned distinctly after the King Cole Trio (then near the zenith of its fame}. Lou would also work as a solo act at various nightclubs and bars in the Los Angeles area, doing his impression of his beloved Nat Cole, playing the boogie-woogie which had become a national rage before the war. He loved playing the piano almost more than anything else in the world, and he loved to entertain people, to make them forget their problems.

But Lou was still torn between showbiz and academia, for he decided to use the G.I. Bill to re-enter UCLA and resume work on a Bachelor of Arts degree that summer. Having thus recharged his academic batteries, he began what was to be a 12-year odyssey through the UC system—a length of time one is sure that he didn't quite anticipate. And for our purposes, the education of Lou Gottlieb, future folksinger, began in this summer at this tree-shaded campus in Westwood.

One must recall the context of folk music in mid-century America to see what an appeal it must have had for Lou, who throughout his life found himself hopelessly attracted to the passions and currents of his times. Folk music had not been part of the commercial mainstream of American music in the first half of the 20th century. It wasn't despised per se; it was simply ignored, thought to be good only for summer camp singalongs, collected only by a handful of visionary archivists who scoured the backwoods and backwaters of America armed with primitive recording machines.

Right under our upturned noses was a wealth of traditional music, with roots going back to the British Isles, grounded deeply in Appalachia, the South, the Pacific Northwest, and other pockets on the continent. Collectors such as Cecil Sharp, Lamar Bascom Lunsford, Robert W. Gordon, John Jacob Niles, and most significantly, John A. Lomax diligently collected the songs and published them, but not until the 1930s did their labors began to bear public fruit.

One can hand it to the Depression for bringing out some of the huge potential of folk music. The hard political Left, then probably at its peak of influence in a country desperate for solutions, seized folk music as an authentic expression of the voice of that great abstract concept, The People. Songs about problems and issues to which average working stiffs could relate. Melodies handed down in the oral tradition (later to be a litmus test of much controversy), retrofitted with lyrics that blamed capitalist excesses for the miseries of the times. Songs that could inspire, uplift, and even educate, but were still simple enough so that anyone could sing them—the ideal of the collective society.

The Depression was one catalyst. A movement, the Left—ranging from the unions to the Socialist and Communist parties—was another. A third catalyst was the need for prophets, or folk heroes if you will. Modern revisionists who say that heroes don't count, that events are driven entirely by historical currents, are way off the mark. Folk music, like political issues, wouldn't have broken out in the open in such a dynamic way in America without strong personalities channeling and defining those currents. And the heroes began to emerge.

Woody Guthrie. Okie, drifter, free spirit, technically only a mediocre musician but equipped with a magnetic personality and astonishing gift for imagery, emerged first as an early radio personality in Los Angeles. He freely plundered the melodies of folk songs for his own purposes, but his lyrics were entirely original—chronicles of optimism, despair, the romance of being on the road, and stubborn defiance against insensitive authority. He was incredibly prolific, writing something like 1,000 songs in a 20-year span before the rare inherited disease Huntington's chorea struck him down. He single-handedly gave folk music a new repertoire, and that legacy was considered exempt from future scuffles over what was folk music and what was not. He also became a fearless role model for countless young rebels, an image that often did not jibe with the difficult, irresponsible Woody whom his friends and families knew.

Huddie Ledbetter, better known to the world as Leadbelly. A Black Louisiana farmer's son with arms of steel, a reputation as a violent man and tireless womanizer, spending a good deal of his adult life in some of the toughest, most racist penitentiaries in the South. He was a human vacuum cleaner as far as music was concerned, sucking up countless folk songs, work songs, ballads, spirituals, blues, dance tunes and reels and spilling them out with a voice of primeval power and a gutsy twelve-string guitar style. John Lomax was responsible for bringing him to the attention of the outside world—and although Leadbelly never completely adapted to the ways of that world, he mellowed somewhat, and a good deal of his legacy was recorded and circulated around. He was the strongest human link between Black folk music—which on another level was busy evolving into jazz and rhythm-and-blues—and the emerging, largely white folk movement. He also stood as a symbol, an indomitable survivor of racial oppression for whites, though some hip Blacks considered him a mere relic of the past.

Pete Seeger. The son of a noted musicologist and composer, a banjo and guitar virtuoso, a tireless and truly fearless fighter for the common man, unions, leftist philosophy, and the vast trove of American folk music. He dropped out of Harvard after two years, picking up his satchel of folk music through his father and the Lomax recordings at the Library of Congress. Eventually he hooked up with Woody Guthrie, roaming the country playing at union rallies and political meetings. If Guthrie created a repertoire and a role model, the disciplined Seeger was the one who really spread the gospel around, making some important original musical contributions of his own, teaching innumerable non-conformists to play fretted instruments and to sing out and speak their minds.

There were other important figures, of course, who would emerge before World War II. There was Burl Ives, probably the most visible folksinger to the general public but whose reputation has been downgraded by historians partly, one suspects, for reasons having more to do with envy and politics than music. One also cannot overlook Josh White and Big Bill Broonzy, two more significant links between the races who blurred categories beyond easy classification, or Guthrie sidekick Cisco Houston, or the mesmerizing, ghostly falsetto of John Jacob Niles.

But Guthrie, Leadbelly and Seeger were the ones who captured the imagination of the Left with the greatest impact. Ultimately in 1941, Seeger, Guthrie, a sardonic son of a preacher from Arkansas named Lee Hays, and Millard Lampell would crystallize into the Almanac Singers, the first important folk group. They sang peace songs that would be quickly taken out of circulation when the United States entered World War II; they made a 78 RPM set of union songs, "Talking Union," that proved more enduring.

Today, they seem like giants, but hindsight being as deceiving as it is, even these powerful personalities created barely a ripple of attention in the middle of the Big Band era. Guthrie and Leadbelly would sporadically record for major labels such as Victor or ARC but their records hardly sold at all and were swiftly withdrawn. As far as much of America was concerned, they didn't exist.

They did, however, exist in the minds of some of the idealistic, intelligent youth who were populating the nation's campuses at the end of the war. One must remember that in those days before Winston Churchill's Iron Curtain speech, Russia was still considered our ally, partners in victory who "broke the backses of the Axis." The unspeakably venal Josef Stalin was still Uncle Joe, the leader of the world's socialist movement, his murderous excesses yet to be thoroughly exposed. The Marxist ideal of how life should be had declined in popularity since its peak in the '30s, thanks to the New Deal and postwar prosperity. But it was still alive, and activists like Seeger tried to keep it that way by forming short-lived but influential organizations like People's Songs—the ultimate collectivist publishing company that went so far as to issue songs without the composers' names on them. Running against the steadily inflating Cold War hysteria, it was a tough order.

Lou himself had never really been interested in politics before, save for echoing his father's hero-worship of President Roosevelt. But when he moved into his father's apartment, he started reading his stepmother's issues of Daily People's World, the local Communist Party newspaper. Ever the artist, Lou was particularly interested in the cultural aspects of the movement at first, and he would read about the beginnings and growing pains of Seeger's People's Songs project. And among the columns whom Lou stumbled upon were those of none other than Woody Guthrie.

On campus, more discoveries confronted Lou. "The first folksongs I ever heard in my life were right here—at UCLA," Lou said when he was invited to speak at a class in his alma mater's Folklore and Mythology Department in 1983. "I learned a few songs from my mother, but they were in Spanish. The first folksinger I ever heard was right over here in the building where the music department used to be. There was a big room downstairs, Room 101, {where} the famous ballad scholar Dr. Sigurd Hustvedt brought a guy named John Jacob Niles. John Jacob Niles was a literate musician—meaning he could read and write music—and he came from Kentucky. He had a fantastic falsetto; he could sing way up high, and he used to play the dulcimer some. And he was kind of a satanic-looking guy, real skinny—and boy, he really impressed me.

"When he first came out, he sang some songs for the children in the audience and made a remark that was frequently made in folklore studies, 'If the children don't like the folksongs, that'll sure stop their existence.' And then he sang 'Edward' {also known as "Gallows Pole," or in a Gottlieb arrangement for the Limeliters, "Hangman, Hangman"}. That made a tremendous impression on me.

"And, then, about two weeks later, Hustvedt brought Bascom Lamar Lunsford, and he had some kids and taught them a few hoedowns and he sang and played. He struck me as being a guy who comes from a university alright, but he's not one of the real scholars. He was more of a folksinger than John Jacob Niles.

"About that same time, around August of 1946, they had a People's World fundraising party—and guess who appeared? Pete Seeger and Josh White. This was a little before the time they were starting to build the Henry Wallace campaign. At that time, there were a lot of kids on this campus who were participating in Students for Wallace. Hanging out with these people was when I first got interested in folk song. They used to have one called 'The Donkey and the Elephant/It's the same old merry-go-round'—the idea of a third party and so on.

"If there's any such thing as a folk song, I would say it's a piece of music that tries to weld together the consciousness of a group for some kind of common purpose which can be considered to be good... so I would say that the context of folk song in my own life started out being a political context because I always used to think of myself as a left-winger."

But Lou's active musical life continued on its merrily eclectic way—studying the European classical tradition at UCLA, grooving on the new bebop idiom in jazz and getting into that scene. He worked in the Western swing band of Art Shackelford and may have made his debut on records with Shackelford in "Guitar Stomp" and "Under the Double Eagle"—on vibes! He wrote arrangements for Freddie Slack's big band (including a piece with the zany title "Viva La Saliva"), some of which were recorded by Capitol. And the Lou Edwards Trio played on.

Yet Lou's political interests were growing. And one of the main reasons why they were growing was a young woman named Zelma "Dolly" Hartz.

Never underestimate the power of testosterone in determining one's future direction. That certainly applied to Lou Gottlieb, who was introduced to his future wife Dolly after a late afternoon meeting sometime in 1947 of the American Youth for Democracy, a short-lived successor to the Young Communist League. Dolly was a member of the Communist Party then, heavily involved in the AYD and the Students For Wallace campaign. Still into his post-Memphis hipster phase, Lou nearly blew it with Dolly on their first date by lapsing into hipster jargon, to which Lou recalled Dolly took offense, thinking that her new suitor was patronizing and/or ridiculing Blacks. Lou quickly dropped that act, and the relationship promptly blossomed. They went to numerous political rallies together, and Lou started studying Marxist/Leninist theory to cement their bond even more tightly. He took a sociology class to "be with Dolly one more hour per day;" his circle of friends widened to include more members of the Party.

At the same time, Lou was completing his senior year at UCLA, due to graduate in the spring of 1948. He had renewed his studies with Arnold Schoenberg, who though retired from UCLA, was persuaded by Lou and several students to conduct private classes on Sunday mornings in his Brentwood home. One of those students, William Malloch—a noted musicologist, broadcaster and lifelong friend of Lou's who passed away only six months before Lou—remembered meeting Lou in Henry Leland Clark's composition class. "There was this very big, tall fellow sitting next to me, this interesting person, and he started talking to me, as he does to everybody," Malloch recalled. "That mind was always at work.

"I wouldn't say he's a courteous person. He's better than that. He always treats people as if they count. I've never heard him bad-mouth anybody. That was all immediately evident when we first met. He was mainly a stimulating person in the midst of people who weren't always that stimulating.

"He always speaks up. He's not aggressive; he never challenges the authority of the teacher or the integrity of the people he's talking to. He was very vocal but always much fun for everyone, not showing off. It's just his natural way."

When UCLA's graduation ceremonies rolled around, Lou decided not to attend. He was already looking forward to the next step in his education, a move to the Bay Area and the University of California at Berkeley.

Again, Lou found himself studying with legendary figures. The first class he took in the summer session of 1948 was a course on Bach's *Well-Tempered Clavier* taught by the aged Swiss-born composer Ernest Bloch. Lou also took a graduate seminar in composition from the revered American composer Roger Sessions. During this period, he was convinced that he wouldn't be able to make the grade as a composer.

"It was Roger Sessions who encouraged me not to become a composer," Lou said. "He said, 'I really don't think you have it,' you know, and I think he was right, actually. As soon as I started studying with Manfred Bukofzer, the idea of musicology became more and more attractive since he was a marvelous teacher and one whose delight at any discoveries or show of interest in musicology manifested by his pupils put him into ecstasy."

So, Lou took an examination for admission to candidacy for a Master's Degree in Musicology. Due to lack of preparation, he failed the exam, but Lou's unquenchable optimism told him to hang in and prepare to pass the exam the following semester. It wasn't until 1950, though, that Lou was finally advanced to candidacy for the Master's Degree and, in 1951 he received the Master of Arts degree for a thesis on the Three-Part Ricercari of Adrian Willaert (1490-1562).

In the break between the summer and fall semesters of 1948, Lou had other things on his mind as well. On Aug. 17, 1948, he and Dolly were married in Baltimore, where Dolly's family lived, and they honeymooned in New York City. As Lou pursued his academic and musical interests at UC Berkeley, he and Dolly moved from a one-room apartment in Richmond to a one-bedroom apartment in a housing project in nearby Albany. While living there, the Gottliebs' first child, Judith Benita, was born on Jan. 27, 1951 (a second, Anthony, would come along soon thereafter).

Meanwhile, Lou's interest in Marxism had become so deep that he joined the Communist Party itself in 1949. In hindsight, it would seem that Lou displayed plenty of foolishness, guts, or both. Joining the Communist Party in 1949, the dawn of America's Big Red Scare, was like signing on for a hitch in the Confederate Army in 1865. But we do tend to forget—or choose to forget—the heady passions that were running among young idealistic students then. "We all loved Russia," Malloch recalled. "We all believed the kindly Uncle Joe stuff, the Great Father; we didn't know what was going on. We were up in arms about injustices in America; it was still just after the union-organizing days."

Also, it's worth mentioning that Lou was never in any danger of being hauled before the McCarthy committee or any other such inquisition. His was one of many "secret" memberships in the Communist Party that were never disclosed to the public. Lou estimated that for every openly declared member of the party, there were about 20 "secret" members back then. In any case, their place in the grand scheme of '50s politics was more on the order of a secret fraternity or club than a dire threat to the American way of life. Their numbers were too small to have any kind of real clout—and that made the tiny American Communist Party an ideal target during the Eisenhower years. What eventually soured Lou on the Communist Party, though, was the conformist nature of the exercise—as conformist in its own outlaw way as the lifestyle of middle America.

During the 1952 election, Lou was suspended briefly from the party as the result of a charge brought against him by a "volunteer" on the campaign committee. The charge was that Lou allegedly phoned this volunteer and asked for her by her maiden name—which she claimed that no one but an FBI agent would have known. Lou didn't remember making the call, but it was still considered a breach of party security in those paranoid days. After his reinstatement, Lou's psychological attachment to the Communist Party lessened—and when the local Communist Party Club voted to disband in the wake of Nikita Khrushchev's secret 1956 speech denouncing Stalin, Lou was delighted.

"I regret to say that I no longer believe that transferring the ownership of the means of production from the bourgeoise to the hands of the proletariat will make a happier society," Lou said in 1983. "In fact, I'm almost sure that it won't. Something happens to societies in which that is done, which makes it impossible for me to live there. Too much thought control. It's very bad to be in a society where people are really listening to what you're saying with the idea of going down and telling someone. It's not possible for me; I have too big a mouth. I cannot watch what I'm saying at all times."

From the perspective of 1989, with the fall of the Berlin Wall imminent, Lou was even more perplexed about his youthful fling on the far Left. "Why it got me, I don't know," he said. "It is the big puzzle of my life, how I ever went for that shit. I mean, how I ever believed, for example, that the national question has been solved in the Soviet Union. It's ludicrous. Everybody wants out. You solved it by putting everybody in the same prison."

One would agree that in America at least, the Communist Party was pretty much of a bust, leaving nothing more than a beat-up corpse sacrificed to feed carnivorous right-wingers. Yet one would have to give the party at least one solid positive achievement. It helped set off the mid-century folk music boom.

Again, Pete Seeger was at the epicenter of folk's latest push toward the mainstream. The Left's utopian visions of a collective world without greed and misery provided the fuel to drive Seeger forward. It even shaped his performing style, for Seeger was a tireless advocate of audience singalongs—the collective society in action.

But then, again, the theory of inevitable historical currents goes smack up against the power of heroes. Sure, ideas were thrusting Seeger forward as a leader, but were the people responding to the material or to Pete Seeger, who was as charismatic a performer as any who ever set foot on a folk music stage? Were they going to a concert to hear "The Hammer Song" or were they going to hear Pete Seeger sing "The Hammer Song"?

The ideas that were driving Pete Seeger probably did not catch on beyond a small coterie of true believers. But on the other hand, there were many, many more young, impressionable musicians who wanted to be Pete Seeger and Woody Guthrie. So they picked up guitars and banjos, bought Seeger's instruction books and recordings, learned the Guthrie canon—and eventually, those who were not content merely to imitate their idols rearranged the shape of the American popular music map.

In any case, around 1948, things started happening for folk music— slowly at first, and then in a sudden popular rush. People's Songs had folded in 1949 in the wake of the ill-fated Henry Wallace 1948 presidential campaign—the victim of that old capitalist evil, financial problems. Yet from its ruins came People Artists, Inc., a booking agency for folk musicians in search of gigs. In May of 1950, Irwin Silber—one of People's Songs founders—started the magazine *Sing Out!* which would serve as a central switchboard for announcements, songs, ideas, harangues, and other thoughts about folk music (Seeger served on the editorial board and wrote a regular column fittingly entitled Johnny Appleseed).

Against great financial odds, Moses Asch issued recordings preserving the great, if then-non-commercial, folk artists of his time. Asch's unique contribution had begun with Asch Records in 1939, releasing 78s of blues and jazz as well as folk and even classical music. But by 1947, Asch had consolidated his various labels, including Asch and Disc, under the single label Folkways. While Seeger and his friends spread the folk gospel in live performance, it was Folkways that expanded its reach, reaching those who could not get to the concerts. Though it is not exactly true that Asch never allowed any of his more than 2,100 recordings to go out of print, the vast majority of them remained available right up to Asch's death in 1986—an invaluable ongoing archive.

Even on mainstream labels, things were beginning to stir. First Asch, then Columbia, and then Decca were recording Burl Ives regularly, making him the most prominent folk musician before the public by the late '40s. Decca was also recording Josh White and Richard Dyer-Bennet, as well as issuing several interesting records of international folk music. Yet the most visible early detonators of the boom, hands down, were the Weavers. Building upon the foundation of the defunct Almanac Singers, Pete Seeger and Lee Hays got together with two young singers named Ronnie Gilbert and Fred Hellerman in Seeger's garret on MacDougal St. in Greenwich Village.

Unlike the Almanacs, whose whole operation had an ad-hoc nature—according to Seeger, Guthrie once jokingly said the Almanac Singers was "the only group he ever knew that rehearsed on the stage"— the Weavers would acquire a coat of polish. That meant more careful rehearsals, set arrangements, an emphasis on instrumental virtuosity, a broadening of the repertory to include international material, communication with audiences.

At first, they would sing for left-wing groups, union rallies and radio programs, passing the hat and barely eking out an existence. But in December of 1949, they landed a gig at the legendary Village Vanguard club (where Seeger had played solo) for $50 a week and sandwiches. The gig was supposed to be for a couple of weeks, but it was extended and extended until it became six months. The Weavers developed a word-of-mouth following—and one of the fans who kept coming back to see them was Gordon Jenkins, then at the peak of his influence as an arranger/conductor/hitmaking A&R man for Decca. It was Jenkins who talked Decca executives into letting this quartet of left-wing folksingers into a studio to cut a 78 with him.

The record was Leadbelly's "Goodnight Irene" backed with a whirling Israeli hora, "Tzena, Tzena, Tzena"—not exactly obvious hit material in 1950 when records by Perry Como, Bing Crosby, Hugo Winterhalter, Nat Cole, and Jenkins himself were dominating the white-bread airwaves and jukeboxes. But "Goodnight Irene" and "Tzena" caught fire, went all the way to the top of the charts, selling over a million copies— soon to be followed by "On Top of Old Smoky," "Kisses Sweeter Than Wine," "So Long (It's Been Good To Know Yuh)" and other unlikely jukebox hits. As a result, the Weavers were in demand at some of the nation's most prestigious night spots, and television soon captured their act. Suddenly folk music was right in the lap of Middle America.

But what kind of "folk" sound was being heard? Just look at the original Decca pressing of The Weavers' first record.

The billing reads as follows:

Gordon Jenkins and His Orchestra
and The Weavers

On "Irene," a saccharine violin solo leads off this pioneering "folk" record, the Weavers then sing the refrain, and then the square Jenkins chorus and strings swoon wordlessly over the tune. Leadbelly's slyly menacing line "I'll get you in my dreams" is smoothed out to "I'll see you in my dreams" so as not to offend prim sensibilities. It all sounds so cozy and domestic, the song of a tough Louisiana ex-con transformed into a middle-of-the-road campfire ballad.

Jenkins took "Tzena" even further into Tin Pan Alley, decorating the dance with swirling bowed and pizzicato strings, snazzy brass, and his trademark choral harmonies. When Seeger breaks through with a solo verse, and the other Weavers gradually start up an intricate round, we finally hear the pure Weavers, with just banjo, guitar and bass backing them up. It's a strange fusion of commercial and folk-minded agendas, very much of its time, and certainly a far cry from the rough-hewn Almanac Singers.

Other Weavers Deccas from this period are similarly confused in style, obviously appealing to what Decca considered the lowest common denominator of perceived public taste. Hence the weird mambo outbreak in the middle of an otherwise relatively straight-forward "Bay of Mexico," or the cute flute and brass obbligatos and Xavier Cugat percussion on "(The Wreck of the) John B." Probably the most spectacular mismatch is "Wimoweh," where Jenkins unleashes a wild, blasting big band sound on this South African tune before the outgunned Weavers even step up to the microphone.

Perhaps the tastemakers were right, that Middle America would not accept the reedy voice of a Woody Guthrie and his stumbling guitar or even the polished banjo licks of a Pete Seeger without candy-coating. Yet the Weavers have been curiously exempt from the contempt of folk purists for their panderings to the Hit Parade. Indeed, the Weavers' early records show that they went much further toward the middle-of-the-road than the Limeliters or Kingston Trio ever dared go. In the back issues of *Sing Out!,* the pages are filled with invective for anyone who dares to add so much as a drum set or electric guitar to a simple folksong—let alone strings or chorus. But the Weavers, self-admitted popularizers of folk music, were still upheld as the living definitions of folk integrity. Surely Seeger's presence at *Sing Out!* and within the inner sanctum of purist folk protected the group from attack.

Seeger himself was profoundly ambivalent about the group's fame and fortune; eventually it would be one of the reasons why he left the Weavers to become a solo artist. He would not even stay at hotels when the group was touring; he preferred to camp out in his friends' homes. The big bands in the studios, however, never seemed to bother Lee Hays, who reveled at the thought of being both "good and commercial." Even Guthrie had little trouble being persuaded to come up with a new lyric for "So Long (It's Been Good to Know Yuh)" just for the recording session.

Yet being good and commercial could not protect the Weavers from the onslaught of the Right. One Harvey M. Matusow of Dayton, Ohio, an employee of an Ohio Un-American Activities committee and an FBI tipster, testified in 1952 that he was a former communist and that three of the four Weavers were likewise. Nothing was ever proved, but in those days, just the pointing of a finger was enough to destroy a career. The Weavers were kicked off the Dave Garroway TV show, engagements were cancelled from underneath them, and those that they kept were under siege by outraged American Legion types. They were placed on the notorious blacklist, and under intense pressure from the McCarthyites, Decca dropped the Weavers in 1952. Bookings fell off to nothing, the group couldn't find any work, and they had to disband.

The Weavers remained out of the show business picture until Dec. 24, 1955, when they appeared at a landmark reunion concert at Carnegie Hall. Even though Sen. McCarthy had been censured in 1954 and his influence was rapidly on the wane, no record company would tape the concert, so the Weavers' manager Harold Leventhal had to contract an independent recording team to preserve the music. When Leventhal shopped the tape around, only the maverick Vanguard label had the courage to take it on.

It is impossible to underestimate the influence of this live album, *The Weavers at Carnegie Hall*. By now, the Weavers were doing it their way, dispensing with the window dressing and relying only upon their own voices and instruments in concerts and on records. The repertoire hadn't changed much since the Decca years—the big hits, the international material, no overt political content—but it had never been performed with more undiluted verve on records. More than any other single record, *The Weavers at Carnegie Hall* paved the way for the folk boom that followed. Many who attended the concert, including some famous names of the future, were inspired to become folksingers by the performance. Even more important, the record set the tone for future so-called commercial folk groups—with plenty of deviation from the original folk sources. There were outbreaks of humor, affectionate parodies (like Seeger's brief off-the-cuff "Greensleeves Talking Blues"), wry lyrics from Hays, impeccable showmanship. In all, it made the concert sound like a joyous gathering rather than a tendentious political rally. Yet during the early 1950s, the Weavers were the lone commercially successful folk group, prophets in the wilderness whose real influence had to outlast McCarthy.

Back in San Francisco, though, the example of the Weavers had made no small effect upon Louis Edward Gottlieb well before the Carnegie Hall reunion. Said Lou, "They showed me and a lot of other people that the songs Woody Guthrie had been releasing on little, for-the-left-wing-only records by Moe Asch had real commercial value."

By then, Lou was a member of the San Francisco branch of People's Songs (a successor to the original defunct version) at the California

Labor School while still struggling to complete his doctorate at UC Berkeley and taking various jobs like playing vibes for a TV pilot film. Emulating the Weavers' example, he and other members of People's Songs decided around 1954 to form their own version of the Weavers to sing at various left-wing functions. With the spectacular view of the Golden Gate Bridge in mind, Lou's group became known as The Gateway Singers.

"We used to sing folk songs, but it wasn't until the Weavers got hits that we thought of making a quartet of that sort," Lou recalled. "And when the Weavers got busted, as it were, we felt there was a real hole in there that we might be able to fill."

Lou's model served him well, for he admitted that at first, he simply copied the Weavers' arrangements note-for-note from the records, while being careful to transpose them to new keys. "We stole everything," said Lou, and they were popularly dubbed "The Re-Weavers" as a result. Nevertheless, the more the Gateways worked, the more new material they had to come up with—and Lou's career as a folksong adapter was born.

The first Gateway Singers were Lou, Jerry Walter—a radio actor (the voice of Jack Armstrong, the All-American boy) and singer from Chicago who played five-string banjo—singer-guitarist Jim Wood and contralto Barbara Dane, duplicating the three-man, one-woman lineup of the Weavers.

All were members of the Communist Party at the time. But Dane was an early casualty due to circumstances beyond their control. "To tell the honest truth, we stopped associating with her under orders from the Communist Party." Lou recalled. "She had become persona non grata, for what reason I don't know. I just saw her three weeks ago (this was October of 1989) and she said it was due to the fact that the Communist club she and her husband belonged to had a fink in it, and somehow things became confused. I hadn't seen her literally since the last rehearsal with the Gateways. I had to apologize to her. I told her, I can't even understand why I never even questioned it. I just left it to Jerry Walter; he told her it was over. I'm sure there are many stories like this."

So, the group had to find another contralto. The first person they turned to was the imposing Black singer Odetta Felious, whose career was just getting started in the Bay Area. She lasted only one rehearsal, for according to Lou, she wasn't terribly interested in singing with a group—and rightly so, given the overpowering nature of her voice and personality. Still, one would give a lot to hear a tape, if one exists, of that rehearsal.

Soon thereafter, Lou and the Gateways asked another contralto, Elmerlee Thomas—a classically trained singer from Oakland who worked as a lab technician at UC Berkeley—to fill the slot. Enrico Banducci, the owner of the hungry i club in San Francisco, gave the Gateways a steady gig in 1955, one that lasted for two years at four shows a night. Wood, who found himself torn between the gig with the Gateways and backing a struggling singer named Rod McKuen at the Purple Onion, left the group. He was replaced by Travis Edmonson, 23, a singer/guitarist from Nogales, Arizona who could sing in fluent Spanish and had followed McKuen into the Purple Onion as a solo act. The lineup was complete.

The Gateways were second on the bill at the hungry i then, sandwiched in between a jazz trio—often that of pianist Vince Guaraldi—and the starring act, usually a comedian of the level of Mort Sahl, Irwin Corey or Don Adams. By now, the hungry i had become the in-place in San Francisco, with celebrities turning up in the audience night after night. In 1956, against Lou's protests, Jerry and Travis came up with the idea of making Adlai Stevenson—then running for the presidency for the second time—an honorary Gateway Singer at a rally in Richmond. It turned out to be a publicity coup of high magnitude, as the story made the front pages of many newspapers.

Strangely enough, the Gateways' manager Abner "Abby" Greshler—a big name in the entertainment business (the man who brought Dean Martin and Jerry Lewis together) whom Jerry Walter knew—was able to procure a contract from Decca for the group in 1955. Yes, Decca—the same label that dropped the Weavers despite the lack of evidence of their leftward leanings. Moreover, this was done at Lou's request because he wanted to be on the Weavers' old label (they had a choice between Decca and Capitol)—and presumably Decca did not know about the Gateways' distinctly portside origins. Lou later thought they should have gone with Capitol, for Decca's distribution policies (i.e., not allowing returns by dealers) probably hurt their sales.

The first Gateway Singers session for Decca—produced by Sonny Burke—took place in Hollywood on Feb. 27, 1956, yielding "The Midnight Special," "Fair Maid" and possibly "Puttin' On The Style"

(MCA's Decca files do not list a date on the latter tune). "Special" and "Style" were coupled on a single that was released in August in both 78 RPM (then a dying format) and 45 RPM versions. Neither song bore a composer credit on the 78, which meant that Decca would come away with all the publishing royalties for public domain material.

"In those days, every record you sold, the publisher got two cents per tune," remembered Lou. "And the publisher then distributed that amongst the different writers. Say you had one guy who wrote the music and two guys who wrote the lyrics; a penny went to the publisher and the other three guys got a third of a cent each. Now it didn't take the record companies very long to figure out that on these folk songs, where there were no authors and lyricists, they would be the publishers and they would take all the two cents.

"I think Pete Seeger or Freddy Hellerman or one of those guys with the Weavers then figured out that's not the way it should be. We'll be the publishers and we'll invent a name. None of us wants to take the credit for writing 'On Top Of Old Smoky.' Anybody who knows anything knows it's a folk song."

It was a bitter lesson that Lou was to learn quickly, for when "Puttin' On The Style" was included on the Gateways' first album of the same name, it bore the legend, "Arranged and Adapted by Fred Regis and Malvina Reynolds." Reynolds, of course, was the housewife-turned-songwriter who contributed many new lyrics to the Gateways' reper-toire of folk songs, and later wrote songs for the Limeliters as well. "Fred Regis," in Lou's wry phrase, was "nobody"; he was a pseudonym for the Gateways much in the way "Paul Campbell" was a pseudonym for the Weavers when they gave themselves composer credit for arranging public domain material. Lou still didn't make any money from "Fred Regis," though; the records apparently didn't sell very well. It was only when he got into the publishing business himself later that he began to reap some rewards from the public domain.

Two more sessions in June and July of 1956 took care of the rest of the Gateways' first album. Another single, Malvina's "Bury Me In My Overalls" coupled with a wry Lou/Malvina calypso takeout of Grace Kelly's wildly publicized wedding, "Monaco" (with Lou singing lead in a weird pseudo-West Indian accent) was released in October. The album finally came out in January of 1957, with a faded, red-tinted photo-graph of downtown San Francisco, with caricatures of the four Gateway

Singers drawn on blank cable car signals. Nowhere on the album are the identities of the four revealed (one wonders if they felt threatened by right-wing heat), yet the background musicians and singers are identified. Ever the jazzman at the core, Lou managed to get the distinguished bassist Red Callender, guitarist Jack Marshall, drummer Alvin Stoller, and on a few tracks, Carlos Vidal on congas. Jud Conlon (best known for his work with Stan Freberg) beefed up some of the vocal harmonies and added some obbligatos with his singers—the Gateways' equivalent of Gordon Jenkins. Thus, while the Weavers' Decca records have echoes of the big band era and Tin Pan Alley in mind, "Puttin' On The Style" comes out of the small clubs with its stripped-down instrumentation and catchy backbeat. It's a bright, cheery, toe-tapping record, clearly setting the tone for the Limeliters with its mood and instrumentation while maintaining its link with the Weavers in the vocal sound. Lou takes a lot of solos in a fresh, youthful, personable voice, clearly exhilarated by his first recordings as a leader. Elmerlee Thomas, ever the classical singer, tends to drag the tempo in her solos, Edmonson sounds like an eager kid, and Walter capably fills in the bass. The vocal blend is rather raucous, the voices clashing but never really striking sparks against each other. Also, the vocal writing is not as sophisticated as Lou's work with the Limeliters would be.

There are some strange interpolations now and then—e.g., when Marshall takes a jarring modern jazz solo break in the middle of "Sally Don't You Grieve" or the horrible discord that ends an otherwise rocking "Rock Island Line." "Midnight Special," in which Lou takes the lead, is a close cousin of the Limeliters version, though the tempo is slower, and Lou's phrasing is freer. And there are some thrilling moments, as in "Rock Island Line" when Lou bellows, "What a peculiar way to run a railroad line!" in his best stentorian baritone on the way to the close.

In contrast to their first album, the Gateways' second and final album with Lou, *At the hungry i*, was made relatively quickly in two sessions (May 2-3, 1957). In a bit of deceptive labeling for which Decca was notorious, the Gateways weren't recorded live at the hungry i at all; it was another studio session. The Jud Conlon Singers are gone, so is Jack Marshall. The backup sound is leaner, more prophetic of the commercial folk sound of the '60s.

Lou sounds huskier, more mature, and Elmerlee lets her gospel influences run freer; she has clearly grown as a folksinger on this second album. On an exuberant treatment of "The Fox," we get something resembling the brio of the Limeliters, and for the first time, there is some vocal counterpoint on "Deep Blue Sea." "The Ballad of Sigmund Freud," later a topical standard in the folk boom, makes an early appearance here with Lou, Ph.D. candidate, as the perfect lead vocalist (one could easily imagine the Limeliters singing this). The whole record sounds tighter and more professional than the first, as if the material had been honed to perfection night after night at the hungry i.

The folk purists, predictably, were not impressed. One Ron Radosh railed in the pages of *Sing Out!* in the spring of 1959 about "Commercialism and the Folk Song Revival," singling out the Gateway Singers as shamelessly showbizzy Weavers imitators. "The major part of their act consists of the fullest type of night club humor, with corny jokes catalogued and repeated with the same ad libs according to what song the group intends to sing," he wrote. "...When the group finally does a number which reveals the possible potential they have, the introduction and their attitude towards the music leaves the audience with none of the excitement which a group like the Weavers produced."

He went on to attack *The Gateway Singers in Hi-Fi,* made after Lou left the group—complaining about the electric guitars, brass bands (some French horns on two tracks) and the "mechanical hand-clapping device" (actually human hand clapping treated with echo). Predictably Radosh finds nothing but sound musical taste, meaning and dignity in the Weavers' souped-up, Hit Parade-bound Decca recordings, although he accuses them of trying to ruin good songs in a 1958 "comeback"— well after they discarded the strings and choir. Such was the level of objective discourse among the old folk guard then.

By the time the Gateways' second album *At the hungry i* was released in February 1958, the whole issue had become temporarily irrelevant for Lou, for he had left the group in the fall of 1957. Lou claimed that the official reason for his leaving—to pursue his Ph. D—was indeed true, or at the very least was part of the truth. Pressure from his professors, plus the genuine desire to finish his dissertation, and a stipend from the Hertz Fellowship, gave him a good deal of incentive. "I just could not work six nights a week and finish the dissertation," Lou concluded.

But there was another, more personal reason. Lou says in his auto-biography that he was being "driven mad" by Jerry Walter onstage, for Walter apparently had picked up on Lou's onstage persona and was imitating it nightly. By this time, Lou's offbeat parody of a high-falutin' professor of music had solidified into his nightly shtick—and Walter's parodies of that parody left a nasty residue in Lou's mind.

Lou's claim was borne out by the unexpected release in 2009 of a private tape of a Gateway Singers concert at Stanford University from Feb. 9, 1957. Right off the bat after the opening "Puttin' On The Style," we can hear Walter doing his Lou impression in his radio voice—and it sounds like a pale copy, perhaps even a bit arch. Lou himself is in very sharp form, his professorial act in full bloom, having already come up with some bits that he would carry over into the Limeliters. The other big presence is Edmonson, full of beans, breaking up "Rock Island Line" with a burlesque of Elvis, driving the group hard with a two-beat rhythm guitar that would play a big part in the popular folk duo Bud and Travis (you can sense that he, too, would not be content to remain a Gateway Singer for very long). This is a remarkable document in that it not only gives us the flavor of a Gateway performance that the Decca albums only hint at—the unified energetic instrumental work, the irreverent banter, the ironic humor aimed right at a college or college-educated crowd—but also points the way to the night-club performing style that subsequent folk groups would adopt en masse.

Once Lou left, the Gateway Singers ended their stay at the hungry i and began to travel. Ernie Sheldon—a fine songwriter, guitarist, and mellifluous tenor-baritone from Brooklyn—stepped in to take Lou's place for a short time. Edmonson would leave in 1958 to form Bud and Travis with Bud Dashiell (who in 1982 said that Lou Gottlieb taught him everything he knew about entertaining people).

Never again would the Gateway Singers reach quite the same high level of visibility they had when they were the Bay Area's folk pioneers—and a few personnel changes later, the group disbanded in 1961. Elmerlee Thomas had quit the road, taking a few solo gigs now and then, choosing to live quietly with her husband and two children until she died of a brain tumor in 1969. Alone, Jerry Walter elected to carry on, forming a spinoff group in 1962 with Betty Mann and Milt Chapman called the Gateway Trio. After recording albums for MGM and Capitol around the height of the folk boom, the Gateway Trio finally gave up at the end of 1965. Walter then stopped performing regularly, turning to producing radio commercials and union activities, rising to become president of the AFTRA local in San Francisco. He, too, died prematurely, the victim of a heart attack in 1979 at home in Sausalito while anticipating a day of sailing on San Francisco Bay. He was only 53.

Long before he quit the Gateways, Lou had found the subject for his doctoral dissertation—"The Cyclic Masses of Trent Codex 89." These were compositions dating from the 15th century, held by the Cathedral at Trent and jealously guarded for centuries. Lou's mentor at Berkeley, Manfred Bukofzer had a friend, Father Lawrence Feininger, who had been appointed head of the library at the cathedral and made microfilms of the Trent Codices 87 through 92. Lou's task was to transcribe the archaic 15th century notation of Codex 89 into modern notation and analyze what he found in this cobwebbed corner of history.

Lou would take his microfilm reader into the dressing room of the hungry i to work on the grind-it-out task of transcribing those strange shapes into something readable. Lou had finished most of the work on his dissertation in early 1957 but he had to wait nearly a year for the doctoral committee to begin reading it. After that came endless rounds of reading, criticism, re-writing, and re-reading—which more than anything, convinced Lou that academia was not for him.

Finally in June of 1958, Lou's dissertation was approved, and he was awarded his long-sought Ph. D. in musicology at the graduation ceremonies at UC Berkeley, a ceremony witnessed by his understandably proud father. But the honor was ashes in Lou's mouth. It had taken far too long—through a world war, a "police action" in Korea, all of the Truman and most of the Eisenhower years, an entire career with the Gateway Singers. In burrowing into some of the deepest, mustiest corners of arcane musicology, Lou had tunneled himself out of the profession.

Lou's finished thesis—available for public perusal in the UC Berkeley Music Library—is a weighty, scholarly piece of work in two volumes, one containing the analysis and the other the transcribed scores. The writing is that of an accomplished scholar deeply immersed in his subject, with frequent musical examples embroidered in the most arcane musical terminology.

Still, if you wade through it, there are passages of whimsy and nightclub slang that could have been written only by Lou. Most entertaining of all is a passage in the introduction, where, after a proposal of high seriousness and scholarly purpose, Lou deflates the balloon in the manner of Lewis Carroll.

"Explain all that," said the Mock Turtle.

"No, no! The adventures first," said the Gryphon in an impatient tone, "explanations take such a dreadful time."

More in keeping with where his head was at in 1958, Lou became a stand-up comedian at the Purple Onion, working as diligently at that as he had trying to get his doctorate.

Then in September, Lou sauntered down to Los Angeles where he would be the comic on the bill at the Avant Garde, a club that folded right in the middle of Lou's engagement. Author/critic Grover Sales remembers catching Lou's standup act at another club in Palo Alto. The audience consisted of Stanford students and their parents; a squarer, more buttoned-down audience would have been difficult to find. "Lou comes out in his professor's uniform," recalled Sales, "and he holds up a copy of *Life Magazine*, and says, 'You've all seen the issue of *Life Magazine* on 'The Birth of a Baby.' It's quite fascinating in their research that they've discovered when a couple are trying to conceive and procreate instead of trying to prevent conception, the sexual enjoyment is immeasurably enhanced.' And he starts popping his fingers and says, 'In other words, fuckin' for kids is better kicks, baby!' There was wholesale walking out."

"Though off the camera he is one of the funniest people I've ever met, he wasn't able to do it in public," said William Malloch. "He tried to be a standup comic and it got all kind of conventionalized and everything. He's a person who makes comedy out of the immediate situation which lies in front of him. But he didn't find a format, a way, that he could do that in public by himself."

Yet Malloch deserves a significant footnote in Limeliter history, for he introduced Lou to the one piece of material that became his enduring comic signature. One day in 1958, Malloch played for Lou a tune from the Michael Flanders/Donald Swann hit album *At The Drop Of A Hat*, a routine about an elderly lecher and his young female prey called "Have Some Madeira, M'Dear." Lou immediately added it to his act, and it wound up as his solo feature with the Limeliters for the rest of his life. Although he grew to dread each performance, shortly before his death, Lou acknowledged his gratitude to Malloch in an email letter to the author; "Performing that song still puts the no-fat, high-fibre, high-carbohydrate victuals on my plate."

During this period, Lou also became better acquainted with a trio of young folkniks whom he had first met during the Gateway Singers period. They were playing first on the bill at the Purple Onion, with Lou following, and Maya Angelou—then a sexy calypso singer—closing. They were Dave Guard, Nick Reynolds and Bob Shane—better known as the fireball that started the next, biggest phase of the folk music revival, the Kingston Trio.

The Kingston Trio was something new and different. They did not think of themselves as folk singers per se; they were eclectics, drawing from whatever forms of music they liked, though the basic thrust of their sound was folk. But they were also in tune with the new energy of rock 'n' roll sweeping the pop charts—not the sound and content, but the energy.

They would take some cues from the Weavers to whom Dave Guard gave credit as the basic inspiration for their sound. But they were not in tune with the political boiler plates from which the folk music revival originated; union songs were for another generation. This was no accident, for despite their liberal upbringing, they wanted to avoid the flak that had cut the Weavers down in mid-flight. They wanted to be entertainers, not protesters, appealing to factions of Ike's Silent Generation who didn't want to mess with rockabilly. (They would lift the political veil a bit in the more opportune '60s, but not in 1957).

They were also listening hard to Harry Belafonte, who after having quit pop crooning in 1950, started carving a path of his own with highly personal, dramatic presentations of folk songs. Due to his versatility—and his immense financial success—historians often pooh-pooh the huge contribution Belafonte made in slipping folk music into almost every middle-class American home, paving what was once a dirt path to poverty into a smooth highway for younger folkies to follow. By the turn of 1957, Belafonte suddenly found himself reluctantly spearheading a calypso craze—which was originally part of his master plan to explore a wide variety of world music but soon turned into the core of his identity with the public. The Kingstons took heed.

And of course, being in the proximity of San Francisco's North Beach, their heaviest immediate influence was the Gateway Singers—and Lou Gottlieb in particular "When we were working at the hungry i there were these guys who used to hang around in the dressing room all the time," Lou remembered. "They were slightly underfoot, to be frank.

I had a whole bunch of arrangements I had worked on for the Gateway Singers and these guys had a chance to make some records. They didn't have enough material to make a whole record so I just got in the drawer and pulled out some stuff I had, changed them around so these three guys could sing them, and they recorded them."

One of the tunes was "Saro Jane," a folk song Lou learned off an Uncle Dave Macon record, and the Kingstons placed it on their first album. This album just happened to be the one that had "Tom Dooley" buried in the middle of Side One. A month after the album's release, two DJs at KLUB in Salt Lake City, Bill Terry and Paul Colburn, fell in love with "Tom Dooley" and played the hell out of the record. Word spread to other cities, and before long, Capitol was pressured to issue "Tom Dooley" on a single. The single went straight to No.1, the album took off in the charts right after it. Eventually, that album sold over 3,000,000 copies—and at two cents per record sold, it didn't take much arithmetic for Lou to figure out that he had just stumbled onto a gold mine.

"I began thinking, whew! this is really a way to make a living, because by this time I understood that you better be your own publisher," he said.

"I had my own publishing company, and I got the full two cents from each one. So, I began really to ransack the public domain for every tune that could conceivably be potchkeed around into something that could be sold."

So, Lou went into overdrive, forming his own publishing company Brio Publishing, coming up with arrangements of folk material and eventually the Trio recorded three more ("Good News," "The Unfortunate Miss Bailey," and "'Round About The Mountain"). Lou even merits a very brief bio on the Trio's *At Large* album as "a San Francisco musicologist and comic."

While the Trio was appearing at the Coconut Grove in Los Angeles' Ambassador Hotel in May of 1959, they were cutting another album at the Capitol Tower, and Lou was invited to submit some songs and sit in on the session. To finance his visit to Los Angeles, Lou got a job working as a solo act at the Ash Grove on Melrose Avenue, where by now, his act had changed from stand-up comedy to comic patter and songs, accompanying himself on the bass. Still very much the academic in those days, Lou always had a music stand in front of him; occasionally the music would fall to the floor and Lou would stoop to pick it up while still singing. The audience would be stunned, not knowing what to make of this off-kilter act.

After his set the night of Friday May 29, Lou's friend Ben Shapiro invited him to drop by a small Hollywood club he co-owned with Theodore Bikel and Herb Cohen in Hollywood called the Cosmo Alley. Lou did—and he stumbled upon two young singers that night who would turn his life around.

Alex as a young man, ever-present cigarette in hand
(Courtesy of Alex Hassilev)

Chapter Two

For Alexander Hassilev, one of the two singers whom Lou saw, the Cosmo Alley gig was a mere side trip from what had been a wandering path of self-discovery apparently without end.

One key to understanding what motivates this brooding Russian is the mind-bending 1951 novel by J.D. Salinger, *The Catcher In The Rye*. The narrative is told in first person by one Holden Caulfield, an intelligent but aimless 17-year-old son of a wealthy New York corporation lawyer who had all the advantages of the good life yet doesn't have any idea of what he wants to do with himself. Holden meanders about for more than half the book's length—and it's tough to stay with him as Salinger has him staggering through one misadventure after another. But while out on the town, our hapless anti-hero upsets his bewildered date with a series of extraordinary speeches that turn conventional wisdom upside down, raging against the materialistic path that society has laid out for him. Nothing is resolved at the end when he goes back home to Mommy and Daddy, but you get the feeling that he won't be there for long. He is intelligent enough to sense that something is wrong with the American Dream, but he can't work out a viable alternative.

Certainly *The Catcher In The Rye* was totally out of step with the self-satisfied, greatest-nation-on-earth image most Americans had in the 1950s. Yet who knows how many teenagers and young adults have seen a lot of themselves in Holden Caulfield, despite the constant reinforcement of so-called mainstream values from television, advertising, the schools, peer pressure and parental authority. Many dropouts of the Beat Generation of the 1950s and the hippies of the 1960s probably first heard the siren song of nonconformity from J.D. Salinger.

And it had a particularly powerful impact upon Alex Hassilev. "I always felt myself to be some kind of European Holden Caulfield," said Alex in 1979. "It (the book) has to do with discovering that things just aren't what you thought they were in adolescence."

"I've been an American for a very long time, but I've never felt, really, that this is my home. Not that I really feel that France is my home,

Russia or any other place in the world. Which certainly doesn't put me in a class by myself; there are many other people like me. It has to do with my temperament, too. I'm a fence-sitter."

"Life, and especially music, presents too much of a smorgasbord to Alex, and he likes too many things on that table," said his longtime friend Theodore Bikel, a multiple career man himself. "He tends to grab for this and grab for that because more than one line is alluring to him. There are too many directions to go, and he often goes toward them and abandons that line and goes to another."

"Alex was eight years old when he started becoming an American," wrote Lou in his autobiography. "The process is not completed. In some ways, Alex remains a European."

Alex's mother Tamara Rudkovsky (later changed to Rudd) was a strikingly handsome-looking, white-haired woman, her eyes and eyebrows having been passed on to her only son almost intact. She was born in St. Petersburg, Russia, and she found it ironic that she spent her last 30 years in St. Petersburg, Florida—where she passed away in 2000 at the age of 90.

Alex's maternal grandfather was quite a wealthy man before the revolution; Alex says he was on the way to being "the Russian Nabisco," with bread, biscuit and flour factories. He invented a process that would keep bread fresh, which an American firm stole from him after he came to the States. He built a factory before the outbreak of World War I that supplied the Russian Army with bread. The family was so well off that they had a vacation estate just on the other side of the Finnish border, about three hours away by car. The estate had three houses on the property, one of which contained a fully stocked library whose contents were later sold to the Library of Congress. It had a field where the family could raise vegetables and potatoes, allowing the estate to become almost entirely self-sufficient.

Came the Revolution of 1917, the Rudkovskys had a tremendous advantage over most of the other refugees from the Bolsheviks—a place to go that was close to home. But Tamara's father lost everything he had in Russia when he fled, and despite the self-contained nature of the Finnish estate, he and Tamara's mother had to find work in Finland. They always hoped that Russia would come to its senses and kick the Bolsheviks out so that they could go home to St. Petersburg. As it turned out, their Finnish "interlude" lasted for 12 years, and they never saw Mother Russia again.

In 1924, economic conditions got so bad that the Rudkovskys had to move to the Finnish capital of Helsinki, where they lived until 1929. Ultimately the goal would be America—and after a sister of Tamara's married an American she met in Paris, all of the Rudkovskys would gradually settle in New York City.

All except Tamara, who suddenly had other plans. She had fallen in love with a Russian-born man ten years her senior named Leonide Hassilev, whom Tamara said came from "Keeshiev" (Kishinev?) in the Bessarabia region of Moldavia.

Leonide's family could be considered middle-class, steeped in European educational tradition, with some money behind it. He was a civil engineer, eventually becoming a specialist in hydroelectric power installations. He studied engineering in Russia before his family fled and continued his studies in Germany and France. Tamara's sisters knew Leonide before she came to Paris, in fact, Tamara recalled that Leonide was interested at first in her older sister who would eventually marry an American. "But then I cried so much at the station when she was leaving that he started paying attention to me," she said. She couldn't have been more than 21 at the time, and Leonide was far less of a go-getter personality than she, more rigid in his ways, more traditional in his beliefs. But the relationship clicked, and they were married in Paris in 1930, determined to make a home there. Tamara cabled her surprised parents in America that she was getting married and staying in France; this after they had just reserved passage for her on an America-bound ship.

The newlyweds settled in a small apartment on the Left Bank in the 15th Arrondissement—and on July 11, 1932, Tamara gave birth to their only child, to whom they gave the Russian name, Alexander. Times were tough, the worldwide economic depression was still on and Tamara had to work, so Alex was left mostly in the care of his Russian nanny, a remarkable, fiercely loyal woman named Pelagie Chibanoff who had raised his mother and stayed with the family throughout their wanderings.

In 1938, the Hassilevs moved to a much larger apartment in a well-to-do residential section. By now, the Hassilevs had become a solid, traditional, Jewish but not terribly religious middle-class family. The language spoken at home was mostly Russian when Alex was a child, with a little bit of French. Leonide eventually would be able to speak at least eight languages; Tamara could handle four fluently and several others to some degree.

Throughout their time in Paris, Tamara couldn't help but notice streaks of brilliance in her son, a native quickness of mind, a vivid imagination, a memory that easily retained new words and most astonishingly, new languages. "He was a very handsome boy, and very clever—too much so," said Tamara Hassilev. "When he was three, he knew so many fairy tales and wanted to always have somebody read to him. At the age of five, he could read already himself in Russian…" Alex was an avid reader; anything he could put his hands on. "We kept him away from French; we wanted him to know the Russian language well. But at the age of five, he went to the pre-school, and we found out that he knows French. He went to the park with Nanny and played with the children and learned without our knowing it."

"I remember very few things, really," says Alex about his native Paris. "I was just a small child. It was a typical French apartment at the time—high ceilings, a lot of wood floors which probably creaked somewhat, a lot of shutters on the windows…I remember going through poison gas drills as a child, having to wear a gas mask, looking at the sandbag placements and stuff, lots of khaki walking around."

In 1939, Tamara received news from America that her father had been stricken with cancer, and his doctors had given him just a year to live (he survived until 1942). There was also a World's Fair in New York in 1939, so the Hassilevs took that as a pretext to visit Tamara's parents in June, with Leonide taking Alex on one ship and Tamara following on a later one soon thereafter. Despite all the ominous talk about Hitler's threats on the Danzig corridor in Poland, they had no intention of staying in America; all had return tickets for Europe. Leonide went back to Paris when his vacation time ended in July, and Tamara and Alex were due back in September. But on September 1, Hitler invaded Poland, touching off World War II. Leonide was stuck in Paris on that date and was immediately drafted into the French Army. Tamara's parents refused to let her go back to Europe—and so Tamara, Alex and her parents had to live in her sister's spacious New York apartment on West End Avenue, where Alex shared a room with his cousin Julian Josephson.

All of a sudden, Alex's world had been blasted to pieces. Here he was, having just turned seven years old, in a strange new country, without his father and his nanny. Prior to this, Alex's mother remembers that he had been a normal, sociable boy in Paris—or as normal as a son of Russian emigres could be. But in America, Alex's personality began to turn inward. "He was quite withdrawn," said his mother. "It happened only after we stayed behind and didn't go back to Paris. His whole life changed. His father was away for 2 1/2 years, and he was worrying about that. He was worrying about the war in general, and in the beginning, he was asking, when are we going home? He was not comfortable; the environment was so different to him. Also, he was considered the older boy and his cousin Julian had all the attention from his grandmother. Alex was used to his nanny, whom we had left behind; she was like a grandmother to him."

Once settled in New York, Alex attended P.S. 87 in Manhattan, initially skipping a grade thanks to his European educational background. "I was way overqualified for that school when I arrived there," he recalls. "I breezed through school, except that I was lousy at shop. I was good at everything in those days because I had this tremendous background from my European days, where they teach at a much higher level. At the age of 6, I was doing 7th grade work in France. I certainly knew a lot more mathematics than any American child."

At first, Alex didn't know a word of English, but given the tender age at which he picked up French, it wouldn't be long before he would master the new language. After only three months, he told his mother not to buy him any more French books, for he was reading fluently in English already. Not only did Alex conquer the languages, he spoke them without foreign accents, a feat which even many lifelong linguists never pull off.

Once he finally arrived in America, Leonide moved his family to Larchmont, New York and worked for Gibson Hill Consulting Engineers, from which he would be on loan for a number of years in South America under President Truman's Point Four plan. Yet Alex never felt that his parents tried to push him in the direction of engineering—or any career direction. Until high school, when he began to experience vague pangs of yearning for the theater, inventing scripts, seating friends and performing before them, Alex didn't have any notion of what he wanted to spend his life doing.

Music wasn't even in the cards in the beginning for Alex, although it was always in the air. Like many traditional well-educated middle-class

European families in those days, music was constantly around the house as a part of everyday life.

Both of Alex's parents played the piano—he recalls that his father played "fairly well," his mother "not as well, but she played"—and one of his aunts, a fine violinist, was a student of the great violinist/pedagogue Leopold Auer back in St. Petersburg. Occasionally Leonide would have his friends over to the house to play chamber music by Haydn, Beethoven, Schubert, Mozart and the other German masters.

Alex's mother remembers him staring at the family piano at the age of six, vowing that someday he'd be able to play. Like a good son, Alex studied classical piano with a cousin and in the '80s, when the Limeliters were short a keyboard player, Alex occasionally dusted off his old skills and chipped in on the piano. "But I never got to be terribly good at it," he said. "I was OK. I loved music, but I wasn't a fanatic about it."

Being more European than ethnic Russian, classical music was the dominant form of music in the Hassilev household. But inevitably, Russian folk songs were brought over from the old country, and one of Alex's aunts was particularly keen upon performing them at family gatherings. They would undoubtedly have a major influence upon young Alex, and his mother said he should have sung more of them over the years.

Yet classical music was all that really mattered to Alex at the time. "I didn't know there was such a thing (as American folk music)," Alex admits. "My interest in music stopped at the 19th century essentially up until that time."

As a child, even after mastering English so quickly, Alex still felt very much as if he was looking in on the outside of American life—and to a certain extent, he feels the same way even today. "I had no window on American street life whatever, except that which I had from going out on the streets of New York, so to that extent I had a little bit," he remembers. "But I would say there was a narrow world. I had no idea what was out there. The kids were supposed to grow up and become doctors, dentists and lawyers and marry preferably the daughter of somebody they know who was in the circle." Though his family was anything but religious, Alex's family went through the motions of putting him through the traditional Jewish rituals of Hebrew school and then the splashy bar mitzvah at age 13—the event where a Jewish male child traditionally enters into manhood. "I was bar mitzvahed but I certainly had no feeling for it; the Jewish religion never took. It was the thing to do, I suppose. Didn't mean much to me."

One of Alex's friends in New York was Miles Kreuger, who became an author and president of the Institute of the American Musical. Miles would usually find Alex whenever he was over at his cousin Julian's home on Central Park West, and he gives us a prophetic portrait of the Alex who emerges when people manage to penetrate his shell.

"He was tall and handsome, very sensible," remembered Kreuger. "He seemed very old, even though he was just in his teens, very sophisticated. He seemed like somebody who could always solve problems when there was a crisis. His presence was warm and made people feel good, a kind of healing quality. I just remember I liked him a lot. He was dazzlingly bright; everybody in that family was. It was a very stimulating household—lots of foreign languages spoken, French, lots of Russian."

At the time, though, Kreuger didn't see any hint of a show business career in Alex's future. Miles and Julian would often go to the movies or take in New York's incredible theater scene, but Alex never tagged along. "I was astonished when he became a Limeliter because I didn't know that he could play an instrument," he said.

Once the family moved back to New York, Alex went to Columbia Grammar School in New York City for a year and then transferred to George School, a beautiful Quaker boarding school in Bucks County, Pennsylvania near Philadelphia where he spent his high school years. "It was not a snob school, but it was a school for privileged kids because it cost money to go there," says Alex. Though the Hassilevs were far from wealthy at that point in their lives, nothing was too good for their brilliant child. "We didn't have money or anything," said Tamara. "But we always took loans from the bank, and we sent him to the best schools, always."

In the summer of 1946, Alex found himself embarking upon what was then the biggest adventure of his life. He went on a bicycle trip of the United States and Canada with about 30 other persons under the auspices of the American Youth Hostels. The trip started in Massachusetts, went north into Quebec, then across the vast Canadian midlands, prairies and mountains to Vancouver, down the West Coast through California, turning east through the hot, dry Southwest and finally working its way back to New York.

The bicyclists camped out often, most memorably in the national parks, and this only child received a valuable learning experience, later calling it "the most important thing I did in my youth. What was extraordinary about it from my standpoint was a kind of camaraderie that I had never experienced before. It also allowed me to see the United States for the first time."

Back in George School, though, Alex was still without a direction, relying upon his extraordinary facility and background to get by. He made his first close friend at George, a young man named Michael Zillahe. By now tall and well-built, Alex went out for tennis—which he enjoyed—and football—which he did not. Ultimately, he couldn't see the point of going out on a grassy field and getting hurt for no reason at all other than picking up a few precious yards of ground. His interest in theater grew, and he was the lead in school plays, but his latent musical abilities had not been tapped at all. He just wasn't interested.

He did pick up another interest, but alas, it was a counter-productive one. "I learned to smoke," he confessed. "I wish I hadn't. There was a group of us who used to sneak out and do that."

Despite his attractive physical attributes, Alex was very shy with girls in his teens, even admitting to being terrified of them. He did have his first "major" girlfriend at age 16, a young woman named Judith Parker, who became a professor at a college in Maine. He also admits to an attempt that was made to seduce him at 13—"one of those youthful insanities when an 18-year-old girl decided she was horny that day. But as far as really losing my virginity, that was not until I was in the Army." Like a typical high schooler, Alex attended his senior prom, but characteristically forgets the name of the girl whom he brought. In any case, he recalls that he didn't have any fun at the prom, coming in as an outsider, hating dancing and the whole ritual. "I was always uncomfortable at those things," he says. "I never got any pleasure out of them then or since. A dance for me is like the last thing in the world I wish to do. I have actually enjoyed dancing a few times in my life, but these moments were aberrations. I have never understood the point of it (except as an exhibition}."

In 1949, Alex graduated from George School and had his mind set upon going to the University of Chicago. He had received a partial scholarship from that school, and besides, Judith Parker was going there and that's where he had to be. But Alex's parents insisted that he go to the prestigious Ivy League capital in Cambridge, Massachusetts, Harvard— school of presidents, Brahmins, Establishment kingpins. Bowing to his parents' wishes, Alex set off for Harvard with Michael Zillahe, and they roomed together in Wigglesworth House right on historic, bustling Harvard Square.

But with only three months of the school year gone, tragedy struck. Michael committed suicide—in the library. "Over a girl, of all things, which made me furious," said Alex, the futility of it all still piercing his memory. "He was a brilliant kid and undoubtedly would have become someone very important. That was one of the reasons I left but, by all means, not the only reason."

"Alex couldn't get over it," recalled his mother. "It made him more withdrawn; it had a terrible influence on him."

Again, alienation had taken hold of Alex. He floundered at Harvard, majoring in nothing but "goof" as he puts it, without much of a social life, intellectually able to make a go of it but unable to concentrate. "Frankly, the whole Ivy league aura of Harvard was not to my taste," he says. "It had to do with a kind of gentlemanly approach to everything that certainly turns out a great many urbane and successful leaders of our country. There was a kind of veiled arrogance that may not be true, but I perceived it as such. I wanted something a little more unbuttoned. I was not ready for Harvard at all." Finally, after a year of this, he was able to prevail upon his folks to allow him to transfer to the University of Chicago. Judith Parker was waiting there, and they had a happy reunion. But as things turned out, things were really over between the two of them, so they started seeing other people. It was hard for Alex to relate to women at the time, for he was still extremely shy. "I sort of had sex with this girlfriend in Chicago, but it was not satisfactory, it wasn't happening," he recalled.

At Chicago, Alex enrolled in the Great Books program, which originated at St. John's College in Maryland (where Glenn Yarbrough had already embarked on the same program). Not unlike today's liberal education, but more rigorous and methodical, the program involved passing a series of courses that the university thought you needed to get a Bachelor of Arts—history, geography, biology, math, etc.—with no electives allowed. Although Alex did well academically, he still found himself in the same general lack of direction he experienced at Harvard. "I was in freefall," he recalls. "I had no idea of what was going on, although I had a good time."

Yet while the Ivy League atmosphere of Harvard alienated him, Alex found himself more comfortable in Chicago's Bohemian student gatherings. He would hang out with them, playing bridge—a game at which he was becoming most proficient—rekindling his interest in theater, playing the Bohemian.

With its proximity to Chicago's tough South Side, curious students at the University were privy to some of the storied blues spots in that area. Being a young, cosmopolitan, urban intellectual, Alex was naturally attracted to blues joints and in these little dives he could hear, in their natural habitat, boogie-woogie players like Jimmy Yancey just before his death, up-and-coming bluesicians like Muddy Waters, the menacing John Lee Hooker, blues poet laureate Willie Dixon, Little Walter and Howlin' Wolf.

But unlike Lou Gottlieb—who was so much into Black music that his buddies in the Army derided him as "Nigger Lou"—Black music never really took hold in Alex. "It was just too far away from me culturally," he concluded. "I liked some of it but never got into it."

But his musical horizons were nevertheless expanding. On a trip to Brazil to visit his parents in 1952, Alex was presented with a guitar for his 20th birthday. Tamara Hassilev had already begun to play the guitar, and she showed Alex a few simple chords. "He played the whole night; he never went to bed," she remembered. "In the morning, he played much better than I had after quite a few lessons. He gave me a complex of inferiority! The guitar became a very, very important thing in his life."

As was his knack in so many things, Alex quickly became fluent on the acoustic guitar, learning several Brazilian folk songs. Brazilian music touched deep taproots within Alex and his mother, who believed that Brazilian and Russian folk music share similar structures, affinities for minor keys, and a melancholy, almost aching feeling. He loved the musicality of Brazilian young people; he would have 10 or 12 of his new friends over to the house, all of them armed with guitars. When he came back to the States, he found that he had acquired an exotic talent that made him stand out at social gatherings, for hardly anyone was singing Brazilian folk songs in America in the early '50s and the first great Brazilian wave known as the bossa nova was a decade in the future.

"My interest in American folk music came later than that," says Alex. "It dates from the time I was in the Army when I was stationed in England in a quonset hut. The radio was always turned to music that I couldn't abide, being outnumbered by the hoi polloi. But one day, I got to choose my station, and that day I heard a record by the Weavers called 'Kisses Sweeter Than Wine' and the one run-through of that particular record electrified me for some reason. I thought, goddamn, that's the greatest thing I ever heard, and it made such an impression on me that it kindled my interest in American folk music. As I recall, I knew Brazilian songs, a couple of Russian songs, a couple of French songs. At that time, I didn't know any songs in English."

Still, the idea of theater had become so irresistible that Alex left Chicago for New York and home, well before graduating. Tamara believed that the biggest influences on Alex at the time were a couple of fellow students, Mike Nichols and Elaine May, then at the start of their careers. He enrolled in the Neighborhood Playhouse in 1952, an acting school where two of his classmates were Sidney Pollack and Steve McQueen.

But within a few months of his enrollment, the draft beckoned. The Korean War was still rumbling—and though at last he had embarked upon something resembling a direction in life, Alex was inducted, undergoing basic training in Aberdeen, Maryland. Luckily for him, he was not sent to the front. Instead, Alex was ordered overseas to England, where he served his entire hitch in relative safety, stationed at a U.S. air base in Chelveston, north of London.

In the Army, Alex had one very good friend by the name of Rudy Peins—like Alex tall and gangling (about six-foot-four)—whom Alex remembers as "a very funny, jovial guy who saw the absurdity of things at all times, looking and laughing at what the Army represented." Attracted by this outsider clown, Alex stuck with him, and they satisfied their rebellious souls by playing pranks, "thumbing our noses at the system, getting out of various details, going on bivouac and disappearing into town, only to reappear at appropriate moments."

The Army inadvertently gave Alex his first crack at a really satisfying sexual relationship. Alex remembers the woman's name only as Vinnie, about his age, "a working-class girl from London, very warm, loving, gentle, on the blondish side, attractive." He doesn't recall where he met her, but he has distant yet fond memories of taking her out to the beautiful English countryside, which he loved.

Perhaps the most influential experiences Alex had in England, though, were in the theater. Theater seats were extraordinarily cheap in London—and those were the days when you could see some of the greatest names in the English-speaking theater live for what amounted to a song. Alex remembers seeing a play on the West End, for example, that had John Gielgud and Ralph Richardson on the same stage—"pretty inspiring stuff," to say the least. Though his direction in life wasn't quite set yet, London certainly nudged Alex further in the direction of theater.

Alex was a Private-First Class throughout his Army career and he could have made Corporal but he got out of the service on an early release program. The Korean War had finally ended in a negotiated truce and manpower needs weren't as great.

The tug of the theater was strong but apparently not strong enough, for when Alex returned to the States, he headed back to the University of Chicago to complete his work on a B.A. By this time, with his extraordinary command of at least six languages, Alex thought he might have a future in the diplomatic service, so he continued his work at Chicago, spending a year in graduate school studying international relations. "But my heart wasn't really in it," he confesses. "(It was) some half-baked thought that I should have some career of a kind as a diplomat."

For one thing, Alex realized that having Russian-born parents would be a terrible handicap once he tried to get a job in the diplomatic service; after all, these were the 1950s. What finally disabused Alex—the outsider, the inward-looking intellectual—of the idea was the Suez crisis of 1956, a confusing, clumsily-executed debacle for American foreign policy. Gamel Abdel Nasser, president of Egypt, had recognized Communist China—and in a fit of self-righteous, Red-baiting pique, American secretary of state John Foster Dulles decided to cancel America's promise to fund the construction of the huge Aswan Dam on the Nile. This blunder precipitated the whole crisis, leaving Alex appalled by the thought of becoming a possible apologist for his government.

So, Alex followed his muse and returned to the Neighborhood Playhouse, studying with Sanford Meisner and the legendary dance master, Martha Graham. By this time, Alex had moved back home with his parents in a large, 3,000 square-foot apartment on 90 Riverside Drive in New York City, overlooking the Hudson at 81st St. Alex remembers this residence as "the best home we ever had." The Hassilevs were perplexed by the vacillating career choices of their only son. But Alex recalls that "my parents always supported me in whatever I wanted to do. If I wished any one thing from my family, it would have been if they had been a lot tougher with me and what I was doing than they ever were."

While he was finishing his work at the Playhouse, Alex's musical talent—up until now a sidelight—was beginning to receive some exposure, for he was invited to make his first public appearance as a folksinger. Now most folkies begin their careers in modest locales, usually working at some dive for peanuts. Alex started at Carnegie Hall! Actually, Alex was appearing as part of a mini-folk festival of up-and-coming but still unknown young folksingers organized by a New York disc jockey named Skip Weshner. For his one and only tune, Alex sang and played a fishing tune he had learned in Brazil called "Curimao," one that eventually became part of the Limeliters' repertoire. "I don't think I was that nervous," he recalls. "I knew I did that song very well, and I got a good reaction."

By this time, the calypso craze had swept the nation—and seeing an opportunity to make some extra bread, Alex got into a calypso band that lasted about a year. The other band members included the young actor/comedian/singer Hamilton Camp and the son of actor Cliff Arquette (a.k.a. Charley Weaver). Alex was the guitarist, Hamilton would sing and cavort around like a madman ("he was insane and wonderful," Alex recalls), and they would do calypso standards and improvise on current events of the day in the calypso tradition. The group, alas, never caught on in any kind of a significant scale—they played parties, mostly—and no recordings exist. But Alex recalls those days with a fond smile, even bursting into a verse in a mock-Trinidad accent.

Alex kept working on his original international folk repertoire, which he would perform at parties—and it was at one such party at the home of Gene and Francesca Raskin that Alex and his family first met Theodore Bikel. A Vienna-born singer/actor who had lived in Palestine and London before moving to America in 1954, Bikel was making a big name for himself acting in films and onstage and singing international folk songs in a zesty, penetrating baritone, always at home in a bewildering variety of languages and dialects. Naturally, he found himself drawn to Alex, for here was a singer/actor who could do the same thing and do it with confident authenticity in languages and accents, a rare quality in America. They would become lifelong friends, and on occasion, roommates and collaborators.

Bikel recalled that in those days, Alex was the new kid on the block, still very much in awe of the personalities he was meeting and rubbing elbows with on the party scene. "I don't know if I would describe him as shy," Bikel said. "It was more that he was younger than the rest of us; in those days, a few years made all the difference."

After finishing up at the Playhouse in 1957, Alex hit the mean streets of New York, looking for work. He got into some off-Broadway plays—nothing major—and taught guitar to keep busy. At one fateful juncture in 1958, an actress/singer named Janice Mars hired Alex to manage her club and sing while she went out on the road to do a play. The club, known as the Baq Room, was a 60-seat joint located on Sixth Ave. in midtown Manhattan. So, Alex had a somewhat steady gig for a while, singing international folk songs as a solo act and keeping things in order at the club.

At one point, Alex finally got a big break—a chance to act in a Broadway show. But he needed someone to take his place at Janice Mars' little club. The first person to come in to try for the job was a folksinger who the year before had been a member of The Tarriers, who scored a big hit with an Americanized folk rendition of "The Banana Boat Song" just before Belafonte's version took off.

The fellow sang a few songs in a desultory way, and Alex perceptively observed that it seemed like he didn't really want the job. He confessed as much, saying that he really wanted to be an actor—which is how we know Alan Arkin today.

But Alan did recommend someone whom Alex could use—a young sturdy-looking fellow from Milwaukee by the name of Glenn Yarbrough. And that is where the professional paths of Alex and Glenn first crossed.

Tamara, Alex and Leonide Hassilev, probably New York City, c 1940s
(Courtesy of Alex Hassilev)

Alex at age 7, 1940
(Courtesy of Alex Hassilev)

Glenn Yarbrough's first record, a 78 RPM disc on the
Stratford label (soon to be renamed Elektra).
Note the misspelled last name.
Released c. 1951. (Scan courtesy of Cary Ginell)

Chapter Three

Alex had known Glenn before he came into Janice Mars' Baq Room. They had met at a Greenwich Village party given by folksinger Cynthia Gooding sometime in either 1956 or 1957. Parties such as these remain a golden memory of a never-to-be-recaptured time in the Village. Folk music was on its way but had not yet been overexposed and over-commercialized. There were still new lodes to be mined, new songs to be revived, learned, swapped, and polished. Everyone seemed to be young, bright, and vibrant, banding together outside the blanket of Eisenhower-era middle-class conformity—and folk music was their common language.

"We all knew each other; everybody who played the guitar knew everybody else who played the guitar, especially if they sang also," said Theo Bikel. "And when there were new people coming up of whom one hadn't heard, the word got around and somehow you met them at a party.

"Nobody cared much about the drinking at all, and only cared peripherally about the eating and mostly cared about the music. That was the kind of party scene we had, which was different from the other parties, where people cared more about eating, drinking, and making out with women. It's not that we disdained that portion of the party scene, but it wasn't uppermost on our minds."

Music may not have been uppermost on the mind of Glenn Yarbrough. At the party at Cynthia Gooding's place, Alex remembers that Glenn was wearing a black turtleneck sweater, sitting on the floor, doing his routine of singing just two songs in the hopes of attracting some comely young thing into his bed. It had to be only two songs, for if you were like Theo Bikel standing there and singing all evening long, you would be the last one there—without a bedmate for the night. That was Glenn's way of getting laid then since he was still very shy with women—and apparently it always worked.

Alex was enormously impressed by what he heard—a clear, flexible, soaring tenor with an unmistakable timbre; it could belong to no one else. In the excitement of the moment, Alex just had to say, "Glenn, you're gonna be a star someday."

"And he looked at me," Alex recalls, "sitting on the floor, and he said, 'Yeah, yeah ... but I don't think I wanna.'"

It was a telling comment. Glenn Robertson Yarbrough ran from stardom for a good deal of his life. The twisted road map of his early life is strewn with routes not taken, whether by choice or circumstance, that might have made him famous long before the Limeliters or "Baby, the Rain Must Fall." His sheer vocal talent dazzled people since he was eight years old, when he became the star boy soprano at the Grace Church in New York City.

Yet Glenn had always been a true loner, anti-authoritarian to the core, a man who would rather be footloose and free than rich and famous. Eventually, late in life, he would come to terms with his enormous talent, trying to fulfill his old promise. But by then, the market had passed him by, and nothing he did would remotely equal the popular success of his string of albums in the '60s with the Limeliters and on his own.

Both of Glenn's colleagues in the Limeliters were in absolute awe of his talent. "I get goose pimples from hearing Yarbrough sing," said Lou. "He's a great singer, there's no doubt about it. Yarbrough is one of the great showmen of all time."

But Lou, speaking in 1978 just after the Limeliters Reunion disbanded, also hit upon the paradox of a tremendous talent trapped in an often-incompatible container. "Glenn, like so many great singers, never really developed an interest in music," he said. "I don't think he listens to music. I know he never plays the guitar. He sings a little bit; he warms up every night, he's interested in his act, he's interested in the structure and arrangements of the songs which he's gonna sing. But as far as what I consider to be an interest in music, he doesn't have it."

Alex had a typically more probing, but equally admiring analysis of Glenn Yarbrough. "Glenn uses sailing as a means of continuing his fantasy that he doesn't sing for a living," he said. "Glenn does not want to feel that he *has* to sing. But like anyone with a talent as great as his, he can't help but use that talent. He has an absolutely overwhelming vocal talent; I would put him in the Top 20 singers in America, period, in terms of sheer ability to sing. God gave it to him, and he has to use it."

Glenn's mother, Elizabeth Robertson hailed from Scottish descent on her father's side and German descent on her mother's side. The Robertsons were a wealthy family in New York City, Glenn's maternal grandfather being Vice President of the Bowery Savings Bank.

Unintimidated by great wealth, Elizabeth struck out on her own for Northwestern University in Chicago and became a social worker, even working in Hull House with the legendary Jane Addams. Never one to simply stay at home, she insisted upon working whenever she could. "She was one of the first liberated women...very dynamic, quite a character." said Glenn. "She was spontaneous, and my father was a rigid kind of guy." As a result, Glenn added, "I never grew up with a mother at home. Women to me have always been equal creatures."

Somehow, Elizabeth Robertson managed to fall in love with younger, quiet, stolid Bruce Yarbrough, a fellow social worker who came from a rural family in Kansas that eventually moved to Colorado. It would be a baffling attraction of almost total opposites, a trait that would be passed onto their son, who also tended to be drawn to women of different temperaments than his own.

"Glenn's father is a very quiet man who loves to be alone," said Jonathan Moore, a longtime friend of Glenn's. "His mother is very funny; she's in her 80s and running around like a 2-year-old. She goes everywhere all over the world, and she's very outgoing. How Bruce and she ever married is beyond me. They've never bothered to get a divorce, those two, and they've never seemed to have any problem. Glenn follows his father more in personality."

After they were married, the Yarbroughs moved to Milwaukee, where Bruce found a job as an athletic secretary at the local YMCA. There in Milwaukee, Glenn, their only child, was born on Jan. 12, 1930. When Glenn was about four years old, Bruce Yarbrough was transferred to the YMCA in Aberdeen, South Dakota. There, deep in the Great Plains, Glenn started school, and the family remained in Aberdeen for two or three years.

Glenn couldn't recall how he became aware of music; he just remembered himself singing from as far back as his memory can carry him. Those who knew Glenn's father say that Glenn inherited his extraordinary voice from Bruce Yarbrough, who also had an attractive, high-pitched tenor. When Glenn was but a toddler, his parents wanted him to take piano lessons, but Glenn hated the instrument; he would only consent to piano lessons if he could sing while he played. Interestingly, Glenn said that he never had any voice lessons, as if his singing just gushed forth like a mountain spring gives water or an apple tree grows apples.

"I really wasn't interested in music," he said. "I just like to sing. Even today I don't have that much interest in music except as I do it myself."

Glenn remembered his early years in Aberdeen as a traumatic time. The YMCA decided to fire the custodian at the building just before his 20th year there to save money on retirement funds. An outraged Bruce wanted to resign in protest—and this being 1937, with America still mired in the Great Depression, it was a risky thing to do. Glenn's parents debated endlessly about it, but in this high-minded family, conscience had to take precedence over mere financial matters. Bruce quit his job in solidarity with the unlucky custodian, and Glenn said that his life changed completely after that.

Just as the Yarbroughs feared, Bruce couldn't find a job anywhere in Aberdeen, so he left town alone to look for work and Elizabeth took young Glenn back to her family in New York City. Glenn's unemployed but enterprising mother realized that her eight-year-old son could sing like an angel—and one day, she took him downtown to Grace Church at 10th and Broadway in hopes of landing him a job there. For the first and not the last time, Glenn's natural wellspring of talent bowled over his auditioners, and the church hired him as the soprano soloist in its boys' choir for $25 a week. In those days, that was enough to support Glenn and his mother in New York City until she and Bruce could find jobs.

Glenn would also attend school at the Grace Church School, though he lived in another neighborhood on the Lower East Side. He used to walk down from the Lower East Side 10 or 12 blocks to school, and since he was attending an exclusive private school, his mother dressed him in what Glenn remembered as cute Little Lord Fauntleroy clothes. To get to 10th and Broadway, Glenn had to walk through a rough neighborhood, and being the odd kid out in that area, he was an obvious target for bullies.

"I used to get beat up all the time going home," Glenn said. "My mother would never take sides; she always thought I should be independent. I'd go home and I'd be crying, and she'd say, 'Well, you've just gotta learn to fight your own battles.' I'd say, 'If you'd stop dressing me up in these Lord Fauntleroy clothes, I wouldn't be so conspicuous!'"

Even then, Glenn's voice had made him a local celebrity at the church. After the services, Glenn found himself having to sign autographs (at 8 years old!) out in front of the church for the girls waiting for the buses to take them back to their girls' schools. Being very shy, he spent the week dreading those Sundays when he would have to sing his solos and mingle with the girls. For those who wonder why Glenn always used to make quick getaways after his concerts, this is where it took root, for Glenn never did get over his shyness.

After long periods of scuffling, Bruce Yarbrough finally found a job in Baltimore. So, at the age of 11, Glenn and his mother moved from New York to Baltimore, where he became the featured boy soprano at St. Paul's Church, a position which also gave him a scholarship at St. Paul's School. Glenn would not be easily forgotten, for when he left New York, the church officials had Glenn's name carved in the wall of Grace Church as the greatest soprano they ever had—and his name remains there to this day.

Glenn lived at home for the first year in Baltimore, but when his parents decided to move back to South Dakota, Glenn stayed on in St. Paul's as a boarding student. From that time forward in his life, except for some relatively brief visits to South Dakota, Glenn was on his own—and the experience shaped his personality as a self-reliant loner.

While at St. Paul's, Glenn's voice broke, as it inevitably does when boys enter adolescence—and the officials there told him that when his voice changed, he wouldn't be able to sing again. So, Glenn, who hated the thought of getting up before people and singing anyway, just stopped—stopped cold. And with his retirement from singing—the first of many to come—came a change of interests. Always a husky lad, and having become interested in sports, Glenn changed his scholarship to football, and before long, he became a star guard on the St. Paul football team. Glenn also played lacrosse, a goal game that uses a long-handled stick with a loose-mesh pouch for catching and carrying the ball. Although Glenn remained a football fan—he' would interrupt everything on Sundays just to watch the games on the tube—he never really liked playing football all that much. It was just a means to an end, another pattern that surfaces a lot in his life, a way to keep his scholarship going.

Glenn's athletic abilities turned out to be as much in demand as his musical talents, for when he graduated in 1948, several colleges offered him football scholarships. But Glenn didn't want to go to college on a football scholarship, and so, in order to figure out what to do next, he went home. Home this time was Deadwood in the Black Hills of South Dakota, where his parents had settled.

Glenn asked his mother what he should do—and most mothers would have probably said, go to college and learn a profession. But ever the free spirit, Glenn's mother told him, "Oh don't go, go off and have some fun." Hitch-hike around the country, see the world, learn, grow, risk. So, Glenn took his thumb and left, armed with graduation money his maternal grandparents had given him. He struck out for the north from Deadwood, through North Dakota into the plains of Canada, then west to the coast through the provinces of Alberta and British Columbia. He saw the city of Calgary, the majestic Canadian Rockies, the mountains and deserts of British Columbia, and the beautiful city of Vancouver. Roughly following the route of Alex's youthful bicycle tour, Glenn's thumb then took him down south through Seattle, the states of Washington and Oregon, down through his future home state of California.

Glenn ended up in Long Beach, California, arriving at the pier near the now-defunct Nu-Pike amusement park. The irresistible urge to move on had finally been dampened a bit, so Glenn put his sleeping bag underneath the pier and lived there for about two months. He would go to the so-called "University-By-The-Sea"—a public gathering place where anyone with a thought in his head could get up and speak. It was set up like a classroom, right up on the pier, and Glenn would be exposed to all kinds of ideas as he warmed himself in the lazy California sun.

Then the graduation money ran out, and Glenn had to suspend his long holiday. He wouldn't ask for handouts, being too proud—or perhaps too shy—to do so, and as a result, he said that he went without eating for two weeks. Ultimately, there was only one solution; he had to look for work. Taking stock of himself, Glenn figured that the only thing he knew how to do was take care of children; singing for a living apparently didn't even enter his mind then. He wrote letters to all the private schools in the area, and finally, he landed a job at the Palomar School for Boys as a dorm counselor and disciplinarian.

It so happened that the owner of the school had a lot of friends in Hollywood's film industry. He heard Glenn singing one day as he was just going about his business, doing his usual chores. Like everyone else, he was stunned by the natural beauty and power of Glenn's voice, and he took his itinerant dorm counselor to his opulent home in Beverly Hills and invited several friends from the studios, MGM, Paramount, and others. Glenn sang for these people, and incredibly, the man from Paramount offered him a $100-a-week job on the spot. He would go to school at Paramount and learn to dance, sing, and act through the Paramount star system, a real foot into the door of Hollywood.

"He was all excited about it and I wasn't," Glenn remembered. "By that time, I was really getting interested in seeing the world; I had seen a lot of stuff and I wanted to see some more. So, I eventually turned it down—and as soon as I made enough money to leave, I left and hitch-hiked down to Mexico." Just like that. By sheer accident, Glenn had wandered through the doorway that thousands of more motivated, starstruck, would-be actors would never even see, and he amiably wandered back out. "If I'd taken it," Glenn mused, "I probably would have been like Donald O'Connor, a big star for a while and then down, over the hill! I wouldn't have been anywhere near as happy as I ended up."

Glenn meandered through Mexico, then north to Texas, through the Deep South into the Florida panhandle. Eventually he landed in Naples, Florida, a small town on the Gulf of Mexico on the opposite side of the Everglades from Fort Lauderdale. Here, Glenn thought he would pitch his sleeping bag once again, on the beach in front of a row of big, expensive houses. There he stayed for another two months, not doing much of anything. He would take daily swims up to two miles out to sea before heading back. It was not too bright a thing to do, for right next to where he was swimming was a shark fishing pier, where they would catch hundreds of the dangerous monsters. Yet Glenn never had a close call, nothing.

One day, while sleeping on the beach, Glenn met an older man who used to be an insurance executive in Chicago, left his wife and kids, left them everything he owned, and made his way down to Florida. Once there, he bought a sailboat in a state of disrepair which he planned to fix up, sail to Cuba and eventually around the world. The two refugees from the straight life became fast friends; the older man would bring

Glenn picnic lunches from the hotel where he worked. Finally, one day, the ex-insurance man asked Glenn if he would want to come along and work on the boat. This is probably the point where Glenn's passion for sailing was ignited, and the sea would never quite loosen its grip.

"I was so excited because I thought, jeez, this is really something interesting," Glenn recalled. "This guy told me, 'I think I can get you a job at the hotel and we could make money and build this boat and get going.' He had just come that morning and said that the next day I would have a job.

"But the cops came, and they got me off the beach. They put me in a police car; it was late in the afternoon. I told the cops, 'Look, I have a job and everything, I'm moving into the '—'hotel, and they wouldn't listen. They took me to the Everglades, to the edge of the city and said, 'Don't come back across this line or you're going to jail!' I said, 'At least give me until tomorrow morning so I don't have to go through the Everglades at night.' They said, 'Nope, you go.' So, I started walking, some guy stopped and took me all the way to Miami."

In Miami, Glenn got his first real taste of Southern racism. Deciding to head north, he hitched a ride with a Black truck driver who worked for a circus. The truck driver had picked Glenn up because he couldn't stop anywhere to eat on the highway, so all Glenn had to do was go in and buy food wherever they stopped. As painful as this must have been to a teenager with growing social awareness, Glenn nevertheless stayed with this truck all the way back to Baltimore. His rambling days were through, for the time being.

With not much else to do, Glenn dropped in at his alma mater, St. Paul's, where the spring lacrosse season was starting, and they hired him as an assistant coach. One day that spring, the dean of St. John's College in Annapolis came to St. Paul's and gave a lecture on the Great Books program there. Glenn's ears lit up. That would be his next direction.

Glenn talked to the dean right after his lecture, saying he would love to go but that he had no money. The dean said to come on down and take an exam and perhaps he could get a scholarship. Glenn did, and he passed. The deal included tuition, plus room and board, plus a paying job as head of intramural athletics.

The Great Books program at St. John's bears only a fleeting resemblance to what passes as a college education these days. Starting from a base in pre-Socratic Greece, the beginning of recorded intellectual activity, the curriculum gradually worked its way up through the chain of civilization. The language program began with Greek, the math classes went through the 14 books of Pythagoras culminating in the Pythagorian Theorem. In science, you started by rubbing two stones together to get a plain surface. There were no electives; each student took the classes that the administration laid out for them to take. Each class would read passages from the designated Great Books, and students would go into seminars with three tutors where they would discuss what they read. Some of these sessions would last all night long.

"They didn't really have exams like you have in regular schools," Glenn remembered. "You go in a room with all your tutors, the tutors would start talking to you, not to find out how much you had memorized or what you know about any particular subject, but to find out how much better you are able to think more deeply through a subject than the last time they examined you. It would last two or three hours, like a seminar. Then after three or four days, they would have the grades, which were really not grades. The teachers would get in a room—about six teachers—around a table and you would sit in a corner, and they would talk about you like you weren't there. And then they would turn to you and ask if you had anything to say and you'd give your two cents worth and that would be the end of it."

Both Glenn's athletic and musical talents were put to good use at St. John's. The school paid him to play semi-pro football on the St. John's team. There was a semi-pro barbershop quartet there, which Glenn joined, and he would also sing in the church.

In addition, Glenn found that although he loathed the pop songs of the post-big-band late '40s, singing them would become a great asset—indeed, the catalyst—for his social life. "They had a lot of great-looking women in Annapolis that would come in for the midshipmen," he recalled. "The midshipmen would go out with them all day and all night, and they'd go into these homes that would have little common rooms where they would sit at night and neck until the midshipmen had to go home at midnight. So, after midnight there were all these horny girls around with nobody to deal with it. The St. John's students would go out after midnight and pick up these girls. The best way to do it, for me, would be to go to the clubs and sing the popular songs of the day. But I never liked the material and I never thought of becoming a singer."

Then one day, Woody Guthrie came through town. Until then—just like Lou and Alex at key catalytic moments of their lives—Glenn had no inkling of what folk music was. Like his two future colleagues, he would never be the same afterwards—and since he was receiving the gospel from the most charismatic singer/songwriter of his time, Glenn may have been hit even harder.

"Every Friday night, we had a lecture, or sometimes a concert," Glenn said. "I had never heard of folk music, and he came on and started singing those songs, and...oh boy, I'll tell you I was just so moved by that whole thing. It was music I had never heard before, but it was music with a meaning. It said something important.

"I was a pretty shy kid but after the concert I went up and told him how much I appreciated what he'd done. And he came with me to my room in the dormitory with about three or four of us, and he sang all night long till about four or five in the morning. So the next day I thought that's what I want to do."

The first "folk" song that Glenn says he learned was a 1942 tune that Carson Robison recorded, "I'm Goin' Back to Whur I Come From," where Glenn quickly learned to play the role of the charming country bumpkin, fingers rolling over the guitar strings in a hypnotic sing-song rhythm. Right next door to Glenn in the dorm, by another amazing stroke of luck, was an electronics-crazy fellow student and budding young entrepreneur named Jac Holzman, who was about to found a tiny record company, Elektra-Stratford, which eventually became the giant label Elektra. He and Glenn became friends, and when Glenn learned to play the guitar in emulation of his new hero Woody Guthrie, Jac—who was recording everything within earshot around St. John's—wanted to record him.

They went down to the commons room of St. John's dormitory sometime in 1950 and recorded two songs, backed only by Glenn's by-now competent guitar. The A-side was a folk standard about directing the slaves out of the old South called "Follow The Drinking Gourd;" the B-side was an old English folk song called "The Reaper's Ghost." These are low-key yet intense purist folk performances; at 20, Glenn already sounds comfortable in his new folk environment, in confident possession of his unique timbre, soulfully using rubato and other expressive devices, already as good as any professional in that field. Jac put the two songs out on a vinyl 78 RPM ten-inch disc bearing the Stratford label, with Glenn's name misspelled "Yarborough." It made a mild impression but there was no follow-up release; Jac was just experimenting.

During the summers at St. John's while school was out, Glenn worked as a lifeguard at the Annapolis Roads Club. At the time, he was still a virgin; thanks to his singing, he dated but never got all the way around the bases. Having gone to all-boys schools and an all-men's college, it was almost impossible to smuggle women into the rooms—and besides, Glenn's shyness was a further handicap.

"Here I was, surrounded with women, and all the mothers and fathers thought I was—as all lifeguards are—a real cocksmith around the club and they all warned their daughters to stay away from me," he recalled. "Of course, that just made 'em more interested, and Peggy was one of those who got interested, and she was smart enough to realize I didn't know a damned thing. So, she just took me under her wing. Taught me everything I needed to know."

"Peggy" was the nickname of Margaret Goodhardt, a determined young woman of German descent who finally broke Glenn's virginity. At the time, the shy young singer thought that the joys of sex would never happen again with anyone else, and he was, needlessly to say, extremely grateful.

After they were married and divorced, Glenn would pay for his early gratitude with some very nasty and very public battles.

Nevertheless, Glenn and Peggy set up housekeeping together in an apartment off campus—a radical lifestyle for the Truman era. It was a large four-bedroom job near the gates of the Naval Academy in Annapolis, and a young cadet named Gerald Sylvester would share the rent with Glenn.

Eventually, they cooked up the scheme of renting the extra bedrooms out to other men who wanted a place in which to sleep with their girlfriends. Glenn and Gerald had a thriving business flouting convention for two years before the authorities found out and placed the apartment off-limits. Glenn may have been living with Peggy but he claimed he had absolutely no intention of marrying her; there was lust on his part but apparently little love. But then in the summer of 1951, he received a desperate call from his father, asking him to come out to South Dakota for the season and help him on his new business. It was a resort called Rimrock Lodge, and for a conservative man like Bruce

Yarbrough, it was his big opportunity to break out of the routine of odd jobs and really make some bucks.

"I agreed to come out," remembered Glenn, "not realizing that here I was living with this girl, and it just wasn't done in those days, and it just never occurred to me that there would be any problem over it. When we got there, I was put in the lodge and she was put in with the waitresses, and I thought wow, wait a minute, this isn't going to work. She said, 'Well, don't get excited, I'll just come up at night and we'll sleep together and early in the morning, I'll go back.'

"Well, somebody told on her, and my father found out and there was all hell to pay. Ordinarily, I would say, 'Hey, you don't like the way I live, forget it, so long.' But I felt so sorry for the man because he really needed me desperately. He wanted to send her back to Baltimore. Finally, I said I guess I can put up with this for a month, send her back to Baltimore. But I felt so badly about it with her for not sticking up for me that I proposed to her, which I really had no intention of doing. And when we got back, we got married at the church there."

Glenn stayed on at St. John's for three years. While he was fascinated with the early courses on the Greeks, Glenn began to get tired of the work after the first year—and when the courses veered into the world of modern philosophy after the second year, Glenn simply lost interest in the whole thing. He was turned off by the ivory tower nature of modern philosophy, without any apparent connection to what Glenn was learning and experiencing in the real world. He also must have particularly dreaded the senior year, in which a student would spend it writing a thesis which was almost like an athletic competition.

"The senior thesis was the thing that everybody got excited about," he recalled. "Each senior would have this huge seminar. In your regular seminar, you would have to defend your position on a small scale, but in the senior thesis, you defended it among the ten top faculty members and any student who wanted to come and challenge you. They had this one room with this huge table and bleachers; it was like an athletic event. We would all go to these things and really lay out a senior and give him a hard time. It was a lot of fun."

At least it was for the lucky ones who weren't being roasted.

By this time, Glenn was getting to be known as quite a character around town. He had grown a long beard; he never wore shoes even in the wintertime (he always had an aversion to clothes). Whenever there was an

Alumni Day, Glenn recalls, the president of the university would come up to Glenn and tell him, "Please do me a favor and get off the campus!" He would then give him a couple of dollars and send him off to a movie until the respectable folk had gone home. "I guess I was the first real hippie in those days," Glenn said with a mixture of relaxed pride and sheepishness.

Moreover, the recurring fever of wanderlust had struck again. Glenn wanted to get out and see more of the world that he had sampled on his year-long hitchhiking odyssey around North America. Shortly after he and Peggy were married, Glenn thought that the time was coming for him to quit.

He stopped doing the work; he was expelled twice from St. John's for "eccentric behavior," though he was reinstated both times. Finally, the exasperated administration took away Glenn's scholarship, effectively ending his St. John's career.

He and Peggy headed West, through the Appalachians, over the plains, the Rockies and the deserts—destination, California. He had a burning desire to go back to Long Beach, to show Peggy what it was like when he was an aimless 18-year-old, bumming around the country. But when they reached Bakersfield, they were flat broke, and they had to work as cotton-pickers in the scorching San Joaquin Valley to make enough money to continue on their way.

"Talk about hard jobs," Glenn said, "I couldn't believe how hard that job was. Hot, bent over all the time. I don't know how they do it today. We had these big bags, dragged them along all the time." Indeed, Glenn must have been one of the few white urban folk singers ever to work at something which they used to sing about.

Once in Long Beach, broke again, Glenn and Peggy both got jobs at the Nu-Pike amusement park—and these must rank as the most bizarre occupations they've ever had. Glenn worked as a "bozo," a guy who sits on a plank in a tank and the customers throw baseballs at him. When they hit the target, the poor bozo goes down in the water. "In those days, you didn't throw baseballs at white guys, you throw them at Black guys, so I had to be in blackface in order to do it," Glenn remembered. Peggy had a job that was probably even worse. She was the assistant to a knife-thrower—the target!

At this time, Glenn had no idea of what he wanted to do with himself. Not even that priceless night with Woody Guthrie had convinced him that singing would be the way to go. Ultimately the U.S.

Government, via the draft, made up Glenn's mind for him; his mail had been forwarded to Bakersfield and then to Long Beach, where his draft notice came sailing in one day. But Glenn didn't object. At that time, he was a fervent believer in the United Nations as an idealistic peace-keeping force. The Korean War was technically a United Nations war, even though the U.S. bore the brunt of the fighting. Had it only been an American war, Glenn wouldn't have been so eager.

Typically, Glenn left everything he owned with Peggy and stepped forward for induction before being assigned to Fort Ord. Unlike many recruits, the former football player breezed through basic training; the hardest part was probably the moment when they shaved off his beard and gave him a G.I. haircut. He wasn't good at target practice; he deliberately made bad marks on his gun tests because he didn't want to kill anybody. As a result, the brass assigned him to signal operations, and it was on to Korea from there. Peggy moved to Greenwich Village, and Glenn went back East on furlough to spend some time with her before he was due to be shipped off. When Glenn arrived in Pusan, the brass didn't know what to do with him, so they gave him a dream job, one with no supervision—exactly to Glenn's liking. He would be running signal operations instructions by scrambling frequencies on the front lines so that the enemy wouldn't know where a certain outfit was on the battlefield. Glenn would only have to scramble the frequencies every three or four days.

Since Glenn had no real boss, no officer in charge, he thought he was the only grunt who came back from Korea as a PFC, but of course, that certainly didn't bother him one bit.

If you hadn't already guessed by now, Glenn was not exactly enthralled with the idea of being an American soldier, and he found the idea of being among the Korean people far more appealing. "I hated the Army so much," he said. "I immediately saw how these people lived; they lived in little tin shacks that were just thrown up for refugee shelter. They cost only about $20 apiece. So, I bought myself one of these shacks, and I never went back to the compound after that. I would go to my job in downtown Pusan just like I was commuting to work and then come back to my shack and spend a lot of time at the University there."

He fell in love with a Korean teacher who ran her classes like a Socratic dialogue, all questions, little actual teaching. His interest in music was reawakened by the Korean culture and, having learned some Korean songs with his quick ear, he was able to pick up some professional singing jobs. The brass, like so many other authority figures in his life, noticed his natural singing voice, and they sent him to Japan to go to an entertainment school with the intent of running recreational activities for the idle troops in Korea. In a separate program, a female colonel would get lists from the commanders on the most talented entertainers in their units and she would pick people from the list. Evidently the commanders couldn't care less about the caliber of the selections, so the colonel was stuck with the goof-offs. She was trying to put together a different program for a package show, and she was getting desperate. She asked Glenn's commander if they would release him for the show, and he did. Glenn and two others, a magician/hypnotist and a comedian, were the centerpieces. Glenn would come on at the end of the show, play the guitar and sing. The other two performers were surrounded by the incompetents who would just dance around them. But Glenn went on alone, and he wondered why. The female colonel told him, "Well, when you got real talent, you don't need anything else."

The threesome and their supporting cast played to gatherings all over the Asian Pacific Rim—in Korea and Japan, as well as bases on Okinawa and in the Philippines. When the act disbanded, the three of them went on to do shows for the hospitals. It was Glenn's first real taste of show business life—and as a reward for making the program work, the colonel gave Glenn the remaining three or four months of his hitch off to do as he pleased. By now Glenn had learned a lot of Korean and Japanese songs—he was even fooling native speakers who, sight unseen, thought he was Korean—so he thought he would try his luck at a Far Eastern show business career. Turned loose in Japan, he went to a Japanese booking agent and became the only American in all-Japanese revues, vastly out earning his colleagues from the start.

Glenn in turn fell in love with one of his booking agents and went off to live with her. He had long since stopped writing to Peggy since he arrived in Korea. But Peggy still wanted Glenn; she kept writing to the chaplain wondering why he never wrote.

Glenn seemed headed for another rendezvous with stardom in Japan, with a big boost from his agent lover. He was really beginning to make it there, getting more work, headed toward star status. His hitch in the Army was up, and Glenn wanted to be released in Japan. But the

Army made him see the aforementioned chaplain who, with one of Peggy's letters in hand, told him to go back to his wife. Glenn promised his Japanese lover that he was just going to the U.S. to get discharged and would be back on the next plane. Her world-weary reaction was, "Sure." Sure enough, Glenn never saw her again and when he returned to Japan many years later, he couldn't even look her up because he had forgotten her name!

In Seattle, Glenn tried to get his discharge and his discharge money so he could buy a plane ticket for Japan. But the authorities made it clear that they were required to discharge him in New York City because Glenn had foolishly put Peggy's Greenwich Village address on his papers. So, Glenn had to fly back East, where he was immediately given a two-week leave in the big city before his official discharge.

"I don't want a two-week leave," Glenn protested. "I want out now."

No dice—take your leave and that's an order.

"There I was in Times Square," he recalled. "I wandered around for about a week trying to avoid going to see Peggy, and finally I thought, well, I'll just go and say hello."

BIG mistake.

"I went down to Greenwich Village," Glenn continued. "She had a voice box there, and said, 'Who is it?' and I said, 'It's Glenn,' and there was dead silence on the other end.

"She said, 'Would you wait down there please for just a few minutes?' So, I waited down there. Pretty soon I see an old college friend of mine from St. John's come tromping out with all his clothes in a duffel bag looking real sad. She had thrown him out!"

Glenn never did become a star in Japan—though this time, it was not for a lack of effort on his part. The fates had other plans for him.

Chapter Four

It was toward the end of 1953. McCarthyism was at its sinister apex of influence and power, though much of white America had already settled into a comfortable pursuit of material goods and wholesome conformity. Not Glenn Yarbrough. His Japanese adventure over and done with, his loveless marriage alive if not perfectly well, he still didn't have a clue as to what he wanted to do with his life. Like many young intellectually inclined people who postpone the day of reckoning, Glenn turned back toward academia. He wanted to study pre-Socratic philosophy, picking up where his favorite studies at St. John's had left off. He had heard of a great philosophy teacher who was working at Mexico City College, he had funds from the G.I. Bill in hand, and the price was cheap. Peggy drove a beat-up station wagon and Glenn had a little motor scooter and off they sped toward Mexico City.

Glenn immediately had a problem with what he called the "machismo stuff" that drives urban Mexican males and, true to form, soon moved out of town to a little Indian village called Quahimalba. Then, Peggy fell in love with a student at Mexico City College and moved in with him, leaving Glenn high and dry and ready to throw over the academic life once again and hit the road, this time trundling north back to his parents in South Dakota. The wayfaring young man was ready to give up roaming again, believing he would end up as a football coach or a philosophy teacher.

But again, Glenn's tremendous singing talent would cause people to sit up and take notice. He soon found a job doing television and radio shows at a station in Rapid City. Glenn didn't recall how he got the job, only that the Bank of the Black Hills sponsored the TV program. The television shows ran on Friday night at 7:30 and Sunday night at 9:00—the prime night for a television show. There was no video tape in those days so Glenn did the TV shows live, and then would go into a studio and tape his five radio shows for the week. The station paid him a princely sum of about $1,000 a week. "My father, who never made more than $3,000 a year in his life, was just amazed at this situation," Glenn said. "I discovered the power of television because after doing these shows for maybe four or five weeks, I went one time to a local high school basketball game and, my God, I was swamped with people and I couldn't stay, I had to leave."

After only six months of being a star in Rapid City, Glenn once again felt the urge to move on. "My father is such a conservative guy when I told him I was quitting to go to New York to try and make it in the big time, he thought I was nuts," he says.

Glenn went from stardom in South Dakota to a $29-a-month sixth-floor walkup in the Lower East Side near Delancey Street, and later an apartment in the Village. By then, Peggy had drifted away from her Mexico City lover and back to the Village, so Glenn moved back in with her—again for the time being.

Glenn had gone back to New York not so much to get into show business as to study philosophy at the New School for Social Research. He would put in a punishing schedule, going to the school by day and working by night from midnight to 8 a.m. as a combination desk clerk/bouncer at the West Side Seamen's hotel on the West Side. He would be the only one there at those hours, where seamen who had just blown their pay on land would huddle inside to try and keep warm.

Glenn's job was to throw them out. "I hated that job, just hated it," he remembered. "There was no reason why they couldn't stay there." During this period in his life, Glenn frequently got invited to Manhattan parties where his two songs-gets-you-laid routine went into effect. More productively in the short run, it was at one of these parties in 1956 where Glenn met Tom and Pat Clancy—the Irish folk singing Clancy Brothers who had started their own folk label in 1956 called Tradition. They, like everyone else, were enormously impressed by Glenn's voice and they offered him a chance to make an album for their label.

Tradition had amassed a small but varied catalogue of folk music from all over the globe—Irish music, of course, Appalachian string music, flamenco recorded in an actual tavern, Ewan MacColl singing Scottish ballads, folk stars like Ed McCurdy, Oscar Brand and the emerging giant, Odetta.

Yet Glenn's first album *Come And Sit By My Side* released in the summer of 1957—with Glenn's name again consistently misspelled "Yarborough" on the back liner—is a distinct departure from the spare, purist folk that Tradition had been dealing with. "Here, Glenn brings folk music up to date, sings in a manner that modern listeners will understand and appreciate," the back liner says in bold print.

The arrangements were made by the Weavers' Fred Hellerman, who was hiding from the McCarthy posse under the pseudonym of "Fred Brooks," but they are nothing for anyone to get excited about. Many of the tracks have a small commercial vocal group cooing along or singing the lyrics in the manner of a '50s TV commercial or pop record (the choral sound on "My Mule Sal" a reworking of "The Erie Canal" could have been used to sell Pepsi). You can also hear a banjo in the background (Erik Darling?) on tracks like "Capitol Ship," "John Hardy" and the gospel/bluegrass-like "Lonesome Valley." Other songs like "Come Again" dispense with all the trappings, just Glenn over a lone acoustic guitar.

Yet Glenn's voice is an awesomely expressive instrument, with a slightly Irish accent that would disappear during the Limeliters days. And then there are times when somehow, everything seems to work, as in Merle Travis' incendiary classic about the plight of coal miners, "Dark As A Dungeon." Here, Glenn overcomes the chorus, the gimmicky echo, everything that Hellerman/Brooks throws at him, and reaches down to the harrowing roots of the song.

Come And Sit By My Side is not a very good record as a whole, but the potential of Glenn's voice, if properly used, is there for all to hear.

Not long afterwards, Glenn's old friend from the dorm at St. John's, Jac Holzman, invited him to make an album for Elektra. By this time, Peggy had been working for Holzman, essentially running the financial end of the small company that was beginning to make some real noise largely through the albums of Theodore Bikel. ("There were three sets of books," Lou remembered Peggy telling him. "There was one for the IRS, one for the artists, and then the REAL books.") Again, a small purist folk label would shift directions especially for Glenn, allowing him to use a variety of backgrounds. Again, Glenn would use Fred Hellerman to create those backgrounds—again, at considerable professional risk.

"Freddy Hellerman arranged the (Tradition) album under a pseudonym, and I didn't think anything of it at the time, although I was sure against the McCarthy era," Glenn recalled. "But then Freddy came to me one day before the (Elektra) sessions and he said 'Pete Seeger is really in bad shape, he needs a job desperately, he can't make any money, nobody will give him a job. Is it OK if we use his banjo on the sessions?' And I said, 'Sure no problem.'

"And then I went home and began to think about this whole thing, and I thought, there's really no reason why Freddy Hellerman should be working under a pseudonym and there's no reason why he (Seeger) can't use his own name. I went back to Freddy and I said, 'I thought this over last night and not only is it OK but I think you and Freddy ought to use your own names in the credits.' At that time—it sounds silly now—that was a serious decision to make. Finally, I made the right decision because, at the time if I didn't, this was a decision I had to live with the rest of my life."

On the album *Glenn Yarbrough*, Fred Hellerman is given his due for leading the backup groups, although the single "Here We Go, Baby" is credited once again to Fred Brooks—perhaps so as not to alienate any DJs from giving it a spin and "Brooks" gets the credit for the adaptations of public domain folk songs. Also on Tradition's first Folk Sampler, issued about the same time as Glenn's first Elektra album, Fred Hellerman's name has been restored on Glenn's track, "Dark As A Dungeon."

But Glenn's problems with the record did not end with dealing with the blacklist. "The problem was that Pete Seeger didn't like the music he was playing on my record, and he was being very petulant about it on the session," Glenn recalled. "I was very annoyed at him. Look, if you don't like the music, it's OK, but just don't ruin the record because of it. You're getting paid to do a job, so just do it, you know? I didn't say anything about it, but everybody just kept their mouths shut until the session was over, and then I talked to Freddy and he said, 'Well I tuned him out anyway, we'll bring in Erik Darling to overdub his part on the record.'"

Not surprisingly, given the presence of Hellerman, *Glenn Yarbrough* is more or less a elaborate continuation of his predecessor—grounded but not chained in folk traditions, keeping an ear open for a possible hit that might come springing out of nowhere. The production numbers could be considered a low-budget foretaste of Glenn's solo career on RCA Victor; even then, Glenn and his handlers saw potential stardom in his future and seemed to be steering him toward the mainstream where stars were traditionally born.

The arrangement for "Here We Go, Baby," a tune credited to Yarbrough, "Brooks" and Erik Darling, is so busy with a solo flute, French horn, vocal group, and bongos that even Glenn's voice sometimes gets buried in the mix. It's an exuberant mess, yet it did make some waves later as a single.

No less than four of the songs Glenn does here would eventually wind up on Limeliters albums. "Rich Gal, Poor Gal" in another busy Hellerman chart, would become "Charmin' Betsy," and "Spanish Is A Loving Tongue," Woody Guthrie's "Hard Ain't It Hard" and "This Land is Your Land" would later be covered by the trio. "Hard" is right out of the Weavers' playbook, a big jazzy backbeat, lots of banjo, chorus, and a clarinet solo; Glenn sounds exuberant and uninhibited.

"All Through The Night," however, has the same lonely, stark quality of the un-orchestrated numbers on the Tradition album. We hear the inimitable Glenn Yarbrough whistle for the first time on the sea shanty, "Goodbye My Lover." Josh White, then recording for Elektra, sits in on guitar on a few unspecified cuts (certainly on "House Of The Rising Sun"), and one can imagine Josh peering over Glenn's shoulder, whether present or not, on the vocal to "Hey, Jim Along."

The New York party scene continued to provide Glenn with leads and breaks when he needed them but least expected them. One of them would be the engagement at Janice Mars' Baq Room at the behest of Alex Hassilev. Unlike Alan Arkin, Glenn did not have to audition, as Alex had vividly remembered the voice that had struck him so unexpectedly at the party. He just called Glenn up and asked him if he could do it. The engagement there didn't last long, but Glenn would certainly remember and repay the favor later.

At yet another such party, after the Elektra album was recorded, Glenn did his two songs, waited to collect his feminine reward—and a fellow from Chicago came up to Glenn and asked him if he would like to work at his club. The club was the modernistic, stark-white Gate of Horn, which had opened six months before, and the man's name was Albert Grossman, the same Albert Grossman who would become a legendary mover and shaker in American music. Grossman offered Glenn $150 a week—more money than he had seen in a long time—to replace Bob Gibson, who had played there since the club opened. Glenn quit the New School—in effect, finally calling a halt to his long-running academic career—and headed off for the Windy City.

When he got there a couple of days early, Glenn recalls the first thing he noticed were the lines around the block for Gibson. Watching the magnetic Gibson, he thought, Geez, I'll never be able to do this. But he managed. Glenn's Elektra album had just been released, and once he started working at the Horn, the single "Here We Go, Baby" started to take off in the Midwest (it became one of Elektra's bigger commercial successes up to that point).

Glenn at first was the opening act for Big Bill Broonzy, then nearing the end of his career. He was mesmerized by the great bluesman, who was losing a slow, painful bout with cancer but kept his music going for as long as he could. "They'd take him out of the club and take him to record every night," Glenn remembered. "He'd record all night long to get all his stuff down before he died. They worked him mercilessly. He taught me so much about entertaining people."

After Big Bill's run, a then nearly-unknown comedian named Shelley Berman came in to open the show. Once they became friends, Glenn graciously decided to let Berman close the show—and Berman's meteoric rise in nightclubs and on records was launched from there. Glenn remembers that he loved to hang out after hours with Berman and satirist Mort Sahl, laughing his sides off at their quips and routines. He did even more for Berman, listening to his marital problems, driving him home night after night.

Yet without a doubt, the most memorable aspect about Glenn's Gate of Horn gig was the influence of the singer whom Glenn replaced, Bob Gibson. Even 30 years later, both Alex and Glenn were still in awe of the performing abilities of Gibson—who, in light of later personal and drug problems, never made as big a mark on the folk scene as everyone thought he would. In those days, Gibson had a fresh, engagingly youthful tenor, played excellent banjo, and had a way of ingratiating himself with an audience based upon and even rivaling the manner of Pete Seeger.

"Bob was probably the most powerful single entertainer in folk music from 1954 to 1961 in the sense that he could completely turn a room around without any effort at all," said Dick Rosmini, who played backup guitar for Gibson throughout his career. "If nobody had known him, they didn't know who he was, he'd do three tunes and every face would be bolted to the stage. He was a blockbuster performer."

"Bob was the consummate entertainer," Glenn said. "I had not thought of what I did as entertainment until he came along. And then I saw what can be done with this kind of material as entertainment. He'd just go up on that stage and knock those people out. Also, the stuff that he was writing and singing were just right up my alley. He stopped being an entertainer after he went on to drugs and LSD and stuff. His nature just wouldn't allow him to be the kind of entertainer he was before."

Glenn worked at the Gate of Horn for six months. While at the Horn, he was approached by a young, local, wealthy Jewish kid named Sheldon Rich—an aspiring writer and reluctant businessman. He wanted to spend his life writing but his parents, like so many parents, thought that he should have a real profession. Determined to go his own way but also eager to please, Rich hit upon the idea of building a restaurant and nightclub in the Colorado ski resort of Aspen. It was a brilliant solution, he thought—making a buck and living in the breathtaking shadows of some of the Colorado Rockies' most picturesque peaks. He soon found otherwise, as owning and running a club turned out to be a full-time ordeal. But in the meantime, Rich was on the lookout for talent—and Glenn landed right in his sights.

Glenn found himself working the 1957 summer season for Rich at the Limelite in downtown Aspen. In those days, the Limelite was just a restaurant and nightclub (today, it is a full-blown lodge) with a handful of private living units for Rich and those who worked there. It had a bar area with a big fireplace and a large picture window where you could gaze right at Aspen Mountain (then Ajax Mountain).

Glenn was not alone at the Limelite that first summer, for he was about to be teamed with a young Californian actress/folk singer with closely-cropped blonde hair named Marilyn Child. An aspiring actress and teacher, Marilyn had discovered folk music when she was in a Girl Scout camp, and the discovery served her well as a source of extra income in college and later landed her a weekly show on Berkeley's left-wing radio station KPFA.

She came to a turning point in her life in 1955, chucked the straight work life, and tried her luck as a fulltime actress and folksinger. "I wasn't like a folksinger," she said. "I had a voice that sounded more schooled than it was. I was not one of the unwashed millions, you know, the barefooted people who sang folk songs. I believed in the performance first, and the whole history and ethnic stuff later."

After trying her luck in New York and Chicago, Marilyn was living in San Francisco in 1957, struggling with a failing marriage, when a call came from Sheldon Rich (who heard her at the Gate of Horn in Chicago), asking if she wanted to work at his new club in tandem with

Glenn Yarbrough. She was apprehensive about working with a singer whom she had never met, but it was a most opportune way to do something about her personal life. So that June, she left her husband and made her way to Aspen—and she discovered a new life.

At this time Aspen was a haven for free-thinking young bohemians who could live cheaply, work in the growing service industries, take in the culture and create some of their own. This was an atmosphere in which folk music thrived, transplanted into an unlikely remote pocket in the Rockies.

"It was a lot better than it is now," Glenn said about the Aspen of the late 1950s. "In those days, a lot of the streets were just dirt roads. You'd walk down the streets, and you'd hear music coming out of every window.

"It was kind of a captain's paradise because you'd get sick of the intellectuals in the summer, then the hunters would come in, and they'd be fun for a while, and then the skiers would come and you'd get sick of sports, and the intellectuals and the musicians would come back. Then of course, all the wealthy people in the world decided they wanted to live in Aspen and things started to change."

"It was a whole different town in the summer," Marilyn remembered fondly. "They had the music festival and at that time, a lot of dust. There weren't any paved streets, and I don't believe there was a boulevard stop. The music students didn't have an area where they were housed so they were staying all over town. When you walked through the town, you heard a violin playing here and a French horn playing over there, and vocal students singing. It was extraordinary how this town was filled with all this lovely music and students and people who cared. But in the winter, here were all these wild skiers, and it was a whole different atmosphere.

"It was a close-knit community. None of us liked the tourists, but we all made our money from the tourists. They were called the 'touri,' and the locals started calling me a half-Aspenite, because they liked me."

Alas, the Limelite wasn't even finished when opening day for Glenn and Marilyn loomed. Marilyn recalled, "When I got there, there was no roof on the building, and the owner Sheldon Rich said don't worry, by the time you open we'll have it finished. Well, they had to postpone the opening a week or two, so I helped paint the orange diamonds on the outside of it."

In the very beginning, Glenn and Marilyn just did their solo acts at the Limelite, and it might have continued that way had fate not intervened about four days after the club opened. "We opened and I got sick," said Marilyn. "I had just left my husband and so I felt very guilty, and I lost my voice." Once Marilyn's voice came back, it was still quite weak, so the duets with Glenn became part of the act because she wasn't up to doing an entire solo set yet. They began rehearsing material in which their voices could merge, folk tunes like "Red River Valley" or "We Come For To Sing." They went back into their solo acts for duo material, and Marilyn drew upon what she had done with Bob Gibson and Big Bill back at the Gate of Horn.

"We were very tentative, and we sat down and started working together, and fell in love," she recalled. "Our voices had the same vocal problems; we both had too much vibrato, we were unschooled vocally, and we both had this quick vibrato. As my first voice teacher (opera star) Phyllis Curtin said, 'It sounds like two sheep bleating in the wind!' Which is true, because if you listen to our album, the vibrato blends beautifully."

Glenn and Marilyn were so close during this period that Aspenites actually thought they were in love—which Marilyn claims wasn't the case. In fact, later in that first summer, she says she convinced Glenn to send for Peggy—whom he had left yet again—and Peggy spent the rest of that and subsequent seasons in Aspen. But the couple's sporadic fighting would continue.

After Aspen and a return engagement to the Gate of Horn as a duo, Glenn and Marilyn, joined again by Fred Hellerman, went into the studio for Jac Holzman to cut a duet album in New York City around Thanksgiving of 1957. This time, there would be no commercial choirs, no French horn, no bongos—no obvious attempts to seek out airplay. Glenn and Marilyn would be backed only by their own guitars and that of Hellerman, with occasional help from the reliable banjo of then-fellow-Weaver Erik Darling. The title was as straight-forward a statement of purpose as you can get in this language—*Marilyn Child And Glenn Yarbrough Sing Folk Songs.*

Score one for the purists, for this is an exceptionally charming record, easily the best of Glenn's three early solo albums. That Marilyn Child—who sported a piping, hollow tone quality and a quavering vibrato then—gets first billing owes more to alphabetical order than prominence, for it is clear that Glenn is the undisputed star of this album. When the two sing together, the effect is like Phyllis Curtin's astute description; the two voices are distinct, but Glenn's is by far the most flexible and striking.

Marilyn had never set foot in a recording studio before, and the whole experience seemed rather weird to her. "It was very disorganized, and I was very naive," she recalled.

"Freddy's mouth was about as bad as mine is now. I was intimidated by it." Not only that, Marilyn got sick again, laid up with the flu, and she claims that is why her voice sounds so high and thin on the record. Indeed, she had to leave the sessions before they were completed, so Glenn recorded solo tracks to fill out the album.

Those familiar with the first lines of "There's A Meeting Here Tonight" will be startled to hear the Child/Yarbrough album opening with exactly the same tune, "We Come For To Sing." The white spiritual "Bound For The Promised Land," "Wayfaring Stranger" and the disarmingly circular tune "Everywhere I Look This Morning" also would turn up on Limeliters albums. With the exception of "Lilli-I-O"—which is credited to E.Y. Harburg and Earl Robinson but sounds like a folk song in this enthusiastic treatment—the songs are English, Scottish and American standards in the public domain, with royalties presumably going straight to Elektra. {Glenn would later complain that he never made a dime off his Elektra albums but Marilyn claimed that he sold all his royalty rights to Elektra, for she still received royalties, however small}.

In any case, Glenn sounds marvelously ingratiating in "Wee Cooper O'Fife," and the sea shanty "New York Girls" gets an appropriately rollicking treatment. In the humorous dialogue song, "Buffalo Boy," Glenn seems to be imitating the flat offhand drawl of his old idol, Woody Guthrie. The album closes with "Everywhere," and even with Marilyn's wavering vocalise instead of the familiar brooding harmonies of Alex and Lou, Glenn offers a moving glimpse of the future just around the bend.

In the winter of 1957–58, the Yarbrough/Child duo became a trio with the addition of Glenn's predecessor at the Gate of Horn, Bob Gibson, by now an Aspen resident. "Ohhh boy, that was an act; that was the greatest folk act that ever was," said Glenn about this Aspen trio. "Marilyn had this terrific voice, and she had a lot of personality. Bob, of course, was the ultimate entertainer.

"It was a magnificent show. I opened the show and did my stuff and then I'd call Marilyn on to sing with me, and then I'd introduce Bob Gibson and he'd come onstage and entertain these people royally. At the end of his act, the three of us would get on and it drove 'em crazy. There were lines around the block every night the whole season in below-zero weather. It was so successful that at the end of the winter, the people who were working in Aspen in all the other clubs when it was time to close down, they begged us to stay open another night so that everybody could see the show that they've been hearing about all winter long.

"We had one final show for the city of Aspen after the season was over and the place was packed. I'll never forget that night; we started singing at 9 o'clock and we didn't quit until about 5 o'clock in the morning. We were supposed to stop selling drinks at 2 and the chief of police and everybody was there, and they said, don't worry. So we kept selling drinks and I was stoned and so was everybody. We recorded the whole thing, but of course, the next day I listened to it and it was just awful!"

"We were all very drunk and the audience was drunk," said Marilyn. "People just kept sending us drinks onstage in milkshake mixing glasses—Singapore Slings. I don't know how we didn't throw up, but we just kept drinking and thinking we were wonderful and ad-libbing a lot. The place was really rocking; there was a lot of love."

The tape of this show still exists—and it reveals a loose, cheery, folk jam session, the vocal and instrumental sound patterned in lockstep after the Weavers. It picks up toward the end of the first show and continues into the boozy wee hours. In Glenn's solo set, he reels off one folk or folk-flavored tune after another, his voice in full youthful bloom, accompanying himself quite competently on solo guitar. We hear Glenn taking the lead in a Crimean tune about a Jewish collective farm "Zhankoye," a version of "Harry Pollitt" tailored with an anti-Communist kicker, and "I'm Goin' Back" with delightfully natural vocal slides—all tunes that he would bring to the Limeliters' repertoire. There is also a flavorful rendition of "So Long (It's Been Good To Know Yuh)," with the picturesque original refrain about the "dusty old dust."

Armed with just a banjo and later a 12-string guitar, Bob Gibson does a long ingratiating routine on a song about a bullfrog, and we hear just why his colleagues were agog over his abilities as a pure entertainer. Eventually the effects of one Singapore Sling after another get to the trio, and the session lurches from one giggly, drunken folk tune to another.

The repertoire strays into Belafonte country ("Tongue-Tied Baby" or "Tie-Tongue Baby," with Glenn as kind of an Irish Calypsonian and Marilyn collapsing in giggles) but they recover and sing some coherent duets. There is some Aspen-tailored material like a saga of reckless skiers based on "The Wreck Of The Old 97," with bombed members of the audience discordantly contributing, and they make up lyrics about the embattled Sheldon Rich in "We Shall Not Be Moved." Later, as they thrash around for something to sing, the loaded trio hits upon on one gospel tune after another. Someone shouts "86!"—bartenders' lingo for "don't serve him, he's drunk!"—as they try to sing "Ezekiel Saw the Wheel."

Basically, the act does not really break much ground that the Weavers hadn't already covered. But there is a smooth, fresh, youthful blend at hand, one that could have been quite successful.

Indeed, Glenn was red-hot about the possibilities for the Yarbrough-Gibson-Child trio that had been knocking 'em dead in Aspen. He tried to get the trio a date at the Purple Onion in San Francisco. The club agreed, the date was set—and suddenly, the mercurial Gibson pulled out of the act. "Bob Gibson was an impossible person; he had a very big ego, and he really had no desire to perform with other people," said Glenn. "He wanted to be a star on his own. Trouble is, he never told anybody until it was too late."

"We had a lot of problems with Bobby," Marilyn remembered. "It was an extraordinary trio, and Gibson was a genius. But he was frequently stoned onstage, and I didn't even know why he was acting so strangely. There were a couple of things that he let us down, where he made almost a definitive commitment and suddenly, he wasn't there for us. Either he was in jail on a dope charge, or he was running off with some woman."

So, Yarbrough-Gibson-Child passed into history. Later on, into the early '60s, Marilyn remembered that Albert Grossman, then looking for a big commercial folk formula, wanted to reunite the three and produce the act—and Gibson pulled out again.

With that idea up in flames, Marilyn claims to have been in an early experimental combination with Peter Yarrow and Noel Paul Stookey, but she felt the vocal blend was wrong. Eventually, of course, Grossman's search would culminate with the formation of the fabulously successful Peter, Paul and Mary.

Meanwhile, that blown Purple Onion date was given to a new satirical folk act from San Jose State College that was just beginning to make some noise, a pair of brothers named Smothers. It seemed that gold could be found on the streets in those days.

After the winter of 1958, Sheldon Rich had had enough of the Limelite. He wanted to write, and the burdens of operating the lodge were just too much to bear. After the season was over, Rich approached his 28-year-old folksinger-for-hire and said, "I can't stand this. I'll sell it to you or let you run it and give you an option to buy." Rich's asking price was $100,000 for the club, plus five choice lots in downtown Aspen—an enormous amount of money in 1958 but a stupendous bargain by today's standards, even allowing for inflation. "It must be worth $10 million now," Glenn guess-timated in 1989, perhaps not with exaggeration.

Like his father before him, Glenn found himself in the resort business. Of course, Glenn didn't have the money to buy the Limelite outright, but he managed to get most of it from an uncle on his father's side of the family who wanted to come up to Aspen and work there. Glenn recalls that he and his uncle did not hit it off, though, and eventually Glenn would buy out his share of the property. In the meantime, Glenn would be delivering his sales pitch to anyone whom he thought could help him buy this club.

Meanwhile, in the fall of 1958, things weren't going too well for Alex. The Broadway play for which he sacrificed his gig at Janice Mars' club was "Handful of Fire," the work of the playwright N. Richard Nash. "Handful of Fire" featured a very talented cast, starring the young Roddy McDowall as Pepe, Joan Copeland as Maria, James Daly as Manuel, with Kay Medford portraying a local madam. Alex played one of three mariachis whose job was to play musical atmospheric interludes and contribute an occasional line of dialogue.

From the beginning, the play was in trouble, going through cast and title changes (one of the more ludicrous proposed titles was "Pocketful of Pesos"). "When I read the script, I really didn't believe in the play," confesses Alex, and his doubts were borne out by the unanimously negative reviews when the play finally opened at the Martin Beck Theatre on Oct. 1, 1958—and closed three days later after only five performances.

As a result, Alex was back on the streets with no job; Glenn's substitute gig at the club was over by then, and Janice Mars came back from summer stock to manage her club. But then, out of the blue, Alex discovered the value of the cliche, "one good turn deserves another." He remembers getting a phone call in December of 1958 from Glenn in

Aspen saying, "Hey, I'm buying an interest in this place, the Limelite, and in the meantime I'm running it, and I need another singer. So why don't you come out and I'll pay you $100 a week and your dinner and a place to live, and you can ski all you want and have a good time." Alex's reaction? "It sounds good to me!"

One of the reasons Glenn invited Alex out to Aspen, besides needing talent, was to try to get him to invest in his club. Alex signed on for the venture and went to his parents, who gave him $4,000 for a share of the Limelite. By this time, Glenn had assumed control of the Limelite, and he generously thought that he would share the place with Gibson, even though it was mostly Glenn's money. Since Gibson had brought in many of the customers himself, Glenn thought that neither he nor the club could lose. He asked Gibson if he was willing to take a share of the club, and Gibson agreed to everything.

"And the next thing I knew, the season was about to open, and suddenly I found out that Gibson had taken a job at the Hotel Jerome as competition," Glenn recalled with more than a trace of hurt. "And this was just after I bought the place. I was really broke, and had to make money and I was in desperate condition because I was the only one there, and I didn't think I could compete with Bob Gibson."

What to do? Well, Sheldon Rich got on the phone and called up Marilyn Child, who was singing solo at the Ash Grove in Los Angeles that January, and then put Glenn on the phone. "I called her up one day and said I'm in real big trouble, Bob's not going to work, and I'll be all alone," Glenn said. "And she was so nice; she said, 'I'll be right out.'"

Yet Marilyn says that she was mad at Glenn at the time. "One of the reasons was I said to Glenn, why don't we form a partnership and buy the club," she recalls. "We'll hire somebody to run the club, we'll have a contractual agreement where you and I will tour together so many weeks of the year, and we're here in Aspen so many weeks of the year because we have a commodity you can't buy; we have goodwill. He said, 'I don't go into a partnership with a woman!' I always thought Glenn was a lovable sexist in those days, and so was I, because when he said, 'I don't go into a partnership with a woman,' I went, 'Oh, of course not.' I really thought he was right in those days. He didn't dislike women, God knows, but he certainly thought we were second-class."

In any case, Marilyn, who was about to start an engagement at Theo Bikel's Cosmo Alley in Hollywood, said she wouldn't come out to Aspen unless Glenn got on the phone and asked her personally—which he did. All was straightened out, Marilyn postponed her Cosmo Alley gig and headed back to Aspen, and Glenn's fears about the competition over at the Hotel Jerome were groundless. Gibson only lasted a month at the Jerome because Alex, Glenn and Marilyn were taking away the town's folk business all by themselves.

Now part-owner and performer, Alex sang at the Limelite for the entire winter of 1958–59, playing flamenco guitar in the bar in the après-ski hours, and occasionally singing his international folk songs. "It was a very convivial atmosphere in there," Alex says of that winter in the Limelite. "In the winter season when the Texans would come to town, all hell would break loose, chiefly the contingent from Houston because it was a dry city (then) and they were heavy and hard drinkers and they loved a good time. When they were in town, you literally couldn't hear yourself think."

By this time, the tall, urbane, strikingly handsome Alex, despite his professed shyness, was becoming known as a ladies' man. "Well, he was very shy with me," Marilyn recalled. "But women thought he was wonderful. He had groupies all around all the time. He may not have been sleeping with them; they may have just thought they were special to him."

Alex would open the evening's entertainment, Glenn entertained on his own, singing mostly standard folk songs and English folk ballads (he said he was heavily into the balladeer Richard Dyer-Bennet in those days), and Marilyn Child followed with her solo act. Glenn and Marilyn would then sing duets, and toward the end of the season, Marilyn, Glenn, and Alex would often sing trios together, the first example of a collaboration between any of the Limeliters of the future.

Again, the final show of the winter season was recorded, and the existing tape has some striking revelations. In her own solo set, Marilyn is clearly more of a finished entertainer, her fast vibrato trilling wildly and her vivacious personality emerging. She even does an early version of the hilarious Leon Pober-Bud Freeman cowpoke-on-the-couch burlesque, "Gunslinger," well before the Limeliters made it famous, and together Glenn and Marilyn do an even more exquisite "Everywhere I Look This Morning" than the one on their album.

But things really get cracking when Alex and his banjo come in on the raucous "Mama Don't 'Low," egged on by Glenn to contribute two verses, and they follow it with a jovial, wise-cracking "Keep On the Sunny Side." A particularly catchy banjo lick by Alex prompts Glenn to take a shot at the absent Bob Gibson, "They need you at the Jerome Hotel!" before they start "Darlin' Corey." "Molly Malone" is strikingly like the Limeliters' version, and the set closes with hard-driving renditions of "Ezekiel Saw The Wheel" and "When The Saints Go Marching In."

This group has an even more exuberant sound than the trio with Gibson, with Alex's ostinato-based banjo giving the group real tension and drive. True, the addition of Alex's direct, steady baritone interferes with the blend of the fast vibratos of Glenn and Marilyn. Still, for the first time, one can hear the terrific edge that Alex would give to the Limeliters' sound—finally, a partial yet unmistakable step out of the Weavers' shadow.

When the winter season at Aspen was over, Alex's thoughts turned to the West Coast he had explored on his bicycle trip as a teenager. He thought of Hollywood, and the all-American dream of breaking into the film industry as an actor. He bought a 1948 Dodge in Aspen for only $100 and pointed it southwest through the Rockies and the deserts.

"It had no handle on the driver's side and the starter motor didn't work," he says. "You had to push-start it and I had to drive that car all the way to California. My plan was to drive into L.A. without stopping, without turning off the engine.

"When I arrived in L.A. around 7 a.m., I pulled into the Chateau Marmont Hotel on Sunset Blvd. because my friend Theo Bikel offered me a place to stay in his suite. When I arrived in my $100 Dodge and pulled into the garage, I was unshaved, greasy, my eyes were red. As I got out of the car, I saw N. Richard Nash walking into the garage. He didn't cringe when he saw me. We just said hi. We both had a flop and we both knew it."

Alex soon landed a curiously uncredited bit part in a Roger Corman quickie horror film called *A Bucket of Blood* which is now considered a cult classic in that genre. A quickie it was, for it took only five days to shoot on a budget of something like $25,000. Alex plays an entertainer in a beatnik nightclub, strumming a guitar with a soulfully dour expression. He sings an Ewan MacColl song about a murderer, then breaks into the Russian gypsy song "Gari Gari" (which would remain a part of his repertoire for decades), and finally strolls around the club playing flamenco guitar.

This brief cameo of the 26-year-old Alex Hassilev captures the essence of his act, although he would become a considerably warmer, more comfortable performer with time. In the meantime, though, he needed a way to pay his room and board in Hollywood while he was looking for acting work by day. Again, Bikel came to the rescue. He, Herb Cohen and Ben Shapiro hired Alex to sing his international folk repertoire at their Hollywood club, the Cosmo Alley, opening for Maya Angelou.

This was May of 1959—and the folk stampede, foretold by the Weavers and ignited by the Kingston Trio, was on.

Singing groups were sprouting left and right. The duo of Bud and Travis was born, the Gateway Singers continued to work in varying configurations, the Chad Mitchell Trio was starting to make some noise. The month before, Harry Belafonte had gone beyond calypso to embrace a whole spectrum of folk music live at Carnegie Hall, the results of which yielded a gigantic hit double album. The Weavers themselves carried on, now recording and performing regularly, with the specter of McCarthy receding. With rock 'n' roll becoming more escapist and insipid by the month. folk music by the young striped-shirt set could offer thoughtful young people a good deal of the exuberance of rock, plus philosophical meaning for their lives, as the Eisenhower years were drawing to a close.

The Cosmo Alley was an offshoot of the Unicorn on the Sunset Strip, which Bikel claims was the very first coffee house in Los Angeles ("We called it the Unicorn because there ain't no such thing," quipped Bikel). Located in back of the Ivar Theatre at 1608 N. Cosmo Street—a tiny, dingy, narrow linkway between Hollywood Blvd and Selma Avenue— the Cosmo Alley was a back room of the theater converted into a small nightclub.

Back in 1959, the Cosmo Alley played host to performers like Maya Angelou, Odetta, Marilyn Child and Bud and Travis. Lenny Bruce used the club to try out new material, and occasionally, Bikel himself would sit in when he wasn't acting, filming or touring somewhere. "It looked like a goodly-sized bar, with a room that could comfortably hold about 125 or so people, uncomfortably about 160," recalled Bikel. "It was a great success; people would line up on the outside to get in because we had wonderful stuff happening there."

Not long after Alex opened there, who should also come down from Aspen but Glenn Yarbrough, in his "official" capacity of looking for talent to fill the Limelite during the impending summer season. "Glenn would drop in to see me and also to sing, we would do some duets," remembered Alex. "Theo used to drop in, and the three of us would sing. I don't remember what we sang, it must have been unbelievable."

Bikel recalled that he, Alex and Glenn would run mostly through Weavers-based repertoire and he, Theo, would make the jokes in between tunes, which is what he did in his solo act anyway. Another key ingredient—humor—had been added to Alex's and Glenn's evolving act; indeed, they enjoyed themselves so much that Alex and Glenn wanted to form a permanent trio with Theo. "They begged me; 'Can't we do this on a regular basis?,' said Bikel. And I said, 'I can't, I have this other life, a career as an actor, and I do this whenever I'm free. To formalize it and tie up with two other people means that you would have to depend on my availability and on my schedule. And I can't hang people up like that.'"

Undaunted by the failed attempt to land Theo, Alex continued to try to get his singing business partner Glenn interested in forming a permanent duo. They worked up a few tunes and made the rounds of a couple of record companies in town; Alex doesn't remember which companies, but he believes one of them was MGM. In any case, there were no takers at that point for a Hassilev and Yarbrough folk duo.

But the two kept at it—Alex acting by day, singing by night, with Glenn scouting around and occasionally joining Alex. On one of these evenings, the night of May 29, Lou Gottlieb dropped by the Cosmo Alley—and although they didn't know it when they came into the club that night, Hassilev and Yarbrough were about to become a trio.

Chapter Five ·

"We never scuffled 15 minutes."
– Lou Gottlieb.

When Lou came to the Cosmo Alley that May night, forming a new folk trio was not exactly at the forefront of his mind.

He had been frantically knocking out arrangements of public domain folk songs for the Kingston Trio in search of gold, but the Trio had only bought two of them, and Lou was pondering the reasons why they didn't buy more. Moreover, Lou was there primarily to see Maya Angelou, for whom he still had a mild unconsummated passion.

But when Alex called Glenn up from the audience to join him in a couple of tunes, Lou's ears perked up. He had heard Alex once before when he was a guest on Theo Bikel's international folk music program on KPFA-FM up in Berkeley. But he had never heard Glenn before, and certainly couldn't have heard them as a duo. "I heard these two guys sing together and said, 'God, they have a very good sound,'" Lou recalled thinking.

"The Kingston Trio at that time had a real need for material. But none of them could read, and none was a particularly quick study unless they had tapes of the stuff. I wrote the thing out and I'd sing each part separately on the tape so that they could follow it. But I thought, God if they could hear the whole thing, I could sell a whole lot of them right away. I'll cut these arrangements I have made with these two guys and myself, and then it will be easier to sell the tune."

As soon as the set was over, Lou wasted no time in finding Alex and Glenn, introducing himself, and launching into his sales pitch for a good hour. On Sunday morning, he would write to Dolly in El Cerrito about his interesting encounter.

"Friday night I met and talked with Glen Yarborough (sic) and Alex Hasilev (sic) two folk singers fa Gahd's sake, with whom I am going to rehearse this afternoon. More about that later.

"Anyway, today I am assembling yet another attempt at establishing a new unit. Glen Yarborough and Alex Hasilev are good singers and they own parts of a night club in Aspen Colorado. They want to organize the unit and put it to work in Aspen this summer in order to whip it into shape. They are fairly sharp cats and perhaps something can be worked out. It becomes increasingly clear that I cannot sit around comfy and cozy in my dollhouse in El Cerrito and make any loot in this business. Could we go to Aspen for a while this summer? They say it is magnificent."

"We didn't know Lou," remembered Alex. "He was wearing this tweedish jacket with leather patches or something and a bowtie. I remember he had a big thick briefcase with him. After the show, he came over and started to talk to us. We couldn't understand what he was talking about, something about arrangements for the Kingston Trio. We didn't know what he meant. He used a lot of words that neither of us understood. So, we were quite fascinated."

"He seemed to be pretty sensible at the time," Glenn wryly recalled. "As I realize now, he was just hiding his craziness from us! He had a whole bunch of arrangements that he had done for the Kingston Trio, and he was being a very successful businessman at the time, something which I know now he absolutely was not."

Puzzled but amused and charmed, Alex and Glenn thought hey, why not see what this erudite Dr. Gottlieb has in mind. The following Sunday afternoon, Alex, Glenn, Lou and a female singer named Sonia Agins gathered at the apartment of Lou's friend Andre Philippe, went through Lou's big briefcase of arrangements, and tried them out. Lou was astounded at what he heard, the three male voices clashing and seeming to draw strength from the clash. Many times over the years, for any friend, musician or journalist who asked, Lou would recall his first impressions as follows:

"From the instant we sang together, I knew that that particular combination of three voices had a memorable profile. The total is larger than the sum of its parts. We sound better singing together than we do individually."

At this point, Lou's thoughts began to turn from forming a demo group to forming a performing group, though as his letter to Dolly shows, it was clearly on the minds of Alex and Glenn from the beginning. He started talking about giving Alex and Glenn credit as writers for the public domain folk material as long as he controlled the publishing. "I couldn't figure out exactly how to talk 'em into cutting these tunes for nothing," Lou said in 1978, his voice getting excited as he remembered that day. "So, I said let's try and make a group together. I know we can go to work for the hungry i. But they one-upped me. They had this club up in Aspen that they didn't have any entertainment for."

The following morning Lou wrote again to his wife, expressing both enthusiasm and anxiety about his new group:

"At 2 o'clock, I rehearsed with Alex Hassilev and Glen Yarborough (sic) and Sonia Agins. The sound is good. Better than the Gates already. I am sorely tempted to go back into the business. We have to talk about it. They own a part of a night club in Aspen, Colorado...and their idea is to polish the unit there...for four weeks starting around the middle of June. I don't know...it can't pay anything much above expenses and I'm not sure we could get along personality-wise. Well, we shall see."

Theo Bikel was at the Cosmo Alley May 29 but his memory of that night was a bit hazy; he was busy rushing around running the club or talking on the phone ("making like a landlord which I was hopeless at anyway," he laughed). But he did remember Alex telling him around this time that he and Glenn may have found a combination that will work as a trio, with Lou as the comic figure in place of Theo. "I loved his kooky sense of humor," said Bikel, who remembered Lou from his days with the Gateways. "I thought he was absolutely hilarious.

"He was a very important ingredient of any stage presentation that the Gateway Singers did, or wherever. He was very funny as a solo standup as well, but it was obvious that wasn't going to endure.

"It seemed natural that they needed somebody to do the connective tissue who could also do the music. They were not actually looking, they just said, 'Isn't it a pity, it was a good idea while it lasted.' But then, obviously that idea stayed in back of somebody's mind, and when Lou appeared on the scene, it fell into place."

But as the next, little-known stage in their evolution shows, the ingredients for the trio were not quite in place. In addition to the trio material, Lou had in his trunk a whole pile of arrangements for four voices left over from the Gateway Singers days.

"If we were really going to do a group thing, let's do it right," Lou thought, still thinking in Weavers' terms. Get a girl singer. As it turned out, Sonia Agins was used only on that first rehearsal. Marilyn Child was briefly considered, but Lou had another singer in mind, whom he introduced at the group's next rehearsal on June 2.

The new candidate for the female slot of the group, then, was Joanelle Shepard, a San Francisco actress and the daughter of a trumpeter who wrote a column for the International Musician newspaper. She had been in the Lenny Bruce show, "A Wonderfully Sick Evening With Lenny Bruce" for which Lou had been invited to direct the music (and declined). "I thought she was a very beautiful showgirl," Lou recalled. "I thought she'd be the one to make the fourth part."

At first, Joan said she would do it, but she never made it to Aspen. Alex recalls that she landed a part in a movie and was committed to traveling to Mexico to film. One can only speculate today how a female voice would have blended with the robust sound of Lou, Alex, and Glenn—and the best guess is that it might have softened some of the edge and tension that made the sound work.

Lou, who at the time was masterminding the musical end of things, shrugged and said let's do the act anyway, as a trio. Soon thereafter, Alex and Glenn went to the Ash Grove to check out Lou's standup act, and they were doubled over by Lou's parody of a highfalutin' music professor. They agreed that this would fit in just fine, giving the act that coveted extra dimension, though different from the one Theo might have added.

They never did get around to recording any demos, though, for the Kingston Trio had already decided what they were going to put on their album. After attending a Trio recording session and trying to sell two more arrangements to folksinger Stan Wilson, Lou was ready for the next step.

He returned to his home in El Cerrito to tell Dolly and the kids that he was going on the road again. "Career obligations," he said. On June 16, he packed his double bass and the trunk which contained his publishing business into his 1954 Volkswagen and took off on U.S. 40 and 50 for Colorado, driving continuously except to grab some sleep in a hotel in Ely, Nevada. He pulled into Aspen the evening of June 17, where, completely bushed from the ride, he slept for ten hours.

Two days after Lou arrived, the new trio gathered in the restaurant club of the Limelite for their first rehearsal—which would give them a potent taste of the craziness to come.

In 1988, Lou told the following bizarre account of that day as only he could, with a matter of fact, laconic delivery that had Glenn—who was in the room—cracking up helplessly.

"I was seated at the little spinet piano there on the stage." Lou recalled. "And we were looking through some scores—and all of a sudden, I noticed a chair...flying through the air. It was Miss Margaret Goodhardt Yarbrough registering intense dissatisfaction with the fact that Glenn, who had promised to move her to Snowmass, where they had a home, had not come through. I understood that she was disturbed, seriously. And Glenn said, 'Oh let's just go right on...' That was my introduction to her, and I fell in love with her on first sight."

Lou later confessed in his autobiography that Peggy was the first woman with whom he broke his fidelity to Dolly. But in a letter to his wife, he diplomatically expressed detached amazement at the turmoil in the Yarbrough family. "How about this," reported Lou. "Yesterday during rehearsal Glen's {sic} wife Peggy came in livid—I mean ANGRY—and said something to her husband that I didn't catch but which ended '... or I'm movin' out NOW.' Glen didn't even look up from the part he was studying on the arrangement we were rehearsing! Man, I don't see how a guy can operate with that kind of a debilitating domestic scene as a base of operations. Hassilev too was completely unconcerned—implying that I hadn't seen anything yet."

After just one full rehearsal, Lou, Alex, and Glenn started their residence at the Limelite that evening, Friday June 19, working up the repertoire, polishing the act, fitting the components together. Alex or Glenn would start the show with their solo acts, Lou would then do a comic turn from his nightclub act, and finally, the three would sing whatever they had rehearsed that day.

To his amazement, Lou found that the comic material that sailed right over the audience's heads in San Francisco and Los Angeles had them rolling under the tables in Aspen, now that he had become a "funny folksinger" as opposed to a comic who sings. Also, he had suddenly become more receptive to suggestions from Alex and Glenn at the rehearsals, whereas with the Gateway Singers, he would tend to "beat down" all ideas from the other members of that group. They were starting almost completely from scratch, having only about three or four tunes they could do right away. And the trio still didn't have a name yet; no one had thought of one. Yet it became apparent that the Aspen audiences were responding to the show's finale with the most enthusiasm. "The people went crazy in Aspen over the act," said Alex. "Lou was funny, the act was fresh, there was true spontaneity because a lot of the time, we really didn't know what the fuck we were going to do."

Paula Jan Holland, an actress and writer, remembered the huge impression that the trio made upon the convivial late-season ski crowd. "I heard Glenn and Marilyn Child singing at Aspen when they were there at the Limelite," she recalled, "and the next year we went back and I said 'Is Marilyn Child going to be there?' and they said, 'No, there's a trio there now.' I said, 'Oh fooey, we're not going to get to hear Marilyn Child?' Then Lou Gottlieb sang 'Have Some Madeira, M'Dear,' and let me tell you, all up and down the chair lifts the next day, everyone was singing 'Have Some Madeira, M'Dear!'

"And all night long and for the rest of our lives, that's what we've said to each other when we want to be naughty!"

Not knowing quite what to expect, Alex's mother came out West to catch her son's new act. She met Alex's new partners, immediately hitting it off particularly well with Lou, with whom she felt an instant bond. Yet being a punctual, precise person, she was completely thrown for a loop by the whole laid-back Aspen experience. Showtime would be minutes away, the audience was already filing into the Limelite, and apparently the stars of the show were completely on their own separate clouds, doing anything but preparing for the show.

"I had with me the book 'Exodus' which I had just purchased," she remembered, chuckling. "Alex snatched this book out of my hands, sat down and started reading. I said, 'Listen, time to get dressed and you have to perform.' Forget it, he was reading. I went out and went to a drugstore to get something.

"There, I see Glenn sitting and enjoying an ice cream soda. I said, 'Glenn, aren't you performing?' He said, 'Yes, eventually.' And Lou was in deep conversation with Gene and Francesca Raskin, who came with me.

"The next day they had a performance at 4 o'clock for the children, and I just couldn't get them together. Glenn was again enjoying the ice cream soda. Alex was reading the book; he said, 'I'll finish soon.'

"I couldn't understand it. I wondered, how can these three function when they do whatever goes to their head a few minutes before they have to go and perform? But they did. It was so informal, so casual."

Lou recalls that it was also a "wonderful summer" at Aspen for other musical reasons as well. The Aspen Music Festival had kicked in at the end of June, and Lou could indulge his by-no-means dormant classical tastes during the breaks when the threesome was not rehearsing. Soprano Jennie Tourel, baritone Mack Harrell, the pianists Vronsky and Babin and William Masselos, and cellist Zara Nelsova were among those who were there that summer, teaching master classes and performing.

Yet Lou, who had become very much the domesticate, was getting homesick. "I don't know what's the matter with me," he wrote to Dolly. "Everything up here is going exactly the way I had planned it. We got in a solid 2 1/2 hour rehearsal yesterday and at least two good recording ideas emerged.

"These cats want to work, and they know how...although I must say the fucking rehearsal did start twenty-five minutes late. I do hope that doesn't happen again or I just get into the Volkswagen and drive home...I keep looking at the Volks and thinking how nice it would be to drive home—not tell anybody they're all asleep anyway—just SPLIT."

Glenn was holding up under an enormous load of his own that summer. Not only did Glenn have to rehearse with his colleagues and work on his own material, he had to run the Limelite and deal with his volatile wife, who was also working as a waitress. "I had a big problem because I had to keep that place going," he recalled. "It was everything I owned."

"Glenn would come in and peel potatoes in the afternoon and sweep the joint out, and hassle with pet Margaret Goodhardt Yarbrough," Lou recalled. "It was a tense situation. And of course, Sean was there, an adorable eight-month-old kid." But Glenn persevered, for he felt that at last, he had stumbled upon a ticket to fame that he could live with. "I knew it was a hit act before we even left Aspen," Glenn said, "because otherwise, I never would have left."

And then suddenly, without warning, around the Fourth of July the trio broke up—or so it seemed at the time. Lou was getting depressed, homesick, perhaps even racked with guilt about his life as an aspiring pop/folk musician for whom security was a sometime thing at best. For all its spectacular scenery and bucolic musical pursuits, Lou hated Aspen, and he longed for the sophisticated excitement of San Francisco.

"There were elements of Aspen that were like a minimum-security prison for me," Lou said. "After you had been around all the different places, it was really very slow, wasn't much happening."

On a deeper level, Lou admitted that "This was the first time I'd ever been away from wife and children, you see. And the situation at our home financially was not exactly what you would call stable. So, I got a call from my wife, probably including a few phrases like, 'These kids need a father,' and so on. I didn't want to discuss it. I packed up my stuff and went back to El Cerrito, leaving a note saying I was going home to Mommy."

The next morning, wondering where Lou was, Glenn went into his room, found the note on his pillow, and reeled in shock. He went to Alex's room and exclaimed, "Lou's split! He left this note." The two looked at each other in disbelief, faced with the possibility of their hit act suddenly crumbling before their eyes.

Glenn was the first to speak. "What do you think we should do?" he asked.

"There is nothing we can do," said pessimistic Alex. "He's gone."

"No, no, no, no, I'm gonna go chase him and bring him back!" responded Glenn.

Whereupon Glenn raced to his car, started it up, and roared northwest up State Highway 82 in the direction of Glenwood Springs, trying hopelessly to catch up with the long-departed Lou. He must have driven 100 miles, through Glenwood Springs, onto U.S. 6 heading west before giving up and slinking off back to Aspen. Alex remembers Glenn coming back, dejected, saying, "I couldn't catch him."

"Glenn and I looked at each other and said, 'Well I guess that's that,'" Alex recalled. "At that point, we started to think about who we could replace Lou with for the season."

But it wasn't over, not by a long shot. Yes, Lou was homesick, and sick of Aspen. But he had not given up on the trio—not at all. "I knew I could get us a job in Frisco, which would be just as good as Aspen because we could work every night and that way I wouldn't have the hassle with the house," he said.

Lou went straight to his old employer Enrico Banducci, and they went for a ride on Banducci's yacht in San Francisco Bay. Lou told the club owner that he had a new act that would be just right for the sophisticated clientele at the hungry i and that he, Banducci, would be delighted with it.

Banducci replied, "Bring 'em in"—this without having seen them and without having heard so much as a tape. It would be a four-week gig at scale wages (about $450 a week for the three of them), which in those days, was enough money to eke out a living.

Banducci, however, did have one question. According to Lou's autobiography, he asked Lou what the group called itself.

Lou answered that the trio didn't have a name as yet.

"I've just had Lambert, Hendricks and Ross here," the practical club owner said. "I'm not going to have 'Hassilev, Yarbrough and Gottlieb' painted on the wall. There isn't room."

Then Banducci had a flash of offhand inspiration. "Where are you working now?" he asked.

Lou replied, "The Limelite in Aspen."

Banducci then said, "OK, you're the Limeliters."

A week after Lou had flown the coop, Alex remembered getting a phone call from their wandering bass player saying, "We got a gig at the hungry i for scale." Glenn and Alex had not yet found a replacement for Lou, so one can imagine their sighs of relief.

Within days, Lou was back in Aspen, convincing his mates that it would be in the group's best interests to make their official debut in San Francisco and let another act play at the Limelite for the remainder of the summer.

"I don't know about this unit," Lou wrote home. "It will be interesting to see how it will be received in Frisco. Individually the singers are better than the Gates were, I think. At least from the hit record point of view."

"Lou was the leader (then)," Alex said. "He said, 'I will manage the act and I don't want any percentage for managing the act. What I want is the publishing and you guys be the writers and share in the writing royalties.' That was the original deal we made. Lou at that time was calling all the shots in the business of getting a gig and record contracts because he was the only one who had had some so-called 'big time experience.'"

Glenn and Alex hired Gene and Francesca Raskin to replace them at the club and a woman to manage the Limelite while he was away. And with those nagging problems solved for the moment, the three played their last gig at Aspen on July 20 and headed for the Bay Area—and sudden fame.

Once upon a time, the hungry i—the lower-case "i" stands for "intellectual" or "id"—on 599 Jackson Street was one of the entertainment hubs of North Beach, which itself was the epicenter of San Francisco's burgeoning, world-famous folk, jazz and comedy scenes. "The hungry i really started this postwar new wave of folk music and comedy," said writer Grover Sales, who was once a publicist for the club.

Originally located in a basement in the old green Columbus Tower building within a triangle bordered by Kearny, Columbus, and Jackson Streets, the club moved across Jackson Street in 1954 to a cavernous former Chinese restaurant on the south side of Jackson at the lower end of North Beach. There were theater seats inside the small showroom instead of the usual sardine-packed nightclub tables and chairs, for this club was more interested in showcasing talent than merely selling drinks. The most famous aspect of the hungry i was the backdrop to the stage, just a stark brick wall against which the club's acts would play. The club's glory days occurred in front of that wall, a look and feel that would be copied and copied to this day by nightclub owners and television directors.

The catalyst behind the hungry i, Enrico Banducci, was a burly, mustachioed Italian American with a gambler's instinct, an almost infallible eye and ear for great talent on the way up—and most important, the self-confidence to put his club on the line behind these instincts. When the young, inexperienced Orson Bean was bombing nightly, Banducci stuck with him, made suggestions, encouraged him, let him develop his act until by the end of his stand, he had the house roaring. When Alvah Bessie of the Hollywood Ten got out of jail and no one would touch him, Banducci hired him to work the lights of the club.

"He was a big, gusty, music-loving, food-loving Italian Diaghilev," Sales recalled. "He had a genius for entrepreneurial panache, with no money, no resources, and always on the verge of bankruptcy. He could sell hell to a bishop. He could talk anybody into anything, and he always had a crowd of hangers-on and worshippers; people hung on his every word. He was a mad entrepreneurial genius, always operating on a shoestring."

"God gave him the gift to be able to pick this talent," said Jimmy Stewart, the versatile jazz guitarist and session man who while still in his 20s was part of the house trio at the hungry i in 1962. "He was picking it himself; people would bring it to him, but he had the feel for it. Every show was usually sold out every night."

In 1953, the fearless Banducci took a chance on a skinny young UC graduate student turned overnight radio announcer named Mort Sahl at $75 a week. "Mort Sahl was the first comic they had that attracted any kind of attention," said Sales. "He did the same thing he always did; he came in with no tie and the university uniform of a cardigan sweater and he had a rolled-up newspaper. He'd come in and start talking about today's newspaper.

"This was shocking in the early years of the Eisenhower administration because people didn't come out and say anything about senile old Ike. He would get up and say things like, 'J. Edgar Hoover has just written a book called How to Turn Your Friends In to the FBI for Fun and Profit.'

"Well, in 1953 you didn't get up and say things about J. Edgar himself, even in the privacy of your own home. The FBI started coming down to the hungry i and hassling Banducci, saying why are you hiring these Communists. Banducci told the FBI to take a hike; he said, 'I run the club to suit myself. I don't hire people to suit you.' They must have a dossier on him that thick."

Banducci was also under a lot of pressure from his "palace guard of unemployables" (in-laws, etc.) who wanted Sahl and his mouth out of there. And Banducci would waver—until he counted the receipts. "By the time Banducci started thinking seriously about getting rid of this fresh kid, there were lines up around the block," said Sales.

Just about every major standup comic appeared at the hungry i after the Sahl breakthrough—and they attracted a sophisticated audience that was a perfect target for the left-leaning, fledgling San Francisco folk scene. Every influence would feed upon one another, creating a merrily bubbling, highly spiced North Beach stew. The comics would get their timing and free-associative flow from the jazz musicians; they even recorded for Fantasy, the local jazz label. Virtually without exception, the comics also leaned to the left, no doubt reinforced by the folkies. The folk musicians in turn would learn about the art of entertaining an audience from the comics, about the value of mixing contemporary satire into what had now become an "act." And jazz-grounded folkies like Lou would pick up on the swinging rhythms of jazz and incorporate that into their music.

It was a special time, in a special locale, with a special audience that often transcended mere economic divisions. It was an amazing unification of the not-so-loyal opposition to Republican values, protected and nurtured by the benevolent Banducci. And, of course it couldn't last, even in the most tolerant big city in the country.

Only half a decade after the Limeliters opened at the "i," the Condor Club at Broadway and Columbus would alter the North Beach landscape forever by introducing Carol Doda as the first topless waitress—after which the other clubs in the area gradually became strip joints. Tastes in music were changing too; the folk movement had been fading away, and not five miles from North Beach, the San Francisco rock scene was exploding in Haight-Ashbury and the Fillmore. "It was the emergence of rock that put the hungry i out of business," concluded Grover Sales.

Standup comedy was becoming the property of television and the pleasure palaces of Reno, Lake Tahoe, and Las Vegas. Moreover, the atmosphere that had bred a satirist like Mort Sahl was changing. Eisenhower was out of office, the martyred Kennedy was an untouchable icon, there was an anger over ghetto uprisings and the Vietnam war that was souring domestic politics, placing it beyond the reach of the comics.

"Political satire doesn't make it anymore, the government appropriated the field," cracked one cynical hungry i mainstay at the time.

Even among those who had not deserted to rock or Nevada, the hungry i was becoming an irrelevance. The customers were pursuing careers, buying homes in Marin County, the Peninsula, or the East Bay, raising a family, unable to spare the time or energy to drive into the city. Tourists increasingly became the audience, and they wanted pure, mindless, unchallenging entertainment.

The hungry i held on far longer than most nightclubs as Banducci tried to cling to his old instincts, but it was a hopeless cause. Forced to close the Jackson Street location in April 1968, he later tried to run another hungry i amidst the tourist traps of Ghirardelli Square near Fisherman's Wharf (loyal Glenn Yarbrough sang there when his solo career was riding high). But that version of the club lasted only ten months, closing in 1970, perhaps a case of a unique plant wilting in foreign soil.

By the early '70s, Banducci had sold the hungry i name to some strip-joint operators who brought it back to North Beach. And so, a so-called "hungry i" stood until 2019 in a cluster of buildings on Broadway near Kearny Street, its glory days long past, now just another home for girlie shows. Banducci would fall upon hard times, battling illness and chronic financial problems. In a sad postscript on the fortunes of one of the most brilliant talent scouts America ever knew, Herb Caen's column in the *San Francisco Chronicle* of April 11, 1990 reported that Banducci had been hired by the owners of Carmelina's, a new restaurant on Nob Hill—as a lunchtime chef. And he made some other entrepreneurial attempts—running a "hungry i hot dog stand" in Richmond, Virginia; periodically reviving his sidewalk cafe, Enrico's—before his death in 2007.

But on the day the Limeliters unveiled their act for the first time outside Aspen, the hungry i fielded as formidable a lineup of talent as any nightclub in the country could have had on a given night. The show on Thursday July 23, 1959, opened with Faith Winthrop, a singer whom Lou only remembers as "a girl with a strapless evening gown." Then the house trio, one of San Francisco's treasures, the Vince Guaraldi Trio—with its pixieish leader's melodic, highly original, always hard-swinging piano—would play a set filling the space in between acts. Then the Limeliters took the stage, followed by more music from Guaraldi and then the headliner, who that night was the screamingly funny musical satirist, Tom Lehrer. This cycle would repeat three times on weekdays, four times on Saturdays, six nights a week.

"When we came into the hungry i, I remember I wrote out a set list for the first show, but that's the last set list I ever wrote out for the Limeliters," Lou remembered. "It was just a disaster. Somehow, it wasn't what was necessary, and from then on, either Glenn or Alex or both would. I have no suggestions for set lists. I still don't know what the proper order for songs to be performed in, is. If they're any good, it doesn't really matter, in my view."

Although the Limeliters don't remember exactly what they sang that night, a review of their hungry i act in *Daily Variety* less than a month later gives us some idea of what their act was like then.

They opened that set with the old high-energy hell-raiser, "Mama Don't 'Low." Then Glenn lowered the temperature with his soaring tenor solo on "Molly Malone," and Alex took the lead on "Zhankoye." A number that they never recorded, Leadbelly's version of "Rock Island Line," catered to the center of hardcore folk. Then Lou delivered his leering calling card, "Have Some Madeira M'Dear," and the set closed with a rousing "Hard, Ain't It Hard." In between much of this, Lou would offer samples of his professorial act, with a keen eye for the headlines as well as asides about the competition.

In all, a rather self-contained 24-minute sampling of what the Limeliters had to offer. "When old pros put their heads together and come up with a new format, an audience generally can count on slick, well-rehearsed entertainment," *Variety's* review on August 12, 1959, said, going on to praise Lou's humor, Glenn's tenor and Alex's way with foreign repertoire.

The Limeliters opened on a Thursday night, to a tumultuous response from the crowd of nightclubbers. They were an instant hit; their timing was exactly right. Here was a wry, original alternative to the Kingston Trio and their packs of imitators, with the finger-popping swing of jazz underpinning the rhythm and an intellectual slant to the humor, a perfect match for the "i's" audience. By Friday, they had been besieged with record offers from no less than four record labels—mammoth RCA Victor; Decca, the home of the Weavers and the Gateways; MGM from Los Angeles; and the local entry, Fantasy.

Alex's reaction to sudden notoriety was, as those who know him would expect, pensive, reflective. "When you are in the forefront of a movement, if you're halfway good at all, you're going to get good response," he said. "And we not only were, we were also in THE primary breeding ground for new talent, namely San Francisco. And we were in THE club in THE place. We were working in a very hip place with the best clientele, which corresponded totally to what we were doing. It was just a golden opportunity."

As the most experienced veteran of major record-company wars, Lou had already decided what he wanted out of any future deals with record companies, given his experiences at Decca. "I was determined that if I ever went back into the folk music business that I would be the publisher of the songs," he said.

"What I also wanted was a contract in which the record company would pay for the sessions costs and the artists' royalties would start coming from record one. Since we were making records for no money, I thought they should eat that and pay us from the get-go. The Kingston Trio's first record for Capitol, which sold easily a million and a half or two, cost a total of $976—and I knew we could do that or better for any company we signed with."

"In those days, Lou was unbelievably paranoid about his Decca experience," Alex recalled. "And Glenn of course had recorded, and he had never seen a penny. I had yet to record anything; I didn't know from nothing about it. All I knew is that people were paying me money to do this insanity."

But while they were sorting out the offers, Herman Diaz Jr. of RCA Victor managed to lure the three down to Hollywood on July 31 to cut a 45 RPM single, just in case his label would win the bidding war. Diaz was in charge of the pan-American activities of RCA Victor—he was responsible for many of Perez Prado's hot-selling mambo-cha-cha discs of the '50s—and he thought there might be a market there for a group that had such fluency and feeling for international folk songs.

The Limeliters entered RCA Victor's Studio 2 for the first time that afternoon at 2 p.m. to cut Lou's arrangement of "Malaguena Salerosa," and "Molly Malone" with Glenn on lead. Diaz used three Los Angeles session men on guitar, banjo, and bass while the Limeliters merely sang their parts. That projected single was never released, although its existence can be confirmed in RCA Victor's session files.

In any case, Lou didn't want to go with RCA Victor because they refused to pay the session fees, and most importantly to Lou at the time, they wouldn't give him the full publishing royalties on public domain material. By this time, a fifth company had entered the bidding war—Elektra, with Jac Holzman dangling before Lou everything he wanted.

"Frankly, I liked Jac Holzman," said Lou. "I always did like Jac. I thought he was a very energetic, imaginative and intelligent man. But Glenn didn't like him, and Glenn had already worked for him. He didn't want to go with Jac, but Jac gave us the best deal."

"Of course, Jac was ready to say anything because he had no intention of paying anything," countered Glenn. "I kept saying that much of nothing is still nothing. RCA was only paying 5 or 6% but at least it was going to turn into money."

"As I recall, I was basically against signing with Elektra from the very beginning, and so was Glenn," says Alex. "If you go with a small record company that is not knowledgeable, that doesn't have either the financial clout or the expertise to sell you as a mass media artist, then all the higher royalties and extra attention doesn't mean much, because nothing is happening...But Lou controlled the publishing, so it was very much in his best interests."

Needless to say, there were endless, heated discussions among the three Limeliters about the whole recording thing. But finally, Glenn—perhaps showing a flicker of inherited business acumen from the prosperous Robertson side of his family—came up with the shrewdest solution to their Elektra dilemma, an escape clause. It would be a contract for one album, and an option on one more—and if Elektra could not sell 50,000 copies of that first album in the span of a year, then the deal was off. That proved acceptable to Lou and Alex and in October of 1959, the Limeliters signed with Elektra. Nevertheless, RCA Victor, then lacking a really hot folk group on its roster, kept on pursuing the Limeliters. Steve Sholes, RCA Victor's A&R director in Nashville, the far-sighted man who snatched Elvis Presley away from Sam Phillips and Sun Records, stopped by often to catch the act. Guitarist/producer/RCA Victor executive Chet Atkins kept approaching them. And most significantly in the long run, Neely Plumb was the most persistent of RCA Victor's line of suitors.

All three of them were on their way to the Monterey Jazz Festival that September and, according to Lou, they made a side trip to nearby San Francisco to see the Limeliters. It was then that Lou told them that the trio had signed with Elektra. And while they were disappointed, they would not give up the chase yet.

Just as Glenn predicted, the Elektra deal turned out to be a costly mistake. "I never got any money from Jac and no one else did either," Lou said. "So, Glenn was right."

Well, not quite, for the Limeliters did get some royalties—and according to Glenn, it wasn't easy. Glenn and his accountant conducted an audit of their account and discovered that Jac owed them what he recalled as a hundred-or-so thousand dollars. Glenn picked it up from here; "Then I went in to Jac and I showed him the figures and he said, 'Uh!, you caught me. What'll you settle for?' I said, 'Settle for? You owe us this amount of money!' He said, 'Yeah, but you're going to have to go to court, you're going to have to get a lawyer, you split with the lawyer...' And I went home that night and thought, he's absolutely right. I went back and settled for like half of what he owed."

"The record business as I have come to know it is the Spanish Main," Lou observed. "It's the only place where pirates really still thrive in the world. And what's more, if you've ever been in it, you'll know why it happens."

So much for the business side of folk music. On the artistic end, the Limeliters seemed to be spending much of their spare daylight hours rehearsing in the hungry i every day. They had hit the ground running so swiftly (remember that they only sang together for the first time in May) that they hadn't had enough time to build a repertoire. Lou had his Kingston Trio material, all contributed key numbers from their solo acts, but it wasn't enough.

Lou was constantly at work hammering out arrangements for this new trio sound he had stumbled onto in Hollywood. Again, as with the Gateway Singers, Lou chose to hide his ransacking of the public domain behind a pseudonym. This time, his nom de plume was Cal Bagby—Cal, because Lou was patting himself on the back for being a California native, and Bagby was inspired by a pianist named Charlie Bagby who played for the old Phil Harris big band. Lou would continue to be Cal Bagby throughout the Limeliters' '60s heyday; only in a few isolated tracks would he drop the pretense of a false identity (a practice that soon would become obsolete in the grab-what-you-can folk gold rush).

After all the experience in arranging voices in university studies, assembling the Gateway Singers arrangement book and the Kingston Trio demos, Lou had at last found his ideal canvas. "Lou finally came into his own with three-part writing," noted William Malloch.

From three different decades in his life, Lou gave his perspective on the Limeliters' sound—how he made it shine. "Any combination of voices has an absolutely specific profile," Lou said in 1978. "We are assuming that the goal is for maximum resonance. (I sometimes think of that as my nickname, Dr. Max Resonance.) That means the most sound with the least effort.

"There is no doubt that as far as Glenn Yarbrough and Alex Hassilev and myself are concerned, the best way to stack those chords is with Alex at the bottom singing the melody, me in the middle, and Glenn singing as good a duet as I can think up. Now if you voice them that way, even if it's a quick-thing for a record date, it'll sound OK. You want to fool around, OK, but it will never sound that good."

"Alex has a loud, heavy, opaque voice," Lou told the *Saturday Evening Post* in 1961. "It has no flexibility at all, but for our purposes that becomes an asset. If the walls were caving in, Alex would still give us a sure, heavy presentation of the melody."

For Glenn, Lou would write, "the kind of harmony that a gifted but musically illiterate folk singer would improvise. My voice has no character and therefore draws no attention to itself. This is no great comfort to me after all my years of study, but it is, I must say, ideal for my role in the kind of *Spaltklang* non-blending arrangements we do."

"When you're doing work for a vocal group, everything has to be hand-tailored," Lou added in 1988. "You try to elicit from the participants what parts they wanna sing, if you can. That makes the thing sound right. If there's any, quote, secret to my vocal arranging, it is that I try to get the people to fake the parts that they're going to get. I'll write something out, then try to see, what do you want to sing?"

"Lou tried to make each part melodic," Glenn said, "and I think that's something that's rarely done, even today. and I think that's important."

"It sure makes the ensemble sound better in my view," added Lou, "and it's also easier to remember the parts." And they worked hard at it—rehearsing compulsively, trying to perfect that sound even more. "One thing we always did; all our tunes we put as much time in on as anybody and we tried to get the sound as good as possible, always," said Lou.

Jimmy Stewart recalled how hard Lou the musicologist drove his colleagues in their rehearsals backstage. "Lou had everything written out on manuscript paper, and he had it on music stands, and they were rehearsing each tune as he had arranged it," Stewart said. "I thought, this is fabulous because it was the first folk or folk-oriented group I had heard that had their music written out. As I remember, Glenn was not a real good reader, but he was good at memorizing his parts, and Alex was pretty good at reading and understanding the music. Lou was a real taskmaster; I loved it."

Lou and a hungry i regular headliner, comic Prof. Irwin Corey, got along famously. Lou thought that Corey got more laughs than any other comic in the business, and one night, he tried to prove it. He sat in the audience with a hand clicker, and every time Corey got a laugh, Lou's clicker would go off. "That's the way Lou's mind works," said Grover Sales.

Occasionally, one of the comic headliners would drop in on their informal rehearsals. One was Tom Lehrer, who was Glenn's hero in particular and whom Alex thought in 1988 was the best act he had ever seen, period. "One of the first songs we began to work on was 'The

Hammer Song,' which at that time we called 'If I Had a Hammer,'" recalled Alex. "Lou, I should say, being the musicologist that he was, took the exact version from the original and we worked on that version. We worked on it interminably because we were sure that it was a potential hit song.

"One day we were rehearsing it endlessly, and Tom came in (it was the afternoon) and was kind of sitting in the back of the room for a while listening to us do this. Then we decided to take a break and he got up and started to walk out of the room singing, 'If I had a screwdriver...' and he walked out the door!

"We tried in vain to get him to write us a song, just for us. Never were able to, at any time. However, we can actually say that Tom Lehrer wrote one line for the Limeliters, and that was in 'Gunslinger.' He upgraded a line."

(For the record, the Lehrer line from the Bud Freeman/Leon Pober song was "Did you come from a broken/Home on the range").

While they couldn't—probably didn't want to—match the two-year mark of the Gateway Singers at the hungry i, the Limeliters did stay there until January of 1960, a six-month run. By the time they finished the gig, they would be making about $900 a week apiece, twice as much as they received combined when they started. And small wonder, for each night, the lines would form along the sidewalk and around the block down Kearny Street as people waited for the tables to clear for the next show.

One evening, the people were standing out in the cold San Francisco night air for hours waiting for places inside. In between their shows, while the other acts were going on, Lou, Alex and Glenn seized the opportunity to make a goodwill gesture. They went out on the sidewalk in front of the club with their instruments and played and sang for about five minutes to their surprised and ecstatic fans. An alert photographer captured the moment for posterity—the young, stoic-looking college-age men in their crew cuts, suits, and ties, with their dates staring adoringly at the three musicians.

Banducci's hunch, taking the trio sight unseen and unheard, had paid off with packed houses. In a widely-circulated quote, Banducci said, "Even the old die-hards who tell me they hate all folk songs and folk singers can't resist this bunch—the Limeliters leave them screaming for more at every show."

One of the highlights of their shows was the audience participation number, "Hey Li Lee Li Lee," a tune from the Caribbean that was in Woody Guthrie's repertoire, then reworked by the Weavers into their "Around The World" medley, picked up by the Gateways, and now inherited by the Limeliters. Lou, Alex and Glenn had no trouble drawing some uproarious "spontaneously invented rhyming couplets" (in Prof. Gottlieb's felicitous phrase) from this hip crowd.

Grover Sales remembered that there were a number of sustaining pillars in this cellar club, including a large central one that was architecturally crucial but a real pain as far as sight lines were concerned. One evening, an unfortunate young man was inspired to come up with the following couplet, "The show down here would be a killer/Hey Ii lee Ii lee lo/If it wasn't for that center pillar!" The show stopped absolutely cold, the line broke everyone up, especially Lou.

The hungry i breakthrough gig also had a profound effect upon Alex on a personal level. He met his first wife there, a woman named Ginger Stagner, part-Navaho Indian, who was the hostess at the hungry i bar. He got to know her gradually as the group's engagement wore on, and by the time December rolled around, Alex decided he wanted to marry her. The marriage itself came quickly after that, in San Francisco at the beginning of January 1960 (Alex believes it might have been New Year's Day)—and it came apart fairly quickly, as they were divorced in 1963 shortly after Glenn left the Limeliters.

"I thought this would make a good first marriage for both of them," said Theo Bikel. "In other words, it wasn't necessarily going to last for either of them. She was a little placid, a little plump but quite pretty. She was rather quiet, and she deferred a lot. She was just there, rather than 'with it;' she just sat in a corner."

"Leonide and I had very warm feelings for Ginger," said Alex's mother. "Nice person. Not right for Alex at all. She was not interested in what he was doing. I remember they would come to New York, and he would say, 'Ginger, just listen to this new tune.' And he would go to the piano, and she would sit, not moving, she wasn't even listening to that. She didn't hide it; she was bored with it. That created certain frictions, an irritation in him."

Alex found it too painful to talk about his first marriage, the reasons why they broke up, what their home life—such as it was—was like, nothing. The fact that Alex isn't sure of his anniversary date says something about his effort to block the whole sorry episode from his memory. "I was not ready for marriage, and I discovered that almost immediately," he says, refusing to elaborate on any of the details. "The marriage lasted as long as it did only because I was on the road so much. I was on the road 80% of the time. When the group broke up, it became clear to me that I had no desire to be married, at least not to this person."

But Alex and Ginger stayed together long enough to produce a son, David Michael, born on Sept. 27, 1960. Like his father, David was destined to be an only child, although he would eventually break the pattern with two children of his own.

While they were making their name and fame at one club in San Francisco, Alex and Glenn still had to deal with the club they had left behind in Colorado. After all, Glenn technically still owned the Limelite, but had to leave it in the care of surrogate managers whom he suspected were draining the Limelite of its income.

"I was doing fairly well with it although I wasn't realizing much because when an owner isn't there, money goes everywhere," Glenn said. "I said to Lou and Alex, I would split the club with them. If we had the club working and if we had time off, we'd go there and work out new material, and furthermore this was all outside income, we could use the sub-chapter S corporation and not have to declare the money as personal income. It was perfect. And Lou said no, he didn't want to be involved in Aspen at all.

"I had to make a decision. I had to either quit and go back to Aspen and work because I couldn't trust the management I had (or go with the Limeliters). I tried to keep it as long as possible, but I lost it and it went back to Sheldon Rich because I didn't pay the mortgage on it. I figured it was a lost cause by then. I didn't think it was worth selling because I felt at the time I paid top dollar for it. I knew it was going to be worth millions someday, but I didn't think I would get anything out of selling it, so I turned it back to Sheldon."

The whole denouement of the Limelite affair left a trace of bitterness in Glenn, although he was no longer angry at his colleagues for not investing in the Limelite. But at the time, he recalled, "I was very annoyed at them because it was a ridiculous decision, and we could have cleaned up. I told them we don't even have to run the club; we could close it up and hold the property and just pay off the mortgage. I couldn't pay it off alone but for the three of us, it was nothing."

It should be added that both Lou and Alex would greatly regret turning down Glenn's offer. Given how real estate has skyrocketed in value since 1959 in Colorado ski country—and jet-set Aspen in particular—the financial state of the Limeliters in later years might have been a lot less troubled. But after such a spectacular launch at the hungry i, with the world of American popular music waiting to be conquered, perhaps one shouldn't blame them for not getting too jazzed about a piece of mountain real estate in a "minimum-security prison."

The Limeliters entertain the line of surprised fans waiting to
get into the hungry i for their next show.
(Photo by Peter Breinig)

The Limeiters with comedian Mort Sahl during their breakthrough Fall 1960 tour.
(Photo by Peter Breinig, courtesy of Alex Hassilev)

Chapter Six

As the 1950s were drawing to a close, the Limeliters made their first contribution to the suddenly crowded folk music record shelves. In December of 1959, they took some time out from their hungry i gig to make their one and only album for Elektra, with Jac Holzman producing the four sessions. Originally entitled *Folk Songs For Moderns*, and later changed to simply *The Limeliters*, much of this album would form the core of their material for years to come. "That was the best album, by far, until we did the album in London without the drums," said Glenn. "Drums never belonged to that act." But there was little or no objection to the drums at the time the album was being made. Although Lou was increasingly giving way to Glenn in business matters, drums there were behind the Gateway Singers and drums there would be behind the Limeliters. Again, Lou drew from the world of jazz for his sidemen—John Pisano, the guitarist/composer who would later find his ticket to fame with Herb Alpert and the Tijuana Brass; Chuck Berghofer, the great stalwart bass player; the drummer Gene Estes.

Right away, the arrangement that they worked so hard upon, the Pete Seeger/Lee Hays song of proletarian brotherhood, "The Hammer Song," begins the record on a robust note, building to the thrilling final chorus. The trio is not above using gimmicks, as canned sounds of musket fire and whistling bombs back the Spanish Civil War song "Battle At Gandessa." In "Charlie The Midnight Marauder," the Limeliters try their hands humorously at one of folk's favorite party games, making up new lyrics to the looping waltz tune that originally was known as "Acres Of Clams." Skewering the conformity of suburbia was a hot topic—perhaps THE topic—among intellectuals in the '50s, and so the unfortunate "Charlie" is Everyman in the grey flannel suit who can't find his tract home amidst the acres of look-alike suburban cracker boxes. It wouldn't be their last rewrite of "Acres Of Clams."

An upbeat "Zhankoye"—paced much faster than it would be later—gives Lou and Alex a chance to show off some idiomatic Yiddish. In its original form, recorded by Pete Seeger and a female group called the Berries, this Crimean song celebrated the achievements, alas short-lived, of a Jewish collective farm in the mid-1920s. But this wouldn't do for the Limeliters, who kept one of the Yiddish verses about the collective farm and dropped the third, adopting instead a vague substitute lyric about universal brotherhood (which Glenn sings on an early Aspen tape). A cop-out? Perhaps, but it's still a fine tune. "When I First Came To This Land," a song that came from German immigrants in Pennsylvania, complete with German lyrics, is given a complete reworking by Oscar Brand, though the LP label gives credit to Malvina Reynolds and Lou. (Brand later complained to Jac Holzman about the erroneous credit, and it was subsequently corrected). The original tune was much like "Twinkle, Twinkle Little Star" but the processes of folk and commercial mutation wrench it out of that context for the benefit of Glenn's casual tenor. Once it became the Folger's Coffee theme some years later, one could say the transition from folk art to commerce was complete.

The hyped-up "Malaguena Salerosa" has something resembling a rocking boogie beat, with Alex playing a none-too-subtle gigolo in a spoken obbligato—and Lou and Alex get in some vocal slapstick in the driving arrangement of the Uncle Dave Macon banjo tune "The Bear Chase." "The Burro" is a thrilling Spanish procession that comes at you at an accelerating pace before dying out as it started. "Gari Gari," a Russian gypsy tune, becomes a pure artifact of the Cold War, with a Gene Raskin-penned English lyric about the consequences of the U.S./ Soviet Cultural Exchange Program of the time—again far different than the more authentic way Alex sang it later. A rather sedate rendition of Lou's powerful chart of "John Henry" follows—with Pisano's guitar commenting wryly between verses—succeeded by a consoling folk tune, "Times Are Getting Hard," with new words credited to the consortium of Brand, Raskin and Lee Hays. This was the recording that improbably surfaced in 2013 on a *Breaking Bad* episode, suddenly bringing the Limeliters back to the attention of the mass media. "Lonesome Traveler" signs off the album on an easy-going note, minus much of the grim tension that would enter their treatment later.

Naturally, the purists at *Sing Out!* were not impressed by the Limeliters' debut on the folk record scene. "A new folksong trio sparked by Glenn Yarbrough; there's not much folk song left in the music by the time the Limeliters finish their 'arrangements,'" sneered editor Irwin Silber. Record buyers were only mildly impressed, and Jac Holzman was only able to sell roughly 35,000 to 40,000 copies before the contracted year had passed. "Of course, in retrospect there's no doubt that (signing with Elektra) was a serious mistake," says Alex. "If it had been on RCA from the beginning, it would have had a much better shot at real record sales simply because the company was so much larger." "The Hammer Song," backed by "Charlie, The Midnight Marauder," also had been issued on a single—with little visible effect. "Of course, it's all hindsight," Alex notes, "who the hell knows; our version was very good but certainly not as accessible or as pop as Peter, Paul and Mary's later version."

With the evidence before us, it's hard to escape the conclusion that even if *The Limeliters* had been on RCA Victor, this would not have been their breakthrough album. The musical potential is there, the personalities of the three are in place, but not the zesty vitality that we would hear shortly down the road—and the studio clowning about seems more than a bit self-conscious. When heard in context with the Limeliters' first few RCA Victors, the Elektra album sounds like a dry run—a good but tentative opening shot.

Watching all of this with immense interest was RCA Victor, still bent upon snaring the Limeliters as their entry to compete with the Kingston Trio. The folk boom was mushrooming, the Kingston Trio was getting bigger and bigger, and RCA was left in the lurch. They could see the tremendous response the Limeliters were getting night after night, but they couldn't do anything about it so long as they stood fast on principle over a few publishing dollars.

And so, approximately six months after RCA had turned down Lou's request for the publishing rights to public domain material, they capitulated. The president of RCA Victor Records, Robert Yorke, came back to the Limeliters and said, OK, we'll give you the publishing and pick up the session costs. And we'll even add something else—a promotional budget. They would put up approximately $25,000 and the Limeliters would put up an equivalent amount of money in advance royalties to form a promotional fund. RCA would then use that fund to send the trio on a promotional tour of 30 major cities, where they would put on private performances for local record distributors, retailers, disc jockeys and other media people.

It was an ingenious idea in which to launch an act, something only a company with an extensive distribution network and a lot of bucks could have organized. "Those shows were extremely successful," remembered Alex. "We made friends as performers, we made friends as people with the entire RCA organization, and when the (first) record came out, all these people knew who we were and were ready to go out and do a job. And the first album took off but it didn't take off all by itself. It took off because we did that work."

Lou went to Jac Holzman sometime in May of 1960 and told him that they wanted out, for that would be the only way the group could stay together. According to Lou's letters, Holzman raised a fuss at first, threatening to reduce their percentages if he didn't get another album from them. Eventually Holzman compromised, asking that the Limeliters cut just one more side for him.

That additional track, the sea shanty "Greenland Fisheries," soon surfaced on an Elektra sampler, *The Folk Scene*, which was the latest in a line of bargain-priced come-ons for the Elektra roster. It has a bright, propulsive arrangement, with an acoustic guitar plugging irresistibly away underneath. The Limeliters would keep hacking away at Lou's chart in the studio well after they switched labels until it finally surfaced again under a different title, "The Whale," on *Through Children's Eyes*.

In any case, Holzman would soon come out a winner anyway, for when the Limeliters hit the big wave on RCA Victor, the undertow pulled the Elektra album along onto the pop charts as well. It rose to the No. 40 position on *Billboard Magazine's* survey in the fall of 1961, competing with two hit RCA Victor albums, and it would remain in print in some form for decades.

The distinguished-looking, easygoing Neely Plumb was an A&R man at RCA Victor's Hollywood headquarters, relatively new on the job. An accomplished musician, Plumb had been a clarinetist, bandleader, and arranger earlier in his career, most notably for Artie Shaw in his heyday. Some 78s exist of Plumb leading a studio orchestra in the manner of contemporaries like Gordon Jenkins and David Carroll, turning out charming novelty instrumentals like "Spring Tonic" roughly patterned after the light masterpieces of Leroy Anderson.

He had had virtually no experience with folk music when word came to Hollywood that there was a hot, unusual new folk act knocking 'em dead at the hungry i. Yet Plumb had an open mind and curious intellect, and he acted.

"I took a plane and went up there, heard the group, and was of course very favorably impressed," Plumb remembered in 1978 in his gentle, Southern-tinged voice (he was working for the Barskin talent agency at the time). "As it happened, I and several other of the RCA executives talked to them at various times but they saw it a different way and went with the very early Elektra record company."

Plumb didn't recall that the main obstacle to their signing with RCA Victor was Lou's determination to be his own publisher. "There was a clause in the standard RCA contract which stated that if they wrote any original material that was recorded under their contract, a lesser mechanical royalty would be paid to them," he said. "As I remember, they wouldn't sit still for that."

But Plumb kept going back to the hungry i, kept in touch with the trio, and kept the heat going under his superiors at RCA that this was an act that ought to be on Little Nipper's label. Eventually, his persistence bore fruit—and when the Limeliters were signed to RCA Victor in May of 1960, Plumb was assigned as their producer. "I had many, many meetings with the guys on the subject of what material they wanted to do," he said. "In many cases, I persuaded them that we could use some additional backup musicians. I not only contributed some ideas to their repertoire, I wrote some of their arrangements. I must say that their opinions about what they should do were extremely important to me because they knew their field. I was not a folknik then and knew very little about it and I listened very carefully to what they said. Some of the things didn't work but on the whole, I think we came off with the best material from just a meeting of the minds of the four of us."

"Great Southern gentleman," Lou would say expansively when the name Neely Plumb was mentioned. "Ultimately there's no substitute for brains—and he has 'em. He certainly didn't start out as a folk song enthusiast, but he became very, very knowledgeable. Not only that, Neely was a great, great employee of the RCA Victor company. He always represented that firm to the utmost. While he was working for RCA Victor, they got 137% of Neely Plumb. He worked for every nickel he got, and I always felt they were ridiculous in letting him go. They should have found someplace further up because they didn't have that many brainy guys working for them at that time. He has self-respect, is a great 'org' man."

"Everything considered, we might have done better with a different producer, but I don't think so," said Alex in 1978. "As a producer, he was extraordinarily right temperamentally for our group because we are all over-communicators—at least Lou and I are, and Glenn in his own way, is. Neely is very laid back, very mellow, very gentlemanly—and very much in charge in a very low-key manner. He is also very knowledgeable musically, which was very important for Lou because Lou would have never been able to interface with a producer who didn't know music."

Interestingly, Alex later said that he probably would have wanted Milt Okun, whom he met backstage in New York after a concert in the early '60s, to produce or at least arrange their recordings. Okun, a classically trained musician who studied opera and piano, had long experience in folk music, getting his first break helping out the Weavers, working with Harry Belafonte, the Belafonte Singers, the Chad Mitchell Trio, the Brothers Four, Bud and Travis—indeed, almost every major commercial folk group except the Kingston Trio and the Limeliters. Ultimately, he would build first a folk music empire—crowned by his work with Peter, Paul and Mary and John Denver—and then a publishing empire with Cherry Lane Music.

Yet Okun never did work with them—and had he done so, the Limeliters would have gone in another, perhaps more serious direction. "During their main career, I would have done it differently," said Okun. "I was less inclined to be humorous than they were, so I would have been a lot straighter with the arranging. You could never go through a whole song and be sure they weren't gonna do a little switch, live. In my arranging, I would have tried to make them straighter and more emotional, try to do songs that were very beautiful, and not try for that cute twist.

"I would have arranged things differently, but that doesn't mean it would have been better. They didn't fight as hard for blending as I wish they did. If they were tighter, it would have been more effective. I would have done some overdubbing; I would have made Glenn a little stronger, doubled Glenn up."

Indeed, it was precisely Lou's jazz leanings, not necessarily the satirical material, that kept Okun away and that probably attracted Neely Plumb, the big band veteran. "They had a jazz touch—and that, I think, is what I mean by the wit or flippancy of what they were doing," Okun said. "I was a little squarer, and I didn't appreciate the jazz element of American music. In my mind, what I thought was weaker in their recordings than my groups was this flippancy and lack of willingness to be directly emotional."

With their gig at the hungry i over at the end of January of 1960, the Limeliters' next destination was Aspen, where they played a couple of weeks at the Limelite. Lou, who still hadn't recovered from the boredom of his last visit to Aspen, was almost apoplectic in his letters to Dolly. "After a triumphant return to the scene of our initial success," he wrote, "I, like every other performer who plays Aspen, am forced to ask myself, 'What the fuck am I doing here?'

"I am going to make it clear today to Glenn Yarbrough that I must never again be asked to come to Aspen regardless of the condition of the business. This town is so utterly boring that it beggars description. It's enough to make me want to try skiing. There is literally NOTHING to do."

But Lou did settle down to record some trenchant observations of life in the secluded ski resort, his wry wit now fine-tuned from night after night in front of a nightclub crowd. "In winter," Lou wrote, "the Limelite is characterized by acrid fumes which emanate from the kitchen, the charcoal broiler, over which US High Grade Choice Gristle is transformed into heartburn. The ski enthusiasts are entirely differnt [sic] from the summer visitors of Aspen. Whereas the latter were sun-burned, raw-boned, mammoth-kneed cretins—the former are wind-burned, raw-boned, mammoth-kneed cretins. But it is the year-round inhabitants who are the most fascinating. Imagine, if you can, a city of two thousand Glenn Yarbroughs..."

By the middle of March, after a gig at Claremont College in Southern California, the Limeliters moved on to Chicago, where they opened for jazz singer/pianist Hazel Scott at Mister Kelly's. Willard Alexander, best known as the booking agent who handled Count Basie, was responsible for getting them into this prestigious nightclub, where the Kingston Trio had made an impressive noise not long before. According to Lou, Alexander was trying to sign the Limeliters himself, and this gig was a deliberate show of his influence. "We had just come from San Francisco where every show literally was a standing ovation," remembered Lou. "All the guys in the Kingston Trio had told me, 'Oh, Mister Kelly's is a great place!'"

They soon found out otherwise. The hip clientele had come to hear Hazel Scott and they didn't seem to have any interest in a sophisticated folk group from San Francisco. They just sat there, responding with polite but tepid applause. In addition, it was still the middle of winter in

Chicago; it was freezing and the mood in the room was, in Alex's word, "Funereal." "They weren't rude," Lou recalled, "they were just totally oblivious to what we were doing." Marilyn Child believed that the lay-out of Mister Kelly's had a lot to do with the inability of the Limeliters to put over their act. "A lot of clubs were so badly set up; they were not floor-show rooms," she recalled. "Kelly's had a bar area, dance floor, the little place where you put a jazz combo and all that, and then bleachers. You can't play to people like this."

Between sets, Lou—who had already had a few drinks under his belt—went into the men's room and an agent from the William Morris Agency, Sid Epstein, followed him in there. With stunning tact, the agent told Lou, "You gotta cut out the pitter-patter," inferring that Lou's humor was slowing up the act.

Now Lou had never encountered anything but instant success in his folk singing career—whether it was with the Gateway Singers or the fledgling Limeliters. He simply wasn't prepared for anything less than total adulation—and he was, to put it succinctly, "pissed off." Before the next set started, he told Alex and Glenn that if the audience doesn't do something (what it was, they can't recall), he would play the rest of the show with his back to the audience. So, when they came on again, and the audience responded as frigidly as before, Lou spun around and did his act to the back wall much to Alex's and Glenn's embarrassment, not to mention that of Jac Holzman, who was in the audience.

"I'd worked in a lot of places where it wasn't so easy and I had already worked this out in my mind that you just keep working and doing your best no matter what happens," said Glenn. "And when Lou didn't do that, I was furious." After the show, when the three went out for a drink, Alex—and most forcefully Glenn—told a repentant Lou that if this kind of "infantile behavior" ever occurred again, that would be the end of the act.

As a result, it was to be the last onstage temper tantrum of Lou's career. But it was also the last time the group played Mister Kelly's, despite favorable notices in the the press ("These boys are every bit as good as the Kingston Trio and the Gateway Singers; in fact, they combine the best elements of the others," wrote Will Leonard in the *Chicago Sunday Tribune*). Even though the owners Oscar and George Marienthal had contractual options for two more engagements by the Limeliters—and they could have done land office business once the group really became hot—the trio was never invited back again. Even later, when the group sold out Chicago's opera house, Mister Kelly's remained off-limits. "That asshole will never play in this club again," the Marienthals reportedly said, and Lou admired them for sticking to their principles.

During the engagement at Mister Kelly's, the Limeliters took time out to make their only political appearance. Senator John F. Kennedy was in a hot Wisconsin primary race with Senator Hubert Humphrey for the 1960 Democratic Presidential nomination, and the trio's attorney Seymour Lazar suggested that they appear with Sen. Kennedy at a rally in Milwaukee along with track star Jesse Owens. After receiving the day of March 23 off, the trio got in a car and drove the 87 miles north to Milwaukee—and lo, Kennedy was not there. A civil rights attorney named Belford Lawson told the assembled, mostly Black crowd that Kennedy was in Washington fighting for civil rights legislation. But the Limeliters played the rally anyway, and if you want to interpret it as a good-luck omen, Kennedy went on to win the Wisconsin primary on April 5—and subsequently the nomination and general election.

During the day, the group visited Kennedy's headquarters, and the ever-irreverent Lou could not resist tweaking the sensibilities of a future senator (possibly Ted Kennedy). "The fact that the meeting was held in the huge Milwaukee Jewish Community Center, plus the fact that there was not one Caucasian face on the platform, caused me to wonder what the Kennedy forces will do for the white Protestant vote," Lou's letter to Dolly the next morning said. "A question which I was impelled to ask in the headquarters. One of Kennedy's younger brothers, a very handsome young putz, found that particular sally most unfunny."

As the gig at Mister Kelly's wound down, the Limeliters suddenly found themselves with no place to go, for Willard Alexander had nothing else up his sleeve after the Chicago debacle. But that changed in a hurry. That February, they started to talk a 23-year-old MBA graduate fresh out of the Harvard Business School named Ken Kragen into becoming their executive-secretary-road-manager. This was the same Ken Kragen who would later become perhaps the most famous pop music manager of the '80s (Kenny Rogers, Lionel Richie, "We Are The World," etc.}. At the urging of Lou, who had known Kragen since he was a student at UC Berkeley where he had been booking shows, the Limeliters gave Kragen his first job.

Kragen vividly remembered his traumatic experience of visiting the Limeliters on his first day on the job. He was heading toward their hotel room in Chicago, and just outside the door, the first thing he heard was Alex bellowing the words, "OK, we're breaking up!" Think of this, a young promising hotshot, having turned down such big-league corporate outfits as Procter and Gamble just so that he could hitch a ride with the Limeliters, and here they were in his first "encounter" with them, saying that they were breaking up.

But soon, Kragen would learn that this irrevocable-sounding decision was just business-as-usual for the volatile group he was about to manage. "They were breaking up every day they were in existence," he said. Like Neely Plumb, Kragen became a referee of sorts for their disputes. When the three, for example, couldn't agree upon a booking firm (each had their own candidate), Kragen ended up making the decision, going to New York City to interview prospective booking agents. And when they had trouble with Jac Holzman trying to get out of their Elektra deal, it was Ken's father Adrian Kragen who mediated, urging them to accept Holzman's request to cut "Greenland Fisheries." The Limeliters were unhappy with the work of the William Morris agency, to which they were signed until June 30th of 1960. True, William Morris did manage to get them two weeks April 5–17 with the Horace Silver Quintet in Manhattan's Village Vanguard, the triangular basement shrine that has played host to many of the greatest names in folk and jazz. It was during this highly visible date that RCA Victor made its biggest and ultimately decisive push to sign the group.

But the agency allowed other gigs to fall through, including a high visibility television show in New York, and the trio instructed Kragen to shop around. After a while, Kragen had settled upon a newly organized firm called International Talent Associates (ITA), a Bert Block/Larry Bennett spinoff from Joe Glaser at Associated Booking Corporation. When they left, they had taken their prize client, the Kingston Trio, with them, and since the Trio was too busy to accept every offer that came their way, ITA could keep the Limeliters working full steam just on the leftovers. When ITA promptly landed them a May gig in New York's Blue Angel nightclub on the bill with comedian Don Adams—for whom the Gateway Singers had opened at the hungry i—Lou was sold on them, and he and Kragen eventually convinced Alex and Glenn that ITA was the way to go.

"They [the Limeliters] were always reliable; never, never had a problem with them," said Frank Modica, who headed the concert division for ITA after he joined them in April 1961. "They did not, like most acts, need a sense of direction in terms of the business."

In a deal that had been in the works before Kragen signed on, Lou Robin and Allan Tinkley of Concerts, Inc. placed the Limeliters for the first time in a theater context, a concert package that included the Ramsey Lewis Trio, cabaret singer Chris Connor and the George Shearing Quintet. They played six shows up and down the state of California in May—and it proved to be a revelation for Lou. "That was the first time I'd ever worked in concert," he said, "and I suddenly saw that it's a whole lot easier to be effective when you are working in a theater situation and it's harder for somebody to look away from the act than it is to look at it. You are not an animated portion of the decor, which is what you usually are in a club."

A friend of Alex's who worked for the William Morris agency managed to get them booked into the Hollywood Bowl in July as the opening act for the sultry Eartha Kitt in a program entitled "Songs From Many Lands." The resurgent Bowl, which had nearly gone under in 1951, was in the midst of an astonishing season. The great French conductor Pierre Monteux had led opening night, and Eugene Ormandy, William Steinberg and Leonard Bernstein with the New York Philharmonic would come visiting. Jascha Heifetz and Isaac Stern headed the violin ranks. Ella Fitzgerald, Nat King Cole, and Benny Goodman were among those who had entertained the multitudes on the well-attended "pops" nights. This was definitely the big leagues. Moreover, the Bowl—a monstrous 17,000-plus-seat, acoustically bizarre concrete amphitheatre—presents its own obstacles to anyone who mounts its stage. Performers have little sense of the vast audience beyond the first few rows, with the bright spotlights glaring in their faces. In turn, to those seated way up in the benches on the paved-over hillside, the performers appear to be little more than somewhat animated insects. In those days, a large reflecting pool of water separated the stage from the first row of seats, further distancing entertainers from their public. Any performer—let alone a folk group used to intimate encounters in cramped nightclubs—would have a tough time communicating under these conditions.

And yet the Limeliters apparently did just that. They were hired to do a 15-minute opening act, and Alex remembers that the crowd "went nuts when we did our thing." The 15 minutes passed in no time, the set was over, and the Limeliters had been told by a time-conscious stage manager that there would be no time for encores, you take your bows and go home. But the audience, supposedly primed for Eartha Kitt but unexpectedly knocked out by this sharp, witty, exciting trio, would have none of it. They started stamping their feet and clapping their hands in that barbaric rhythm familiar to anyone who has heard a crowd come alive—thump! thump! thump! thump! They would not let them go. Trying to please both the crowd and the stage manager, Lou, Alex, and Glenn came back for another bow. But it wasn't enough. Thump! thump! thump! thump! went the crowd, yelling and screaming all the way, with even the solid concrete Bowl seeming to shake with their impact. There was no choice; they had to do an encore, and to hell with what anyone in the Eartha Kitt camp thought.

And there was hell to pay, for Kitt was so mad she couldn't even utter an intelligible word. "After we did our little show, she was going backstage and she was like a woman insane," Lou remembered. "She was just talking in tongues, I'm telling you."

"She wanted to kill us," Alex concurred. All Glenn could recall about it was how much he wanted to go to bed with her.

Albert Goldberg, the classical music critic of the *Los Angeles Times* who found himself covering pops concerts on the Hollywood Bowl beat, was nevertheless moved to write that the Limeliters "injected fun and high spirits" into the show. He also reported that two encores had to be added during the Limeliters' second appearance the next night since they had "stirred up such a storm of applause." "They probably could have stayed on over the weekend if the management hadn't insisted the show must go on," wrote Margaret Harford of the *Los Angeles Mirror News*. If there was a flashpoint for the breakout of Limeliter-mania into the mass media, this Bowl appearance was it.

The Limeliters began to make a disconcerting habit of stealing the show as the opening act to a mainstream pop headliner. They were asked by Johnny Mathis' manager Helen Noga to open the show for him at Los Angeles' outdoor Greek Theatre in August of 1960. In an amusing unintentional faux pas, they didn't know that after their 20-minute opening set, they were supposed to wait around backstage until the end of Mathis' elaborate act to take a final bow, as if they were a part of the entire package. Instead, on opening night, the trio did their act, tore up the audience, and went right home. Well, Kragen was on the receiving end of the first obscene tirade from Ms. Noga the next day—and after withstanding another such fusillade themselves ("You call yourself show business? You're not shit!" Lou remembered her saying), the Limeliters made sure that they were around for the curtain call that night.

Later, the trio opened for Mathis in September in San Francisco's Geary Theater—and Jim Estes' *San Francisco Chronicle* review bore the sensational headline, "Limeliters Steal Show at Johnny Mathis' Opening." Estes went on to call them "masters of their own particular style of folk and pseudo-folk singing," lauding Lou Gottlieb in particular as "one of the funniest men in show business." There were no pretenses about the Mathis company being one big happy family the next day. "When we walked into the theater that night, nobody would talk to us," Glenn said. "It was like we had arranged this review."

Ed Sullivan, one of the shrewdest talent scouts this side of Enrico Banducci, was quick to pick up on the trio's ascending career—and at 8 p.m. on a Sunday night, Oct. 16, 1960, the Limeliters appeared in black-and-white on television screens all over the nation. It had been the electronic equivalent of playing the Palace, for by this time, the Sullivan show had already triggered cultural breakthroughs, most notoriously that of Elvis Presley.

The videotape of their appearance has been preserved, and it captures a magic moment. The tape reveals Lou, Alex and Glenn on the rise—young, cocky, rehearsed to the teeth, brimming with confidence, punching home their two songs in front of the hungry i's classic brick wall.

It is mind-boggling to realize how drastically performing logistics have changed since 1960, for here the trio is, huddled around a single microphone, stepping back and forward in carefully coordinated choreography as each soloist takes his turn. Yet it must have been a very good microphone, for the Limeliters' blend and each soloist come through beautifully, and the sound of their unmiked, unamplified instruments (even Lou's bass) is also surprisingly clear. There is something to be said for such primitive technology; it teaches you showmanship, how to move onstage, how to get the best out of limited means with no place to hide.

In only six minutes, the time traveler gets a capsule summary of what the Limeliters were like in their prime, with Lou's highbrow humor, Glenn's extraordinary voice, Alex's boyish charm, instrumental expertise, a dash of history and sheer professional razzle-dazzle all at work. Alex and Glenn tune up while Lou goes into one of his convoluted professorial monologues about whether all this fuss is necessary. Then with heads full of barely suppressed energy, they launch right into "Headin' For The Hills," a stirring tune about the American Revolution credited to John Stewart, the future member of the Kingston Trio.

Later on in the hour-long program, they would perform "There's A Meetin' Here Tonight," which preceded by its brief preamble, "We Come For To Sing," had become a rousing, can't-miss opening number. The live, obviously adoring audience can't resist clapping along. The Limeliters would appear on the Sullivan show at least two more times during their heyday, yet in hindsight, this first appearance was the moment that middle America at large first heard the trio that had conquered San Francisco.

But Lou and Glenn believed that the big career break for the Limeliters was a five-week concert tour with Mort Sahl in the fall of 1960—arranged through Alex's friend as a result of the Bowl triumph. They knew that in October and November, the 1960 Presidential campaign would be going into its red-hot home stretch. And there was no hotter topical comedian in America than Mort Sahl, then riding at the very peak of his career, with almost every intellectual and liberal in America hanging upon every word of his extemporaneous nightly lancings of the Eisenhower administration.

The tour went all over the United States and Canada, selling out virtually every house in which they played. Indeed, they were at the Queen Elizabeth Theatre in Vancouver in the wee hours of a November morning when John Kennedy's whisker-thin election as president was announced. Being on the ticket with Sahl around election time gave the Limeliters priceless national exposure. "That is really what did it," said Glenn. "That was the most important gig we ever did." It was also, in another crucial way, one of their most enjoyable tours because they were able to go out and whip up hysteria without having to worry about how the headliner would react. "I must say that Mort Sahl was the best," said Glenn, "because Mort Sahl didn't have that insecurity that the rest of them had, because we just went out and tore that audience up. And Mort, it never bothered him. He went out and did his show and it was great."

But Sahl—a fearless iconoclast who would shortly thereafter find his career on the ropes when he dared to satirize liberals in general and the Kennedy administration in particular—was a rare exception.

Entertainment is a precarious business at best, one that feeds any shreds of self-doubt even when a performer has hit the top.

For an extreme example, take Glenn's old after-hours buddy at the Gate of Horn, Shelley Berman. If there ever was a comedian who had the world on a string, it was Shelley Berman in 1960. His *Inside* and *Outside* albums were required listening at suburban dinner parties all across the country. His simulated crank phone calls in his weird, almost perverted accent had people breaking up uncontrollably.

And yet Berman felt almost mortally threatened by his old friend's new trio when they opened for him one June night in Hawaii. "Now I want you to go out there and just sing," Glenn remembered Berman telling them. "I don't want any jokes." They looked at each other incredulously. But hey, Shelley was the boss that night, whatever he wanted. So, they put together a show in which they wouldn't have to tune their instruments—so Lou would not get his comic licks in—and they did their show sans jokes. The audience went crazy anyway and wouldn't let them out of the house. They came backstage to find Berman pacing back and forth furiously like a deranged psychotic. "OK, go take a bow," he barked, and just as at the Bowl, the Limeliters took a bow, and another bow. The applause kept coming.

Finally, Glenn had had enough of his erstwhile friend's ego. "Fuck off Shelley, we're not going to keep going out there taking bows," he remembered saying. "Either we do an encore or forget it, you go out." Berman relented, and they weren't in tune! So they went back into form, Lou doing his comic turns while he, Alex and Glenn tuned up. "These people who didn't know us to start with anyway didn't realize what Lou did," Glenn said. "And then, oh my God, they just went absolutely crazy. We came offstage and Shelley was back there, and he was shaking his fist and he says, 'I'll get you barred from the Musicians Union!'"

Glenn then went to a spot in the back row of the audience, which was still yelling for more, and he noticed a stool being placed onstage from behind the curtain, a signal that the comedian was about to come on. Suddenly the house was enveloped with loud boos.

But no, this amazing madman did not cave in. "Shelley Berman went out there and did the best show I'd ever seen him do," Glenn flatly said.

"He was fucking brilliant!" added Lou. "I wanted to see if a guy could come out of the nuthouse where he was and be even coherent.

I'd seen him at the hungry i, I'd seen him a dozen times before; he was fucking on fire! I don't know how a man like that could live.

"But I made a mental note, though; if he ever, ever came near me with that same kind of thing, I was gonna punch him. He wants it. He wants to be hit."

Having finally captured the Limeliters, RCA Victor put the group to work in July of 1960 on its first album for the label. Neely Plumb had heard the Elektra record, and Lou said that Neely thought it was comparatively stiff to the way the show went. So as far as the Limeliters remembered, the intention all along was to record them live.

However, in the week prior to their gig at the Ash Grove that would supply the tapes for *Tonight: In Person,* an attempt was made to record a studio album in RCA Victor's Studio 1 in Hollywood. RCA Victor's session files reveal three studio dates on the afternoons of July 20, 21 and 26, which yielded a total of nine songs, none of which were ever released. On July 20, they would work on "There's A Meetin' Here Tonight," "Molly Malone," "Seven Daffodils," and the Elektra leftover, "Greenland Fisheries." The next day, the agenda contained Travis Edmonson's thoughtful "The Time Of Man," Woody Guthrie's "Hard Travelin'" and "Whistlin' Gypsy" and the last day, they tried a stirring Lou Gottlieb/Malvina Reynolds song "Western Wind" and a tune credited to Gene Raskin and Lou Gottlieb, "Careless Love."

The sessions couldn't have gone well; the take numbers were piling up ("Greenland Fisheries" reached 17 takes and "Western Wind" hit 19). Eventually everything except "Careless Love" would come out in re-recorded live versions, usually accomplished on one take. The experience must have reinforced Neely's belief that he could only capture the essence of the Limeliters in their live habitat, although attempts to make acceptable studio tracks would continue.

All three Limeliters, along with Neely, believed that the group was never effective in the studio, and that they preferred to record out in front of their audiences. "I never did think we captured that same thing (an 'alive' quality) in the studio," said Neely. "We got a lot more technical perfection very often, we had better sound, and by going over and over the things many times, we got what you might say is a better performance. But some of the excitement was lacking, as compared to the live albums."

In addition, the closed, private conditions of the studio would bring out all the prickly edges of the three. Glenn would complain about how slow Lou and Alex were in learning new material. Alex would rail about Lou's "pedantic" ways in running the musical end of a session, and less vehemently about Glenn's impatience. Lou would say that in later years, Alex as a producer was happiest when procrastinating endlessly about which take to choose, racking up hours of extra studio charges if someone else was footing the bill.

Whatever the truth, if any, behind all this bickering, the group eventually did come up with some worthy studio material, some of which stands high among their finest moments. However, if you go by percentages, a much higher proportion of their released live tracks have truly clicked, as opposed to those made in the studio. And there is also no question that their live albums have sold better than their studio albums.

In any event, around the time of their Bowl debut—and just two days after their last attempt to cut tracks for an abortive studio album— the Limeliters and a remote unit from RCA Victor went into the Ash Grove for the first of four straight nights of live recording. Usually, the trio would work without backup musicians but for this date, as well as the earlier studio sessions, they had some help. Two veteran studio players, guitarist Allan Reuss {whose adventures the teenaged Lou once followed in the Benny Goodman band} and drummer Earl Palmer Jr. were on board and would become fixtures on later Limeliters albums.

The second guitarist was an eager young folkie by the name of James McGuinn, who was working on what Alex claims was his first professional job. Again, the Limeliters proved themselves to be astute talent scouts, for Jim (later Roger) McGuinn would later form the Byrds, which ironically would be one of the catalysts behind the merger of folk with rock. They couldn't have known that their young sideman would play such a major role in shattering the mass media's infatuation with the folk revival. But that was five years down the road—which in the hyperspace speed of events in the 1960s seemed like an eternity.

A lot of material was taped on those four nights, but Neely and the group only chose to use material from the July 28, 29 and 31 performances. What they got was a breakthrough, a record that captured much of what was exciting club audiences in the big cities. From the slow "We Come For To Sing" intro to a rousing "There's A Meetin' Here Tonight," one is in the presence of something electric. "Molly Malone," with bongos in the background, features Glenn's tenor against virile vocal harmony, a breather before the group's extraordinary rapport with its audience begins. This happens in the most unlikely of material, a French tune entitled "Les Moines de Saint Bernardin" dealing with a young man who discovers a monastery within which the activities are far from devout. By the time the Limeliters get through with it, it is no longer an esoteric import. "Well, I can see you're all dying to know what that chorus means," says Alex after he and his colleagues sally forth on the lusty, driving chorus for the first time. "Well, it means exactly what you think it means."

Another ballad for Glenn, "Seven Daffodils," sets apart the philandering monks from the singalong "Hey Li Lee Li Lee." Here, the Limeliters give their surefire audience participation number near-definitive life, with Palmer's drums kicking it along. Lou assumes the role of a slightly bent professor doubling as summer camp counselor, establishing the tone of this gathering with his "camp" motto: "Clean mind, clean body—take your pick!" The real fun comes when the audience starts coming up with often really inventive verses. RCA Victor's executives no doubt flipped over the fan who was moved to sing, "The Limeliters put on a show/Kingston Trio, out you go!" A stirring performance of "Headin' For The Hills," leads off Side Two, with Alex interpolating "Yankee Doodle" on the banjo over Glenn's brief narrative. It's a pity that the Limeliters never recorded more of John Stewart's material but also understandable, given that he would soon become a member of the competition over at Capitol.

Morgan Ames' exquisite ode to wanderlust, "The Far Side Of The Hill," must have struck an autobiographical chord in Glenn; his soulful whistling and sensitively phrased vocal are completely at one with the wistful, restless loner in the song. In an exciting rearrangement of "Rumania, Rumania," with a boost from Malvina Reynolds on the English chorus, Lou fuses it with his professor shtick while retaining the vivacity of Aaron Lebedeff's original recording, sprinkling all kinds of contemporary references (such as rhyming "pastramola" with "Stan Kenton-ola"). The drums really push it forward, giving the tune a swinging jazz feeling, and Alex's interpolation of "Greensleeves" is a delightful burst of European sophistication.

"Madeira M'Dear" makes its first appearance on records, with Alex's flamenco-like guitar backing Lou's zany, lecherous vocal. The Russian

"Proshchai," which Artie Shaw had cut way back in 1939, becomes an upbeat, multilingual farewell and an invitation to come see them again—astute programming that leaves you panting for more.

All of this comes through with tremendous immediacy on the compact disc version that RCA put out in 1989. You are practically seated in the old Ash Grove with the clinking glasses, dishes and silverware and other extraneous noises, with an audience attuned to the Limeliters' satirical mindset and fine musicianship. Despite the topical references that pin it firmly to its time,*Tonight: In Person* still leaps out from the speakers.

Only one tune looked as if it might have some potential on its own—and as unlikely as it seems, that was Lou's Yiddish extravaganza "Rumania, Rumania." It was this song—the calling card of Lebedeff, a leading light of the now-legendary Second Avenue Theatre of New York City's Yiddish theater scene between the world wars—that really broke the Limeliters in New York, with its vast Jewish population. A disc jockey named William B. Williams played "Rumania" on his show one Saturday morning, and the result was pandemonium ("The switchboard exploded," recalled Lou). The demand was so great that RCA Victor released a seven-inch 33 RPM EP of "Rumania" backed with "Hey Li Lee Li Lee" in May 1961 on its Compact 33 Double series—a short-lived attempt to jettison the 45 RPM single. Released in a hardcover jacket with the *Tonight: In Person* photo on the front, this little disc is now an attractive collector's item.

It was even responsible for getting the Limeliters on the high-riding Perry Como television show. In a letter to Dolly, Lou wrote that the producer of the show came up to him and asked, "Which one is the mam-elige?" [sic]. However, the fact that the producers had asked for such an ethnic bit of material nearly backfired on everyone. "They wanted us to sing 'Rumania, Rumania' and I was against it," recalled Glenn. "And we sang it and Bert Block and Harry Bennett (of ITA) almost went crazy because they had had a tour already booked and people were calling up to cancel the tour." In a later bit of correspondence, Lou wearily recorded his impressions of big-time television: "Yesterday was hard work. Those 'network' shows are the most insane rat races I've ever seen. This one is worse than the Dinah Shore show because they do it in an old theater and there is no room for anything. The orchestra rehearses in the mezzanine of the theater, for instance...Perry Como seems to be a good guy. But this business is so hassled up that one can't get a clear impression."

But although the seven-inch LP didn't sell outside the New York area, the idea of having a hit single was never far from the minds of the trio and Neely Plumb. They went into the studio again on January 8 and 10, 1961 to cut tunes for a follow up album but all they ended up with was a single, Cisco Houston's "A Dollar Down," backed with "When Twice the Moon Has Come and Gone" and one side of a future single, "Jonah." The other songs were "Aravah, Aravah" and the first of many futile attempts to cut the Clancy Brothers' treatment of "By The Risin' Of The Moon." Again, there appeared to be some problems in getting acceptable takes out; the January 8 session went 1 1/2 hours into overtime but still yielded only one tune ("A Dollar Down").

Yet "A Dollar Down"—a bouncy picture of modern suburban life fueled on credit—is a fine example of the Limeliters' wryly contemporary slant, and it was their only single that came even close to being a hit, rising to No. 60 during a three-week stay on *Billboard*'s pop singles chart in April. "Twice The Moon," a German song colored by Jimmie Haskell's accordion, was a more commercial-sounding piece of work. The real masterpiece of these sessions was "Jonah," with a swinging, finger-popping arrangement by Lou that lifts the trio's heavy voices into its plane, driven by jazzman Howard Roberts' catchy guitar riff. But "Jonah" didn't come out until some 10 months later when Neely needed a flip side for "Just An Honest Mistake."

Yet even if the chase for the singles charts was a futile one, everything else seemed to be going incredibly right for the Limeliters in 1961. They had made a decision to go for the money—and while the big money was still a couple of years away, with the help of the promotional punch of RCA Victor, they were well on their way toward the upper strata of American show business.

A publicity shot from the early 1960s.

Above Left: A rare Limeliters 7-inch EP taken from the "Tonight: In Person" album. It was marketed in a failed format from the early '60s, the Compact 33 Double. Released 1961.

Above Right: Picture sleeve from The Limeliters' first – and only charted – single. Released 1961.

Right: The Limeliters' self-titled first album, usually referred to as the Elektra album. Released 1960.

The Limeliters in a forest
setting, August 1962.
(Photo by Jerry Stoll,
Jerry Stoll Photography)

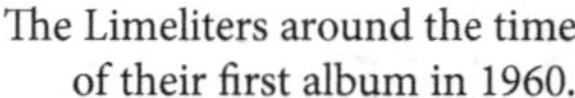

The Limeliters around the time
of their first album in 1960.

Glenn with the hills of San Francisco in the background, early 1960s.

Alex Hassilev, banjo virtuoso, early 1960s.

Title page of an RCA Victor press kit, probably 1960

The Limeliters at Basin Street East, June 1961.
(Photo courtesy of Alex Hassilev)

Chapter Seven

"We never turned down a good offer
Commercials for coffee and Coke
We published, promoted and hustled, 'cau-ause
We were afraid to be broke"
– Gene Raskin/Byron Walls: *"Acres of Limeliters" (1973)*

Folk music never had it so good as it did in the early 1960s—and in all likelihood, never would again. It was certainly a beneficiary of the persecution and problems that rock 'n' roll was undergoing at the time. As rock 'n' roll—crippled by the 1959-60 payola scandals, and the deaths, arrests, disgraces, or sellouts of most of its heroes—retreated to the control of the moneymen in the Brill Building in New York, the folk boom picked up speed. There was plenty of money to be made by the record companies, even as no-longer-naive artists were increasingly grabbing a piece of the public domain action.

The record companies were beating the bushes to sign their own versions of the Kingston Trio. With Capitol and RCA Victor owning the No.1 {Kingston Trio} and No.2 {Limeliters} groups, almost every other label seemed to have at least one such group in hand—Columbia (The Brothers Four), Liberty (Bud and Travis), Warner Bros. (The Gateway Trio), United Artists (The Highwaymen), Philips (The Serendipity Singers), Mercury (The Smothers Brothers), Kapp (The Chad Mitchell Trio). Elektra and Vanguard, the two small independents who were there early and fast, were growing into major players in the record business, fed by their large folk rosters. And even persistent little Folkways reveled in its role as the prophet that was right from the start.

No one could know how long the boom would last, but everyone with a banjo or a seat in the boardroom was out there mining the Mother Lode. And as a result, the rest of 1961 and almost all of 1962 was a delirious blur for the Limeliters.

They were pushed from one end of the country to the other by their grateful record company and ecstatic booking agents. Couch potatoes of the time couldn't miss them on television, which was loaded with their variety show appearances and their commercials.

They were cranking out three albums a year for RCA Victor right up until 1964, even after they stopped touring—and every one of them made the charts. In 1961, they were on the road 300 days out of the year, 1962 increased the total to 310 days, a punishing pace in any era—and one which put additional strain on all three of their marriages.

Yet Alex doesn't necessarily agree that the Limeliters were becoming tycoons from their strenuous labors. "We were making a good living, but we weren't making a fortune by any stretch of the imagination," he recalled. "I suppose if we collected everything in cash instead of putting some in investments or doing whatever we were doing...but it wasn't huge. The big money really came that last year (1963), and the paradox is when Glenn left the group, that was the year we would have really made a lot of money."

In a way, this was true, for the Limeliters had worked out a plan of deferred compensation with RCA Victor, a concept that was invented by Ken Kragen's father Adrian. Lou claimed he didn't get a penny of royalties from RCA Victor until 1966, which he estimated at roughly $150,000 each over the boom period.

In any case, they paid themselves $500 a week apiece to live on—and for three once-struggling young intellectuals, who remembered how tough it was to scratch out a comfortable living in the 1950s, it must have seemed like the Klondike gold strike. "None of us had ever seen any money and then suddenly you are making easily $3500 a night no matter where you are working," remembered Lou. "In those days, that was big money. I really was bulge-eyed—and we got so we couldn't turn anything down."

At this point, Lou, ever the entertainer, would simulate the typical dialogue between a rich yet bedraggled folk singer wheezing with fatigue and his sharp-eyed booking agent.

"The classic scene is, you get the call from the booker who says, 'Whaddya doin' after the gig on Saturday night in Chicago?'"

"'We're takin' the day off, Larry.'"

"'Hey, listen, they called up from Champlain-Urbana and they wanna know if you can make it for Sunday afternoon.'"

"'Can't do it, man, exhausted, finished.'"

"'Hey, they got the front money in.'"

"'Front money?'"

"Hey, I said they got the $1750 mailed in."

"And you think, yes, I'm going to give up what is $1000 to me to lie in a hotel room in Chicago on a Sunday? You can't see yourself doing it. Couldn't turn anything down."

Indeed, ITA now had the two biggest-selling folk acts in the country under its belt (the other being the Kingston Trio), and they were wasting no time capitalizing on the Limeliters' first hit album and all the rave reviews piling up. They had become too valuable for the intimate nightclubs that had launched them.

"It was my business to get on the phone and start moving them out of the clubs now that they've broke with a hit album," said Frank Modica. "We took them to a college convention, the forerunner of the National Entertainment Conference that was originally called the Southern University Student Government Association. It was a group of schools predominantly from the southeastern part of the country, from Virginia as far west as Mississippi. The directors of student activities would come to this annual convention, and the first one I went to was held at Clemson University in Clemson, South Carolina. I think at that time ITA was the only entertainment agency represented."

"We would put on a show for the students all the time, and we presented people like the Limeliters, exposed them to the students, we would sit there and give out albums. By the end of the conference, we'd probably walk away with 15 to 20 one-nighters for them in that geographical region."

To help their agents do their jobs better, the Limeliters added a startling degree of professionalism. They made it a point to arrive on time, fully rehearsed, ready to do the necessary preliminaries before the concert, ready to give their all at the concert.

All three had nothing but absolute praise for each other's professional work habits—Lou's tantrum at Mister Kelly's notwithstanding—and one wonders if this also perversely contributed to the criticism by folk purists who still worshipped the beloved but wayward Woody Guthrie.

For example, Frank Modica recalled how unusually reliable the Limeliters were in doing the advance work for their college gigs. "I always made a point of making sure that the agents made sure there was a telephone number given to the artist to call the school at least two days before to let them know what time they were arriving, if there were any changes they needed, technical riders, any help or assistance they may need," he recalled. "This was done, and the students or the faculty people who were in charge of this operation felt very relaxed.

"We had a problem with different acts running around the country showing up late, not showing up, not calling. They (the Limeliters) were very, very good at that, good business people."

One sometimes tends to forget about the dramatic physical differences in show business between the early 1960s and only seven or eight years later. Listeners had not yet become used to having everything amplified. Vocal groups would still sing into one microphone, acoustic instruments would not be miked, stage monitors were not nearly as much a staple of concerts as they would be a short time later. Logistics of travel were much less complicated; all the Limeliters had to do was load and unload their guitars, banjo and bass and let the houses in which they were playing take care of the electronics.

Stage dress was a world apart from the casual revolution soon to come. For men, suits and ties—even tuxedos—were de rigueur if they wanted to appear before an audience. Even rebellious jazz musicians had to dress in suits and ties like any middlebrow pop crooner. Interestingly enough, the most noticeable non-conformists prior to the rock era's explosion in the '60s were the folk singers, many of whom were earnestly trying to identify with the working class. Even there, there was no set pattern. Harry Belafonte would do Carnegie Hall in his trademark casual shirts, open at the chest, while his backup bands wore the usual male concert uniforms. Meanwhile, the male Weavers would be smartly outfitted in show business tuxedos at their Carnegie Hall concerts. The Kingston Trio achieved a compromise with their collegiate striped shirts which nevertheless definitely constituted a uniform—and an example to be imitated by their many copycats.

We bring up the issue of dress because, believe it or not, it was one of the major points of dispute among the Limeliters—perhaps a case of making mountains out of molehills but still an issue. It was an issue for the free-spirited, non-conforming Glenn Yarbrough, who made it a flashpoint in his lifelong love-hate relationship with show business. When he found out that the trio would be clad identically, he says that he nearly quit the group before it ever reached the hungry i.

"Dress is a really strange thing with me," he said. "I don't like clothes and I don't like to be told what to wear either. I hated the idea of dressing like everybody else.

"If anything, the interesting thing about this act is its really diverse people on the stage, each with his own unique style of personality and to try and make it a uniform kind of group was ridiculous to me...for the whole time that we had this act going, I was of the minority opinion to stop wearing the same kind of clothes."

Indeed, Lou recalled that just before they opened at the hungry i, he made Glenn go down to the Cable Car haberdasher in San Francisco. There Lou bought him a suit with a midnight-blue, single-breasted coat, the first suit made of the same material that Glenn ever owned. Although Glenn gave in, over the next four years, he continued what really was a pathbreaking assault on the idea of uniforms. "It was a constant argument, and it was so serious, and it was so meaningless because when we finally did it, nobody even cared," Glenn said. "When we went to Europe to perform, we left the suits home and now we're gonna just not wear the same clothes. And when we got to Europe, everyone got so paranoid that we went into this Italian tailor and we had suits made, all alike!"

Clothing would be only one aspect of the inevitable and numerous clashes among the three highly opinionated Limeliters. The music would often provoke fights; we have already seen that Glenn didn't want to do "Rumania, Rumania" and he would voice objections to another Lou comic extravaganza, "Vikki Dougan." The three had come into the group with their own distinct repertoires; each could be perfectionists in their own ways; each would bring formidable intellectual and forensic resources into the debates.

"Alex would sometimes be almost pompous in his analysis of the way something should be, and Lou would make some remark that would crack everybody up," Neely Plumb recalled. "There was very little that wasn't fun and funny with them. The kind of things they used to do between takes when the tape was still running—the little arguments they would get into.

"I took an hour or two one day with Al Schmitt (the group's engineer) and we made a recording of the remarks and various sounds they would make. They were talking about how to interpret this or that particular line, and we cut these things together and made a two-minute record out of them and it was hilarious just to hear them with their 'Uhhh I don't think, No, you don't, I will not.' I actually cut a disc of it and tried to get RCA to send it out to the disc jockeys. RCA in those days was not the most adventuresome record company and I never could get it off the ground."

When there were two-against-one splits in the consensus, either Glenn or Lou would tend to be the holdout. Alex, the junior partner in the team, still watching and learning, seems to have sided with one or the other. Lou would later give this tempestuous trio the whimsical nickname, "The Bicker Brothers." Glenn, the compulsive loner, would withdraw into himself for long periods of time when he was unhappy about things. For him to feel like an outsider was probably a natural state of mind. He felt closest to Alex at the time, no doubt because they had known each other in New York and worked closely together in Aspen, and there was a polite distance between himself and Lou. But still, Glenn just couldn't see himself as a truly integral player in a group situation. "In those days, I never really thought of the Limeliters as *me*," he said. "I always thought of the Limeliters as 'this outside thing I'm looking at.' The music was important to me, and we would have great arguments over the material. But as far as the performance was concerned, I left it to Lou mostly."

In a sense, Glenn's working relationship with Lou and Alex was also clouded by his own virtuosity, the natural musicality and quickness he had ever since his days as a boy soprano. "Lou and Alex are real good performers and I like working with them from that point of view," he said in 1978. "But to learn something with them is the most tedious task in the world because they're very, very slow and their intonation is not exactly right. It takes ages to get a song down so that the intonation kind of works itself into a groove, you know, and everything becomes right."

Lou and Alex were the first to concede the point; they simply were not in Glenn's league as instinctive musicians.

"With our particular group, recording in the studio was never successful," said Alex. "It was always a chore and always a drag. Glenn has nothing but—I wouldn't say contempt—but let's put it this way, he does not consider Lou and me to be singers by his standards. And that's understandable, given the kind of singer he is.

"Onstage, it was different because it was a totality, and the nature of our sound was such that it had its greatest effect live. And we knew the material, so when we were recording live, it was a breeze. But in the studio, there were always problems because Glenn was able to execute things that took Lou and me a long, long time to get to—and maybe we would never get to it because we didn't have the same facility as Glenn has.

"Glenn is a very impatient man," Alex probed on. "Very impatient. He is cursed, in my opinion, with how easily everything came to him. When you have a vocal talent of the kind he possesses, it's virtually incomprehensible that singing could be an effort."

But Glenn's differences with his partners seemed benign next to the major chasm between Lou and Alex—a full-blown personality clash. It was a clash between two different attitudes—Alex the debonair Continental, Lou the brash American. Lou would later call Alex "one of the more contentious individuals I have ever known," adding that if he said "A," Alex would say "non-A" as an instinctive reflex "in the spirit of debate."

"During the group days, there was a problem between Lou and me, but it was usually a business problem; there never were any personal problems," said Glenn. "I enjoyed his company, and he was fun to be with. But between Lou and Alex, there were these terrible fights.

"I remember one time we were up in some hockey arena in Canada and before the show there was this huge dressing room. There must have been 50 people in this dressing room—and suddenly they got into a fight and they started screaming at each other. And as intelligent as both of those guys are, all they could say to each other was, 'You're a horse's ass!' And the other one would say, 'No, YOU'RE a horse's ass!' this went on for like 10 minutes. In those days, we had fans who were almost worshipful and they stood around and were just amazed at this."

Jonathan Moore was an English comic and actor who met Glenn back in 1959 when he was an exchange student tending Enrico Banducci's yacht in Sausalito. Glenn and the irreverent young Englishman became fast friends, and eventually he would work for the Limeliters on salary selling programs at California concerts and looking after Glenn's kids when the trio was on the road.

He remembered the Limeliters' concerts—as opposed to the early nightclub gigs—as being "very tense," the three distinct personalities and egos grinding and grating against each other. "In the beginning they were not so tense," he recalled. "The hungry i shows were much more relaxed and easy in the club but on the road, they all came from different directions; they never arrived together. Something would always go wrong, and Alex was the most difficult one to deal with in those days. Lou never argued with anybody in the beginning, but then Lou got stuffy about the music. Who would sing what songs. And there was a lot of jealousy about who was the best performer."

Moore remembers playing schoolboy pranks on Alex, sometimes in league with their road manager Burt Zell, since Alex seemed to be the least likely one to take the nonsense in stride. "Alex would always piss us off," he recalled, "and we'd get his 12-string guitar; it was supposed to be tuned ready for him onstage and we'd detune it so it would go bluuuhahh."

Glenn, for one, found it hard to believe that Alex was ever shy toward women. "He was the sex symbol," said Glenn. "It was more than just enjoyment with him, it was a very deep need. Even after various venereal diseases, he still didn't quit. Backstage after the show, he would try and pick up somebody who would come in and say hello. If he didn't succeed there, he would go to the stage door where they would gather. If he didn't succeed there, he would go back to the hotel and check out the bar and hang around the bar until closing time. And if he still didn't succeed, he'd go walking the streets trying to find someone. And if he didn't find a girl, he was a bear the next day. I used to try and set him up all the time so he wouldn't be difficult to deal with the next day."

Lou and Glenn were both in awe of Alex's successes as the group's Lothario. "I think this was a natural knack he had—and he was magnificent at it," said Glenn. "Lou never made out at all and I wasn't much better. I've often wondered about it. I think women don't go for the comedian very much; they go for the singer or the appearance, but they don't go for the joke."

In his autobiography, Lou wrote that occasionally he would seek out the services of prostitutes as a sexual safety valve. He claimed that an RCA Victor promotion man in Chicago used to carry around two typewritten pages of names of prostitutes, along with a one-line commentary on their particular physical characteristics or specialty, as it were. The information was said to be very reliable, as the promotion man conducted the research himself.

Yet Moore's recollection was that "Lou was a tremendous womanizer; Lou would screw everything. See, when you're a performer you don't have any trouble finding women. Women find you." Indeed, Lou apparently was very fond of Black women in particular, wanting to be closer to the culture he respected and loved. Lou would quote the great blues singer Bessie Smith, who allegedly said, "There's always been integration between the sheets."

Since they tended to conduct their social lives separately, the three could not recall much about each other's adventures. But Glenn did recall stumbling upon one encounter that must rate as one of the all-time road classics.

"One day, I walked over to Lou's room and knocked on the door and there was no answer," Glenn said. "It was kind of open and so I opened it up and looked in—they had gotten this old hooker with no teeth. And (our road manager) was on the bed, and she was going down on him, and Lou was standing in the corner, stark naked, bowing his bass!" Glenn laughed uncontrollably when he recalled this truly twisted happening. "It was the funniest scene I'd ever seen in my life!"

The Limeliters' concert schedule would increase to the point where Alex was only aware of a blurred picture without any outstanding details. Only Lou could recall, for example, a prestigious gig at Basin Street East in New York through the month of June 1961, with Mort Sahl again as the headliner and pianist Peter Nero, then beginning to make some noise on the easy-listening album scene, as the opening act.

Nero remembered the Limeliters in those days as "very clever, very funny, very slick. It was interesting that they were coming up during the folk craze and were considered a folk trio. But to me, what they were doing was good old showbiz and satire. It was the satirical part that I liked."

They would play in the Valhalla of the American musical world, Carnegie Hall, where the demand for tickets was so heavy that they had to seat people on the stage. After each performance, Alex's parents would hold an open house in their big, spacious apartment on Riverside Drive. Over one hundred people would drop in on the Hassilevs; Alex's grandmother cooked dinner for 70 people, and Tamara would help out after she got home from work. "I was a little embarrassed because instead of praising the Limeliters, they praised the food," laughed Tamara.

Back in the recording studio, the Limeliters again made fitful attempts to try to put together a studio album—with absolutely no success. A March 30, 1961 session in Hollywood yielded two unreleased takes of "Jehosephat"—a zany self-mocking saga of the trio's life on the road by Lou and Gene Raskin—and Travis Edmonson's "Leaving a Song." On May 2, they tried to cut "Gunslinger" and Lou's stirring collaboration with Malvina Reynolds, "Western Wind;" May 3, they tried "Jehosephat" again and a swinging adaptation of the spiritual "You Can Tell The World" called "Joy Across the Land." None of these were released either and the first two sessions went into a half-hour of unproductive overtime.

Dick Rosmini, who had known Alex since the Village days, was invited by Alex to play on the May 3 date. "They fought continuously," he recalled. "There was real hostility between the three of them. I got there a week early to rehearse because I didn't read music hardly at all, and they rehearsed one tune for the whole seven days. Just constant bickering and fighting. Stupid things—quarter notes, you fucked up, you didn't remember this. It was Glenn who was doing most of the accusing. Glenn would say something, then Lou would say something, and all of a sudden the room would be icy. And I'm sitting in the corner trying to rehearse."

"They were their own worst enemies," Rosmini went on. "They could have made a lot more money if they had managed to avoid fistfights. Their personal disagreements were pretty violent; the amount of emotional heat that went on in the 1961 album was constant. Just physical gestures of body about to be violent and then more words, and then they'd grasp themselves saying it was dumb and turn away. But they would go through something like this every 20 minutes. It was a miracle they ever managed to get through the next two years."

However, the May sessions were probably meant to be studio rehearsals, for plans were on the boards to repeat the tremendous artistic and financial success of *Tonight In Person* by recording its sequel live. With tongue firmly planted in cheek, the album was called *The Slightly Fabulous Limeliters,* featuring a classic cover shot of the three, arms joyously outstretched, perched on Lou's old Volkswagen. Although the liner notes say the album was recorded at a concert in San Francisco, the session files place it on May 6, 1961. Five of the tracks (Hard Travelin/ Mount Zion," "Mama Don't 'Low," "Gunslinger," "Vikki Dougan," "The Time Of Man") were recorded the previous day in Berkeley.

While Lou wryly says on the album that RCA Victor requested them to knock some of the polish off their act, if anything, the Limeliters sound even more polished, more focused, more invigorating, and more entertaining than ever. This is the record where they hit cruising altitude, now thoroughly in command of their craft.

The group's strengths are even more evident in the broad international repertoire—particularly in "Curimao," Alex's haunting Brazilian showcase. There is the definitive "Gunslinger," with perfect choral burlesques of the typical Western movie theme, and fine versions of "Aravah, Aravah" and "The Time Of Man." The record closes with three rowdy throwbacks to the Limelite days ("Harry Pollitt," "Hard Ain't It Hard," "Mama Don't 'Low"}, rendered with even more gusto in the '60s, with "Hard" now a vehicle for all kinds of dialects and fooling around.

The hilarity reaches a high (or low?) point with the notorious "Vikki Dougan," a Gottlieb/Reynolds opus about a young actress who got her name temporarily in the spotlight in 1957 by wearing a daring dress to the Golden Globe awards at the Coconut Grove in Los Angeles. The dress was cut so low that, in Lou's inimitable words, "it revealed a new cleavage," particularly since the cheaply made garment stretched even further when Vikki sat down. "When she rose to give an award to Earl Holliman," her public relations man Milton Weiss told the *Los Angeles Times* in 1978, "all hell broke loose."

Whereas once Lou and Malvina would celebrate a contemporary event in a calypso idiom ("Monaco"), this time they try their hand at teenage rock 'n' roll. Lou's stage persona would suddenly turn into a wild parody of any number of teenage idols, much to the distaste of his two colleagues. "I hate that number," Alex told the *Saturday Evening Post* in 1961. "A change of pace is fine but with 'Vikki,' all of a sudden, we're aiming very, very low."

Apparently, Miss Dougan was flattered at the time by the trio's half-leering ditty. "I'll never forget," recalled Glenn, "we used to sing in the Crescendo down in Hollywood and every time we'd come there, she'd come and sit in the front row. That song was a satire, but she didn't seem to understand it. We'd sing the song and then she would get up and take a bow! It was the most ludicrous thing I ever saw. She thought that was going to be the start of her success."

(In a postscript to this tale, Dougan evidently was not amused when the *Times* caught up with the long-retired actress in 1978 in Westlake Village. She claimed that the whole thing was blown up out of proportion, and the dress was not designed to show any "cleavage." But Lou's amusing ditty was brought before the attention of the public once again—and a decade later, the Limeliters would revive it in their act. And more than two decades after the *Times* article ran, Dougan evidently had had another change of heart. She showed up at a Limeliters gig in Beverly Hills where she was then living and went to the post-concert party, armed with scrapbooks of her brief brush with fame and eager to talk about it.)

With one hit album still lodged firmly on the charts, and the Elektra album finally starting to make some noise, *Slightly Fabulous* looked like a hit right out of the box, as they used to say in the record trade. Lou recalled that the Limeliters were working for the famous jazz impresario George Wein at Storyville in Boston for three weeks in August of 1961 when *Slightly Fabulous* came out. A visiting RCA Victor executive told them breathlessly, "Boys, we've already sold 90,000"—and it had only been out about two days. Like its predecessor, *Slightly Fabulous* rose into the Top 10 on *Billboard*'s pop album chart, stopping at No. 8. Alas, although they would come close in the future, it would be the last trip to the national Top 10 for any of the Limeliters.

Once *Slightly Fabulous* was in the can, the Limeliters wasted little time in getting back to RCA Victor's Hollywood studios for another go. This two-day session (May 18-19) was only a little more productive than the others, yielding a single containing a Civil War centennial salute, "A Hundred Years Ago" and one of the strangest records the Limeliters ever cut, "Paco Peco." With electric guitar and Fender bass pumping along, the Limeliters give a robust rendition of tongue-twisting nonsense Spanish lyrics as Glenn punctuates the instrumental breaks with hysterical laughter. Then at the end, the tape starts speeding up, the Limeliters gradually turn into the Chipmunks, Glenn cackles, and the song mercifully fades away.

"I ran across a nursery rhyme in a Spanish grammar book I was studying called 'Paco Peco,' Neely remembered. "And I just lifted this right out of the book, wrote the music to it, wrote a bridge to it, where Lou helped me along." As for the wacky ending, Neely said that the purpose behind the original nursery rhyme dictated it. "Paco Peco" is the same thing as 'Peter Piper Picked a Peck of Pickled Peppers,'" he said. "It's a thing that the Spanish children are taught to do and the faster they can say it—you know, it's a tongue-twister. So, we just sped up the ending on that. I don't remember whether I think it's a good idea now or not."

"Oh God, that was a ridiculous record," said Alex when reminded of something he probably would just as soon forget. "It should never have seen the light of day." In any case, if the idea was to invade the pop singles chart with a novelty, it backfired, for "Paco Peco" didn't even chart when it came out in July. The session also found the group trying and discarding "Joy Across The Land" yet again.

Undaunted, back into the studio Neely and the trio went for four days in July (18-21), cutting eight songs of which only three were released. The record business in those days was still driven heavily by what was happening on Broadway, and labels that owned the rights to current shows would have their artists cover the tunes from the shows. Hence, in the manner of most of their RCA Victor label mates, the Limeliters found themselves covering the title tune from Jerry Herman's *Milk and Honey* and a song from the Jay Livingston/Ray Evans show *Let It Ride!* called "Just an Honest Mistake," (along with a folk-pop ballad, "Red Roses and White Wine").

To their credit, though, the trio would not record any old Broadway ballad simply to placate RCA Victor executives. "Milk and Honey" is a love song to the nation of Israel, not too far outside the scope of the Limeliters' international repertoire. "Just an Honest Mistake" was originally sung by a group of inept cops in the show, and it falls rather flat on the cast album. But with a few judicious cuts, it was transformed into a very sharp piece of material for the Limeliters, opening with a brief skit by Lou and going through a repertoire of imaginary and genuine contemporary faux pas—e.g., "Mr. Gallup said that Truman was the losing candidate/Mr. Ford put out the Edsel/Mr. Nixon said, let's debate."

"One of their main thrusts was to do material that was topical, and that was a very topical song," said Neely. "It was the material, really, not because it was from a show."

"Milk and Honey" would go out with "Red Roses" in September while "Mistake" and the resurrected "Jonah" went out in November. Neither single sold—and none of the singles released in 1961 made it onto regular Limeliters albums. "They were probably excluded from the albums because they didn't make it as singles," Neely speculated.

Otherwise, these sessions were a wreckage of failed experiments— including 18 unsuccessful takes of "The Lion and the Lamb" and 19 of "This Train." The others were another attempt at "Greenland Fisheries" (now retitled "The Whale"), "By the Risin' of the Moon," and a title that was an unintentional commentary on their studio fortunes at the time, "The Well Has Run Dry."

But the well would not be dry for long. In four Hollywood sessions in September (25-28), with hardly a wasted track, the Limeliters pulled their studio act together and came up with a terrific album. *Sing Out!* proved beyond any doubt that the Limeliters were perfectly capable of making superb music inside the studio. And the title itself perhaps served as an ironic, goading jab at the poison pens from a certain New York folk magazine!

Lou counted *Sing Out!* as his favorite Limeliters studio album. "*Sing Out!* had some nice ideas on it," he said. "It had some stuff we never did in public that were really written for that session. 'Pretty Far Out'—I loved that tune, although we never did it in public."

A familiar sideman from the Gateway Singers days, jazzman Red Callender, would add his booming bass to the sound, which did away with the extraneous electric guitar and piccolo of the recent singles. Alex by now had become an astounding virtuoso banjo player, with the driving quality heard in the Aspen tapes coupled with even greater coordination and imagination. Guitarist Allan Reuss, by now a regular on the Limeliters' live and studio sessions, gave Alex a backhanded accolade as related by Neely, "Just because he plays in a folk group gives him no right to be that good on the five-string banjo." "Alex played the hell out of it; he really made it talk," added Neely.

Glenn was in brilliant voice on his lead vocals, from an encore from Aspen days, "Everywhere I Look This Morning" to a spine-chilling "Wayfaring Stranger." Lou himself is in top wry form analyzing big white lies in "Pretty Far Out," and the three have a fine time sending up the American credit card fetish to the tune of the "Battle Hymn of the Republic" in "Marvin." "Golden Bell," which they started rehearsing during the Storyville gig, is a thrilling arrangement of a Mexican folk tune by Lou and Malvina. "Joy Across The Land" finally makes it onto records in a blazing take that still sizzles. The canned atmosphere, of course, is quite different from that of a club or concert stage, with no room for Lou's professorial mock-lectures or spontaneous outbursts from the audience. But this time, at least, it doesn't matter.

By now, Malvina Reynolds had become an invaluable contributor to the Limeliters' repertoire, as she had been for the Gateway Singers.

A late bloomer, finally she was beginning to reap recognition for her songwriting talents outside leftist folk circles. Her prolific imagination never failed to amaze Lou, who by now was so busy trying to come up with material that he needed whatever help she could offer.

"If I'd get an idea, I'd call her on the phone, and she'd call back in less than an hour and she'd have a whole tune written," Lou said shortly after Malvina's death in 1978. "It was unbelievable how quick she was. Believe me, there's no substitute for brains and she had a mind like a steel trap. She was an incredibly brilliant woman.

"For years, I'd written out lead sheets for illiterate songwriters, and she was one of them who I did it for. But one day I said 'Mal, you gotta learn how to do this yourself.' She turned around and went to UC Berkeley, took a course in music fundamentals, and in a year, she was making better lead sheets than I was. She's the only one who's ever done that."

Unfortunately for the Limeliters, despite the obvious quality and care that went into their records, they were caught on the wrong side of the authenticity shootout of the time. Matters of commerce did not sit well with the pure folk defenders.

The purists were prophets—longing, praying for the day when America would sing "If I Had A Hammer" and "Black Is The Color Of My True Love's Hair" and now that day was here.

But it wasn't enough. Money was the great corrupting evil to them; they thought of Lou Gottlieb as a buccaneer raiding their precious duffel bag of pure folk, watering it down, selling the tainted goods to the masses in the form of entertainment.

One can point to a kind of trench mentality among the pure folkies, the warm feeling that infantrymen have when they are hunkered down together fighting the good battle against long and dangerous odds. Folk was once a forbidden music as far as commercial appeal was concerned, only leftists and rubes need apply. For the original folkies, it was the few of us versus the many of them, and one mustn't underestimate the powerful feeling of camaraderie that united and sustained them. But now that the mainstream had come to them, the old feeling was gone.

Sing Out! appointed itself the bulletin board for the controversy, first with various columns defending or excoriating (mostly the latter) the commercial folk singers. Ron Radosh would complain pompously in the spring of 1959 that the folk revival was "devoid to a large degree of any of the content or understanding of the folk tradition which characterizes the form." In the Oct.-Nov. 1960 issue, one G. Legman wrote a piece provocatively entitled "Folksongs, Fakelore, Folkniks and Cash"—a rambling run-on diatribe that in effect damned practically anyone who accepts money for singing or compiling or collecting folk music.

Not all the true believers felt that way. Pete Seeger, for one, was delighted by the boom, embracing new young folkies of whatever grade of purity as his children and disciples. Seeger would write in 1960, "If human beings didn't plagiarize, we would all still be living in caves." Also springing eloquently to the defense of commercial folk music was Malvina Reynolds, who in a summer 1959 piece entitled "Walla Walla Bing Bang" (taken from David Seville's pop hit "Witch Doctor") found that the ends certainly justified the means. "It gave new life to popular music," she wrote regarding the popularity of groups like the Kingston Trio. "And whatever the lousy intentions of the commercial song pur-veyors, they had to become bearers of this stream of force and beauty. They corrupt it, they dilute it—but it comes through, and reaches those thirsty ears and tapping feet."

Into the 60s, when the readership of *Sing Out!* reached its apogee along with the folk boom, a greatly expanded letters-to-the-editor sec-tion picked up the ball, raging back and forth about whether commercial folk music has a right to exist. Quite often, the primary example of a typical money-mad folk entertainment group was the Limeliters—par-ticularly from 1962 on, where you could not escape their presence on television and radio commercials.

"Much of the folk music performed in the city and on campus today is a straight case of bastardization," wrote Peter Wyborn in Oct.Nov.-1962. "The current gods are the Limelighters (sic) and the Kingston Trio, and many youthful exponents are playing with a desperation which hasn't been equaled since the skiffle mania which took hold of Britain five years ago."

"What the heck has happened?" asked Bobb West in Oct.-Nov. 1963. "I was sitting in front of the television when, by God, Oscar Brand started singing. When I started to listen, it was a DOG FOOD COMMERCIAL!!!

"Now it is hard for me to stomach the commercial folks, such as the Limeliters with their cigarette commercials. This is simply too much."

Even after the Limeliters stopped touring, the letters still came. "All we students of folk music can hope for is that people interested first in the Limeliter-type of groups will realize the shallowness of their entertainment and then delve deeper into folk music," wrote John Lockwood in a grudging admission of the Limeliters' value in 1964.

Edwin A. Butenhof was somewhat more generous. "I don't believe that true folk music needs protectors who regard anyone liking the Limeliters as sub-human," he wrote in 1964…"The Limeliters may not be true folk, but they are fine entertainers."

Yet even with hindsight on their side, these correspondents did not grasp the fact that the Limeliters had already recorded an album that did more for the cause of pure folk music than most of the true believers ever would. That album, which would soon follow *Sing Out!*, was *Through Children's Eyes*.

The Limes rehearse in their hotel room somewhere
on the road, early 1960s.

A Limeliters' recording session for RCA Victor in their mini-heyday, early 1960s.

Alex and Theo Bikel jam at Alex's New York apartment with Marilyn Child, Glenn and Lou looking on, early '60s *(Photo by Marvin Bolotsky, courtesy of Alex Hassilev)*

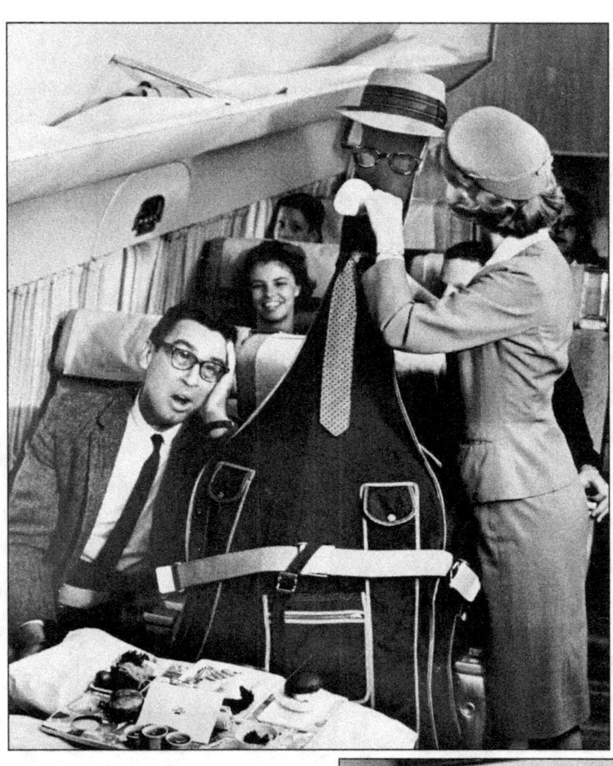

Gag publicity shots with
Lou and "companion."

This recording session photo was featured on the back cover of the *Sing Out!* album but with their producer Neely Plumb (left) cropped out of the picture. Here is the entire photo. 1961.

The Limeliters on the set of NBC's *The Today Show*, Oct. 1961 *(Photo by Ernie Newhouse, courtesy of Alex Hassilev)*

A rare 33 1/3 RPM pressing of "Paco Peco," an artifact
from RCA Victor's failed attempt to establish a new
speed standard for 7" singles., Released1961

Album cover from The Limeliters' "mini-heyday." Released 1961.

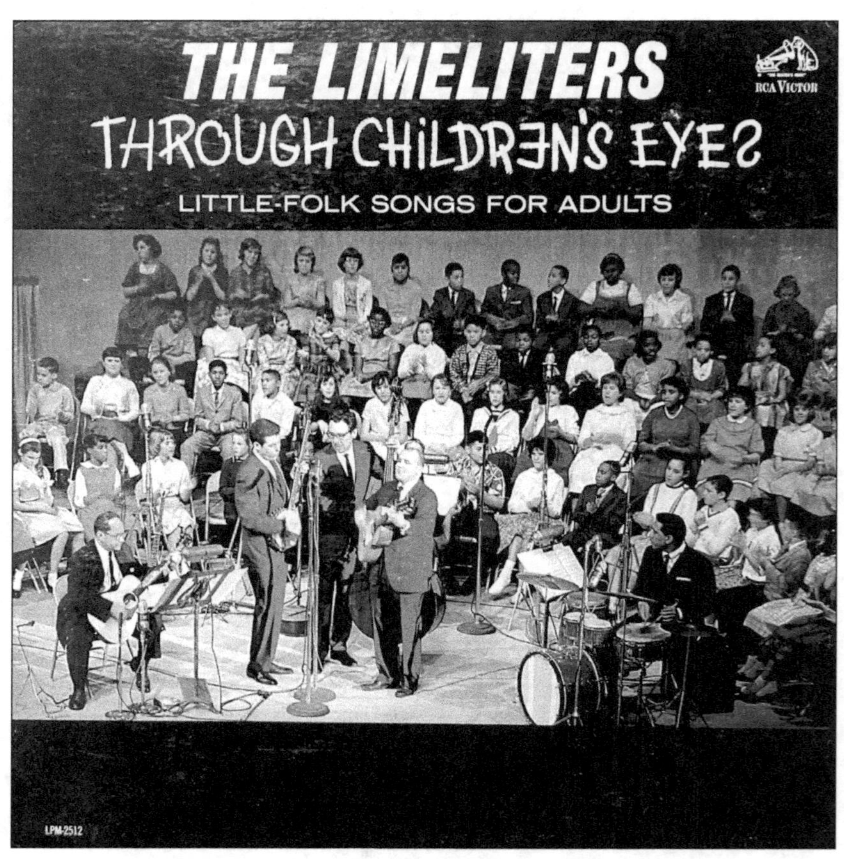

The album that inspired several generations of children and adults, released 1962

Chapter Eight

In *Through Children's Eyes*, the Limeliters would get right back to the heart of what folk music is supposed to be about—the oral tradition, the idea of songs being passed down from one generation to another. That is how the record was made, and that is the effect it has had over countless young people of the time who first hooked onto the Limeliters by singing and memorizing these songs.

It is also the main reason why the record has remained dearest to Alex's heart. "I would say that *Through Children's Eyes* is my personal favorite, and the reason I do really has to do with the nature of folk music," he said in 1978. "Folk music is a very fragile kind of music, its essence in terms of what it has to say aesthetically is very hard to render in any large-scale manner. It's a living room music. It is music that was transmitted by folk to folk in a very small setting. To the extent that we were able to reach the larger audience with it, to the extent that it was diluted from its original strength, in my opinion, that album captured the best of what we did."

"I would say that truthfully, if I had to listen to an album of the Limeliters, I would prefer to listen to *Through Children's Eyes* than anything else." said Lou. "*Through Children's Eyes* is the only really great record we made. All the rest of them were OK, but that was a great record."

"It was a mammoth project; the logistics of it were incredible and how it ever came off is still kind of beyond me," remembered Neely Plumb, who also counted *Through Children's Eyes* as his favorite Limeliters album. "I recall making five or six trips to San Francisco just for rehearsals."

Glenn, however, took a more measured view of *Through Children's Eyes* than his colleagues. "That was one of my favorites, too, but it wasn't my favorite concert," he said. "It was one of those concerts that got beefed up after the recording with applause from somebody else because the concerts themselves were not very successful. But working with the kids was a lot of fun and the songs were fun."

Folk songs for children, of course, had long been a subsidiary staple for singers like Woody Guthrie, Leadbelly, Burl Ives, Pete Seeger, and Lee Hays (The Babysitters). Using children's voices on records was nothing new either; Mitch Miller had taken a children's chorus with him into the higher reaches of the pop charts in the '50s, and later, in 1963, Tom Glazer would score a freak hit with "On Top of Spaghetti" using the folk-plus-kids formula. But at first glance, it would seem to have been a daring idea for a sophisticated, satire-minded, distinctly adult-oriented group like the Limeliters.

According to Lou, the idea for *Through Children's Eyes* came from Al Brackman, a music publisher who worked with the Howard Richmond organization. One day in 1961, Brackman approached Lou with a notion of making a record with children's voices. At that point, Lou said that a series of bells went off in his head—bing! bing!, like the bells of St. Mary's. He wasted little time in getting on the phone to Dr. Earle Blakeslee, the head of the Berkeley public schools music department. Blakeslee said he would be delighted to help out—and he held auditions among the 14 Berkeley public schools, picking the five best singers from each school for a chorus of 70 kids from the fourth through sixth grades.

The biggest problem, though, was the Limeliters' own tremendous success and their inability to turn anything down. They were constantly running from one gig to the next, and Lou had to hammer out the arrangements literally on the run. "I know we were in Dallas when we finally got the arrangements into some kind of shape," recalled Lou. "We hired a young lady there who was singing commercials and stuff like that and we ran through the arrangements with her singing the children's parts. We made this tape with this girl singing on it and we sent it to Neely, and he made acetates of it and sent them to Earle Blakeslee. Blakeslee sent these acetates out to the various music teachers of the 14 schools, and then for about six or eight weeks, these kids would listen to this record and sing along with the lady."

Interestingly, despite the pressure and the rush, *Through Children's Eyes*—the title of which comes from a lyric in the chorus of "Hey Jimmy Joe John Jim Jack"—was one of the few projects the Limeliters undertook where there were few if any fights over the material. "We had a lot of arguments; we had very dissimilar tastes in everything," said Glenn. "It would take ages just to decide on a song. But in this particular project, for some reason or another it just fell together. We all seemed to like the same things—and I think it showed on the record."

In writing the arrangements, Lou found himself up against a new problem, trying to make them simple enough so that a child could sing them comfortably. "I made it very conservatively; I wrote two parts for the children on only one song," he said (the song was "America the Beautiful"). "If we were to do it again, I would write two or three parts for the children everywhere because they were far more capable of singing parts than I had any idea at the time."

December was usually the vacation month for the Limeliters at this stage of their heyday, but they decided to use their time off for making this recording. First, on Dec. 23, there was a studio date at RCA Hollywood in which the Limeliters rehearsed and cut safety versions of five prospective *Through Children's Eyes* songs in two sessions in the morning and afternoon. Then they flew to the Bay Area, where final rehearsals were underway for the concerts at the Berkeley Community Theater Dec. 29 and San Francisco's Masonic Memorial Auditorium Dec. 30.

"When we got there, they (the kids) were singing fantastically well... but...the arrangements were no good," Lou said. "The layout wasn't right. Same old problem. As an arranger, my major failing is the larger line. I love to fool with sound. But we couldn't change the kids. They had already learned what they were (singing) on that record, and it was like trying to change the course of a General Sherman tank, 70 kids singing one way."

Ralph Gleason's liner notes and RCA Victor's own session files indicate that the selections released on the album came entirely from the Berkeley concert. However, Neely distinctly remembered that the album was a composite of the two concerts—and Lou backed him up on that.

"We did this performance in Berkeley and it came off well and the next night we did it in San Francisco and it came off well," Neely said. "But as things happened, some of the numbers in Berkeley were not as good as the ones in San Francisco, and I edited those two performances together. The sound was almost completely different in the two auditoriums, and my engineer Al Schmitt and I devised a way to blend these performances together so that when you went out of one, you weren't really aware that you were crossing the bay to San Francisco. It was done with prudent use of reverb and equalization so that we wouldn't have a drastic change when we jumped from one side of the bay to the other."

In any case, *Through Children's Eyes* holds up marvelously today because it isn't a typical children's record. There is nothing cloying about it, as many children's records are; kids who grew up with it can still listen to it today as adults. The Limeliters never lower themselves for a second to a perceived child's level; they entertain them, they involve them in the action, they make jokes and let them tell jokes, but they are always in charge. Lyric sheets were standard issue on folk specialist labels like Folkways and Elektra back then, but it was a breakthrough for a major company like RCA Victor to supply one on a mainstream album like this.

The Berkeley kids had been well-prepped for the concert, for they sing beautifully, wrapping the robust Limeliters harmonies in kind of a spatial halo. Even when Glenn's solo on "The Whale" bursts into its familiar rhythmically free pattern, the kids hold on tightly to the straight melody they have been taught. Lou holds back on the topical discourse of the first two live albums but enough of his style remains so that adults can still smile knowingly. The subtitle "Little-Folk Songs for Adults" is as accurate a statement of purpose for this joyous record as one could imagine.

Through Children's Eyes gives the Limeliters a chance to salvage some material they have been unable to bring to release in the recent past. With a driving burst of jangling, jazzy guitars, "This Train" launches the album down the right track, a great swinging arrangement considered for release on a single. With "The Whale," at last, the trio has found the song after numerous grounded studio attempts; Lou's recorded comment about the song being "suggested by the children themselves" rings a bit hollow in that context.

"Hey Jimmy Joe John Jim Jack" isn't even a folk song; it's yet another show tune from *Let It Ride!* Yet it is the warmest, wisest, and most moving selection on the record, a gentle admonition to parents to let their children be themselves and encourage them to develop their own special talents. It must have had a tremendous yet underestimated impact upon both children and adults who heard it then; the '60s were underway, and this song was right in tune with the eventual greening of the Dr. Spock generation. Indeed, decades later, fans at the Limeliters' concerts requested this tune perhaps more than any other from the early repertoire, but they haven't revived it since the '60s (one reason may be the prominent solo parts for the children).

And of course, there are the priceless spontaneous moments that almost every fan of this album holds dear. Malvina Reynolds' "Marty" finds a designated young boy coming onstage at the end to utter the priceless line that Art Linkletter would have envied, "My name is Steven!" There are the overzealous kids who keep shouting an unauthorized third "Help!" to their part in "Grace Darling," Lou and Alex's affectionate kidding of Glenn's sweet tooth just before "The Lollipop Tree," the wonderfully pointed verses that the pairs of children come up with in the calypso "Run, Little Donkey (Tingalayo)," the raucous jokes in "Stay On The Sunny Side" (another revisit to the Aspen days) that must have been chaotic in live performance.

Two of the numbers recorded in San Francisco, "I Had a Mule" and "The Riddle Song" were also released on a single to a quiet response. For the record, four songs, "Paw Paw Patch," "Down by the Riverside," "Marching to Pretoria" and "Be Kind To Your Teachers," were recorded at the concerts but left off the album.

As enduring as this record turned out to be, it is amusing to hear Glenn say that RCA Victor's executives were not exactly dancing in the aisles when *Through Children's Eyes* was presented to them. "At the time, RCA Victor didn't want it," said Glenn. "We finished it and gave it to them, and they were just gonna throw it in the can and leave it and they didn't want any more. We wanted to do another one because we had so much fun doing it and they refused to take another record. I told them at the time that I was very mad at them and said, 'Someday when everything is dead and gone on this Limeliter nonsense, you're gonna have that record and people are still gonna request it. That'll be the best-selling record in the long run than anything we've ever had.'"

If that is what Glenn said, he was right on the money. *Through Children's Eyes* stayed in RCA Victor's catalogue longer than any other Limeliters album. Even though its short-term chart action wasn't as good as that of its three predecessors (it only got to No. 25), it continued to sell steadily in the manner of a classical album. Even when RCA finally deleted it, the demand from schools was so high that they had to reissue it on RCA's special educational line in 1973—and it remained in print somewhere for decades.

Through Children's Eyes has now worked its way through the lives of several generations of kids—and some remarkable stories can be told. Kathryn Goria was working as an occupational therapist at

Bellevue Hospital in 1967 when she used the Limeliters' rendition of "The Lollipop Tree" as a group sing project for autistic children. One child in particular was severely afflicted, completely shut off from the world, couldn't relate to anyone. Yet "The Lollipop Tree" proved to be a breakthrough, for one day, the boy recognized Kathryn as the lady who sang the "Lollipop" song. "It was the peak experience of my life," she said 23 years later.

If any single artifact guarantees the Limeliters immortality, *Through Children's Eyes* is the one.

But there was little time for the group to rest on its laurels in 1962. The pressure for more product for RCA Victor's ravenous dealers continued, and Neely and the Limeliters would go into RCA Victor's Hollywood studio February 7 and 8, 1962 to start on their next album. But nothing came of those sessions, only five unreleased tunes.

April 2, they tried again, but this time they went to Nashville, Tennessee, the headquarters not only of country music but an increasingly sophisticated recording operation headed by guitarist Chet Atkins. Out of this session, where the trio was joined by a crack team of experienced Nashville session men, they came up with the rousing "Sing Hallelujah," written by a promising young folk singer from Muskogee, Oklahoma named Mike Settle. They kept in touch, and Settle would eventually play an important role in the Limeliters saga.

Three days later, the Limeliters were in New York City's Webster Hall, trying to finish the album once and for all. Out of the 12 selections, 11 came from the four New York sessions which, combined with Nashville's "Sing Hallelujah," formed the Limeliters' next album *Folk Matinee*. Yet as cosmopolitan as *Folk Matinee* is—the Limeliters even venture gingerly into German ("Die Gedanken Sind Frei")—one gets the feeling that their frenzied workload is beginning to wear them down. The close-miked vocal blend is beginning to fray, particularly on the numbers recorded on the last day of the session and, by and large, the material isn't quite as strong as on previous albums. True, the happy-go-lucky "Funk," driven by Osie Johnson's swinging drums, has the old jazzy gusto, if anything more infectious than ever now. They also get first-class support from the New York session men, particularly guitarists Tony Mottola (whom Lou acknowledges on his "Tamborito") and Al

Caiola. "Sing Hallelujah" is a fine performance, with a more reverberant sound than the rest of the album, reflective of Nashville engineering. Still, the strain of coming up with three albums a year—standard practice then but unheard of today—is inevitably taking a toll.

Yet *Folk Matinee* would prove to be historic since it contained two songs that would eventually provide tickets to the top of the charts—for other artists. They were Pete Seeger's opus based on a passage from the Book of Ecclesiastes. "Turn, Turn, Turn," and Gene Raskin's rewrite of a Russian folk song, "Those Were the Days."

"Turn" would be picked up by former Limeliters sideman Jim McGuinn, given a majestic, electrified arrangement, and turned into a No.1 hit single for the Byrds in 1965. In 1968, Paul McCartney was producing Mary Hopkin for the Beatles' new label Apple—and from the recesses of his memory, he recalled hearing Gene and Francesca Raskin's performance of "Those Were the Days" in a London nightclub three years before. Thus inspired, McCartney chose the song for his young Welsh protegee's first single (interestingly, "Turn, Turn, Turn" was the flip side!). Backed with a schmaltzy arrangement, Hopkin's naive soprano took "Those Were the Days" all the way to No. 2 in America—and had the Beatles' own smash "Hey Jude" not been in the way, it might have gone to No.1. Stung, RCA quickly re-released *Folk Matinee* that year with a new cover in a timely but unsuccessful attempt to cash in on the Limeliters' prescience.

As with "If I Had a Hammer," the Limeliters again had shown what shrewd A&R men they were, even though they could never turn the same trick for themselves. "If we had had the hit versions of the songs we recorded before they became hits, we would have been…huge," says Alex wistfully.

Beyond that, there were also some tunes that got away, songs that for some reason or another the Limeliters decided not to record before other artists turned them into hits. Tamara Hassilev had not wanted Alex to make folk singing a career, but once he did, she loyally and energetically threw herself into the arena, making suggestions about repertoire and handling money. Since Ginger apparently did not take an interest in what her husband was doing, Tamara became Alex's musical confidant, his critic. She was always trying to prod Alex into recording more of the Russian and Brazilian folk songs that they knew and loved. She even kept a songbook in which she had written out about a hundred Brazilian folk tunes, and she constantly tried to pitch some of these tunes to her son's group.

Indeed, Tamara may have had an unsuspected commercial knack. There was one Brazilian tune, "Meu limão, meu limoeiro," that Tamara was particularly fond of, one with a simple, lilting, nursery-rhyme melody that would have made a good singalong. "Alex knew it when he was in Brazil, it was played all over," she said. "And I loved it. I took it out of my book and said, 'Do something with this song.' He said, 'Mother, you do not understand.'"

Well, Will Holt understood. Somehow, he got ahold of this Brazilian tune, found an English lyric, and came up with a song called "Lemon Tree." The Kingston Trio understood, recording it in 1961 on a very successful album called *Goin' Places*. Peter, Paul and Mary certainly understood, for when they recorded it with far more finesse and delicacy than the Kingstons, "Lemon Tree" became their first hit single in 1962, launching a career that would ultimately flourish even after the demise of the folk era. In 1965, Trini Lopez had an even bigger hit with it, taking it up to No. 20, and it was featured on Herb Alpert's biggest-selling Tijuana Brass album, *Whipped Cream And Other Delights*. With some satisfaction on being right, Tamara said, "Then Alex was biting his nails."

Just two months after *Folk Matinee*, the Limeliters were back at RCA Hollywood for five days in June, picking up the thread of "Sing Hallelujah" to fashion an all-gospel album called *Makin' A Joyful Noise*. On the surface, it would seem like an out-of-character choice for a group so closely identified with what was new and satirical and, yes, commercial. But perhaps it was also a deliberate gesture to use their mass platform to expose their eager public to the gospel side of life and perhaps muzzle the fire of a few purists as well.

Though it lacks that extra ounce of spontaneity, *Makin' A Joyful Noise* finds the Limeliters sounding more vigorous than on the previous album, with everyone soloing well—particularly Glenn, who may have been remembering his boyhood at the Grace Church.

Some contemporary touches of pop are offered by Ernie Freeman's organ here and there, and the atmosphere is clearly in tune with the title. It's funny to hear this sharp hip-to-the-times group sing a moth-eaten fundamentalist hymn like "Old Time Religion" perfectly straight, but they pull it off with Freeman's organ pitching in. The civil rights anthem

"We Will Overcome" has jazzman Bob Florence playing triplets on the piano in a brighter treatment than it usually gets. "Bound For The Promised Land" gets the nod for the most red-blooded performance; "How Bright Is The Day" is "Acres Of Clams" again; with no need for the overworked Lou to change the vocal arrangements from "Charlie, The Midnight Marauder." The most striking idea, though, occurs on the chilling "Who Will Join," where an ominous organ pedal and banjo drone run underneath Glenn's lovely vocal. A most enjoyable project it is, spanning a generous 16 songs.

Yet RCA Victor held onto *Joyful Noise* until March 1963, preferring to release the next live album *Our Men in San Francisco* ahead of it. The main reason may well have been that *Our Men* was part of a mass release of *Our Man in...* albums that RCA Victor was marketing then—hence *Our Man in Nashville* for Chet Atkins, Our *Man in Boston* for Arthur Fiedler, *Our Man in New Orleans* for Al Hirt, and so forth. One wonders whether RCA Victor also feared a cool reception in the marketplace for such a specialized album.

However, judging from the malicious reaction of Josh Dunson, who mentioned the album in his broadside against commercial folk in *Sing Out's* Oct./Nov. 1963 issue, any attempt to please the purists was bound to fail at this point. "A clumsy and tasteless collection of gospel and religious folk music," Dunson fumed. "The songs, like 'Amazing Grace,' represent the cream of American religious folk music, but are done with such callosity and lack of dignity that it would be a rare person who, exposed only to the Limeliters, would be able to listen to Doc Watson sing 'Amazing Grace' without wondering, 'who let that hillbilly onstage?'"

No doubt Dunson would have been horrified when Judy Collins took "Amazing Grace" to No. 15 on the singles charts in 1971, followed improbably by the Royal Scots Dragoon Guards who scored a No. 11 hit with it in 1972. Again, the Limeliters could be said to have been slightly ahead of their time.

In any case, the Limeliters would record their next album *Our Men in San Francisco* live—and not only live, but back in the hungry i that had originally launched them in 1959. Recorded over three days in August 1962, all eyes were on reversing the Limeliters' diminishing track record on the charts—and *Our Men* stayed there longer than its studio predecessor.

Still, the fresh, wryly hip style that had taken record buyers by storm in 1961 has worn just a little thin on *Our Men*—perhaps again the consequences of too much work, too much traveling, too many recordings in too short a time. Not that it is a mediocre record; on the contrary, the three Limeliters are always entertaining, still interested in venturing into new areas, even tighter as a group. It just doesn't make as big an impact as the previous live albums.

After a rollicking "Wabash Cannonball," "Max Goolis" now sounds like a labored attempt to update "John Henry"—even with Lou's wry interpolations. "I'm Goin' Back," a leftover from Glenn's Aspen repertoire, receives a driving bluegrass-tinged rendition, the lyrics described by Lou as "the quintessence of Yarbroughism." "Corn Whiskey" is deliberately weary and harsh in the chorus, a hauntingly effective performance, and a lengthy Civil War medley is thoroughly dominated by Glenn.

"The Risin' of the Moon"—which the group later performed as part of its Irish medley—takes the dignified Irish fighting tune at a march-like clip. "Yerakina," a Greek dance tune in 7/8 time that had been Americanized by Lou and Malvina Reynolds, had been attempted previously in the studio without success—and even in this version, with its hilarious false start, they don't have the tricky odd-meter rhythm quite under their belts. Also, the coupling of the hoary old "Goodnight Ladies" with Travis Edmonson's swaying "Leaving A Song" does the latter a favor by comparison. Originally, "The Maids of Australia" had been set to appear on the album, but it was pulled before release. "Too dirty," Lou said, but its replacement, "The Lute Player (Le Joueur de Luth)"—which comes from the *Slightly Fabulous* concerts—couldn't be much less salacious. In any case, Neely's editing is so unobtrusive that one isn't aware of any editorial sleight-of-hand or change in locale, and Alex's French vocal oozes mischievous Continental charm. It is telling that "Lute Player," a mere outtake from a previous album, is the zestiest cut on the entire record.

Four days prior to the hungry i concerts, the Limeliters were in RCA Victor's Hollywood Studio 2 for a double session to set down some safety tracks for the upcoming album and to cut another single. Again, RCA was beating the drums for a hot theater album, *Oliver!* and the Limeliters were prevailed upon to cover one of its tunes, "Who Will Buy?," backed with the unusual jangling sounds of a Hungarian cymbalom and a spare effective rhythm section. They also cut a tune called "Particul'y Funicular" for the flip side, but that was scrapped in favor of a slightly different mix of "Funk" from the *Folk Matinee* album. In all, an engaging recorded footnote, though again nothing that grabbed the attention of the nation's deejays.

Yet all the Limeliters' records combined, even the biggest hits, didn't bring them anywhere near the attention that one 60-second commercial could. As early as 1960, they received their first offer, an opportunity to do a commercial for Folger's coffee. It was a simple matter, as jingle writer Bob Pritikin converted Glenn's bedrock folk showcase "When I First Came To This Land" into a smooth, catchy sales pitch loaded with verbal hooks:

> *"When I say coffee this I mean*
> *Coffee from the mountain bean*
> *Nurtured by the mountain soil*
> *Coffee beans for Folger's ...*
> *"Have yourself a Folger fling*
> *Brewed with beans that really swing ...*
> *"Just one sip*
> *And you'll flip."*

Undaunted by their first fling with real commercialism, the Limeliters recorded it in a studio within Hollywood's famous circular Capitol Records Tower in just 25 minutes. It caught on immediately, becoming a hugely popular spot that lasted for years on the airwaves. In California, one could see billboards up and down U.S. 101 bearing the name of a nearby city followed by the tag line that Glenn sang ("In Oceanside, When I say coffee/I mean Folger's.").

In their zeal to capitalize upon their hot hand, the Limeliters would go on to record commercials for Ford automobiles for the J. Walter Thompson ad agency, punching out the lines with all the gusto they normally would save for "John Henry" ("Which Ford will it be/It's as easy as 1-2-3/Falcon, Fairlane, or if you please/The beautiful Galaxie."). In 1961, a producer for Damper, Sample and Fitzgerald named Arnold Brown hooked up with the trio during an appearance for RCA Victor distributors in New York, and he got them a contract to do jingles and TV commercials for L&M cigarettes.

Therein lies a humorous tale. According to Lou, L&M had been using the same ad slogan for about 12 years ("L&M has found the secret/ That's sure to give you flavor") and was looking for a new treatment. Slowly it dawned on Lou that the slogan would be an uncanny match to the well-worn gospel tune, "Down By The Riverside"—and so it was decreed.

But the irreverent Lou wasn't taking the "skull sessions" for L&M terribly seriously. During a break between discussions, he was walking down a hallway when a devil-may-care urge caused him to burst into song "L&M has found the secret/That's sure to give you cancer!" Even though the link between cancer and cigarettes had been established years before, these were the pre-Surgeon General's report days, and the notion was still somewhat avant-garde. More to the point, Lou's off-the-cuff rewrite was overheard by the humorless advertising manager of L&M, Larry Brough, who happened to be in the hallway. After Brough heard it, Lou reported that "his face was a mask of nausea." Yet the group was permitted to complete the commercial anyway.

One ad led to another, and the Limeliters eventually recorded what they regarded—with tongues firmly planted in cheeks—as their "biggest hit," the Coca Cola commercial. They came up with a vocal arrangement that beat out a competing treatment by Paul Anka, along with those of other musicians. Coca Cola flew the Limeliters down to their corporate headquarters in Atlanta to sign the contracts, and there was tension in the air, as the board of directors didn't know what to make of this folk act that they were about to sign. Glenn, avid connoisseur of anything with sugar in it, thought he would break the ice with an irreverent opinion. "You know, you guys have a great product," he declared. "But Pepsi's better!" For a few seconds, Atlanta might as well have been in Siberia, for a chill ran through the room as the Limeliters and their lawyers could see thousands of greenbacks vanishing before their eyes. But Coke's advertising director, a man named Deloney Sledge, thankfully had more of a sense of humor than Larry Brough. He burst out laughing, the rest of the board followed right along, and the deal was signed.

"Things Go Better With Coca Cola" ran for at least three years—with and without Glenn's voiceover. Once the Coke ad became a lucrative smash, the Limeliters formed a commercial production company with Brown, a short-lived yet successful one. By 1963, it would be nearly impossible for an American to escape the Limeliters' harmonies on television or the radio.

It is here where the charges of "sellout" by the folk brethren bear the greatest ring of truth—particularly when they were allowing real folk tunes to be mangled in order to serve Madison Avenue. The Limeliters were taking advantage of virtually every angle that American capitalism could throw at them. In the case of the L&M ads, clearly the money was more important than any qualms about encouraging a public health hazard.

To be fair, in those days, it was a rare public figure who did not jump to attention whenever a cigarette company offered a chance to do an ad (Sandy Koufax, the Hall of Fame pitcher for the Dodgers during that era, was one of the few who declined). And it is probably true that the Limeliters gained many more fans through their commercials than they lost from the folk crowd—which, though growing rapidly, was still a sect in comparison to the gigantic American mainstream. Thus, they would take the money, and the attention, and try to turn a deaf ear toward the rantings of the letters section in *Sing Out!*

Of the three, it was Glenn who took the heartiest shine to doing commercials. The Folgers and Coke jingles and voiceovers probably did more to keep him in the public eye than anything as he made the transition from Limeliter to solo singer. He would later cut another ad for Folger's on his own, along with numerous spots for Italian Swiss Colony wine, Ken-L Ration dog food, Pillsbury breakfast rolls, Cribari and Sons wine, and countless others over the years.

Indeed, Glenn genuinely relished using his relaxed voice as a tool to move merchandise. "I enjoy doing commercials," he said. "For one thing, they put more effort into the 30 seconds or one minute than anybody ever does for a song. I like that kind of perfection."

In 1962, the Limeliters took another leap into the mainstream that would not bear public fruit until 1963. They participated in a pilot for a proposed television series that would bring folk music to the tube on a regular basis for the first time and widen the bitter chasm within the folk movement. The show was called *Hootenanny*. The idea behind *Hootenanny* was simple; go around to several universities on the concert circuit and shoot a variety of folk music performances live before predictably enthusiastic student audiences. Jack Linkletter, son of *House Party's* Art Linkletter, would be the good-looking, non-threatening, all-American emcee. The results would be edited down to the perceived half-hour attention span of a mass audience presumably groomed on Perry Como and Ed Sullivan.

With an eye on the growing folk boom, ABC bought the pilot and gave the go-ahead for a weekly series, which made its debut April 6, 1963 in the Saturday 8:30 p.m. slot as a late-season replacement for *Mr. Smith Goes to Washington* opposite *The Joey Bishop Show* and *The Defenders*. Amazingly enough, throughout its short history, *Hootenanny* would serve as a lead-in to the antithesis of everything new and hip in popular music, Lawrence Welk.

The timing for mass acceptance was exactly right; ABC had caught the folk boom on its upward arc nearing the peak—and the thirteen initial shows did so well that the series was renewed in the fall, expanded to a full hour, and moved up to 7:30 p.m. The word "Hootenanny" caught on like the proverbial prairie fire, and American industry wasted no time cashing in. Thorn McAn put out a Hootenanny brown suede shoe, Playboy magazine ran ads for a Hootenanny sweatshirt, grocery stores would carry Hootenanny candy. Record companies started issuing Hootenanny albums, usually anthologies drawn from the back catalogue, by the cartload. By the winter of 1963, Izzy Young of *Sing Out!* claimed that he had counted 87 albums bearing the magic word in their titles.

Ah, but was the folk press ecstatic now that their music, or something resembling it, had conquered the airwaves? Don't wish for anything, you may get it, goes the old saw—and the hardcore could see nothing at all redeeming about *Hootenanny*.

"A vaguely unsatisfying half-hour every Saturday night containing little more than a kiss-and-a-promise of the vast riches of our folk heritage," sniffed Irwin Silber in *Sing Out!* that summer.

Later, he would cry out, "The Hootenanny of yesteryear has become the Lootenanny of 1963," and the catty letters just kept pouring in.

But there was more than just petty pique at work here; the folkies did have a forceful reason for hating *Hootenanny*. ABC, to its credit, tried to invite a wide cross-section of folk musicians besides the obvious stars. But the decision had been made from the beginning that Pete Seeger, who made the word "hootenanny" a part of the language in the first place, would not be invited on the show. Even though Joseph McCarthy had been dead for six years, the blacklist was still in effect—and the shroud extended to the existing lineup of Weavers as well.

As a result, several outraged folk acts refused ABC's invitations to appear on the show. Joan Baez, Tom Paxton, the Greenbriar Boys, Barbara Dane, Ramblin' Jack Elliott, Phil Ochs, Peter, Paul and Mary and Bob Dylan were among those who boycotted *Hootenanny.* Others found the lure of prime time too powerful to resist—the Chad Mitchell Trio, the Smothers Brothers, the Carter Family, Ian and Sylvia, Will Holt, Josh White and the Kingston Trio, though the latter group later added its name to the boycott.

For better and worse, the Limeliters became the group most closely associated with *Hootenanny.* After having made the pilot, they were the star attractions of at least six of the first thirteen shows, and they could be seen on the promotional spots that ran elsewhere through the week on ABC. Surely, they must have been aware of the firestorm of controversy about the blacklisting of Seeger, but they carried on with the show anyway until the group broke up.

Alex and Glenn beg amnesia; neither of them can remember any of the protests or picketing that the show underwent as it shuffled from campus to campus, always attracting full houses of around two or three thousand students. But Lou, thinking back to his adventures on the left, certainly felt twinges of guilt about doing *Hootenanny* then. "We were aware of the blacklist, certainly never approved of it, perhaps hoped that we could do something working from within to change the policy, but not willing to take any heat by refusing to appear on the show ourselves," he wrote in his autobiography.

Lou also remembered a purely coincidental Freudian slip on the part of Linkletter, who brought no folk background whatsoever to the show. One seriously doubts if he was aware of Josh White's reputation within the folk community, unfairly or not, as a sellout figure who cooperated with the House Un-American Activities Committee and allegedly watered his music down for white audiences. In any case, White was performing a hootenanny-style singalong with the audience, and midway through the number, the director asked him to start again. Lou asked a technician why, since the number had been going so well. It turned out that Linkletter had blown the intro on the cue cards. He said, "And now, ladies and gentlemen, the white of folksingers, Josh King!"

In any case, *Hootenanny* could not long survive the dilution of talent from the boycott, robbing the show of many of the vital new young performers who were revitalizing and redefining folk. That, and more importantly, the swift collapse of the commercial folk boom and accompanying "Hootenanny" fad led the show down, down, down in the Nielsens—and ABC axed it after its last airing on September 12, 1964, moving *The Outer Limits* into its slot.

Lawrence Welk, meanwhile, would polka on and on into the 1980s.

Photo from the "Through Childrens' Eyes" concerts
in Berkeley and San Francisco, Dec. 1961.
(Photo by Jerry Stoll, Jerry Stoll Photography)

Photo from the "Through Childrens' Eyes" rehearsals
in Berkeley, December 1961.
(Photo by Jerry Stoll, Jerry Stoll Photography)

The Limeliters, looking awed and serious, at the
Lincoln Memorial in Washington DC, early '60s
(Photo by Marvin Bolotsky, courtesy of Alex Hassilev)

Chapter Nine

As 1962 rolled inexorably into its holiday season, the Limeliters looked forward to another prosperous year. There was television, commercials, one sold-out concert and eagerly-awaited album after another, a European tour to prepare for in February, and the prospect of vast quantities of money beginning to roll in as the folk boom neared what turned out to be its crest.

A Keystone Kops-like incident from their heyday perfectly captures the mad merry-go-round of fame and fortune the trio was trapped upon. As Alex recalls, "We were in an airport and Lou at that time was carrying a big acoustic bass with him. It was one of those things where we had literally 30 seconds to catch a plane.

"We were running to catch the plane in an airport where there was a long hall and then you could either turn right or left. Glenn and I went in the right direction and Lou with the bass came careening down this incline and zipped off to the left. As Glenn and I were running, I yelled, 'Lou, where are you going?' And Lou yelled back, still running down the hall, not missing a beat, 'THE WRONG WAY!'"

And then, on December 7, 1962, the rush-rush-rush madness of flinging themselves all over the continent in pursuit of the big payday caught up with them in a most unexpectedly macabre way. They were involved in a plane crash in Provo, Utah, from which they were incredibly lucky to survive. To put it another way, as individuals they survived—but the group ultimately would not.

"Actually, I think the plane crash broke up the group, more than any other factor," said Alex in 1979. "It was never the same after that."

"I think the plane crash is what decided for them that they didn't want to go touring anymore," said Glenn, adding that "it had nothing to do with my decision. I remember when the plane crash came, I was tickled to death because I thought, now we get some rest."

The Limeliter whom the crash affected perhaps the most profoundly was Lou—with repercussions that would become increasingly bizarre. Lou believed that December 7 and its surrounding dates is a bad time of the year, citing Pearl Harbor Day, the death of his revered mentor at Berkeley, Manfred Bukofzer (December 7), and John Lennon's murder (December 8) (one can also add Otis Redding's plane crash December 10), along with that terrifying night in Utah. "He (Lou) wasn't anxious to get on airplanes after that," said Glenn. "Lou always used to say, 'We almost met our Zion in Provo, Utah.'"

"After the crash, my desire to continue fooling around was severely curtailed," Lou said. "Scared me to death."

The Limeliters had been in some close calls in the sky prior to this. Every performing artist who spends a good deal of time touring in planes probably has some harrowing war stories to tell. And the Limeliters—who by now were keeping up a frantic schedule, a punishing 310 touring days out of the year in 1962—may have been pressing their luck.

By 1962, they were chartering an Aero-Commander private plane to keep their road schedule humming along, often bypassing the commercial airlines. At about $80 to $100 an hour for both the plane and the pilot, the group had reached the financial stage where they could consider traveling in this fashion. "We were making enough money and it was just cost-effective to do it that way," recalls Alex. "We had all kinds of hassles with Lou's bass and getting on the airlines."

In addition, their adventure-seeking tenor had learned how to fly, and eventually would serve as the co-pilot on the Aero-Commander. "I used to fly over the Rocky Mountains with no visibility," remembered Glenn. "I remember the first time I landed it. They (Lou and Alex) always played cards, bridge, in the back and they would have these terrible fights all the time about the card game, and they were always screaming at each other. And this first time, the pilot said, 'OK now I'm going to let you land it.' Suddenly there was dead silence in the back. And I landed this plane and, when I finally got it landed, I said, 'Phew, I was really nervous.' And Lou put his hand over to where I was sitting and he says, 'You were nervous? Look at us!'...and there was this drip, dripping sweat!"

Nothing to worry about there, but there were other, more harrowing incidents. One time, they found oil oozing out of a wing. Another time in the Aero-Commander, they came in on the wrong runway in a snowstorm; the runways were plowed in the wrong direction and the plane smashed right into an eight-foot snowdrift.

Still another time, while on his own in North Dakota, Glenn lost an engine on a two-engine private plane. There were no landing fields, they were piled down with gear, and Bismarck the destination was about 200 miles away. "We started to lose altitude little by little," he recalled. "By the time we got to Bismarck, it was about 300 feet off the ground."

In one epic adventure, the Limeliters were scheduled to take a commercial United Airlines flight out of Cincinnati to play an afternoon gig at the University of Connecticut in Storrs, a small farming community/college town in the eastern part of the state. Well, United was on strike, and when the group got to the airport that Sunday morning, there were no planes. Frantically, they tried to catch a plane to Cleveland and transfer to a Hartford-bound flight that would place them within an hour of Storrs. No way.

Finally, Lou, Alex and Glenn settled for a ride in a small wooden plane known as a Moonie, while road manager Burt Zell and the instruments had to go in a separate craft. By the time they arrived in the vicinity of New York City's La Guardia airport, the ground winds in the region had kicked up to 60 miles an hour, and there was doubt as to where they could land.

"The plane was just like a leaf in the wind," Lou remembered. "We were just about at La Guardia and the guy hears over the radio that the instruments have been put down in Wilkes-Barre, Pennsylvania, they're not going any further. But this guy, who was going to try and sell us a Moonie, he wanted to show us that this plane could get where it was going. He did—and we finally landed there in Storrs." But it was hardly a routine landing. "As we were losing altitude, the clouds were whizzing by us," said Alex, picking up the story. "He couldn't land the thing because there was too much wind. He had to do a crosswind landing which is kind of tricky. So, he came in like a crab and he shut off the power and the plane still wouldn't sit on the runway. He had to finally pancake down on the runway and then he had to do a pinwheel with the tail to keep it from running off the end of the runway."

They arrived at the gig without their instruments—Zell having not arrived yet—had to borrow some from the music department, and instead of taking an intermission, they did their whole show all at once. "The university did not want to pay us," Alex said. "They said, 'You didn't do your whole show, and you were late'—and we had risked our lives to go play the show!" (Eventually they were paid).

Obviously being a folk musician had come a long way from Woody Guthrie's train-hopping days.

Thus, it was a familiar predicament with which the Limeliters were faced on the morning of December 7, 1962. The previous evening, they had played a gig at the University of Colorado in Denver—and they were booked on a 10 a.m. United Airlines flight to Salt Lake City, where a sold-out house would await them at the University of Utah. They got on the plane, which flew uneventfully to Salt Lake only to find the whole city fogged in. The plane circled for about 20 minutes, found no break in the murk, and found itself shuttling back to Denver.

What to do? "There we were in Denver, it was about 1 o'clock or 2, and we were thinking about how that lovely payday was just flying away," said Lou, who had morbidly detailed total recall of the whole misadventure. Glenn went searching around Stapleton Airport, called the air taxi service and found a man named Harlan Mitten who had a twin-engine Beechcraft that was under contract to the executive echelon of the Ringsby Trucking Company. Mitten boasted of his 30,000-or-so hours of flight experience, claiming that he had been a bush pilot in the Alaskan wilderness. Mitten told the stranded trio, "Look, I'll fly you over to Provo, we'll be there by 6 p.m., you can rent a car, drive to the show, and it will be no problem, 40 minutes and you're there."

As Glenn was talking to Mitten, another man by the name of Herbert Sobel, an architect from Chicago, came up and heard Glenn making the deal. "Let me go with you," he piped up. "How much will it be? We'll divide up the sum by five instead of four." The figure turned out to be about $85 and Sobel paid it right there in cash.

Then there were six passengers—the three Limeliters, their road manager Burt Zell, Sobel, and this showboating pilot. Mitten did not have a co-pilot at hand on such short notice, so Glenn volunteered as a hasty substitute. Unforgivably, in his haste to service his famous passengers, Mitten forgot to file a flight plan, so no one on the ground in Provo knew about his plane.

Most of the roughly 500-mile flight went beautifully that afternoon. The Rockies are always magnificent to look at all year round—and it was early December, the beginning of the snow season. "I remember it was an absolutely stunning flight because if you fly the Rockies in a little executive aircraft, it seems as if you could reach out and touch these beautiful peaks," said Lou.

Provo itself lies about 40 miles south of Salt Lake City, in the southern portion of the valley that begins on the Great Salt Lake's south shore. To the immediate east stands Provo Peak, elevation 11,068, part of a high wall of mountains that hugs the city's eastern limits. Hemming in the city on the west is a good-sized body of water called Utah Lake—and the municipal airport is located on its east shore. It can be tricky country to land in, what with unstable weather in the mountains and ground fogs in the fertile valley around the lakes. Only a little over a year later in early 1964, Provo would be the site of another noted private plane crash, one that took the life of the young, promising Chicago Cubs second baseman Ken Hubbs.

When the plane entered the Provo area, though, the weather was clear for the most part, except for a patch of haze about 15 feet off the ground. It was six o'clock at night, the sky was pitch black, but the lights of the Provo airport could clearly be seen from the air. Yet Harlan Mitten, alleged bush pilot, was confused. His altimeter was set improperly; they had been at 13,000 feet through the Rockies but when the plane hit the floor of the valley, the altimeter still read 400 feet.

"I saw the lights in the field," recalled Glenn, "and the only thing that happened was that we then went right into some ground fog, and the ground fog is what caused the problem. I think if I'd been with my own pilot in the Aero-Commander, I would have said let's go up, get our bearings and then go down again. But I didn't want to be a smart-ass with this guy, so I just let him do his thing. We were banking to the right, and I was looking out the window and I was feeling real funny about this.

"Right away I saw the ground and I hollered 'Look out!' And when I said that, he pulled back on his stick and tried to go up, but luckily it hit right flat. After that, I was out."

Lou was animatedly involved in another endless bridge game with Zell and Sobel in the back of the plane while Alex, who was closest to the door of the plane, was napping—all unaware of the impending danger. "We're playing bridge there in the back, Burtie, Sobel and me," said Lou, "and then I hear the inimitable tenor voice of Glenn sing out, 'Look out! We're gonna crash!' And then there was a period of absolute fear. I'm talking about real fear. Then there was a sound, like when you hit your head on the bottom of a swimming pool, then some (at this point, Lou made some discombobulated random sounds) and then, boom, we stopped. I had my safety belt on, it was broken loose."

Though Glenn says that the pilot grabbed the stick, Alex claims it was Glenn who pulled back on it, raising the nose of the plane just enough so that it pancaked into a farm field in the valley. The plane was still doing about 120 knots—or takeoff velocity—so it was going very fast. It skidded on the ground and the wheels were caught in a dead furrow (a deep drainage trench), thus tearing off the plane's undercarriage and sending the craft into a terrifying spin. The engines were torn out of the wings, the tail assembly broke up, and several seconds later, the shattered plane finally came to a stop.

Incredibly, no one was seriously hurt, for they received a number of lucky breaks. For one thing, having spotted the ground before the confused pilot, Glenn probably saved their lives, giving them just enough time to raise the nose of the plane and avoid a more crunching impact. Also, they landed in a freshly plowed field, which cushioned the impact of the crash with several inches of mud. The field was surrounded by a barbed-wire fence—which they missed—and there were some sizable trees in the field which they could have hit. There was fuel all over the place, and had there been just one spark, the whole group would have been trapped in an inferno.

Still, Mitten blew what should have been a routine landing. "He was apparently trying to show off," said Lou. "Glenn said he did everything too fast."

Alex was the first one out of the plane, being nearest to the door—and he hightailed out of there in seconds. Though thoroughly shaken up, the only injury Alex sustained was a cut under the bridge of his nose that required stitches. Lou, who came out next, suffered five cracked ribs; neither Zell nor Sobel were hurt. Mitten's teeth went through his upper lip but otherwise, he came through unscathed.

But Glenn had been knocked out by the impact of his head going through the windshield of the plane. Only when he regained consciousness did he leave the plane, and he was an alarming sight. According to Lou, "I remember looking up and seeing Glenn come out and he had head cuts and face cuts and there was blood all over him. But he was apparently walking under his own steam." "His mouth swelled up so that he couldn't talk at all," says Alex. "He looked as if a thousand bees had stung him all around his mouth."

At this point, standing in mud under a black Utah sky loaded with stars, Alex came up with what Lou later thought was the greatest line of his life. As Glenn finally emerged from the plane, bloodied, staggering, Alex looked at his watch and said, "I think we can still make the gig!"

The rest of the group stared at him aghast in disbelief.

Since they were the most ambulatory ones in the party, Alex and Mitten took off looking for help. Luckily, they didn't have to go far, for the plane had crashed in one of several adjacent farms owned by a family of brothers who, as it turned out, all happened to be doctors! An ambulance came and took the shaken-up survivors to a hospital in Provo. Lou was taped up and given Novocaine for the pain; Alex, Glenn and the pilot received stitches for their injuries. Lou recalled that when he was assigned a room in which to recuperate, the first call he received was from his insurance agent, for Lou had just bought a $450,000 life insurance policy. "How are you, Lou…" the agent said unctuously, for had Lou been killed in the crash, the company would have gone belly up.

While Glenn was getting stitched up, he narrowly managed to intercept a macabre, scandalously inaccurate news flash. "I remember right in the middle (of when) they were sowing my lip up," he recalls, "I thought, 'God if Peggy hears about this.' I said, 'I gotta call my wife.' And the doctor said, 'Wait until I sew you up.' And I said, '*No*, gotta stop right now and call.' I dialed the number, she was watching television, and just as she picked up the phone, they flashed on, 'Limeliters Killed in Airplane Accident.'"

Glenn and his colleagues would be out of performing action for nearly three weeks. Glenn had temporarily lost his marvelous ability to whistle, and he had trouble speaking, let alone singing. Naturally, a Limeliters appearance on the Roy Rogers/Dale Evans television show a few days after Provo had to be cancelled, along with two sold-out shows at the Santa Monica Civic Auditorium December 9. Nevertheless, they had to play a date in an ice rink in Squaw Valley near Lake Tahoe around December 27, where, still a bit shaky, they went on with the show despite Glenn's puffed-out lip. For his part, Lou drove to the gig from his El Cerrito home in his Volvo station wagon with his two children.

"I remember him (Glenn) doing a concert after that (the crash) with the Limeliters in Stockton or Sacramento and he had songs where he had to whistle," said Jonathan Moore. "His mouth was still stitched up, and he couldn't whistle it, so he wanted me to stand at the side of the stage. Well, I couldn't whistle. I forget how he managed to do it but somehow he managed a kind of whistle."

Bravely, the trio would continue to fly when they had to in 1963. They would take a plane to Europe in February, and there was a whole Limeliters tour in the spring that was booked on a chartered plane—another Beechcraft. But neither Alex nor Lou would ever completely recover from their brush with death in Provo. "I never really loved flying, ever," says Alex. "Now I'm not scared, but 60% of the time when the plane comes in for a landing, my palms begin to sweat. Takeoff, I'm a little apprehensive but it doesn't bother me a whole lot."

And so, they rested—taking some time off to recuperate, thinking about life, the future, their families, the price of fame and fortune. "Up till that time, everything had been going our way," says Alex. "We had had it really easy. It was a miracle we escaped, completely a miracle. And after that, I think all of us started to think in a different way. We were working like crazy. We had worked way too much, too many shows."

Yet Tamara Hassilev discounted the influence of the plane crash in the Limeliters' breakup. Seizing upon Alex's theme of how easily success came to them, she believed that the breakup was due mainly to the inability of her son, still only in his 20s, and his colleagues to realize how early success can distort the big picture.

"When you are very successful at the age of 27, you somehow lose the perspective of what life is," she said. "In my opinion, that's what happened. I think when success started to come, they realized it's really serious work. In Aspen, it was like being on vacation. The audience was vacationers, and they were grateful for what they got."

But, deep within the foundation, there had always been a built-in time bomb for the Limeliters' destruction, quietly ticking away. "Glenn, of course, had always had his eye on being a single; we knew that when we formed the group," says Alex. "And after that [the crash], I think Glenn simply said if I'm going to do it, I'd better do it. I think Glenn would have left the group in any event, but I don't think he would have left right then. We had originally made an agreement for five years, and I think he would have stuck to that agreement."

Indeed, the group had made a five-year commitment to stay together way back in 1959. However, Glenn recalled that he first gave notice back in mid-July of 1962—well before Provo—when they were staying and playing at the Chase Hotel in St. Louis.

In 1978, Glenn insisted he gave notice because he had just counted his money one time and figured that if he was very careful, he could live for about 20 years on his boat with what he had made, raise his kids and be with his family. But ten years later, Glenn revealed another, perhaps less noble motivation—the issue of inequality among the three. Lou not only controlled the publishing of the group, he would also get extra pay at the recording sessions since he was designated as the leader of the session. Of course, Alex and Glenn agreed to this tilting of the balance up front, but at the years went by, Glenn began to wonder about the fairness of the deal.

Indeed, one should not rule out the issue of inflated heads as a reason for the group's eventual breakup. "I think what happens with all these groups, they stay together but the tensions get greater and greater because everybody has an individual ego," said William Malloch. "There were three very strong egos in that group. Lou was the only one who was able to handle the ego problem in any sense at all. I don't think Alex could handle it and I don't think Glenn could handle it. Glenn was a star, wanted to be more of a star; Alex wanted to be a star. Lou wanted to be a star, too, but I think he realized that he just couldn't do it alone."

At this time, though, Glenn was disturbed primarily because he thought Lou felt he was the most important member of the trio—the founder, the sparkplug. Now they had given Lou the publishing out of free will, but Alex and Glenn thought that meant Lou would take on other burdens of the group—management, getting concert dates, programming their concerts. Indeed, hadn't Lou procured their breakthrough gig, the immensely successful 1959 run at the hungry i? As it turned out, Lou was less inclined to take charge of these matters after a while—and it was Glenn who was increasingly handling money and management matters, and it was Alex who would research the music and, with Glenn, sequence the show. They felt as if they were junior partners, shortchanged.

Glenn claimed that it wasn't the money that made the difference. Glenn was not really hung up about money; throughout his life, he would repeatedly allow fortunes to pass him by or slip through his fingers. But although he didn't lust uncontrollably after money, he didn't like to think he was being cheated. "We were making so much money that it didn't make much difference and I sure as hell didn't care about it, but I did care about Lou feeling I was not an equal partner in this whole arrangement," he said. "I didn't know that for sure, I just suspected it."

Finally, Glenn decided he would bring everything to a head. He came up with a simple plan in which everything the group made would be placed in a "pot" and split three ways.

It was in the Chase Hotel in mid-July 1962 that Glenn made his proposal. "God, I'll never forget that night," Glenn recalled. "When I made this proposal, Lou got up out of his seat and became a madman. He paced up and down, ranting and raving, saying 'I could've done this with any two people, I don't need you,' and on and on and on. I said to myself at that time, that's the way he felt and I just couldn't work with someone who felt that way. And so that night, I said to him, 'Lou, I thought that was the way you felt about it, so I think it's time for me to give my notice.' I gave him a year's notice to quit."

Half-heartedly, Alex and Lou began their search for a replacement right there at the Chase Hotel. The noted folksinger Will Holt was in town, and they thought he might be a possible replacement for Glenn. Holt went through an audition but Lou and Alex felt that he wasn't right for the part.

"Big mistake," opined Milt Okun. "Holt has a very wide range, an excellent musician, marvelous voice. He didn't have the star tenor quality of Glenn—it didn't gleam at the top you know—but he had a beautiful tenor sound. It was a good idea to audition him, but it's too bad they didn't take him because I think he would have been a marvelous addition to the group with his writing ability."

A bit later that year, the Limeliters were in Norman, Oklahoma playing a date and they took time out to hear Mike Settle. Settle—young, vibrant, part-Creek Indian, briefly a member of the Cumberland Three—was just beginning to shine, selling songs to various folk acts (including the Limeliters), and would soon record two albums on the Folk Sing label in a youthful, sustained, almost vibrato-less tenor. Indeed, the previous year, Settle had been a leading candidate to succeed the departing Dave Guard in the Kingston Trio, a slot that ultimately went to Cumberland Three colleague John Stewart. Glenn listened hard and exclaimed, "That's the guy to replace me." ("Mike Settle would have been perfect," Glenn reiterated in 1989).

But Lou and Alex never did make a really serious effort to line Settle up, mostly because they didn't believe that Glenn would actually quit. After all, how could any sane man turn down all the money that was gushing into their bank accounts in ever-increasing amounts—especially after *Hootenanny* hit the airwaves? "But I must have reminded them every month," Glenn recalled, "'you now have ten months to find somebody to replace me.'

"They never understood that it didn't make any difference to me how big the money got. When the time came to go, I was gonna go. I thought I gave them plenty of time."

But Lou and Alex thought that making preparations to contain the explosion of the built-in time bomb could wait. While still in their recuperation process, in January of 1963 they played both the Salt Lake City date and the two Santa Monica concerts that were cancelled after Provo. Then at the beginning of February, they got into a plane and headed for Rome, the first stop of their first and only tour of Europe. Essentially the tour was designed for them to promote the sales of their records abroad, playing mostly television shows in Rome, Brussels, and Amsterdam, along with some concert dates in England. Lou, who had never been to Europe, hugely enjoyed playing the role of tourist, but Alex mostly remembered suffering from hepatitis throughout the trip.

In Rome, they performed on a popular Italian TV variety show; "performing" in the sense that they could only lip-sync, as that is what the director of the show wanted. Lou related a funny anecdote in which the director sent his assistant down to the offices of RCA Italiana to get one of the Limeliters' albums for playing over the air, only to find that there was a Sonny Rollins record inside the jacket. The flustered girl had to go back, returning with the only item that they had available, the "Who Will Buy?" single, of all things. They had to "perform" a song that was not part of their concert repertoire, something which they never really learned and could barely lip-synch.

While they were in Rome, the Limeliters took time out to visit RCA Italiana's huge recording studios—usually reserved for opera sessions—to record a pair of sides. One was an Italian folk song, "Questa Bella Che Mafa;" the other was a World War I tune called "La Rivista del Corredo," which later found its way onto *Leave It to the Limeliters* in a re-recorded version ("Inspection Time") after Glenn left the group. But it was a wasted exercise, for neither track saw the light of day.

The most tangible souvenir of the tour is the *London Concert* album, which was recorded during the Limeliters' February 7, 1963 date in London's Royal Festival Hall. Glenn counts this as the Limeliters' best post-Elektra album, mainly because they used no backup musicians for the first and only time on records made during their heyday. They had to stand or fall completely on their own power—and stand they do, brilliantly, without even a hint of post-Provo trauma.

The album supports Glenn's claim that the Limeliters did not really need drums and backup musicians on their records (although Alex believes it was a mistake not to record with backup help). Their work may not be as polished as on the previous albums, but it is more than merely competent; it bristles with drive and vigor. The strength of Glenn's rhythm guitar is never as much in evidence as on this album, particularly on the hard-charging "Wabash Cannonball." Alex, as always, is right on target whether on banjo or flamenco-influenced guitar, while Lou occasionally adds a jazzy grace note to his otherwise straightforward bass lines.

None of the songs are new to the Limeliters' catalogue; six of the ten are from the Elektra album, yet all of them are superior to the originals (two more songs from the concert, "Gunslinger" and "Those Were The Days," were recorded but not issued).

The tempos are mostly slower, yet the energy level is higher, and their confidence in the material never more assured. Glenn's performance on "The Far Side of the Hill" is even deeper than his already masterful one on *Slightly Fabulous*; perhaps he was anticipating his impending departure from the group in the hope of emulating the song's drifter. "Hard Ain't It Hard" is a vehicle for even more uninhibited wise-cracking than before, particularly by Alex. The high point of the record for many is undoubtedly "Hey Li Lee Li Lee," where Lou is in top form as the professorial camp counselor and the British audience indicates that it has been listening to the group's records very closely. At one point, as Lou prattles on, the instruments drop out except for Alex's banjo, which launches into a mocking parody of the Kingston Trio's record of "Tom Dooley." Lou comments, "You KNOW how that song upsets me," and he may not have been kidding. Although in interviews, Nick Reynolds of the Trio has denied that a feud ever existed between the Limeliters and the Kingstons, Lou still must have been envious of these former upstarts who used to follow him around at the hungry i in the '50s. An old colleague of Lou's at Berkeley, Alan Rich, once ran into Lou in the streets of New York around this time, and the Limeliter spent a good part of an hour in a harangue about what was wrong with the Kingston Trio.

The one part of the singalong that no one will ever forget came at the end, when a Welshman with bushy red hair stood up in the rear of the balcony and bellowed a verse in a wildly comic, near-operatic, incomprehensible tenor. At this point, the trio completely lost it, laughing uncontrollably with the rest of the audience. Finally, Lou recovered enough to say, "We MUST hear your verse, sir!"—and the man responded with more gibberish. None of the Limeliters, nor Neely Plumb, nor the author, ever figured out what he was saying.

"It was easily the biggest laugh we've ever had in a concert hall," recalls Alex. "It was incredible, as you can hear on the record. It was brilliant. We practically fell off the stage."

Curiously, RCA Victor saw fit to sit on the tapes of *London Concert* until January of 1965 before putting out the record. Perhaps they did so in fear of competing with the Elektra album, which shared many songs with the *London* album, or the versions previously issued on RCA Victor—or perhaps they didn't want to put it out so soon after the live *Our Men in San Francisco* album. In any event, when they finally did, it was too late; the folk boom was all but over, the Limeliters had long since stopped touring, and few people bought it or were even aware of it. It was an inconspicuous sendoff for a remarkable document of a folk group at the height of its powers.

Later on in England, the Limeliters played in Cambridge University's Debating Union, where they discovered there was no public address system and had to borrow one from a campus rock group. As the group animatedly discussed the situation in the yard outside in front of the hall, Lou remembered seeing a university don, clad in the stereotypical cap-and-gown, shuffling down the sidewalk with his back bent in the manner of Groucho Marx. He paused briefly to listen to the conversation and then strode off, commenting out loud, "Ah, lusty trans-Atlantic voices!"

Back in the U.S.A., the Limeliters returned to Nashville less than two months later to record what would be their last album with Glenn during the early '60s, *Fourteen 14K Folk Songs*. They completed the album in seven sessions from March 26 to 29, really slugging away at the production, with RCA's Nashville chief Chet Atkins overseeing the operation.

By now, Nashville was well en-route to becoming a major recording center for all kinds of music, not just bread-and-butter country. Since the late 1950s, Atkins at RCA Victor, Owen Bradley at Decca, and later, Don Law at Columbia had been developing the "Nashville Sound," which loosely defined, was a watering down of straight hard country music with softer-edged elements from middle-of-the-road pop. As the records sold, existing studios were upgraded while others sprang up throughout the city, creating a real alternative to the East and West Coast hit factories. More to the point, visitors from Los Angeles and New York were attracted by the versatile, intuitively flexible talents of a tightly knit coterie of musicians who roamed from session to session. They could quickly settle into almost any kind of groove in their relaxed, good ole boy manner, making any session a breeze. Burl Ives was one of the first folk stars to discover Bradley's Nashville Sound machine at Decca, covering song after song by young hotshot writers like Hank Cochran, Harlan Howard, Roger Miller and Mel Tillis, scoring pop Top 10 hits with the country-politan songs "A Little Bitty Tear" and "Funny Way of Laughin" in 1962. And while the Limeliters eschewed the more commercial trappings of the Anita Kerr Singers or the strings of the Nashville Symphony, they definitely wanted to make use of the good ole boys.

"I remember being absolutely overjoyed at working in Nashville because those musicians understood guitars," recalls Alex. "I remember we hired this banjo player [Bob Johnson] and he came into town every day from about 30 miles away; he lived in a cabin somewhere in the hills. He would come in and his wife—she had long hair down to her waist—would massage his neck all the time he was playing these intricate things during the session. It was bizarre."

A good deal of the album's artistic success could be laid at the feet of Neely Plumb, who flew in from Los Angeles to assume the usual production duties. Atkins' polished sonic footprints can be heard too—and Alex's recollection is that Chet was more involved with the sessions than Neely. Yet Atkins himself recalled that Neely was definitely in charge, and he believed he might have lent a hand on guitar. "I'll bet I'm playing on some of the sides because I remember spending quite a bit of time with them," Atkins recalled in 1980. However, the session files do not include his name anywhere, and Lou confirmed that Atkins did not actually play on the session.

The back cover is a deceptive display of tongue-in-cheek humor—a three-way interview that pokes fun at the gathering purist storm about who is more-authentic-than-thou in folk music, and a photo of the group turned 90° on its side with the weird caption, "Why Do The Limeliters Always Record Standing Sideways?" Which is odd because the album itself is a dead serious attempt to make a really good record of standard folksongs as if to prove once again to *Sing Out!* and the *Little Sandy Review* that they can cut it. Again, there are no drums this time, just the Limeliters and crack Nashville guitarists Harold Bradley and Ray Edenton, and bassist Henry Strzelecki. On several tracks, Bob Gibson lent a hand on guitar and also contributed some fine reworkings of "Sweet Betsy From Pike" "John Riley" and Leadbelly's "Dink's Song." Wrapped in the superb acoustics of RCA's "Nashville Sound" Studio, the Limeliters' bass-heavy gusto had never been recorded so well.

For all the poker-faced professionalism on every track, there are many emotionally moving moments—the exquisite performances of "Dink's Song" and "I'm Goin' Away," the pound-it-out dignity of the chain gang song, "No More Cane." Alex believes Lou's vocal on the latter was the best of his life and there's no denying its thundering power. They tackle some blues in "Betty and Dupree," with Lou belting with a freedom that had been hidden for a while, and even worn-out folk warhorses like "Whoopee Ti Yi Yo" ("Git Along Little Dogies') and "Hangman, Hangman" ("Gallows Pole") are reinvigorated. This is not the Limeliters of their stage act; at last, they have become a seasoned, assured recording group—and next to *Sing Out!,* this is the studio album that has held up the best over the years. It also sold somewhat better than *Makin' A Joyful Noise,* though not nearly as well as *Our Men In San Francisco..*

Despite the rekindled vigor of their recordings, the end was near for the group as Glenn's deadline came closer. The plane crash had badly shaken Lou up, and a good deal of his interest in the group had drained away. Toward the end, Glenn says that Lou simply stopped talking to him. At this point, Alex assumed the role of the keeper of the Limeliters flame, a part he has played ever since. He still could not bring himself to believe that Glenn would leave just when big money for engagements was piling in. He kept after Glenn, nagging, cajoling him to remain in the group.

The breaking point for Glenn finally came at a June month-long return engagement at Basin Street East, the month before his deadline. They were now the headliners at a highly-visible show, with singer Nancy Ames opening the evening, followed by baritone sax giant Gerry Mulligan's quartet featuring trombonist Bob Brookmeyer. Alex's campaign intensified, and one night in the dressing room, Glenn simply couldn't take it anymore. He hoisted Alex up in the air, threw him against the side of the dressing room wall, and said, "Alex, I am not staying one minute longer!"

"That shut him up, and he never mentioned it again," said Glenn. "I felt so badly afterwards because I don't have much of a temper, but if I get mad—it doesn't happen very often—it's not good."

Not even the most devoted Limeliters fan was more appalled by the news of the breakup than Alex's mother. Always trying to look after her son's long term security, she thought that Alex was just a year away from being financially set for a good portion of the rest of the life. "In '63, I went to see their agent, and he cried on my shoulder," she said. "He said, 'Listen, do something. I have here contracts for half a million dollars and they don't want to sign them.' Half a million dollars. I was shocked to see that they were so stupid to throw it away. I used to tell Alex, 'Work another year while the going is good, and put aside a nice sum of money, and then you can choose what you want to do.' But they just couldn't get along anymore."

While they were in New York, Lou, Alex and Glenn had but one more recording task ahead of them. On June 27, they went into RCA Victor's Studio A with their TV-radio commercial producer Arnold Brown to cut "McLintock's Theme" ("Love in the Country")—a rare studio session without Neely in the control room. The tune, written by Hollywood's Frank DeVol, came from a John Wayne comedy Western film called *McLintock!* and the backing sported three French horns presumably to give it some commercial oomph. Issued on a single with the vastly superior "The Midnight Special" from *Fourteen 14K Folk Song*s as the B-side, it went belly up just like all the Limeliters' singles save one. It was a most atypical and innocuous way to bow out. Their last concert together for at least 10 years would be held July 13, 1963 at the stunning Red Rocks Amphitheatre just above Denver, Colorado. After only four years together, the first fabulously successful incarnation of the group would be history.

Hindsight tells us it may have been a lucky thing for the Limeliters that they got off the concert circuit when they did. True, Alex says the group walked away from a million dollars in bookings when they stopped touring, but the long-term signs of continuing at that magic pay level for much longer were not good. Only two weeks after the Limeliters' last concert, the folk revival would come to its crest at the Newport Folk Festival where the young Bob Dylan captivated the crowd with his pre-electric songs of protest. Although no one could have really predicted it at the time, commercial folk music would hit the skids within a year and be all but buried two years later.

Not only that, the Limeliters' own record sales then were in the midst of a zigzagging but unmistakably slow decline with each release, even as the paydays for live gigs were getting bigger. Even the Kingston Trio was coming to the end of its peak period during that time; the group would not score a Top 40 single after August 1963. The only folk group that really did well, indeed gained strength, from the summer of 1963 onward was Peter, Paul and Mary, for they had latched onto the songs of Dylan and other young folk-influenced songwriters from the next wave and still enjoyed the full backing of their label, Warner Bros. One generation of folkniks was suddenly giving way to another, and they would soon make it clear that they had different ideas about which directions they would like to send their music.

Yet despite a late start, the Limeliters did have a smashing run right through the heart of the folk revival years. And their collective commercial timing would never be as keen again.

The Limeliters contemplate the wrecked plane in a field near Provo, UT, Dec. 1962. *(Photo from Biddulph-STUM Fine Photography, courtesy of Alex Hassilev)*

Chapter Ten

At this point, the Limeliters' saga goes underground in a sense, for technically, the group no longer existed. All three were preoccupied with solo pursuits or projects, strained or broken marriages, or just trying to make sense of what had happened during the four years of runaway success. The group was no longer the focus of their lives, and they would just as soon leave it in the past.

But the bottom-line watchers in the Manhattan headquarters of RCA Victor had other ideas. More to the point, they had a signed piece of paper, a 1962 contract that said the Limeliters owed RCA Victor at least three more albums before they could hang up their spikes. "The company naturally had the momentum going, and they're money oriented—they felt like the name of the Limeliters would sell some more records whether Glenn was there or not," recalled Neely Plumb. "I never fully agreed with that."

And so, under pressure from the bean counters, Neely set about the task of trying against all odds to find an adequate replacement for Glenn. Neither Alex nor Lou would go out on the road again, so this replacement would simply be someone who could get them through their recording commitments with a minimum of problems. Neither Alex nor Lou wanted any part of the hunt for a replacement at this point, and they would later regret their lack of involvement when Neely came up with an old familiar face as Glenn's successor. That man was none other than the honey-voiced figure who succeeded Lou in the Gateway Singers: Ernie Sheldon.

"Actually I blame myself—and Lou, I suppose, blames himself to some extent—in that we did not find somebody more suitable to replace Glenn," said Alex. "Neely was the one who searched out a singer, and Lou and I just accepted it. We had known Ernie, and that was why in a way he was acceptable. He was a very nice man, and it was easy to do with him, and so on and so forth. But musically, it was a disaster."

"Ernie is an extremely facile singer," said Lou. "He can fit into anything. He's a good folk-type singer and a very nice man. Actually, Neely got him, but I certainly didn't object."

Yet Lou wasn't as harshly critical of the three albums and the single that Lou, Alex and Ernie made. "It was an interesting sound," he said. "We sang together a couple of old charts, and I said, well sure, what's the difference because I wasn't going out on the road anymore. So, if Neely wanted to use him on the rest of the dates, I couldn't disagree."

"Ernie, of course, is a dear friend," said Neely, "and I think we settled upon Ernie because Ernie did a good job, and the reason it didn't work out is because of the uniqueness of Glenn's voice. There was no other voice like Glenn. Ernie had the tenor range to reach the notes and he had the folk orientation—he was a good folk writer himself—but I think we settled upon Ernie because he was the best we could find, and Ernie didn't do anything wrong. I don't think there is anything wrong with the records we made with Ernie, except they were not Glenn."

Glenn himself noticed something else which was lacking in the recordings with Ernie that he heard—an inward censor. "There was a tendency in the Limeliters to do a lot of phony bullshit stuff, and I think I was the one that was always saying, 'Let's not do that crap,'" Glenn said. "There was too much of an effort to be commercial, to be funny in an artificial way, and I've got a button in me that says, PHONY. I noticed on those albums there didn't seem to be anybody being self-critical enough to say, 'This is phony bullshit, throw it out.'"

Now Ernie Sheldon—born Ernest Sheldon Lieberman in 1930—was a respected veteran of the hardcore and commercial folk scenes. He did a handsome job of replacing Lou in the Gateway Singers—and Lou kept in touch, at one point trying to use him to represent his Brio publishing outfit in New York. As Ernie Lieberman, he recorded a solo album of peace songs in 1955, *Goodbye, Mr. War*, for the small Amerecord label. As Ernie Sheldon, he made another album of tall tale songs for Columbia in 1959 called *The Big Men—Bold and Bad*, and a few years later, a duo album of mostly adapted folk songs and a few originals for Mercury in tandem with Joyce James—all workmanlike stuff that went nowhere in sales yet enhanced his reputation.

What the Limeliters gained in Ernie was a solid songwriter, the most consistent and prolific one the group ever had. For a trio that in Lou's words had supposedly "exhausted its creative potential," Ernie would prove to be a wellspring of new folk-pop material. He would have a hand in the writing or adaptation of five of the tunes on *More of Everything*, and three more on *Leave It to the Limeliters*. In a sense he was fulfilling the same role as Dave Guard's replacement in the Kingston Trio, a singer-songwriter named John Stewart.

What they lost, though, was something that would prove to be more precious—their sound. For whatever reason, Ernie's heavier, almost baritonal tenor clashed abrasively with the voices of Lou and Alex. Whereas the clash with Glenn resulted in a soaring, energetic yet flexible blend, the Lou-Alex-Ernie combination was weightier, huskier, saddled with a buzzsaw-like edge and often noticeably out of tune.

Would more rehearsals or working out the bugs on the road have improved the blend? It's hard to say—but the loss of Glenn would haunt the entire series of projects.

Nevertheless Lou, Alex and Ernie wasted little time in booking RCA Hollywood's Studio 2 in the middle of December 1963. The result, *More of Everything*, is on balance a worthy record of mostly strong material, hardly the disaster that an incompatible blend of voices would be expected to produce. The Limeliters themselves do not play instruments on the sessions here, nor do they on any of the sessions with Ernie. Glen Campbell, then one of the busiest session men in Hollywood, is the lead guitarist while longtime sidemen Allan Reuss and Earl Palmer are in place on guitar and drums respectively.

"There's Many a River" gets the new collaboration off to a rousing start, and "The Best Is Yet To Come" an adaptation and rewrite by Ernie of a French-Canadian logging song, continues the streak. One's hopes go up; maybe the boys can pull it off despite losing their matchless tenor. But "Last Class Seaman," one of Woody Guthrie's lesser-known shanties, is a fine song poorly performed; the horrible intonation really grates even though one imagines the effect of wine-besotted sailors is probably deliberate.

Lou gets his chance to sing an honest-to-goodness country song, a tune written by Scott Wiseman for T. Texas Tyler called "Remember Me." Again, the prophets would fail to reap the profits from their acumen, for Willie Nelson would revive "Remember Me" on his *Red Headed Stranger* album in 1975, the record that made him at long last an American megastar.

Bob Florence plays tack piano on "Minneapolis-St. Paul," a story song of bigamy in the Twin Cities that gives Lou some comic things to do. The bluesy "Why Don't You Come Home," set to a mild rock beat, comes off well as long as Lou does his ringing Leadbelly impression on the solos, and Campbell gets off a fine swinging acoustic guitar solo on the break. "Bring Me A Rose" is reminiscent of Pete Seeger's "Where Have All the Flowers Gone?" in theme and melodic structure almost a brazen rewrite but Ernie's sincerity pulls it off. "No Man Is an Island" is based on a John Donne sermon from which Ernest Hemingway found his title "For Whom the Bell Tolls," but the idea of Lou speaking the words underneath proves to be a misfire.

All three Limeliters do well as soloists under the protection of RCA's echo chamber; it's when the voices combine that the listening becomes tough. Indeed, the record would have been a triumph of tasteful A&R and tasty session work—if only the group vocals were recut.

Lou, Alex and Ernie were whisked into the studio again in late April and early May to cut another album that would hit the record racks in August. If anything, *Leave It to the Limeliters* is an even better album than *More of Everything*, full of solid material that with more rehearsal would have made a killer record. While nothing much can be done about the jarring blend of voices, at least the three are more in sync and in tune this time, and Glen Campbell and the L.A. studio aces are back to provide the crack accompaniment.

"Farewell," which comes from a Bob Dylan demo tape, is the Limeliters' first realization that the times they are a'changin,' even though they picked a mild Dylan reworking of an old sea shanty, "Leavin' Of Liverpool." More whimsy can be heard in "Tani, the Lady Bullfighter;" "Port au Prince," a lovely Gene Raskin-credited ballad with a gentle calypso rhythm, is sung beautifully by Ernie even if one can't help but be reminded that Port-au-Prince then was the poverty-stricken capital of the Duvaliers' Haiti. "Inspection Time," getting a second chance after the group's unsuccessful Rome recording, finds Lou trying to provide a running spoken translation over the verse, finally admitting in mock-defeat, "I guess it does suffer in translation."

Lou's treatment of Leadbelly's "When I Was A Cowboy (Cow Cow Yicky Yicky Yea)" (aka "Out On The Western Plains") is terrific, with a charging, funky rhythm track built on a single, revolving banjo lick. This would have made a great item for revival once the group started perform-ing regularly again; indeed, in the '80s, the Limeliters would periodically try to dust off this chart, but they never did get around to performing it.

Alex, by now the automatic recipient of all songs involving playboys, takes the lead on "Sportin' Bachelors;" "My Love Doth Walk the Picket

Line" is very sharp and satirical, with Linus Pauling, J. Edgar Hoover, sit-ins, nuclear testing, HUAC and other topics all getting a mention. "The 8th Day of the Week" is the best of Ernie's songs, a lullaby riddled with cynicism about the intractable state of the world, marred only by the raggedly sung chorus. And "C'est l'aviron," the last tune to be recorded, has another catchy, repeated banjo line.

Clearly the Limeliters at this point still had something to say.

Even though the Limeliters ceased to exist as a touring group, albums continued to flow out of RCA Victor in 1964 as the corporation tried to squeeze the last ounce of profit out of their leading folk act. In July, an anthology, *The Best of the Limeliters*, was assembled by A&R coordinator Brad McCuen and dumped onto the market with a liner note that gave no hint that Glenn had left the group and that they were no longer performing. Moreover, the album was cleverly stitched together, often with no breaks between tracks, whether studio or live— as if RCA was trying to create a new quasi-live package.

What followed, though, would be perhaps the least representative and least successful album the Limeliters would ever make. Shortly following the belated release of *London Concert* in January 1965, the trio went into RCA Hollywood to cut a concept album, *The Limeliters Look At Love...In Depth.*

It was easily the most expensive record the Limeliters had cut up until then, for Neely Plumb wanted to make a grand production of the Limeliters' last obligation to their label. For the first time, the Limeliters took a creative bye and left the driving to others, just dropping in to sing their parts.

As Lou recalled, "We took a flyer and Neely got Leon Pober and Bud Freeman to write an album for us and that was a very bad bomb. The only reason it was a bomb was because it cost so much to produce. But Neely said 'Look, we've got money ahead, we're a hit, this account is way over-earned, let me take a flyer,' because we had had a lot of luck with a tune that Leon Pober and Bud Freeman wrote called 'Gunslinger.'

"So, they dug us, and they did work very hard and there was some funny stuff on it. But it was just arch, and you know, this act can't read arrangements off a score and make a record. Never could."

"That was not a bad idea for a record," mused Alex. "But it was not a good idea for a non-working band. If we had done that material live, I think the album would have sold like gangbusters at the time." But Alex also added, "I think we performed it atrociously. A lot of the material was inferior."

What Neely did was rip the Limeliters away from their folk base and place them in a curious swamp of over-arranged semi-pop and mock-rock. One of Hollywood's busiest arrangers, Perry Botkin, Jr., was brought in to provide charts for winds, brass, harpsichord, electric guitars, and some cooing female (and occasionally male) singers. It was another of RCA Victor's hidebound attempts during the mid '60s to get a piece of the rock and easy-listening action simultaneously.

Even more pathetic was the material. Whatever zany inspiration the Pober-Freeman team had for "Gunslinger" had evaporated by now, and they tried in vain to spin off all kinds of contemporary variations on the theme of love, often cramming so many words into phrases that they collapse. The lyrics are so sneering, so self-consciously "clever," so overloaded with contemporary references that they cross the line between satire and outright meanness. "The Trouble With You, Fred" is a tired attempt to extend the psychoanalysis theme of "Gunslinger;" "Come A-Bed, John" somehow tries to apply baroque counterpoint to the words, "leaky transmission seal." In "Buddy Bike," the Limeliters are actually forced to sing in a puerile teen-pop style; the song was probably intended to be a parody, but it doesn't quite come off that way, certainly not as hilariously as "Vikki Dougan." To be sure, "Billy Bean" is a pretty sharp skewering of right-wing patriots, seemingly inspired by W.S. Gilbert. Yet for the most part, Pober and Freeman commit the biggest sin for any would-be satirists—they are simply not funny.

The cover art—with the three ex-folkies dressed in lab coats in a sterile computer room, staring quizzically at a piece of computer tape while a blonde-haired model leers at Lou—made no apparent sense, and certainly didn't help sales. Indeed, if RCA Victor thought that the Limeliters name alone would sell albums in the post-Glenn period, they had a shock coming. *More of Everything* rose to only a feeble No. 118 on the *Billboard* album survey, and none of its successors—including *London Concert* and *The Best of*—even charted.

Two leftovers from the *Look At Love* sessions were issued on a single, which also predictably went nowhere. Pober's "Seventeen Wives" is a feeble burlesque of Western and Middle Eastern marital practices, with an irritating mock-Arabian arrangement. "Rose," on the other hand, is the first Limeliters encounter with a song by Rod McKuen, who had already hooked up successfully with Glenn. Though saddled with a maudlin spoken verse quite at odds with the Pober-Freeman archness, "Rose" boasted a catchy chorus, and it holds up fairly well today. It would also be the last song the Limeliters would cut for RCA Victor, for when the trio's contract came up for renewal, RCA passed.

Not that anyone really cared at this point. "That was okay with me," wrote Lou in his autobiography. "I had lost interest in singing with the Limeliters."

In any case, it was too late. The music world had changed by 1965—irrevocably, as it turned out.

The one crucial musical event that laid the folk revival low occurred on Feb. 9, 1964, the day the Beatles first played the Ed Sullivan Show. After its wild, earthy start, rock 'n' roll had been emasculated during the early '60s, the beat muted, the charts dominated by manufactured teen-age crooners, dance crazes, whining vocal groups, novelty records, and hack tunes from the Brill Building. If the youth of the time wanted music with any kind of brains or swing, played by their peers, the Kingston Trio brand of folk was the way to go.

Then the Beatles blew in from Liverpool, armed with charisma, charm, irreverence, a huge musical talent that had not even begun to assert itself, and the long-lost sounds of America's rock 'n' roll. From the hindsight of our fragmented, market-targeted age, it is hard to believe how dominant they were in the spring of 1964, with exposure on the variety show that EVERYBODY saw, holding down the Top 5 singles at once.

They and their co-conspirators from England had captured the imaginations of a generation—and the folkies must have known their time in the spotlight was up. "The Beatles, as far as I'm concerned, immediately monopolized the attention of people who listened to popular music," said Lou. "They were so unique and so darling, you know, and so completely original in terms of what had been going down that it just mangled everybody."

Especially hard hit by the British invasion was the Kingston Trio—particularly since they, like the Beatles, recorded for Capitol Records. "It was like shooting you right in the heart with an M16," said the Trio's Bob Shane of the coming of the Beatles. "It was dead—phhhft! We saw the writing on the wall. It was a whole change in music, and it was a good change, too, because the Beatles are fantastic."

As Lou put it, "From being the absolute kings of Capitol Records, they became office boys. 'Get outta here, we can't handle Kingston Trio records, we got something that's selling.'"

"At the time the Beatles came in, we accounted for 14% of all of Capitol's record sales," said Shane. "And I thought it was kind of a crappy thing to do for them to turn their backs on us when they saw us not selling as many, and the change with John (Stewart) and not pumping it up and advertising it."

At the same time, the Young Turks of the second folk wave were listening carefully and hard to these Anglo-rockers. Bob Dylan, of course, had started his musical life as a rock 'n' roller back in high school in Hibbing, Minnesota and, unbeknownst to the folk crowd, recorded an electric version of "Mixed-Up Confusion" back in 1963. He had also hooked up with the Animals; indeed, the Animals' rendition of the old New Orleans bordello tune "House of the Rising Sun" in 1964 was an electrified version of Dylan's acoustic recording.

After the assassination of President Kennedy, Dylan backed away from protest songs to the dismay of the Left, writing by degrees romantic, inward, then nihilistic, free-associative, sometimes sloganeering lyrics that spoke of disillusion and dropping out rather than getting involved. He was bound to return to the home church—and did so with a vengeance in March of 1965 with a scorching side of ambiguously anti-Establishment rock 'n' roll on his *Bringing It All Back Home* album. Thus, it shouldn't have been such a shock to the crowd at the 1965 Newport Folk Festival when he turned up with an electric guitar and the Butterfield Blues Band.

Jim McGuinn, the ex-Limeliters sideman, saw George Harrison playing a Rickenbacker electric 12-string guitar in the film *A Hard Day's Night* and immediately had to have one. Before long, he had become excited by the new music, putting together a rock group called the Byrds and recording a new elliptical Dylan song called "Mr. Tambourine Man" that the composer had already put out on the acoustic side of *Bringing It All Back Home.*

The Byrds' "Mr. Tambourine Man" went straight to No. 1 on the singles charts as McGuinn's inspired, jangling intro on his 12-string electric guitar shot a 1000-volt bolt of electricity into the pop world of

June 1965—and simultaneously electrocuted the remains of the fading folk revival.

If the Beatles' appearance on the Sullivan show was the warning sign that commercial folk was on its way out, Dylan's rampaging "Subterranean Homesick Blues," followed by the Byrds' "Mr. Tambourine Man" and Dylan again with the apocalyptic "Like A Rolling Stone," slammed the door shut. Rock had suddenly become a viable intellectual outlet for those who were once captivated by Woody Guthrie.

Also the country itself had changed. Without a doubt, the brutal murder of John F. Kennedy on Nov. 22, 1963 cast a heavy pall upon the nation, dampening the idealism that had been whipped up by the young president, the civil rights movement, and the folk musicians who provided the most emotional soundtrack for those years. Part of folk music's appeal was based on flattery, appealing to the belief that its listeners were basically righteous Americans at heart, ready to stand up against evil.

But Kennedy's murder shook the nation's self-confidence badly, and further shakes were coming in the 1960s. Idealists would put their faith in heroes, only to see them gunned down and the plots behind the murders covered up. They marched for civil rights, only to see the movement seized by Black nationalists who told them to go find their own revolution. They believed that technological progress would make this a better world, only to see it result in a poisoned environment and a pace of life speeding out of control. They thought they could bear any burden, pay any price, to make America live up to its ideals, and that led to the grotesque distortion of patriotism that was the Vietnam war.

Disillusionment would give way to anger and protest—and by 1965, the high-voltage jolts of rock were a far more satisfying conduit for that anger that the relatively sedate singalongs of Pete Seeger. The timing of the Beatles' first visit was also uncanny, coming as it did just a few months after the Kennedy assassination, giving young people new heroes to look up to. America also lost a good deal of its collective sense of humor around that time, and the decline in the popularity of satirical stand-up comedy also produced an undertow that made a lot of folk group shtick obsolete. It seemed that there wasn't much to laugh about anymore; even the brilliant Tom Lehrer soon became convinced of that and quit the stage for good.

Finally, there is an obvious, simple, non-political explanation for the sudden fall of folk; the repertoire was worn out through overexposure. A good deal of this repertoire was shared by virtually everyone, leading to a simultaneous burn out.

Over and over and over again, one would hear "John Henry," "Michael Row The Boat Ashore," "I Gave My Love A Cherry," "Black Is The Color Of My True Love's Hair," "Rock Island Line," "Midnight Special," "Sloop John B," and other standards—whatever the group, whatever the locale, whatever the album.

Even Woody Guthrie's durable repertoire—or at least the dozen or so of his thousand songs that became folk staples buckled under the strain. "This Land Is Your Land," shorn of its broadside against private property, would become a cliche, a routine concert closer or an innocuous campfire tune. There are only so many times that all these groups could sing these tunes before either the group and/or its audience finally says, Enough!

The overexposure theory is the one that most satisfies Alex. "The thing that killed folk music was nothing more or less than the cyclical nature of all mass pop art phenomena; namely, anything that is overexposed becomes an artifact very quickly," he said. "The word 'commercialized' is one I don't understand because the fact that people make money from things that are exposed is, in my judgment, incidental. It doesn't have anything to do with anything. What is important is that when you do overexpose anything, the dilution created by overexposure is a sign of death. If you overexpose Bach—let's assume that the entire nation heard nothing but Brandenburg Concerti on the AM morning show for four or five months—people will get damned tired of Bach, as great as Bach is."

"I don't think folk music will ever be what it was during the Kingston Trio era," said Glenn. "That was a fluke anyway. "Folk music was never meant to be that kind of Tin Pan Alley popular. That's why it died because there are only so many folk songs, and whenever you try and write a folk song, you can't do it. You can always tell a fake folk song; it's not the same thing as the real old-fashioned stuff. In the old days, when Tin Pan Alley discovered that there was a lot of money in folk music, they began writing it. The minute they began writing it, the whole thing died. It had to die because they exhausted practically all the songs in the folk repertoire."

Gradually folk artists and groups who survived found that the old acoustic ways and the old traditional repertoire would no longer do. The self-contained singer/songwriters like Dylan, Tom Paxton, Phil Ochs, Gordon Lightfoot, and others would point the way—and their paths would stray out of the pure folk realm, often toward accommodations with the resurgent rockers over the howls of the purists. As we have seen, the Limeliters made an extremely half-hearted attempt to change their style. Even the Kingston Trio briefly capitulated. "We tried with the *Something Else* album to add rock sounds, and some of the songs were kind of interesting," said Shane. "But we got letters like, 'What is this trash you're doing? We want to hear 'Tom Dooley!'"

Inevitably, even the indefatigable Kingston Trio—which had survived nearly as traumatic a plane crash in 1959 as the Limeliters' but kept going out on the road 300 days a year—was becoming exhausted. They held out until 1967, switching over to Decca (which predictably didn't know what to do with them) until they finally ran out of gas. "We had gotten to the point where we realized how heavily the record sales had failed and how tiring it was getting to be on the road," said Shane. "It started off as one guy saying, 'Boy I'm sure getting bored with this,' and we all agreed, 'Let's just do one more thing at the hungry i and get out.'" (Shane, it should be said, was the sole voice of dissent who wanted to carry on).

So, the folk purists could take some grim satisfaction in seeing the implosion of the great commercial folk dragon. Almost everyone who remained true to their sources would soon be scuffling again. But the ex-Limeliters weren't looking back.

For the next ten years, starting in 1963, they would be trying to find themselves in increasingly diverse and often bizarre ways as the 1960s unfolded.

Leave It To The Limeliters, the best of the
albums with Ernie Sheldon (right)

Chapter Eleven

On Oct. 10, 1963, Lou Gottlieb turned 40 years old. By mainstream standards, he had achieved the American Dream. He was well-off financially, all his debts paid, with securities that were doing well, with about $100,000 in deferred record royalties coming his way from RCA Victor over three years. He had a wife, two children, lived in a modern home with glass walls on a hillside in beautiful El Cerrito just north of enlightened Berkeley. He was famous, a household name to those who had seen the Limeliters work and who had heard and seen their commercials. No longer would he have to endure the grind of 300 performances a year, the rickety private planes, the loneliness, and exhaustion of the road.

All he needed was something to do...and something to relieve the growing feeling of emptiness inside.

Lou began to dabble in various ventures. In the fall of 1963, he signed on as Master of Ceremonies for a six-week tour of one-nighters with the Modern Folk Quartet, The Knoblick Upper Ten Thousand, and Bessie Griffin and the Gospel Pearls. This was an opportunistic attempt by International Talent Associates to cash in on the *Hootenanny* TV Show (another similar ITA package tour was emceed by Glenn), appearing mostly on college campuses. The tour used chartered Greyhound buses, so Lou didn't have to worry about planes, and he also admitted having a clandestine affair with one of the Pearls.

Once the tour was over, Lou thought he would try personal management. Malvina Reynolds turned him on to Calvin Grayson, a 15-year-old Black singer from Berkeley whom Lou swore sounded like a teenaged Ray Charles. An immense raw talent, Lou thought, and he promptly had Calvin record a few demos of Lou's songs and rushed them down to Capitol Records' A&R man David Axelrod. While Axelrod was not taken with Lou's tunes, he liked the singer, and signed Grayson to the label.

Lou then formed a management company with a man named Richard Lewis and tried to assume the role of star-maker. But Grayson's career with Capitol was a bust; he recorded only a pair of mediocre

R&B singles that didn't sell, and Lou suddenly found himself playing surrogate father to a teenager who liked to run around with the wrong crowd. What Lou learned from that experience was that he was temperamentally incapable of being a manager of an entertainment personality. (Interestingly, Grayson's singles are now prized by collectors of "northern soul.")

1964 found Lou wading in and out of the music business, never staying at one thing for too long. Neely Plumb asked him to chair a NARAS meeting in February, where the biggest buzz at the meeting was over Capitol's campaign to bring the Beatles to America for the first time. Undaunted by this harbinger of the future, Lou drifted back into the folk world. He formed an alliance with David "Buck" Wheat, guitarist and former bass player with the Kingston Trio and they began to rehearse an act together. According to Lou, Wheat was known as a very successful drug dealer on the sly, and given Lou's leftist past, they thought of calling their act "Dope and Communism." They even had the zany thought of adding a beautiful Black girl singer and renaming the group, "Dope, Sex and Communism."

In any case, "Dope and Communism" played one performance at Disneyland of all places, following the fiery singer/guitarist Jose Feliciano. But the duo laid an egg. Lou claimed the act was doomed from the start because whenever they started to rehearse, he was so knocked out by the high-grade Acapulco Gold marijuana that Wheat was passing him that he could barely keep his eyes open.

While based in Berkeley, Lou would drop into Los Angeles about five days out of each month, either to cut new Limeliters sessions with Alex and Ernie or try and sell his tunes to other artists. By now Amadeo Music had become Amadeo-Brio, Inc., and Larry Shayne—a Los Angeles publisher whose main client at the time was Henry Mancini—had been running the business for Lou, trying without any success to get other performers to cut Amadeo's songs. Nevertheless, Shayne still got 20% of Amadeo's income off the top due to royalties from Limeliters recordings—and Lou thought he could save money by eliminating the middleman and doing the tune-hustling himself, just as he did in the '50s.

Lou walked into Shayne's office, grabbed his business records and left. For six months, until Shayne threatened him with a lawsuit for breach of a multi-year contract, Lou tried to run his publishing business out of his briefcase again, renting a room on Sunset Blvd. as his

Los Angeles headquarters. But he soon tired of song-plugging, finding that he could no longer stay interested in the nuts-and-bolts of running a business. Once Shayne's high-powered lawyer read him the riot act, Lou meekly gave the administration of Amadeo-Brio back to Shayne.

Lou next turned to acting, appearing in Eugene Ionesco's provocative *The Bald Soprano* and *Jack* in a small Santa Barbara theater company, and as the mad professor in Ionesco's *The Lesson* in Walnut Creek, California with his daughter Judith playing the student. He re-enrolled at UC Berkeley as a student, taking classes in traditional English and Scottish Balladry and playwriting. In between classes, he would take in the birth of the Free Speech Movement, feeling totally alienated from the protesters who were half his age. He was really drifting by now, unable to find anything that would hold his attention.

Also Lou's normally robust health was beginning to give way. On March 4, 1964, while walking uphill in Hollywood, he began to feel a new strange discomfort in his knees and legs. He had rashes and nerve tingles in his legs. His joints hurt when he clenched his fists. On April 1, he had a basal cell carcinoma removed from his nose; luckily the cancer was arrested but his other symptoms continued. A year later, he submitted himself to a battery of tests, including a wrenching spinal tap, and the doctors concluded that he was suffering from pernicious anemia. They prescribed injections of Vitamin B-12, which did no good at all. Lou was convinced that all these aches were due to an allergy to his lifestyle—and the symptoms would last for three years.

What Lou was experiencing was a mid-life crisis, a whopper of one, particularly since it occurred after some major upheavals in his life—the plane crash, the breakup of the group. "I got hit by a big one," Lou said. "I didn't know what it was. It comes in the early 40s. First, it's the attack of what-does-it-all-mean-itis and then it is a paternal urge, the desire to procreate. You start to sit back and think, now what is really interesting to do? I just knew I had to absolutely get out of my situation, because I felt like I was dying...Suicide, a kind of tremendous emptiness."

The first thing that dawned upon Lou was that everybody was cheating him. Being thought of as rich meant having to put up with phone calls and letters from friends, alleged friends and total strangers who needed a donation, an investment, or a loan. Lou would joke that he could tell by the way the phone rang what the size of the touch would be. He would later write in his press biography, "Having money made me suspicious, competitive, pessimistic and ultimately physically ill."

It was also in tune with a wave of subversive thought that was just beginning to make itself known in America during the 1960s.

Today, we think of the youth revolution in the '60s mostly in terms of its artifacts—the music, long hair, beads, psychedelic clothing, open sex, drugs. Yet the most dangerous, most revolutionary idea to come out of the '60s was that of rejecting the money culture, the principal engine that drives America. The idea that the pursuit of financial success isn't the most important goal in life was the one that really frightened the Establishment in the '60s—and it was the one that first took hold of the sensitive cultural antennae of Lou.

Everything else would flow from that realization. In the spring of 1964, Lou's friend Andre Philippe would push his odyssey a little further along by giving him a couple of pamphlets by Ramana Marharshi (*Who Am I?*) and Gerard Heard (*Lion Prayer*). Taking his cue from the former, Lou began to chant "Kokham, Soham, Naham—Who am I? I am He. I am not the Body." It was his first exposure to Eastern spiritual thought, and it began to fill a part of the gap that Lou felt within himself, something he described as a "God-thirst." Later that year, Lou tried a glamorous hallucinogenic drug that was breaking out of national security circles and psychiatric offices into the open—LSD. By 1964, LSD had invaded Hollywood—and few among the area's curious resident and visiting intellectuals in the middle of spiritual crises would have been more receptive to this experience than Lou Gottlieb, Ph.D. Lou's rented Los Angeles room happened to be the backroom of Virginia Dennison, fiancée of Andre Philippe, friend of the Huxleys and an acquaintance of LSD guru Timothy Leary. Virginia, who had given Lou a lesson in Hatha Yoga some time before, got him to ingest five pills, after which they walked on the Santa Monica beach. Lou felt nothing new; he reported that it felt like taking marijuana and benzedrine at the same time. Being a large man, Lou apparently did not react to a mere 125 micrograms of the stuff. A month later, he tried again—this time with 450 micrograms. This time, he "definitely got the message."

It would be a gradual process of change in consciousness for Lou, one that would not take full effect for about two years. But once one has tried LSD, even just once, that person is never quite the same. People who have taken LSD report that they feel differently about their relationship to the earth and its living things, that they feel more as one with them. They find that it unlocks portions of the mind that they never thought existed; colors become more vivid, inanimate objects pulsate. It tends to dampen ambition; career goals become less important. One is less aware of passing time; one feels strongly bonded to other people who have taken trips. And one also tends to become more receptive to self-styled gurus peddling Eastern spiritual philosophy.

"I think it may have made him a bit less purposeful, a bit less focused," said William Malloch. "Lou wanted to do something on his own; he wanted to amount to something separate, and if he couldn't do this, he'd do that. From not perhaps having enough power, he had too much power. He was in the position—as anybody who takes a lot of dope is—to be charmed by the sound of his own voice. Therefore, he was like the Mikado; the Mikado says something ought to be done, it's as good as done—and the difference between having an intention and carrying out an effective action becomes blurred."

The most significant action Lou would make in the post-Limeliters '60s, however, had already been taken. Back in October of 1962, during the Limeliters' four-week gig at the hungry i that produced the *Our Men in San Francisco* album, Lou had noticed a tiny ad in the KPFA monthly bulletin. The ad said that 31.7 acres of land in Sonoma County redwood country 70 miles north of San Francisco were up for sale. By sheer coincidence, the next day, Bud Reynolds (Malvina's husband) rang Lou up, saying that he had seen the ad and that we ought to check it out.

So Lou and Bud drove across the dramatic Richmond-San Rafael bridge from Berkeley, up Highway 101, took the cutoff route 116 through Sebastopol, turned left on Graton Road, and a few miles later beheld a beautiful sloping hill with a ten-acre apple orchard, a few redwood groves, a couple of houses, a storage shed and a barn. The ranch could be entered from the north on Dupont Road, where a narrow lane separating two adjacent properties empties out into a forest meadow. A dirt road continues gently across and down the hill, crossing a stream in a narrow ravine until it comes to an end on Graton Road near an area of flat land that was bulldozed to make way for a housing project that never came about. Part of the land was being used as an egg ranch, and a Catholic lay group from San Francisco, the Third Order of Dominicans, would occasionally celebrate Mass on a knoll near the orchard.

According to Lou, one day the group put all of the names of the Litany of the Blessed Virgin into a hat and someone pulled out one of the pieces of paper at random, and it happened to be Morningstar. Thus came the name, Morningstar Ranch. The owner was John Beecher, a faculty member in San Francisco State College's English department, and his asking price for the property was $36,000, with $5,000 down and $250 per month. As was Lou's impulse-buying nature, he said that he mulled over the idea for approximately 30 seconds before deciding to buy the ranch. Bud Reynolds agreed to manage the upper house, collecting $40 a month rent, in return for being able to use the lower one as a country retreat. Other than occasional day trips to the ranch with his family, Lou just left the property alone for the next few years, with the egg ranch having been shut down. It was there as a nest egg, an idyllic retreat made possible by the financial success of the Limeliters and once RCA Victor's deferred royalties arrived in 1966, Lou paid off the property and owned it free and clear.

In 1965, Lou thought he'd give his standup comedy-plus-music act another try. He contacted his erstwhile partner, Dave Wheat, who suggested that Lou use Jimmy Stewart, his old hangout buddy from the hungry i, as an accompanist. Stewart, who was aiming his sights at becoming a Hollywood session man, was reliable and serious on the musical end, able to play in a multitude of styles with the jazz feeling Lou always treasured. But he also had a crazy side, a love of practical jokes and a mind that was right in tune with Lou's more demented comic flights.

Stewart drove to Lou's house in El Cerrito, where they started going through some tunes for the act. "When I walked in there, I was knocked out," he remembered. "I was in the right place because I saw all these books on folk music. Here's somebody I can grow with; this guy's a master of this stuff. I enjoyed playing the odd meters and learning the new tunes, having to come up with patterns of classical things, using my chops to add to the tunes."

With his new, young, skilled guitarist in tow, Lou found himself booked in some of his familiar haunts, a club near Stanford and back at the Ash Grove in Los Angeles, as well as a folk festival in Palm Springs. It was at the Palm Springs event that Stewart remembers Lou enlisting him on one of his more bizarre practical in-jokes. "He said, 'Jimmy, what I want you to do is go to each dressing room and tune these people up,'" Stewart recalled. "So, I went to each dressing room and tuned their guitars up. I was walking in some heavy dressing rooms, and I said, 'Well, Lou Gottlieb sent me in here to tune up your guitars.' They started laughing.

"That's what I call real humor, yet it's humor in two sides. For one thing, he showed me respect because he knew I was the best musician there. And that's appropriate, that he should have me come in and tune their instruments and teach them something. There is a perfect example of Uncle Lou's sense of humor."

Luckily Stewart was level-headed enough to tape one of Lou's shows at the Ash Grove, probably in the summer in 1965, and a good part of that tape survives despite some serious deterioration. Alas, Lou seems to be bombing here. The delivery is great, but his monologue wanders all over the place, the punch lines aren't getting through, and many of them just lack punch. He uses the same professor character that he developed in the '50s, now just a little bit stoned. The subject matter—usually sexual—is often way out there, and he has to explain some of the arcane cultural or linguistic references. If you want a perfect capsule of the type of intellectual hard-on humor Lou was doing then, one sentence should suffice: "That reminds me of the old slogan the Anti-Freudians used to use in Berkeley; 'A telephone pole is a telephone pole."

The act really takes hold, though, when Lou and Jimmy start making music ("I think we've had enough of this interminable palaver," Lou says). First Jimmy plays "Satin Doll," with Lou just managing to keep up on bass. He digs into the final two Limeliters albums for songs that they never performed live—"Johnny Todd" and "My Love Doth Walk The Picket Line" from *Leave It To The Limeliters* and "Fellow Man" and "Ties That Bind," from *Look At Love*. The latter two numbers actually sound much better here, now that Lou has had a chance to work them out without the elaborate orchestrations and unrehearsed trio vocals.

Lou then takes a nostalgic flyer into Wynonie Harris' "Good Morning Judge" in a lively two-beat arrangement, and even the Seekers' "I'll Never Find Another You," then a recent Top 10 hit.

The tape ends when "My Love Doth Walk The Picket Line" cuts off in mid-verse, but enough is there to show how ingratiating Lou could be on his own—that is, when he or Jimmy weren't sampling the latest fragrant, mind-bending herb. "There were times when he gave me some grass, I couldn't stop laughing," Stewart remembered. "Now, when you're sitting watching the fellow you're going to go onstage with, and you understand his mind, and you're a little ripped, I absolutely was almost getting sick laughing. There were times I almost couldn't go up and play...He had me on the floor, in tears, out of my mind."

In any case, Lou soon found once again that his kind of humor, once separated from the Limeliters, still didn't travel very well outside a small sexually liberated, intellectually hip crowd. Moreover, even though Lou now had a famous name, Stewart believed that he was still weighted down by the Limeliters' shadow. "He must have gotten tired of answering all the questions of why the Limeliters aren't together," observed Stewart. "Once you have a visible group like that, your audience identifies with the group. They don't want it to go away; they don't want it to change; they want the same people in it. It's an emotional rigor mortis of the soul. If the group doesn't change, they don't change. They don't get older."

Lou was to make one last attempt to find a job he could live with in January of 1966. Dean Wallace, a music critic on the staff of the *San Francisco Chronicle*, had left the paper to write a series of books, and Robert Commanday—an old college friend of Lou's at UC who had succeeded Alfred Frankenstein as chief critic in 1964—suggested that Lou apply for the vacancy. It seemed like a reasonable suggestion: Lou could write with his own brand of original flair, had the Ph.D. as an academic credential, and most of all, still had contagious enthusiasm for classical music.

With the endorsement of Ralph Gleason, another old friend who was the *Chronicle's* highly influential jazz columnist, Lou got the job and set to work, reviewing music and dance concerts, theater and recordings, interviewing passing stars, and contributing a music column. Before long, it became apparent that Lou had embarked upon one of the most bizarre classical music reviewing careers that journalism has ever known. Throughout most of the eleven articles that Lou was to write for the *Chronicle*, one gets the feeling that his mind was more preoccupied with psychedelic or spiritual matters than the music at hand. Also, there are times when Lou's libido was clearly in control of his critical faculties. The Jane Lapiner Dance Company probably never received a notice quite like the following cold-shower special: "Maybe mine was a fairly low-level reaction, but these chicks turned me on far stronger than all the topless dancers, bare-chested revues and torrid Swedish movies that I've ever seen all put together."

Yet while swinging wildly, Lou does occasionally hit a wrong-field home run. On cellist Robert Sayre's performance of the Kodaly Sonata for Unaccompanied Cello, Lou wrote, "Sayre should record the piece, but he should first take it on the road and play it at a different Jewish Community Center in the Bay Area every night for a month or so. Then record it while drunk. I felt the performance could have been a bit more vulgar in the Slavic manner."

Alas, Lou burned himself out after only three weeks on the job. Commanday recalled that whenever Lou heard a pianist who could play better than he—which was almost always the case—he would lose all objectivity and rhapsodize uncontrollably.

As January came to a close, Lou grew to loathe writing about music after so long a time in the performing arena, and his final reviews show a definite drop-off in enthusiasm. The last straw was an all-Bach recital by pianist Rosalyn Tureck on Jan 30., which Lou wrote, "It stirred me so deeply that my review was incoherent." The piece was sent back to him for a rewrite, and Lou just snapped. At this point, he realized what he wanted to do with his life. He should be playing the piano, not writing about pianists. As a result, Lou quit virtually on the spot, and the Tureck review (a rave) ran Feb. 1 under the name of John L. Wasserman, a general assignment entertainment critic who probably was assigned the rewrite.

Thanks in part to Rosalyn Tureck, Lou finally had conceived a goal. He would give a classical piano recital at New York's Carnegie Hall on Oct. 10, 1973—his 50th birthday—and he had over seven years in which to put in the grueling, all-consuming training that concert pianists must undergo. But he couldn't do so at home in El Cerrito. His marriage was beginning to sour, no doubt exacerbated by the changes of consciousness and mid-life crisis, and Lou would eventually blame his various physical ailments on an "allergy" to "my best friend, the mother of my two beautiful children, and the house in which we lived." At first, Lou thought it was the eucalyptus trees surrounding his El Cerrito home, but he soon convinced himself otherwise, for whenever he would go up to Morningstar Ranch for a day visit, his ailments would fade.

After he left the *Chronicle*, Lou hired Sven "Pete" Petersen and his sons to convert a 12-by-20-foot egg storage shed on a lovely meadow near the northern border of Morningstar into a music studio, big enough for one rather large man and a shiny Bösendorfer grand piano. On May 17, 1966, the job was completed, and Lou and his piano moved out of El Cerrito, hearth and home, into this small room in Sonoma redwood country. On the concrete-and-brick foundation, Lou inscribed the words of St. John: "Disquietude is always vanity, for it serves no good."

Disquietude, alas, would be a chronic condition of Morningstar Ranch in the days ahead.

While Lou was at the *Chronicle*, another event triggered his growing appreciation of the trends ripping through the 1960s. The San Francisco rock scene was about to explode. Some of its sparkplugs like Paul Kantner, Marty Balin and Jorma Kaukonen of the Jefferson Airplane and Jerry Garcia of the Grateful Dead, had started out as folkies, only to be dazzled by the Beatles and the electric conversion of Bob Dylan. The Dead were also mesmerized by Ken Kesey, author and crazed inventor of the Acid Test, an event combining rock music, dancing, wild lights, projected images and ample quantities of LSD to heighten the experience. The music was getting louder, longer winded, depoliticized, more eclectic in its sources and more experimental in its forms.

Inevitably someone had to come up with the idea of showcasing the emerging San Francisco counterculture in one concise package—and so, the Dead, Big Brother and the Holding Company, and other San Francisco bands were hired to play at the three-night Trips Festival Jan. 21–23 at Longshoremen's Hall, only blocks from the tourist traps on Fisherman's Wharf. Augustus Owsley Stanley III, the soon-to-be-famous acid king, helped fund the fest while fueling it with some of his high-grade, homemade chemicals. Bill Graham, who had been the business manager of the satirical San Francisco Mime Troupe, signed on as producer and publicist.

In the latter role, his natural target was the largest newspaper in Northern California, the *Chronicle*—and he paid several daily visits to the paper's editorial offices. Graham found two sets of sympathetic ears in particular—Ralph Gleason and Lou Gottlieb. Alone among San Francisco's jazz critics, if not the nation's, Gleason had made the leap to rock well before rock criticism became a profession. More and more, he was using his widely read "On the Town" jazz column to encourage young rock musicians in the Bay Area and beyond, and the Trips

Festival got a sympathetic plug from him on Jan. 7. As for Lou, he was assigned to meet with some of the organizers—photographer Stewart Brand (later the author of *The Whole Earth Catalog*), composer and San Francisco Tape Center co-founder Ramon Sender, the synthesizer inventor Don Buchla, and Open Theatre founder Ben Jacopetti—at a press conference, and he was knocked out by the idea. Lou devoted his first (and only) "World of Music" column to the Trips Jan. 18, wildly endorsing it with no questions asked. "If I were to tell you that an event of major significance in the history of religion is going to take place in this City of Saint Francis this weekend," he wrote, "you would say, 'Lou, you stayed out of work too long.' And if I were to tell you that an event of major significance in the history of the arts is going to take place simultaneously, you would pat my hand and say, 'Drink this glass of warm milk slowly and try to get some rest.'" No publicist could have asked for more.

As it turned out, Lou wasn't that far off the mark. The Trips Festival *was* a major event in the history of the '60s. It crystallized the currents that were sweeping through the San Francisco underground, a combination of old-fashioned sock hops, new-fangled abstract light shows and extended-play rock music, with LSD as a liberating lubricant. It had the effect of launching the San Francisco sound, as well as the fabulously lucrative career of impresario Graham. It fused acid, rock and lights together indelibly in the minds of a growing number of disillusioned, rebellious American kids and rock concerts with light shows would become a staple everywhere.

It also celebrated something quite frightening to outsiders—anarchy. Do your own thing. Gleason, in his review of the festival, mused that the only evening which really worked was Saturday (the 22nd) when the music was top-notch. But the most vivid reporting was on the chaos of the event—the stoned anonymous blonde-haired girl who took off her blouse and danced bare-breasted with her partner, the young man who climbed an aluminum ladder and cracked an egg on a woman's head. The counterculture was off and running and it would achieve mushrooming publicity as the national press fell under its spell.

It also must have made an indelible impression upon Lou. The festival organizers, particularly Sender, became his friends, and he would take them up to Morningstar a few weeks later in March for a good look around, hiking and getting stoned in the country. All kinds of new ideas were fusing in his mind. The paternal urge and the "God-thirst" worked hand-in-hand with learning about contemplative Eastern religions, experiencing spiritual, musical, physical, sexual or pharmaceutical ecstasy—or just simply goofing off. Morningstar Ranch would be an ideal place to fan these flames.

1966 was a marvelous time to be at Morningstar. Around Easter time, having been denied camping access to Mt. Tamalpais in Marin County, Ramon Sender remembered his visit to Morningstar in March and Lou's kind offer to his new friends that they could stay there if they wanted to get out of the city. He asked Lou if he could camp at Morningstar and Lou had no objection. Thus, Sender was the first Morningstar resident—and by June, Ben and Rain Jacopetti, Stewart Brand, several other artistic types and their families, eight in all, were living in the Morningstar houses while Lou set up housekeeping in his studio.

That first year, Lou put in a lot of work at the piano, practicing as much as 36 hours a week, playing mostly the music of Bach and Mozart. His reading agenda went into overdrive; books of almost every religion bought or borrowed from the Pacific School of Religion library in Berkeley, every issue of the Psychedelic Review, George Ohsawa's teachings on the Zen Macrobiotic diet. He would go home to the straight life in El Cerrito on the weekends and spend the weekdays at Morningstar, a rustic "office" of sorts. He grew his hair long, adding a black bushy beard so that he took on the imposing yet gentle appearance of a hippie patriarch.

As a group, he and his new friends would read aloud from various religious and psychedelic texts every night, taking group acid trips, reveling in the beautiful natural surroundings. Turned on by the teachings of Ohsawa, they once went on a ten-day macrobiotic diet during which they ate nothing but brown rice and tea. One day, Lou and two women residents were practicing yoga in the verdant northwest corner of the ranch and they experienced what Lou described as "an ecstatic shower of golden particles of light," a dazzling religious experience he had been seeking.

It was a time when Lou was increasingly seeking knowledge of God in whatever form, and one cannot doubt that his piano work—particularly in Bach, who spent most of his life constructing hundreds of musical monuments to the Almighty—was closely linked with that search. And with that search came a gradual revelation. He saw that others needed his land as a sanctuary from the frantic rat race as badly as he did.

He hated the practice of collecting rent on God's land, and he could not bear the idea of evicting people. So then, he eventually decided that he would never ask anyone to leave Morningstar Ranch. It would become "land to which access is denied no one."

With his religious readings fresh in mind, Lou developed a philosophy around the idea of accessible land. "Exclusive ownership of land is original sin," he would write, "and man commits original sin when he slices up his Mother Earth's 'sweet flowing breast' in order to buy and sell the pieces."

It was not a new idea in world history; Lou claimed that Islam had cities of refuge and there was a commune in Hawaii where people who had violated the taboos could come and repair without fear of persecution. But Morningstar Ranch was a dangerously radical idea for America, where private property is almost a national birthright.

"Something very unique was discovered there, truthfully," Lou said in 1978. "One of the most difficult things to do is to figure out how to juxtapose human forms. Who should live next door to whom? Now in the world at large, in the straight life, it is determined by how to maximize the net in the rent.

"It's my impression that there is a more creative way of juxtaposing human forms, and that is, to take a piece of land and never tell anybody to split. And what you succeed in doing then is building a tribe, because there is a proper set of coordinates on the earth's surface for every human being. Perhaps it has to do with magnetic currents or something. But I mean, if you really want to be healthy, you gotta live in the proper set of coordinates, the right place—and you can't find the right place because most of them got No Trespassing signs upon them.

"Very interesting things happen when you take a piece of land and never tell anybody to split. You gotta sit there sometimes a long time before the place builds a tribe. But it will build a tribe, and you will find that amongst the people who stay on that land voluntarily, a curious interpersonal relationship emerges which is a family sort but more intense. It doesn't have the allergies that develop in nuclear family relationships."

That first year, however, was not one for building of tribes—not yet at least. It gets cold in the coastal mountains at night when winter comes around, and by November, many of the original eight had left—the Jacopettis back to Berkeley, the Brands to New Mexico. Carried away by their religious studies, there was talk among the remaining guests about turning Morningstar into a Hindu ashram, affiliating it with one in India. But Lou was content to let the ranch drift along in peaceful contentment.

In November, though, seven young hippies came up from Haight-Ashbury, having heard about Lou's ranch and the house policy of letting anyone stay on the land. Two months later, four more showed up. By this time, Lou had fallen into a state of total beatific acceptance, convinced that he was just a vehicle for God's decisions on the land. He let them stay and quite unintentionally, he found himself on the cutting edge of social history.

Chapter Twelve

Much has been written of the heyday of Haight-Ashbury and its high noon year, 1967. It has become a touchstone for a whole era's worth of events that flicked past us with enormous speed. Merchandisers have cleaned up on its artifacts; the Republican party continues to run against it to this day. Many ex-hippies look back upon the era with a mixture of longing and embarrassment, many of today's kids openly wish that they had been alive then. Few, however, have managed to come to grips with the most radical implications of the whole experiment—not the drugs, not the free love, not the music; rather, the whole idea of questioning the validity and goals of the American Dream. But Lou Gottlieb, a 43-year-old convert to the movement that flippantly vowed never to trust anyone over 30, jumped with glee into just about all the Haight's fashions, fads, facets, intellectual pretensions and hedonistic thrills. It would be a long period for Lou, lasting at least until 1979—and even after that, the Haight left its mark on Lou for the rest of his life.

The most serious, committed activists were the Diggers, a faction of intellectual hippies that broke off from the San Francisco Mime Troupe sometime in 1966. Named after a 17th century sect of English mavericks who distributed free food to the people, the Diggers were in full rebellion against middle-class values and goals. After corning down from the highs of psychedelic drugs, they questioned why the tripper would want to go back to the suburban conformity of the straight life.

They tried to come up with increasingly ingenious ways of surviving in the city without a plan for material success, on the premise that the man with nothing has nothing to lose. The Haight was their theater, and while they could, they played it with tendentious zeal.

Emulating the original Diggers, they made their first big splash in October of 1966, handing out leaflets that promised free daily food for all in the Panhandle, a long narrow strip of parkland that borders the Haight-Ashbury district. "Free Food Everyday Free Food. It's Free Because It's Yours!" the leaflets cried. No matter that the bread was a day old, the vegetables and meat discards from local grocery stores and the city produce market; the Diggers figured out how to keep the dole going for almost a year and reaped a windfall of publicity. They also opened a "store" called Free Frame of Reference where they gave away clothing and household items. They declared money to be dead in the post-scarcity age, in which America was so prosperous that hippies could live off the surplus; they even held a Death of Money parade that December to make the point.

The Diggers and other factions of the growing alternative communities in the Haight and Berkeley hit upon the idea of a Gathering of the Tribes, or a Human Be-In Jan. 14, 1967 in Golden Gate Park's Polo Field, a spacious, tree-surrounded lawn tucked away from the park's main roads. It would be a mass gathering of at least 20,000 kids, dressed in outrageously colorful garb, who came mostly to mingle, get stoned in the open, revel in the oneness of a generation, and only incidentally listen to a parade of guest speakers and San Francisco's finest rock acts. Politics was out. Left-minded speakers like Jerry Rubin were ignored, and even Timothy Leary, touched by the leaderless spectacle before him, could only utter his by-now-familiar mantra, "Turn on, tune in, drop out," before getting quickly off the stage. The Diggers handed out free turkey sandwiches, Owsley supplied a batch of his strongest acid yet, no one was arrested, and Allen Ginsberg led a clean-up brigade afterwards that left the Polo Field spotless.

Once word of this spectacular event spread through the omnipresent national media, San Francisco would be the destination of every alienated, fun-seeking, rebellious kid with access to a VW van in the country that summer. Where would they all stay? How could even the generous, tolerant Haight support a gathering of anywhere from 50,000 to 200,000? The Diggers' thoughts began to turn outside the city, toward the country where food could be raised to support the invasion, where self-sufficient communes could be formed. They had heard about Lou's benign experiment in Sonoma County, so they sent a delegation of seven to Morningstar on March 14 to talk to the bearded would-be classical pianist. The Diggers offered to work on the ranch's apple orchard and to start a vegetable garden elsewhere on the property in return for a percentage of the crop.

Lou was in Golden Gate Park for the Be-In, and he thought that he recognized in the gathering the same mellow, anything-is-permissible spiritual aura that shone throughout Morningstar. He thought about the Diggers' proposal for a couple of days and decided, why not? Never mind that the earliest apple harvest would not be edible until August. Never mind that the San Francisco scene was starting to receive tons of publicity in the straight press. Lou would trust God to make the right decision on this land—or at least that was his rationale.

Even after Lou gave the go-ahead, he didn't know until much later that the Diggers had posted a sign in their free store giving out the address to the "Digger Farm" near Graton. Thus informed, Diggers and hippies from the Haight started to descend upon Morningstar, and Lou, of course, could not bear to tell them to leave. Various unused structures from the egg ranch were being pulled down to supply raw material for constructing lean-tos and makeshift homes for the new arrivals. A list was circulated in March by the Communications Company around the Haight asking for additional building materials and supplies for the "Diggers Farm." Whether Lou wanted it or not, he now was the proud owner of a hippie commune. "I never set out to live in a commune," Lou wrote in his autobiography. "One simply developed where I was staying."

Everything that was simmering in the new counterculture came to a boil in the summer of 1967. The war in Vietnam intensified, with no end in sight; the draft threatened the safety of every able-bodied young male in America. The non-violent civil rights movement that Pete Seeger and Bob Dylan sang about was in a state of shell shock as one inner city after another fell to the torch. Arguments between parents and their enlightened, disillusioned children increased—over politics, draft dodging, long hair, sexual freedom, drugs, rock music, middle-class conformity—as did peer pressure among the young. By its collective action that year, the Establishment unwittingly provided some of the most effective advertising for the alternative lifestyle that the Haight seemed to offer.

In the straight press, the subject of hippies became one of the hottest stories of the year. It made great copy for publishers out to sell papers; with liberal doses of sex, drugs, color, the dreams of the young and the worries of their parents, everyone would be hooked. Probably the most famous and influential piece of the year came from ex-LSD-tripper Henry Luce's *Time Magazine*, whose July 7 issue led with a glowing cover story, "The Hippies: Philosophy of a Subculture."

"Hippies preach altruism and mysticism, honesty, joy and non-violence," *Time's* writers rhapsodized. "Its disciples are mostly young and generally thoughtful Americans who are unable to reconcile themselves to the stated values and implicit contradictions of contemporary Western society and have become internal emigres, seeking individual liberation through means as various as drug use, total withdrawal from the economy, and the quest for individual identity." Which is not a bad assessment of the attitudes floating through the Haight in those days; even some hardcore hippies were impressed by *Time's* insight.

As the long, liberally illustrated article moves into its home stretch, it focuses on a "major new development in the hippie world," the rural commune. And whose commune did it zero in upon? None other than Lou Gottlieb's Morningstar Ranch, where the proprietor supposedly had his band of hippies hard at work ("rarest of all hippie trips") growing vegetables for the Diggers. Lou claimed that he wasn't around when *Time* correspondent Robert Jones visited the ranch, but Ramon Sender gave him a guided tour. Jones writes about neat rows of cabbages, turnips, lettuce and tomatoes, naked girls lounging in the buffalo grass, a sheepdog playing with the children. According to *Time's* editors, he even attended a yoga session with the residents, during which he was the only clothed participant. The Morningstar section concludes with the observation that Lou's commune is "perhaps the most hopeful development in the hippie philosophy to date."

The accompanying color photo says it even more graphically. We behold an idyllic Sonoma County hillside, with bright blue sky, big trees and yellowed tall grass. In the foreground is an open A-frame structure, two clothed curly-haired hippie boys, and one completely nude hippie girl with long blonde hair. With a barely suppressed leer, the caption says, "It's hip to unzip at Morning Star Commune, where the formula for living is do what you want, wear or not wear what you want." Yep, that did it. When *Time's* article hit the stands, Morningstar suddenly became a hot destination for countless starry-eyed hippies and more than a few curious tourists and voyeurs. Lou never kept track of how many people were camped at one time on his land-to-which-access-is-denied-no-one, but the traffic really picked up from *Time's* estimate of about 30 to 50 residents. Psychedelically-painted cars, some from out of state, would be parked for quite a distance on Graton Road leading up to the ranch. Most would just visit for the day, revel in the do-your-own thing freedom, do a little dope, perhaps join the nudists in wardrobe-free splendor, and then take off for other Bay Area countercultural landmarks.

Alex, his mother, and his father, who was on his way to Tokyo to present a paper on hydraulic power, visited Morningstar once during its peak of activity. "Lou was fully in his role as reigning guru and executive hippie," says Alex, shaking his head as he recalls walking around a scene that must have been totally disorienting to his European parents. More than that, Alex's father accidentally stepped into a wasps' nest, and the swarming insects sent him to the hospital, nearly killing him. "I took that as an omen," concludes Alex. "We didn't belong there."

The always-sympathetic Ralph Gleason visited his old friend Lou at the ranch on August 11 and devoted his "On The Town" column in the *Chronicle* three days later to what he saw. "Gottlieb Lane," which earlier surveyors had named the dirt road that goes from the bottom to the top of the hill, was blocked off at Graton Road by a huge wooden cross—and Gleason wandered up to the top of the hill under a broiling sun. There he saw several structures, including Lou's studio which contained little more than a shelf of books, a cot, a desk, and his grand piano. There were tents made from blankets, sleeping bags spread out in the brush, mattresses placed across tree stumps in the ranch's major redwood grove. A sign tacked on a redwood tree nearby read "Eros Cathedral—House of Faith"; one of the old hen houses had "Jesus is the Way" lettered upon a wall; and an older resident was constructing a three-room house of his own in another tree grove. He and Lou would walk by a deeply tanned naked girl and not even take much notice; although Lou said he didn't accept nudity fully for himself until 1968, most of his "guests" indulged at will.

Lou himself appears "resplendent in full beard and glowing in health." "We are running a pilot study in survival," Gleason quotes Lou. "The hippies are the first wave of the technologically unemployed." Lou goes on to compare his al fresco commune to earlier communal experiments like Brook Farm, Oneida, and New Harmony, carrying on the tradition of intentional community. "The problem is to get a piece of land and see who it attracts," he adds.

Gleason came away enraptured by the place. "In the flower-scented air of the hill," he concludes, "even the hippie panhandler seemed sweet, if sad and somewhat cynical and unable to dampen the suspicion that this 'pilot study' may be more important than we think."

In the first half or so of 1967, life still was generally quite sweet on the ranch. But trouble began brewing for Lou as early as March 25. On that day, Lou was tipped off by a furloughed inmate from Sonoma County Jail that Morningstar was about to be subjected to a drug bust. He had been sent by the police to look for evidence of drugs but instead, finding himself enchanted, he warned everybody of the imminent bust, giving them time to get rid of any contraband. A week later, April Fool's Day, the Sonoma County narcotics squad came, searched everyone's possessions but found nothing. But this was the opening shot of what would turn into a series of daily visits by the police.

There were no restrictions whatsoever at Morningstar, no rules other than no campfires (this being a high-risk fire area). There were no assignments of work detail at the ranch; everyone pretty much fell into what they enjoyed doing the most. This was a central tenet of Lou's philosophy on life, that no one should be required to do anything that he or she does not feel suited for since somewhere, somebody has a knack for it or gets a kick out of doing it. Some of the residents were resourceful gardeners; that coupled with the rich redwood-mixed soil resulted in a very productive vegetable garden.

The ranch attracted architecture students from UC Berkeley who would hold classes there on Sunday afternoons with the goal of designing structures to fit the needs of the ranch's inhabitants. They even drew up plans and constructed a model for a modern mess hall that would be made from materials from the existing hen houses on the property. It never got built, though, for the ranch's freewheeling lifestyle didn't exactly encourage planning or for that matter, any hard sustained work.

Glenn said that he visited Morningstar frequently during this period, perhaps feeling some kinship between himself and the young dropouts. After all, Glenn was a free spirit and former hitchhiker himself who loathed clothing, grew a beard and went barefoot long before some of these kids were born. He also agreed wholeheartedly with Lou's anti-private property philosophy.

Yet Glenn had to conclude that the "pilot study" was doomed precisely because it had no structure. "Some of them were industrious; they would work the organic gardens and stuff like that," he remembered. "Then the others would sit down on the plants and smoke weed and destroy the garden. All the leech types would hang around in the parking lot and get you to pay for parking (about $2.00!).

"Lou never participated in anything," Glenn continued. "Even when the police started coming and giving him a hard time, he wouldn't even take his money out of the bank. They would attach his bank accounts for the fines. I said to him, 'God, Lou, at least put it in a box someplace and bury it, but don't leave it in the bank for the state to get.' And he said no, he wouldn't act in any way. He was completely passive."

Since no one could be asked to leave, inevitably the promise of a no-restrictions lifestyle at Morningstar attracted some low-life elements. The trouble began when a pack of five winos who got tired of hassling tourists in the Haight came to Morningstar, where they nearly turned Lou's innocent experiment into a hellhole. They had outlaw names like Nevada, Gypsy, Chief, TW and Crazy Annie; they would harass the peaceful hippies and panhandle visitors in the parking lot near Lou's studio for wine money. Lou, who detested alcoholics of whatever stripe, described them as "loud, profane, pugnacious, egomaniacal, you name it...no self-respect, just terrible people."

Eventually Gypsy went too far, pulling a knife on a shopkeeper in nearby Graton. Lou's benign tolerance was shattered, and he and all the regular Morningstar residents held a meeting—their first ever—while the winos were out swimming in the Russian River one day. They naturally came to the conclusion that since this was Lou's property, he should be the one to ask the winos to leave.

When they came back, Lou steeled himself and ordered them off the ranch. Amazingly they took it gracefully and said they'd be gone in a couple of days. But the next day, Gypsy was back, begging Lou to let him stay.

At first, Lou stood his ground; Gypsy had to go. But then, strange things started to happen to him. He developed a headache, broke into cold sweats, felt mild nausea and had fits of "uncontrollable weeping." His interpretation? It was God's will that no one be ordered off his ranch. If he denied sanctuary to anyone, it would cease to become a sanctuary for himself or anyone else. "That was the last time I ever asked anyone to leave Morningstar Ranch," he wrote.

But Gypsy and his inebriated gang weren't the main threats to Morningstar. Even though Morningstar seemed to be located out in the wilderness, Lou had neighbors—and these neighbors were not exactly fellow hippies. Many were middle-class, retired, or otherwise hard-working folk who were finally able to afford a country home far from the madness of the city. Then their tranquility is shattered when this semi-retired musician next door has a mid-life crisis and becomes

Uncle Lou to an ever-changing mob of hippies, druggies, nudists, crazies, winos, and who knows what else.

Mainly it was the nudity that got Lou in hot water. "Nudity will freak out straight life quicker than anything else in the world, far quicker than dope, far quicker even than rip off," said Lou. "And there were some hippies up there who didn't have a wardrobe." Nudity visible from public highways is illegal, and if one looked up the hillside from Graton Road, some naked hippies could conceivably come into view.

That Gypsy told his victim in Graton he was living up on the ranch with Lou didn't help Morningstar's image either. Neither did the dope scene; a ranch-wide bout with STP one night produced an evening full of whoops, crazed laughter, shrieks, and other sounds guaranteed to interrupt a night's sleep. There were no toilets or washrooms on the open property; the hippies were left entirely to their own devices. There were incidents of ripoff, starting with the capitalists in the parking lot. There were moments of freaky humor, like the time a stoned hippie girl thought that a pair of prized Arabian horses next door were having trouble seeing through their forelocks. So, she took a pair of scissors and cut their forelocks into neatly trimmed bangs. Needless to say, the owner of the horses was not amused.

Lewis Yablonsky, a sociologist from San Fernando Valley State College (now Cal State University, Northridge), paints a much darker picture of Morningstar in his book, *The Hippie Trip*, than either *Time* or Ralph Gleason. He visited Morningstar during roughly the same period as Gleason, but noticed instead of a rural nirvana, a palpable atmosphere of fear. People were wandering about or laying around on the grounds with expressions of "grimness" or outright "hostility" on their faces. A four-year-old child was stumbling about unattended, reeking of urine and fecal matter; his mother was said to be freaked out on acid somewhere in the woods. An 18-year-old girl told Yablonsky that she had been raped by two Black men the first day she arrived at the ranch, and no one had bothered to call the police. He heard sounds of gunfire on the property; luckily no one was hurt.

True, everyone loved Uncle Lou—who was in Los Angeles when Yablonsky visited the ranch—but there was a depressing sense of indifference throughout the place; almost everyone seemed totally absorbed into their own head trips. Admittedly the tense scene may have been a temporary condition, although the residents whom Yablonsky interviewed said that this was a typical state of affairs around the commune.

In late July of 1967, about ten or fifteen Black men from the Fillmore district had noticed a sign at the Diggers' Black free store giving directions to the "Digger Farm"—and they went up to check it out. Upon grasping the implications of total freedom, they moved into the big upper house on the property and began terrorizing the commune, getting loaded on booze and ordering people to leave the house. They were led by a large bully named Mystery who exuded a self-styled, intimidating form of charisma. For a couple of weeks at least, Mystery's word was law around Morningstar, even superseding that of Lou, who really didn't want to be bothered.

Eventually, on August 12, a group of Hell's Angels were called to pay Mystery and his friends a visit and flush them out of the house. The gentle experiment in land-to-which-access-is-denied-no-one was running headlong into the violent age that spawned it.

And the neighbors had had more than enough of it. Ed Hochuli, a crew-cut assistant to the president of Sonoma State College (now Sonoma State University), lived on an adjacent property and he was appalled by the hippie lifestyle and frightened by the potential hazards of unsupervised campfires. He took it upon himself to rid the Graton-Occidental area of this eyesore, and he and some likeminded neighbors went to the Sonoma County District Attorney's office to get some action.

Hochuli was nothing if not persistent, collecting 396 signatures from Sonoma County's registered voters protesting Morningstar's existence as a public nuisance and health hazard. The state's building codes were invoked regarding the ramshackle structures scattered around the ranch. Violations of the fire laws, despite Lou's sole rule of no campfires, were cited.

On July 1, Lou was arrested for operating an organized camp without a license. Out immediately on bail, he entered a plea of innocent on July 11, protesting that Morningstar was anything but an organized camp, that it just materialized with no leadership at all from him or anyone else. On September 15, Lou's lawyer Richard Wertheimer had him plead "nolo contendre" to the charges, and Lou was put on probation and ordered to clean up the ranch and provide proper sanitary facilities in a year's time. That wasn't enough to satisfy Hochuli and the neighbors, so the Superior Court issued a Temporary Restraining Order which became a Permanent Injunction prohibiting anyone other than Lou from staying on the property overnight.

At this point, the Morningstar dream had degenerated into the theater of the absurd. Sheriff's deputies would make visits at almost all hours to the ranch, reading the injunction to various residents of the commune and returning 24 hours later to see if they had left. The Border Patrol would march into the ranch looking for Canadian runaways on the grounds that since the California border was only six miles to the west (the Pacific coastline) they were within their jurisdiction.

Lou tried one legal gambit after another, no doubt straining even his considerable ingenuity. At one point, he even claimed that Morningstar was up for sale and that residents were interested buyers looking around to see whether they liked it. In case anyone tried to take Lou up on his offer, his asking price on the land was $7 million! But the Establishment bore down hard, and on October 7, Lou was ordered to make citizen's arrests of 15 Morningstar campers or pay a $500-a-day fine for as long they remained on the property and possibly face jail for contempt of court. On the advice of Wertheimer, Lou complied, at first asking the 15 to leave and when they refused, had them arrested for trespassing.

Lou's legal defense began to collapse. Upon visiting Morningstar and determining that the charges of unsanitary facilities were essentially true, Wertheimer withdrew from the case, and after a while, his successor Rex Sater did likewise, concluding that Morningstar was "essentially indefensible." At this point, rather than find another attorney, Lou decided to be his own lawyer, spending days in the Law Library of Sonoma County poring over volumes of litigation. It left him with, if nothing else, a lifelong distaste for the American legal system.

The charges against the hippies whom Lou "arrested" were dismissed in November, but the exhausted landowner finally gave in and spent $7,000 to have communal lavatory and shower facilities built not far from the picturesque well near the parking lot. "I always thought that an entrenching tool was a proper sanitary facility," said Lou. "You bury the shit. 'Proper sanitary facilities' is meaningless unless you know how many people are there." But they were there, and for good measure, they never worked adequately anyway.

As if Lou needed any more distractions to keep him from practicing the piano—his practice time had fallen to about 20 hours a week in 1967—by the fall of 1967, he had another; a full-blown affair. Somehow, he had managed to resist, for the most part, the temptation of being around dozens of nubile, often attractive, naked teenage girls on the ranch. But even celibate visitors to the ranch from Hare Krishna chapters were having a tough time keeping their libidos dormant under these conditions—and Lou, too, would fall.

That summer, he began to notice the enticing presence of an 18-year-old flower child named Rena Blumberg. In a way, her story is typical of many a pampered suburban teen of that era. Having grown up in posh Westchester County, New York, the daughter of wealthy parents, Rena dropped out of high school to come West for the Be-In—and eventually she found herself at let-it-all-hang-out Morningstar. There she seemed to find meaning in her life for the first time, and she would become known as Rena Morningstar.

Lou recalled seeing her at a communal dinner in the lower house and many times afterwards sitting on the well—naked to the world. "She looked like a Yemenite, with frizzy black hair, lovely quick expression, and a beautiful bod," recalled Lou. For Lou, Rena brought back memories of his political days at UCLA; she could have been any young activist girl then. He became infatuated with her, and in November, exhausted by his legal skirmishes, he asked her out. He took her to a motel that night, but ravaged with guilt, he couldn't perform. But it was only a temporary setback, for Rena soon began visiting Lou regularly in his studio.

It was an unlikely steady liaison in the first place—Rena being a year and a half older than Lou's own daughter—and on top of that, a tempestuous relationship at that. There were frequent times when Lou would just throw her out of his studio and drive her to nearby communes like Rancho Olompali in Novato or the Wheeler Ranch in the Coleman Valley. His meticulous diary, a remnant of the straight life, would record the exact dates of their breakups and reunions at a clip of almost once a month in 1968. Each time, in the classic manner. Lou would swear to himself that his little fling was over, done with, but a few days later, he would do an about-face after paroxysms of jealousy. And all through this period, Lou would continue to return to El Cerrito on weekends to his wife and children, who though puzzled by Lou's increasingly far-out lifestyle, were unaware of Lou's mad love affair with Rena.

However, Rena definitely had a good head on her shoulders, otherwise Lou probably would not have stuck with her for so long. She reinforced Lou's faith in his steadily evolving theories about the evils of private property—and together, they would come up with the "Open Land Movement," otherwise known as the "Morningstar Philosophy." By 1968, the always voluble and articulate Lou was in demand as a speaker at various clubs, colleges, conventions, and other gatherings, talking about his "pilot study" and its implications.

Frequently Rena would join in and offer her views, which sounded mighty convincing coming from a genuine flower child. She also helped devise a survey which she and Lou passed around to the diminished number of residents at Morningstar in February 1968. In March, Rena moved into Lou's 12 X 20-foot studio—and their collaborations, fights, and frequent sessions of wild sex continued full steam ahead.

Amidst all the tumult, the hedonist/philosopher of Morningstar also became a film actor late in 1967. That summer, Andre Philippe had suggested to his friend, writer/producer Paul Mazursky, that Lou would be perfect in the supporting role of a guru in a new Peter Sellers film, *I Love You, Alice B. Toklas*. Eager to try his hand at something else new, Lou went down to Los Angeles to audition, and aided by his bushy black beard and by-now-instinctive familiarity with guru-think, he got the part.

The film is one of Hollywood's better attempts to cash in on the Love Generation, where Sellers plays an uptight nebbish of a lawyer who leaves his bride and the straight life at the altar for a series of mis-adventures in the counterculture with a beautiful hippie chick (Leigh Taylor-Young). Right before the opening credits, we see Lou in his white robes strolling with a pair of hippies, babbling about flowers and self-knowledge in a strangely disembodied voice. Later he urges his flock to turn on straight life, make them "love junkies."

In his most extended scene, Lou and the newly-converted Sellers stroll beside the waves at Leo Carrillo State Beach near Malibu—Lou gliding serenely along doing his guru rap, Sellers comically stumbling on driftwood, freezing his toes in the cold November surf. At one point, Lou just can't help himself; he virtually cracks up after one of Sellers' lines, swallowing his reply. Then Lou drops all pretenses of acting and reverts to his professorial act, ad-libbing a story about a holy man in India as they fade behind a rock. It's a funny scene, very much in keeping with the film's gentle pokes at the excesses of the counterculture.

Lou had a ball working with Sellers—riding to the on-location site in a limousine with the great comic busting Lou up with his Indian accent, watching Sellers improvise the hilarious physical business on the spot. But Lou also experienced all the hard work that goes into acting, getting the lines down and improvising some, enduring the vast gaps of dead time waiting around the set in between takes. After two run-throughs of the beach scene, director Hy Averback, seeing Lou's inexperience before the cameras, came up and started to say, "Now Lou…" whereupon Sellers cut him short with the assurance, "He's got it." In any case, Lou didn't return to Hollywood until 1973, when he briefly reprised his guru character in another Mazursky film, *Blume in Love*.

Meanwhile at Morningstar, conditions continued to deteriorate as 1968 went on. Despite the new lavatories, sanitary facilities continued to be inadequate. Dirty dishes piled up in the mess hall, the sinks were clogged, many refugees from the Haight refused to do any work to help out.

The residents had to endure continuing visits from the Sonoma County sheriff's department trying to enforce the Permanent Injunction against camping, nudity, trash dumping, campfires, and trespassing. Many grew tired of the constant legal hassles, and they split to new communes in New Mexico where the land was wide open, and the peyote ran wild. Lou's fines to the county for allowing the hippies on his land were eating into his stash of cash from the Limeliters years.

Lou was still hard at work at the piano, mainly the Bach partitas and some Mozart but also studying Chopin waltzes, Beethoven sonatas, and occasionally taking a piano lesson in Berkeley. But he would be spending more and more time thinking of new legal strategies to save his open land, as well as making love and quarreling with his flower child.

It all came to a head on Sept. 3, 1968, when Lou was found guilty of contempt of court for violating the injunction and was sentenced to 15 days in the Sonoma County jail. He was also fined $1,500, which brought his total of fines for 1968 up to a whopping $15,500. It was a turbulent scene at the courthouse that day, for Don McCoy, owner of Rancho Olompali, came to Lou's defense demanding to be heard. Upon being ejected from the courtroom, he stood outside in a corridor and loudly sang, "God bless the people and God bless Lincoln F. Mahan" (the presiding judge in the case). For his antics, he was sentenced to five days in jail, which he served with Lou in the same cell.

Undoubtedly jail was a harrowing and humbling experience for Lou, shooting new messages of fear through his system. Mostly he feared the "dingbats"—truly disturbed inmates who would occasionally be locked in the same cell. Other than Lou and Don, there were 11 other prisoners in that cell, ten of them serving time on dope charges. Unrepentant as ever, once Lou got out, he would write a letter to the *Santa Rosa Press-Democrat* in which he recommended the use of open land as a place to house hippie violators of the taboos rather than the Sonoma County jail, thus saving the taxpayers some money.

If anything, though, jail drove Lou even further into the counterculture than ever. The day he got out, he "married" Rena after a torrid sexual reunion in the Morningstar apple orchard, performing the ceremony himself. Never mind that he was still married to Dolly; Lou never believed in divorce.

Following the latest countercultural line, his thoughts gravitated more and more toward India. He read Paramahamsa Yogananda's *Autobiography of a Yogi*, learning about the relationship between a guru and chela. At a party in Haight-Ashbury, Lou and Rena met a Bengali ashram head named Ashok Fakir who was organizing a four-week group trip to India in November 1968. The trip was due to begin in only ten days, but they made a snap decision to pay the $3,000 fare for two to search for their own bonafide guru. As far as Dolly knew then, Lou was traveling alone—and on Nov. 3, after stops in New York and London, they landed in Bombay. The U.S. presidential election took place a couple of days later, but Lou's mind was thousands of miles away; indeed, his once formidable left wing had nearly atrophied completely in the heat of the counterculture.

They visited the city of Madras, an ashram at nearby Pondicherry, and a model city of the future called Auroville; they took in the heart-wrenching scenes of human misery of Calcutta. And it was in a Calcutta hotel that Lou, upon the recommendation of other God-thirsty, globe-hopping Americans like Don McCoy, came into the presence of one Chiranjiva Roy. Once a beggar, Chiranjiva had become a guru preaching the coming of a new era, the age of Shiva's Omnipotent Imagination, and he claimed to be the Creator of the Universe in Human Form.

Incredible as it may seem, Dr. Louis Gottlieb, product of a Western academic education, believed him. Lou had suddenly seen another spiritual light; indeed, his imagination lit up, in his words, like Copenhagen's Tivoli Gardens. "It's Him! It's Him! By God, it's Him!" he reportedly exclaimed—and from this point onward, Lou and other disciples would always refer to Chiranjiva as "Father."

When Lou got back to America, all he could talk about was Father. A month after Lou returned from India, his natural father died of a heart attack on Dec. 23 at the age of 87, leaving a big emotional gap which this surrogate from India was only too happy to fill. One didn't need to do good material deeds to save the world; all that was necessary is to love Father. Chiranjiva would flatter his disciples; he told Lou that he was Moses, and he dubbed other genuflecting American members of the cult "The Emperor" or "Chitraratha, the King of the Gandharvas" or "Hari, the Lord of Yoga." In turn, in his autobiography, Lou wrote, "I felt like soon all the Jews would see me as I saw him, a natural hierarchy would fall in like a squad of infantrymen in close order drill and march off to a future free of ignorance and greed...One has the feeling of being in a cosmic drama, for the betterment of all and the punishment of evil, in which one creates the script, acts in the drama, and watches the show simultaneously."

By this time, one imagines that Lou's friends and family—if they hadn't thought so already—felt that Lou had really gone off the deep end. Grover Sales remembered running into Lou around this time after not seeing him for many years.

"Lou was very deep into his New Age mysticism period where he had gone into all kinds of extra-sensory perceptions," he said. "He was sounding like an older edition of Rennie Davis and these revolutionary mystics. I didn't buy any of it, and still don't."

Yet even in the 1980s, Lou could write, "I feel sorry for anyone who has no guru. I feel sorry for anyone who has never believed another human being who says, 'I am the Creator of the Universe in Human Form.' Someone you know instinctively is much smarter than you, much more evolved spiritually. Someone whose advice you seek. Someone in whose presence you feel safe. A wonderful Father."

After many months of trying to enforce the injunction against Lou's "guests" at Morningstar, the county came in and bulldozed all the ramshackle structures and houses on the property to the ground, leaving only Lou's studio. "The county didn't want to; it (the ranch) was kind of entertaining for them," Lou said. "But finally, they had to." After this, only "the hardiest of the hardy" remained on the land, a handful of hardcore hippies who could put up with the al fresco conditions and constant harassment.

In May of 1969, Lou came up with the zaniest and most profound legal gambit yet in his effort to preserve beleaguered Morningstar Ranch. Acting on a suggestion by Joan Bransten, Lou decided to deed his ranch to God!

He marched into the office of Sonoma County recorder Herbert Snyder, who at first refused to record the deed. Only until after Lou had it notarized did Snyder throw up his hands and go through with the act.

"I didn't argue," he told a reporter from *United Press International.* "If he wanted to waste his money (all of $2.80), let him."

No longer could Sonoma County hold Lou responsible for providing sanitary facilities or keeping the hippies off his land. It was God's problem now, not Lou's. Nor was it Dolly Gottlieb's problem, for Lou had worked it out so that he traded his half-ownership of the El Cerrito house to Dolly in exchange for her half of Morningstar Ranch. However, Lou did say that he would continue to pay property taxes on God's land. "It's preposterous to pay taxes for God, but for God's sake, I'll pay them," he told UPI with a straight face.

Lou approached Justice Joseph A. Rattigan in the Law Library of the Santa Rosa Hall of Justice and prevailed upon him to compose a "Nature of the Controversy" draft. This chance meeting further convinced Lou that Divine Purpose was at work again regarding this land.

With rhetorical flourishes reminiscent of the writings of Timothy Leary, Lou set forth his case most passionately in an appellate brief delivered to the State Court of Appeals September 9, 1971. Some short excerpts from this lordly document will suffice:

"The earth is the mother of us all; and to pay rent will one day be understood as turning mother into a prostitute and hiring her services.

"Deeding land to God opens land-access-to-which-is-denied-no-one; land whereupon permission to live is not required; land from which no one may be ordered to depart; land on which God is the Casting Director assembling, juxtaposing and re-tribalizing those human forms He has chosen to help free Mother Earth from the ecologically lethal grasp of exclusive ownership; land on which life becomes an ongoing encounter for the mutual benefit of the participants who are abandoning materialistic goals and incentives...

"Deeding land to God can prepare refuge for the survivors should radioactive catastrophe accidentally strike an urban center...many of the surviving city dwellers will not feel safe anywhere but on God's land...

"Deeding land to God is for the defendant-appellant a ritualistic offering to the Divine, at once the pinnacle of deeply held religious convictions and the synthesis of primitive, medieval and contemporary devotional practice, fully protected by the free exercise clause of the First Amendment to the U.S. Constitution from legislative and judicial infringement.

"But, deeding land to God is superfluous, is it not? Since God created the universe, He certainly 'owns' his creations and does not require a grant deed to prove that ownership. I know that. You know that. Everybody knows that. Only the Superior Court of the State of California in and for the County of Sonoma, Departments 1, 3 and 4 does not know that."

Well, once word got around about that, an avaricious individual decided to put Lou's deed to the test. A woman from Phoenix, Arizona, Betty Penrose, sued God for $100,000 property damage in an Oakland court. It seems that God acted with "malice and ill will" when He struck her home with lightning on August 17, 1960. Now that God owned land in California, He had tangible assets and was liable for damages. Ms. Penrose also attached a $25,000 demand in punitive and exemplary damages because "the acts were committed with malice and ill will and with intent and design of injuring and oppressing the plaintiff." That'll teach Him never to do it again.

Then, to add to the loony atmosphere, one Paul Yerkes Bechtel, then an inmate of San Quentin, filed an answer to the suit. He said he was God.

The ensuing trial attracted international attention and had plenty of moments of weird humor, such as the arguments over which God was the grantee. "I remember when he (Lou) was taken to court about the Morningstar Ranch," recalled Grover Sales. "He had told the judge that he had deeded the property to God. The judge said, 'Which God is that?' And he pulled a quarter out of his pocket and said, 'That one there!'"

Finally Superior Court Judge Kenneth Eymann, with a perfectly straight face, ruled that God was unfit to own land in the State of California. He had no property rights, for the law requires that "the grantee must be a person, either natural or artificial, in existence at the time of the conveyance and capable of taking title." *Time Magazine*, which reported on the outcome in its July 20, 1970 issue with the misleading headline "God As Landlord," referred to Lou as a "rich, retired folk singer" who was so well off that he thought he could afford to give away some land. In any case, Judge Eymann gave Lou another 30 days to clean up the mess at Morningstar.

While all these legal shenanigans were going on, Lou and Rena decided to try to procreate, enthusiastically and often—and before long, Rena was pregnant. Rather than go to a hospital, having observed and helped at several births among hippie mothers, Lou would deliver the baby himself and on March 27, 1970, Lou's new son was born, tumbling headfirst onto the mattress in his studio. "Anyone who has missed witnessing or better participating in this indescribable miracle has missed the greatest show on earth," wrote Lou.

Right in line with the hippie mindset of the time, they named their child Vishnu—which is not too far-out when you consider that Grace Slick and Paul Kantner named their child "god." Later, Vishnu would understandably want to be called William or Bill, for he was constantly teased about his unusual name in the fourth grade, and he chose the plainest substitute possible. But for now, he would be named after the Son in the Hindu equivalent of the Father, Son and Holy Ghost trinity.

Lou never could find the courage to tell Dolly, his older son Tony and daughter Judith about Vishnu. They had seen Rena, and didn't like what they saw at all, but they still had no idea about Lou's tempestuous affair with her, let alone his "marriage" to her. As it turned out, Lou didn't have to make the announcement; it was done for him in a most embarrassingly public way. While Lou and Rena were attending a fund-raiser in San Francisco, a photographer from the *Chronicle* spotted Lou holding his five-month-old son and snapped a picture. The photo ran the next day in the paper, which circulates all over Northern California, and it reached a certain shocked household in the hills of El Cerrito. "Very bad form on my part," Lou admitted in his autobiography.

That shattered Lou's marriage once and for all, though there still was no divorce. Instead, the practical-minded Dolly drove out to Morningstar to have Lou sign some papers guaranteeing her financial interests and those of her children in case Lou was tempted to fritter away all his assets.

And there were more "financial eccentricities" to come. With a loan of $1,200 from former Limeliter lawyer Seymour Lazar, Lou got Chiranjiva out of India on a plane to San Francisco, and he was taken to Morningstar the next day. He enthralled the seated, stoned hippies in the Morningstar redwood grove with long raps on the holy book *Bhagavad Gita* and Lou, the showbiz mindset still not entirely out of his system, was sure his guru was the greatest entertainer who ever lived, "bigger than the Beatles," if given time and exposure. At least Lou was savvy enough to notice that Father would try to cut down previously cherished beliefs of his disciples with ridicule, not out of conviction but to break their attachments to them and thus cement his own links.

Father didn't get along well with Rena, though, after she dosed him with LSD in the middle of a serious spiritual rap. Nor did he approve of Lou's wild-eyed efforts to publicize his arrival in San Francisco, and a personal rift grew between guru and disciple that lasted for years, though Lou continued to worship Chiranjiva all through this time. Though apparently not out to get rich like other self-appointed messiahs, Chiranjiva kept himself busy acquiring eight American wives among the worshipping hippie women—all at once—and siring at least one child by each of them! Lou sometimes mused about emulating Father in this manner (shades of the obscure Limeliters single, "Seventeen Wives"), but practical considerations kept these thoughts under control for a change.

Don McCoy, whose even more irresponsible financial behavior had caused his family to appoint a conservator for his property (once a wealthy man, he had vowed to give away all his worldly goods), moved onto the ranch once his Rancho Olompali had been closed down. A new girlfriend of his from Los Angeles was a member of the Charles Manson gang, and she told Lou that anyone could visit the jailed cult leader (who was awaiting trial) if they had identification. Eager to get a glimpse of Evil itself, Lou decided to go down to the L.A. Hall of Justice and pay Charlie a visit.

Lou had in hand a letter of introduction which he presented to the three Manson girls living in a parked Dodge van in front of the hall (one of whom was Lynette "Squeaky" Fromme, who later tried to kill President Ford}. They told him to come back the next day—and when he did, bearing gifts of acid, they guaranteed that Manson would see him provided that he mark his application for the visit with a swastika made of backwards sevens. Well, once Lou got into the hall, and a loud voice over the public address system announced, "Will the visitor for Manson step over to the elevator, please," Lou was beginning to lose his taste for this latest wacky escapade.

In any case, Manson twice denied Lou's request for an audience, and when Lou returned to the girls asking what more he could do for them, they answered "AK 47s." With that, Lou hightailed it out of downtown L.A. in a hurry. This was too freaky a scene even for him.

By 1971, Lou had virtually abandoned his dream of becoming a concert pianist. His practice time was dwindling due to all the distractions and recreational pleasures, and he had all but admitted to himself that he just was not cut out for the classical world. His musicologist friend William Malloch claimed that it was just another of many examples of good popular musicians who simply cannot cross over to the classics. To Malloch, Lou's playing lacked the rhythm that a classical pianist needs, and each note wasn't given its own character and shape.

Lou stopped driving and refused to wear a wristwatch or glasses in the early '70s. He wouldn't even subject his new baby son to the usual round of inoculations until it was time to get a passport. Lou had dropped out almost as far as he could without starving.

Finally, getting restless for a change of scene, Lou abandoned Morningstar as a resident, leaving in the fall of 1971 for a period of compulsive travel. First, he visited the Atlanta estate of a onetime Morningstar resident for about a month and then it was on to the Gate of Heaven in Kentucky, the only other piece of land that Lou knew of that had been deeded to God. The "former owner" of the land was Noel Singer, and he and Lou came up with another wacky idea.

According to Lou, the plan was to buy a piece of land in India, deed it to God, and see if they could go from God's land in the United States to God's land in India without a passport! For this little escapade, Lou cashed in his G.I. life insurance policy, received $2500, and off he, Rena, Vishnu and the Singers went. The two families traveled all around the subcontinent, through the interior from Bombay to Calcutta, down the east coast, across the southern tip. They stayed in India for about four months, visiting and staying at ashrams, thoroughly absorbing themselves in the Indian mindset. While in Allahabad, Lou researched land ownership law in India, but found it was almost impossible for a non-Indian to purchase land in that country. So much for that scheme.

Meanwhile, without Lou, what was left of the Morningstar commune had virtually collapsed. This is how the last days of the ranch looked to Sarah, a young Englishwoman who came to visit for a day in 1972, well after Lou stopped living on the ranch full time. "It was very pretty, quite overgrown, lots of wildflowers," she remembered. "I don't remember seeing many structures. We ran into some zoned-out-looking folk, half a dozen or so...mostly guys, long-haired, kind of looking funky. Someone was playing a guitar.

"There was this woman walking around nude with a child. When we asked her what she did in the winter when it was cold, she said she just sat and watched the rain or read. But it was summer and she was roaming around.

"It had fallen apart; nobody wanted to do their chores and cooperate. They just wanted to bliss out and do who knows what. So, it disintegrated."

By the time Lou got back from India—this was March of 1972—the joyride was almost over. He had no place to stay; the tiny studio at Morningstar had been disassembled and razed to the foundation. El Cerrito was off limits and, in any case, he had already signed it away to Dolly. He, Rena and Vishnu ended up living out of a Ford Econoline van that he purchased upon his return.

Moreover, Lou's time as a leading light of the counterculture had passed. Too many unthinking suburban kids had ignored Tim Leary's cautionings about proper supervision and pleasant surroundings when trying psychedelic drugs; that, plus the countervailing freewheeling Ken Kesey school of trip-taking, and the impure acid on the streets led to many family tragedies. At last, after years of considering rock music a short-term fad, the record industry was fully awakened to its financial potential—and the moguls embraced it, smothering whatever consciousness-rousing qualities it once had.

The greatest economic boom in recorded history had come to a screeching halt with the 1970 recession; people would have less leisure time in which to contemplate new ways of living. In the emerging Republican era, it would be a time to keep one's mouth shut and concentrate on finding and keeping a job in order to survive. Long hair, blue jeans, and freer attitudes toward sex and marijuana smoking remained in fashion—and for many part-time hippies, that would be enough.

So when Lou and Rena had mailed out some 1,500 flyers announcing Lou's availability as a speaker on the open land movement, they shouldn't have been surprised when they got only two or three responses. The economy of abundance was over; who would want to give away their land now?

Despite the changing cultural climate, Lou's hippie period was far from over. Even though his last night camping on the ranch—meticulously recorded in his diary as always—was Dec. 12, 1972, after a lecture at Sonoma State, Lou spent the rest of the '70s trying to hang onto his countercultural lifestyle and appearance. He would never again confront the powers-that-be, be they the government, the courts, the police, or his future neighbors, on any legal level, but he was far from apologetic about what he had done and how he chose to live.

Lou always believed that the most important thing he ever did was deed Morningstar Ranch to God, leaving it as a blueprint for some form of refuge in the event of a future nuclear or environmental holocaust. He believed that he added an original contribution to the Western world's storehouse of knowledge, calling God's ownership of land "a powerful force for the amelioration of the human condition."

For all the differences in personality between Alex and Lou, Alex always had much respect for the idealistic motivations that caused Lou to deed his land to God. "There is a great deal to be said for that idea," Alex mused. "It's a facile idea for parlor conversation. The central problem of mankind in society from the first day that man formed any kind of society was the conflict between the rights of the individual versus the rights of the mass. That has always been so. What are your rights vis a vis your neighbors or your fellows? And isn't that always the clash, the right of private property versus the right of public good versus what constitutes the common good?"

About Lou's hippie period in general, Alex was less generous. "I thought it was an exercise in futility," he said.

"He was trying to change the world," observed William Malloch. "He was trying to enjoy himself but at the same time, make a social contribution. (But he) blew his marriage apart, started another marriage, blew his whole life apart, I guess."

Lou summed up this tumultuous period in his life quite simply. "Well, it was a lot of fun. It was living theater. But I ran out of loot, so I had to go back to work."

Chapter Thirteen

All three Limeliters always assumed that the group would be a means to an end, rather than the end in itself. From his public statements then, none seemed more convinced of this than Alex, the youngest of the three and the one with the most options.

He was only 31 years old when the group broke up, with four years in the big-time behind him. His growing command of folk music, expertise in several languages and virtuoso standing on stringed instruments might have given him a good shot at capturing ground in Theodore Bikel's international folk territory. He was versatile and open-minded enough to go the other way into pop singing, as Glenn was about to do. He might have continued pursuing his first love, the theater, where he was starting to make a bit of headway until Glenn and Aspen beckoned. Still unusually handsome and debonair, he might have tried Hollywood again, now armed with his Limeliters fame as a powerful crowbar to get in the door. And there were plenty of behind-the-scenes options that he felt like exploring—like producing records, commercials, or television shows, or writing songs.

So many choices, so much time ahead of him. By the time the 1960s ended, Alex would have tried them all, and some options would work out better than others. But none really satisfied him. Essentially, Alex had no plan, no idea of what he wanted to do in this life, no idea of which venture should come next.

"I have a tremendously analytical mind in terms of the way I approach a given problem," he says. "But in terms of how I approach my life, I would say that I do exactly the opposite."

The first thing Alex did after Glenn left the Limeliters was to straighten out his personal life. He left Ginger in September of 1963, ending a marriage that perhaps never really was a marriage, what with Alex being away for so much of the time.

He then changed his base of operations. For an aspiring player in the entertainment business, Mill Valley is nowhere, an idyllic retreat whose psychological distance from the power centers of Los Angeles and New York City is more than a phone call or one-hour jet flight away.

Alex moved into a bicoastal existence, leaving his Mill Valley house to Ginger, living with his parents in New York and renting a duplex apartment with his old friend Theo Bikel at the corner of La Cienega Blvd. and Fountain Ave. in West Hollywood. His time in New York would be spent with his parents, winding down the Limeliters' office there, or dabbling in the company the group was running with Arnold Brown. In Los Angeles, his agent would try to rustle up acting parts for him in film, television, or the theater, and the Limeliters' last three studio projects would keep his hand in the music business. Deferred royalties from Coca Cola, RCA Victor, and other outfits were coming in until 1966, a substantial sum of money that kept Alex going while he looked around to play his options.

Alex couldn't recall whether a solo career was on his mind when the group broke up. But the desire to try to make it on his own surfaced soon after Glenn's first solo recordings started coming out. "I guess it was, well, Glenn's doing it, why can't I?" he recalled.

In between Limeliters sessions, Alex tried to capitalize upon his fame by making his first solo album in New York in July 1964. Released in December, the album was called *Man Of the World*—and it was a fortuitously little-noticed bomb. Instead of the reliable Neely Plumb as producer, Alex was assigned Jack Somer, whose production was a master class on how to completely misjudge and misuse a singer. "As a result of that album, he was fired," said Alex with a rueful laugh, although Neely countered, "That's not why he was fired. He was fired because he did something that his boss absolutely told him not to do. But (the album) could have contributed to it."

Alex didn't mince any words about his solo debut. "It was a tragedy," he says. "The entire production and creation of that album was a total disaster. I knew absolutely nothing of what I was doing. What I did for that first album was what many people do. I said, 'OK, you guys know best, you do it, and I'll do what you say.' And it was a terrible idea."

Despite the misleading album title, Somer tries to turn the urbane, sophisticated Alex into a banal pop crooner, a novelty singer, even a fake hillbilly yokel—anything but an international folk balladeer. Not once does the liner annotator mention Alex's Limeliters credentials. In the early-bird Limeliter tradition, Alex did record a Jacques Brel tune with Rod McKuen lyrics, "Seasons in the Sun," that eventually became a No. 1 hit for bubble-gum-rocker Terry Jacks in 1974, but the Kingston Trio beat Alex to that song by seven months.

Alex's singing is wooden, his voice too inflexible for the material, the parts often written too embarrassingly high for him, with only token bursts into French and Portuguese. The arrangements are horrible, busily intruding on the vocals. The July sessions were string-laden affairs, arranged by Manny Albam, that smack of a low budget. Later sessions, presumably to avert total catastrophe, were held in September under the direction of Dick Hyman, the extremely talented pianist/arranger who really should have turned in better work than this.

Almost a year later, Alex made one more attempt to get a solo career going on records. This time, Neely took the production reins, and borrowing from his then-successful recordings with Glenn, brought in L.A. chart whizzes David Gates (later a member of the multi-million-selling group, Bread), Mort Garson, and Perry Botkin, Jr. to handle the arrangements. "I wanted to call it *The Folk Sophisticate* and the company wouldn't let me do it," said Neely. "Because that's what he was, a really suave, dapper man—a ladies' man. But they didn't think that the words 'folk' and 'sophistication' went together at all."

Instead, the record went out in October of 1965 as *Affairs Of The Heart*, a melange of show tunes, current film songs, orchestrated soft-rock, Latin and pop material vaguely centered around Alex's Lothario persona. Alex sounds more comfortable and confident with pop now—Neely clearly knew how to get more out of his singer and the charts are considerably more hip to the times, but again, mediocre material often places a drag on the project. Two exceptions stand out, though. Neely had the good sense to give Alex "Chove Chuva," a fine Brazilian bossa nova by Jorge Ben, before Sergio Mendes could get his hands on it, but again the line lies too high for the singer and he doesn't quite do it justice.

Yet Alex is perfectly suited for "Young Man," a rocking Gates-arranged track with a cynical lyric advising young would-be Don Juans to make hey while the sun shines.

"There was one good cut on that album called 'Young Man' which I don't apologize for," recalled Alex. "David Gates was the perfect arranger for pop/folk, as he later proved in his own work. It came out as a single, and one of the reviewers at the time wrote a very accurate review of the record. He said, 'This is a wonderful record, beautifully arranged, very well sung. There's only one trouble; it won't sell, because the lyrics do not speak to the young.' And he was absolutely right."

Affairs Of The Heart didn't do any better than its predecessor in the shops, and Alex's recording career was effectively over for the time being. "That was a better album, but it was also not very good," concludes Alex.

Around this period, Alex's roommate Theo hired him and Fred Hellerman of the just-disbanded Weavers to back him in a concert in London's Royal Festival Hall. "Freddy played guitar and I was like Theo Bikel, Jr.," he recalls. "Theo would mainly do a solo thing, then he would bring me out and we would do duets in French and Russian. I do remember we had a hell of a good time and Theo, of course, is a great performer, a joy to work with, a consummate professional."

After the concert was over, Alex stayed on in England to cut some demos in the London recording studios, where he came away with total awe of British recording techniques but nothing worth releasing.

On another occasion, probably in 1968, Bikel was asked to do a series of folk programs on German television in Munich—and Alex helped out on that project as well. The Bayerischen Rundfunks released a live record of one of the sessions called *Lieder der Voelker* ("Songs of the People"), in which we get a tantalizing idea of what two-thirds of the Cosmo Alley trio would have sounded like. Alex was clearly in a jovial mood, and these resonant Jewish-European baritones blend in rich, electrifying harmony, with Theo's voice taking all kinds of shapes and guises. There are things like a magnificent duo version of "The Little Burro" in Spanish using the Limeliters' arrangement, a comic turn on Woody Guthrie's "Put Your Finger in the Air," a Civil Rights movement-era tune "Sail On, Freedom" which neither of them had ever sung before. It's a pity this record was never released in North America.

In the last half of 1965, in his only serious attempt to perform live as a solo during this period, Alex put a trio together and opened for Lenny Bruce not long before the latter's death from a drug overdose at Basin Street West in San Francisco. Like Lou, Alex called upon Jimmy Stewart to help him as music director and guitarist for the new act, and they would rehearse in Theo Bikel's duplex. The program was a collection of pop/folk songs from his two solo albums ("Black Is The Color Of

My True Love's Hair" "Chove Chuva," etc.) which Stewart transcribed and arranged for a small combo.

But Alex quit his act after only two weeks, discouraged by his performance. "I was terrible," Alex says. "I played guitar and sang standup, had a collection of songs that, looking back on it, was idiotic. And I was scared, not comfortable at all."

Yet Stewart believed that Alex was being overly hard on himself, that his sense of organization and his work ethic were solid, and eventually he would have become more comfortable once he gauged what Lenny Bruce's audience wanted.

"I would have liked to see him continue the act," said Stewart. "It was a good idea, may have even been before its time because his taste in music was really good. All he needed to do was stay in there with it a little longer."

But again, the old "where's the Limeliters?" questions came flying. Alex simply thought he could not compete against his expectations from his early wild success—and he withdrew.

During his period adrift, Alex immersed himself in a broad variety of other projects and schemes around this time. In 1964, he and Burt Zell tried their hands at promotion, taking on a project where they bought the rights to set up closed-circuit theater showings of a Beatles concert. "We lost our shirt," says Alex ruefully. "Some locations I guess did well, but they charged too much money for it; you know, they essentially got a bunch of suckers to buy into this thing."

While in New York, Alex produced a one-man off-Broadway play, *The Madman* by the bizarre Russian writer Nikolai Gogol, with a score by George Delerue. He tried to buy the rights to *The Magic Christian* after reading Terry Southern's novel, thinking that it would make a really kooky movie. He lunched once with Southern, who said that he wanted to write the screenplay, but Alex backed off when he realized that the novelist "was too far out for me." (Later, of course, it became a successful film starring Peter Sellers and Ringo Starr.)

Still keeping some eggs in the acting basket, Alex did a respectable guest spot as a debonair KAOS killer in TV's *Get Smart*, a minor part in a theater-in-the-round production of Lerner and Loewe's *Paint Your Wagon*, other TV series, whatever his agent could get him. Yet the only time a real Class A part came around was when Lynn Stallmaster called one day and asked Alex to play the part of a Russian sailor, Hrushevsky, in a Norman Jewison-directed Cold War comedy film, *The Russians Are Coming, The Russians Are Coming.*

Based on Nathaniel Benchley's novel *The Off-Islanders*, the plot was an ingenious setup for comic misunderstandings. A Soviet submarine was grounded off the coast of Nantucket Island and the captain of the sub (Theo Bikel) sent some of his men ashore to find help. To the impressionable people of the town, it is as if the Russians were invading America, just as the Cold Warmongers had been warning all along—and all hell breaks loose, with World War III looming grimly on the horizon.

Yet along with the slapstick and satirical skewering of super-patriotism, there is an underlying warmth, an unspoken message that Russians and Americans are equally guilty of demonizing each other. As a result, the film was a resounding hit in its time, except in areas too obsessed with anti-communism. The film had a team of gifted actors like Theo, Carl Reiner, Jonathan Winters, Paul Ford, Alan Arkin, Brian Keith, Eva-Marie Saint, Ben Blue and John Philip Law. To give the film a really authentic touch, Jewison populated his Soviet sub with sailors who could speak Russian dialogue—a rare species in Hollywood. "They rounded up every Russian actor they could find in Los Angeles," says Alex.

Indeed, he nearly got Arkin's lead part—that of Rozanov, the commander of the Russian landing boat. It seems that Arkin, who would be making his motion picture debut in the film, had some trouble trying to get a release from his starring Broadway role in *Enter Laughing*. Jewison told Alex they might not be able to get Arkin out of his contract, in which case the lead might go to Alex. It didn't happen, but for a while, Alex found himself in the ironic position of possibly filling in for an old friend who nearly substituted for him at that New York club in the '50s. And in any case, Alex was still left with a lucrative role of some visibility.

The filming took place not in the actual location, but in the small Northern California town of Mendocino, which was designed by its founders to look like a 19th century New England village. It was a happy reunion for the folkies from New York—Alan, Theo and Alex—working for a period of months on the breathtaking Mendocino coast, with its sheer bluffs overlooking wild seascapes. "The parties were especially wonderful because it wasn't only Alex and I who could play the music," said Bikel. "There was Alan Arkin, a Russian language expert on the set who played the violin, and then there was a guy named Gino who spoke Russian and played the accordion. Lee Hays (who was in the Babysitters with Arkin) came to visit and stayed three weeks on the location."

After Alex had been living in Theo's duplex for a couple of years, his lawyer suggested he buy a house. Alex agreed but was unable to participate in the search since he was just going out on location in *The Russians are Coming.* So, in an amazingly casual manner, he left the decision to his mother, who selected a lovely yet unpretentious two-story home on West Knoll Drive in an unincorporated patch of Los Angeles County (now West Hollywood). On a break from filming one weekend, Alex took one look at the house, and simply said, "This one will do."

The house rested on a gently sloping hillside a block or so south of the Sunset Strip. There was a detached one-car garage off to the left, a spacious backyard, a modest enclosed front porch, very much a byproduct of suburban America. Down a flight of stairs on the bottom floor was a large room that Alex immediately thought would make a good music room. This house would make a useful center of operations, being only minutes away from most of the power centers in town—and Theo, who had given up his duplex, rented the back bedroom on the main floor as his L.A. base of operations for about three years.

At about this time, Alex's wavering internal compass was beginning to point in the direction of behind the scenes. He started writing original songs, spending a good deal of his free time on the *The Russians Are Coming* set trying to compose a hit tune. One day, in about 25 minutes, he came up with the idea of using the metaphor of months to describe a stone-hearted lover, and he called the tune "Cold December In Your Heart."

Fortuitously, Alex had become friendly with Glen Campbell when he was playing all those dazzling guitar parts on the Limeliters' later recording sessions. Just when Campbell's own solo career was taking off in 1967, Alex showed Campbell his clever song with its descending guitar hook—and Glen thought enough of the tune to include it on his next album wrapped in a fine country-pop arrangement. That album just happened to be named after a Jimmy Webb tune, *By The Time I Get To Phoenix,* a record that sold some 1.3 million copies. Alex had found a tiger to ride, and he later estimated he made about $100,000 in royalties on "Cold December" from that one album alone. Alas, it would be the only song of his that made any big money.

Alex also started taking a more active interest in the goings-on in the control room in the Limeliters' post-Glenn sessions, trying to pick up bits of recording wisdom wherever he could. "The whole time we were recording, particularly in the studio, I became aware of all the parameters involved and how easy it was to blow it," he says. "And after I made my two albums, that's when I really began to get interested because I realized what was going wrong."

Meanwhile some production opportunities were gradually turning up. In New York, he was asked to produce a television special based on the *Through Children's Eyes* album—basically a "Hootenanny" for kids, with performers like Mike Settle, Jill O'Hara, Scott McKenzie and Alex himself leading the singalongs. Alex found it to be a nightmarish experience.

"I found that television was not the medium for me at all," he says. "I was in way over my head. I was nervous, uptight, insecure, didn't know what I was doing." But the experience did whet his desire to become involved in production in some way, if not via television. Gene Norman, founder of GNP/Crescendo Records, came along with an offer to produce a "Hootenanny" record, a grab-bag of various folk performers with Jack Linkletter reprising his TV emcee role. The record didn't sell—the "Hootenanny" days being well on the wane—but Alex found record producing something he enjoyed, particularly when it meant working with engineer Wally Heider, a seminal figure in the recording industry. "He was one of the few people who had the foresight to buy eight-track recording machines when there were none and he made a fortune renting out equipment. He loved his work; I learned a lot from Wally; he understood recording."

The next step for Alex was forming a production company in tandem with Mort Garson, who had worked on his second solo album. They set about looking for projects to produce—and after a couple of misfires, they hit upon the idea of doing a pop orchestral album based on the signs of the zodiac. They took the idea to Jac Holzman, still head of his now-booming Elektra label, and he gave them the go-ahead. Composed and arranged by Garson and produced by Alex, with narration written by Jacques Wilson, *The Zodiac Cosmic Sounds* became a moderate hit in the summer of 1967, rising to No. 118 on the *Billboard* charts and staying on nine weeks.

Today, *The Zodiac* comes off as a series of aimless pop vamps, with the spaced-out narration and trendy sitars tying it irrevocably to the doomed Age of Aquarius. Yet the feature that made the record so unusual in its time was its extensive yet restrained use of electronic music, then a rare novelty in the recording industry. Up until this point, serious electronic music composition was mostly in the hands of the academics at no-public-access facilities like the Columbia-Princeton Electronic Music Center. The general public knew little beyond the slithering sound of Paul Tanner's Electro-Theremin in the TV series *My Favorite Martian* and the Beach Boys' "Good Vibrations." When Garson needed electronic sounds, Alex had few choices other than Paul Beaver, the pioneer electronic musician-about-town in Hollywood.

But soon they were to find another. Robert Moog was showing off his first commercially available Moog synthesizer at the AES Convention in Anaheim just as the *Zodiac* project was approaching its final stages. Finding themselves in need of yet more bizarre electronic effects, Alex and Mort went down to the show—and just as Lou was impressed by the Buchla synthesizer around this time, Alex was knocked out by the Moog's seemingly limitless capabilities.

"We hired it right out of the AES show and brought it into the studio, and when we played it there, I went crazy," Alex remembers. "I thought this was the most amazing thing I'd ever seen. (Later), we each got one—and at the time there was hardly anybody in town who knew anything about these things. There were probably no more than half a dozen people into electronic music in Los Angeles in any serious way at that time. I saw the possibilities immediately; it seemed to me to be the wave of the future."

Soon thereafter, Alex and Garson parted company—an "amicable" split, Alex says, which it seemed to be since Alex would use Garson's charts again in the future. With the small pile of money he made from the *Zodiac* record, Alex decided to convert his new music room into a home studio, another far-seeing idea that had not caught on yet.

One day, Alex noticed an ad in a San Diego newspaper from a man named Jack Williams, offering to sell a pair of Concertone two-track tape recorders, a professional mixer, and other recording paraphernalia for roughly $1200. Alex called the number, and not only would Williams sell, he offered to drive up from San Diego to install the equipment and teach Alex how to run it. "It was in beautiful condition, a great buy for somebody starting out," Alex remembers. Then he soundproofed the downstairs room with acoustical tile and invited various musicians to come down and try it out. One young singer/songwriter who ventured there was then-unknown Van Dyke Parks.

After some more successful experiments, Alex was ready to gamble. "Let's go all the way, all out, and build a real studio," he thought—and with the rest of his *Zodiac* and *Russians* money, plus a few bank loans, he set to work. The whole conversion of his music room, complete with control booth, came to somewhere in the $8,000 to $10,000 range, and over the next few years, Alex would add another $90,000 of pro equipment, including a coveted eight-track tape machine. He ended up with a studio comparable in quality to just about anything else in town other than the major labels' complexes. He started renting his room out for about $45 an hour, well under the going rate in L.A. (then around $75-100 an hour).

Word quickly got around about this advanced home studio with reasonable rates and electronic music capabilities—and by 1967, Alex was flooded with work. Armed with his new Moog, Alex was in demand for commercials, and he cranked out quite a few of them for Chevrolet cars, Chevron gasoline, Dole pineapple, and several others.

Major stars like Johnny Mathis and Bobby Darin booked time there, attracted by the privacy Alex could offer. Carole King recorded several demos in the studio. Producer/musician Terry Melcher, often accompanied by friend Candice Bergen, made some masters there with a rock group; Seals and Crofts cut a single there. Dialect virtuoso Paul Frees recorded the vocals for an album of then-current pop tunes in celebrity voices for MGM in 1970. The cream of L.A. session men, The Wrecking Crew—Larry Knechtel, Hal Blaine, Joe Osborn, Leon Russell, Tommy Tedesco, Mike Deasy, and so many more—would work at Alex Hassilev Studio, and Alex even had a rack of cups inscribed with their names installed downstairs for their regular use. In addition, Alex's own producing activities went into high gear, yielding a varied, often off-the-wall series of albums. Although the results show that Alex was thoroughly in touch with contemporary hit sounds, he seemed to go out of his way to look for projects that interested his wandering, eclectic mind first, thinking of chart potential second.

Ananda Shankar, Ravi Shankar's nephew, made a progressive East-meets-West record for Reprise under Alex's direction that sold well in Europe. Dick Rosmini, who had become a regular visitor to Alex's studio, even recording an album of his own there for Imperial, says that he had a ball playing on Shankar's album, jamming on the cross-cultural groove. "The job was almost inconsequential, and it made Alex rather angry because we were having more fun playing than tending to business," he said.

Malvina Reynolds, quavery in voice but still as prolific as ever in her 70s, made a couple of idiosyncratic records with Alex in the 1970s. Rosmini remembered that Alex, ever the fence-sitter, actually abdicated control over the final mix when he couldn't make up his mind on which mix he liked best.

"He said, 'I can't make any sense out of this. I'm listening to this so much that I don't know what I'm doing. You and John (Horton) do it and call me when you're done and I'll either pass it or reject it.' He got to the point where he couldn't make decisions."

One of the best Hassilev productions was Hoyt Axton's 1968 Columbia album My *Griffin Is Gone*, a thoughtful, tastefully set collection of some of Axton's most absorbing, highly original, off-center songs. Though it didn't sell many copies, it was a favorite of Alex's, as well as Hoyt and his late mother, songwriter Mae Axton. Theo Bikel, who was still living at the house, came in with the Pennywhistlers, an all-female vocal septet, and made what Alex calls a "totally uncommercial" record, *Songs Of The Earth*, for Elektra in New York. The finished record is a joyous, uncompromising smorgasbord of folk music from Russia, Serbia, Ukraine, Macedonia, Scotland, Spain, England and Greece, plus one song in Yiddish. "He was not a high-pressure kind of producer," said Bikel of Alex. "He guided it with a soft hand rather than an iron fist."

From 1967 to about 1970, Alex's life had become a mad merry-go-round of work—running and renting his studio, producing records, doing commercials, selling projects to record labels, supervising a staff of three people. At times, he would play a simple banjo or keyboard part if somebody needed it, but for the most part, he had quit performing entirely in order to run his studio. After Theo moved out, Alex lived in the upstairs bedroom all this time, often while sessions one after another were going on beneath him.

"I was doing this 16 hours a day," he recalls. "I was living it and breathing it. I had weeks where this studio was booked around the clock. Looking back on it...at the time, it seemed perfectly normal."

Moreover, Alex's once-hyperactive social life had apparently dwindled down to near zero, what with all the work occupying his time downstairs. Instead, he would hang around with the steady stream of musicians who would come and go. "My social life was my work," he says.

Yet almost inevitably, Alex's past would return to play a part in his new life. While searching for new projects to produce, Alex occasionally crossed paths with his old colleague Glenn Yarbrough; indeed, Glenn had cut an early version of Alex's "Cold December In Your Heart," in January 1966. Now a star solo attraction, Glenn had just left RCA Victor for Warner Bros., and Alex was busy producing a pair of singles for him. As part of Glenn's new contract, Alex had suggested that Glenn negotiate a one-shot reunion of the Limeliters for an album that he, Alex, would conceive and produce.

Alex made it clear that the new album would not be a mere instant replay of the old folk sound. It would be a thoroughly contemporary record that could find favor with Glenn's new middle-brow audience and the young, as well as those who remembered the Limeliters. It would take advantage of the advances in recording techniques since the early '60s; it would be a reflection of the new superheated political and cultural attitudes in the air. And there would be potential hits aimed toward Top 40 airplay, the stubborn territory which the group could not conquer back in its heyday.

When the subject was brought up at a Warners conference, the brass, remembering the Limeliters' gold mine of not so long before, gave Alex an immediate go-ahead for the project. Now at last the prime motivating force behind the group, Alex rounded up the musicians, hired the arrangers, picked the songs, reserved the studio time, and essentially ran the show. Glenn arranged for time off from his busy performance schedule so he could go into the studio and track his vocals. And Lou emerged from his piano and "retirement" at Morningstar Ranch to come down to Los Angeles for a few days to punch in his parts.

For Lou, returning to the recording studio in January 1968, even after only a three-year absence, was a distinct shock. Suddenly, instead of everyone being in the same studio at the same time, here he was cutting the vocals while listening through headphones to a rhythm track that had been already recorded, running from studio to studio that happened to have some time open. Not only that, the balance of power in the group had been overturned. The project was in Alex's control, Glenn was the star, and Lou was now just along for the ride.

"I remember the very first time we carne to the rehearsals," Lou recalled. "Alex passed out arrangements he had had made and Burt Zell, our road manager, was there. I started, you know, to criticize the voicings, and Burtie pulled me off to the side and said, 'Lou, for once, why don't you just shut up and do what you're told.' It was God speaking and I did. I sat back and said, 'I am a studio singer, I'm going to do these parts as good as I can,' and I didn't say doodly-squat about anything."

For Glenn, singing with Alex and Lou in the studio again reminded him with a jolt of how slow his partners were in learning new material. "It was difficult to do, which everything always was with the Limeliters," he recalled. "By this time, after working for five years alone where I just go in the studio and do it in one or two takes, it just became awfully tedious. I swore I would never do it again."

As one of the players on these sessions, Dick Rosmini noticed a world of difference in atmosphere between the Limeliters of 1968 and the explosive sessions of 1961. "The enforced brotherhood was not there at all," he said. "As a result of that, they got along far better."

It took many months and $37,000—a lot of money at the time, particularly for a group that hadn't had a hit album in many years—to make *Time To Gather Seeds*, and it shows in the playback. Clearly influenced by the Beatles' George Martin, Alex went crazy on the production, using six different arrangers (counting himself), piling on orchestras, female voices, sound effects, and rock rhythms to such a degree that the Limeliters themselves almost become bit players.

Not only that, the Limeliters often sound like a static facsimile of themselves, recessed way back in the mix, drowning in the production. The vocal arrangements are rather staid, desperately in need of the spatial splendor of Lou's own hand. And yet one still feels great affection for this record, a brave product of its time in which the Limeliters finally stand up for their socio-political beliefs. Alex and Glenn were becoming active in the antiwar movement of the time—indeed, Alex had sung at rallies for Sen. Eugene McCarthy during the 1968 California presidential primary campaign—and the songs here would often lean conspicuously in this direction.

The album starts off strongly with a gem, a Gilbert Becaud tune with a Rod McKuen English lyric, "The Importance Of The Rose"— upbeat, samba-influenced, optimistic, a real candidate for airplay. The Limeliters seem to be hugely enjoying the sheer act of singing together again; toward the fade, when the three ad-lib a sardonic parody, "It's the dough that's important," they nearly break up, and Alex wisely keeps that joyous burst in.

From here, though, the record veers off in several weird directions—the odd ersatz-Afro-Cuban groove of "Only 18," the grim picture of 1968 in "L.A. In The Summer," a polished remake of "Cold December," the apocalyptic title track with its tricky 7/4 meter. All the above material except "December" was written by a new discovery of Alex and Glenn named Peter Boyd, an unconventional writer contracted to Alex's publishing company Tamara Music {named after his mother} at the time.

By the middle of Side Two, even as the production becomes increasingly bizarre, Alex finally finds a consistent theme, a fervently pacifistic one. Boyd's "Were You In Berlin?," with its clever Kurt Weill-like arrangement by Lincoln Mayorga, savages the onlookers who were "just doing their jobs" throughout the terror of the Third Reich—and by implication, those who were silent on Vietnam.

The mockery of the "The General" misfires, but Glenn has the final, eloquent last word in what is probably Alex's best song, "A Hundred Men," an indictment of the stupidity of all wars that ends in a blaze of drums, solo trumpet, and air raid siren.

Glenn's manager Rein Neggo, Jr. remembered the *Time To Gather Seeds* sessions, as well as those for Glenn's concurrent *Let Me Choose Life* album (which Alex also produced), as marathons that took forever to complete. "He was the master of uncertainty," Neggo said about Alex as producer. "Both albums were overproduced like crazy, and they spent a lot of money where they had to redo things and redo things. Alex was a great producer, but he didn't walk into the studio knowing what he wanted, so he would experiment in the studio, and he would always be looking at people trying to guess what they were thinking. It was always, 'What do you think? What do you think?' and then build on the reaction. You can't do that when you're paying for the studio and the musicians."

Ever his own worst critic, Alex himself acknowledges the flaws in the record. "I didn't really do a great job producing that record, but in a way, it was also not entirely my fault," he says. "I was unable to get my colleagues, Glenn and Lou, to put enough time into the project—and as a result, we went in and made that record in too brief a time. They didn't spend enough time woodshedding it with me. If they had, I think it would have come out a whole lot better.

"The results were very uneven; however, there are some cuts on it I really like very much. My favorite song on that record is 'Were You In Berlin?' It's a completely non-commercial song; it is an astonishing piece of material."

"That's not a bad album, by the way," said Lou. "It's stiff. Alex picked some good tunes, but the only thing is, we didn't know the charts, man. It was one of those things where we never had a chance to really get into those tunes. Glenn had three minutes off from a successful tour somewhere, you know.

"'The Importance Of The Rose' was the best tune on the album, although I did like that tune that I did, 'Were You In Berlin?' I wish I could have learned it so I could do it. If I would have had, say, three months on the road with that tune, I could have made a very good interpretation of that. Sight-reading recordings, that's what I hate."

A paradox—a record that took too much time to produce and not enough time to get the songs right. Undoubtedly the months Alex spent trying to fine-tune it did not endear him to the Warner Bros. executives footing the bill. When it was finally delivered, they just dumped it onto the market with little or no promotion, and very few bought it or even knew about it.

Alex feels Warners gave up way too soon on the album—and he is probably right. The second single from the album, "The Importance Of The Rose," had "hit" written all over it—and it nearly broke out in several markets. It was just beginning to get some serious airplay; Lee Barker, a broadcaster and devoted Limeliters fan, remembered hearing it in Salem, Oregon on the radio one morning with an encouraging back announcement, "That's who's back together again: The Limeliters!" Even Lou roused himself from Morningstar to do some promotional work on the single in San Francisco and Sacramento. But Warners refused to get behind the promotion and the single vanished from the airwaves.

"I don't think Warner Bros. ever thought of it being a commercially viable product," said Neggo. "They didn't push it; they had no intention of pushing it; they just wanted to get it over with and get it done. Warner Bros. was very happy to see that thing die."

Credit Alex with one significant achievement—prying the Limeliters out of their amber encasement of the early '60s and placing them into the tumult of the late '60s. But musically, this was Alex's achievement alone. "My desire at the time was to get into music that they really were not interested in," he concludes. "That's what happens when you don't collaborate actively over time; your interests diverge."

A few years down the road, about 1971, even the life of a successful studio owner began to pall upon Alex. For all the records he produced down in his music room, none had hit the charts in anything resembling a big way. In a sense, Alex wanted to have it both ways. In the spirit of the game, he desperately wanted a hit record but often would not consciously go after it by tailoring his productions to the marketplace. True, this was the period—a rare one in pop music history—in which you could be adventurous and still have hits, but Alex never punched the right combination of buttons. Once, Alex thought he had struck gold with a young singing duo of Richard Atkins and Richard Manning who ingeniously called themselves Richard Twice. Alex believed that he had found the next Simon and Garfunkel but now blames himself for not finding outside potential hit material for them to sing. But really, the problem went beyond Atkins' so-so original material; their vocal blend was anemic, a weak imitation of S&G and the Monkees—and Richard Twice quickly disappeared from sight.

In addition to the frustration of not having hits, Alex was simply exhausted. Burned out. The exhaustion of presiding over round-the-clock sessions would feed on the frustration, not only of the lack of chart success, but Alex's own insecurity. He felt that he didn't have a thorough enough music education to compete on the top levels of the business. He knew how to interface with artists as a producer but not, so he thought, on a technical nuts-and-bolts level.

Also, there was a practical consideration—money. Technology was advancing at an ever-rapidly-increasing rate; new products, each more bewildering and versatile than the one before it, were flooding the marketplace. Alex may have been one of the first to have an 8-track board but before long, they were being supplanted by 16-track and 24-track boards. Alex's cumbersome prototype Moog would be superseded by the new, simpler, smaller Minimoog, which really ushered in the electronic age, as well as a wave of synthesizers from ARP. Alex simply did not have the funds to be able to stay with the electronic revolution and compete with Los Angeles' top, well financed recording studios.

And finally, he thought he just wasn't getting anywhere aesthetically. "It wasn't satisfying," he says. "I loved production of records, of talent. Commercials were sort of interesting and paid very well. But I couldn't see myself continuing to do this. It got to be kind of a treadmill. The things that drew me to the process still intrigue me, but that was the only thing that intrigued me."

In the early '70s, the calls for work at Alex Hassilev Studios started to taper off, partly because he deliberately began charging higher rates, which led to fewer bookings. That, plus Alex's lack of chart success, plus perhaps incidents like the cost overruns he incurred producing records for Warners which subsequently didn't sell, led to a "winding down" period in his life.

"I think something was saying to me, 'You don't want to be going this way, 24 hours a day,'" he thought.

By 1972, Alex had settled into what he calls "a retirement without port-folio," a state of mind where he didn't feel like doing much of anything at all. The studio was still rented out occasionally, so some income was coming in, but the master of the house was out of commission, sunk in depression, searching for something he would enjoy doing.

He rarely retreated into the stupor of drugs, though. Alex hated dope; pot made him sleepy and nauseous, he never tried LSD because he was terrified of what it could do to his personality. There were, however, a few wild experiments, particularly during his European tour with Theo. "I remember a crazy mad scene with a couple of English girls and some hashish," he recalls, smiling. "The girls had the hashish, and Theo took a few drags on this pipe and promptly lay down and fell asleep on the floor—and I wasn't too far behind him. That stuff was paralyzing. I don't like drugs; I don't like what they do to me. Sexually, they certainly never did anything for me."

Essentially, he remained an outsider to the whole countercultural scene—an observer and commentator to a culture whose philosophical core fascinated him but whose artifacts and lifestyle repelled him. "In many ways, that whole '60s period—where Lou's head was during those years, as opposed to where mine was—was madness," he says. "It was a scene that absolutely held no interest for me. Where they were coming from had no meaning for me. It seemed to me imbecilic, and still does. It was so non-rational; it was so ignorant in the main.

"Now, that doesn't mean that there were not people who benefited from the liberating power of leaving their bourgeois existence and following Tim Leary's 'Turn on, tune in, drop out.' I thought of that as horseshit, but that doesn't mean the basic philosophical underpinning of that idea is bad—get in touch with yourself, the universe, and get off your point of view so you could turn the kaleidoscope, in other words.

"Yes I understood there was some value in it, but you didn't have to be a hippie to do that, except that a lot of people in this culture needed to become hippies because where they were coming from was so unbelievably banal. But I like to think that the world from which I came was not banal. I came from a background which gave me, I think, more of a perspective on life so I didn't feel I had to drop off a cliff in order to see different possibilities."

Yet for the most part, in the early 1970s, Alex couldn't see the possibilities for himself. So, he retreated, contemplating the state of the world from his cocoon on West Knoll Drive. And there he remained—until his past beckoned yet again.

Time to Gather Seeds - Warner Brothers, 1968

Chapter Fourteen

*"I intended not to work anymore.
I thought it was time to do something else."
—Glenn Yarbrough.*

When Glenn said he was leaving the Limeliters, and hopefully show business, he wasn't kidding. There was no thought of resuming his long-delayed solo career. He completely severed his professional ties with Lou and Alex. He gave them his share of any rights to the material they performed jointly, even gave up his share of the name, The Limeliters, so that he couldn't cash in on it later. Glenn had carefully saved his share of Limeliters money, anticipating his emancipation from the concert circuit. And the vehicle for his freedom would be the open seas.

But again, the old charmed pattern in his life would surface. No matter how many times he adamantly turned away from material success, it came his way anyway—thanks to his golden voice. And in the late '60s, fame and wealth would come to Glenn in larger waves than ever.

Ever since his experience in Naples, Florida with the Cuba-bound retired Chicago insurance man's boat, Glenn had been fascinated with the sea. When he was at St. John's College, he used to go to the waterfront and watch the old skipjacks with huge, tall masts sail into the docks. Since they were used to collect oysters, by law the skipjacks had no engines; they would rely completely on windpower out on the sea.

Glenn thought, wouldn't that be a romantic idea, to sail around the world relying only on one's instincts, skills, and the power and direction of the wind. Those memories, and the fact that he had missed out on that adventure to Cuba so long ago, were always in the back of Glenn's mind.

So, he resolved to do it. Just prior to the Provo air incident, Glenn bought his first boat, a 40-foot cutter which he christened the *Armorel* after a legendary disappearing island in the Atlantic. "Glenn knew buggerall about boats," remembered Jonathan Moore. "He thought he did. And we went over to pick it up in Oakland, me, Glenn and Peggy, and

Glenn insisted on doing everything himself. So, he cranks the engine up, goes roaring out of the dock, the boat swings sideways. He'd forgotten to untie one of the lines up front! Brilliant beginning to a great sailor. But he certainly learnt a lot after that."

Soon after the breakup of the trio, Glenn had the *Armorel* ready to go in a dock in San Rafael, California. Part of the idea was to take Peggy, Sean, and Stephanie along with him so he could be with his family at last after so many months on the road. Peggy couldn't believe Glenn was going to go through with it. "I guess she wasn't too crazy about that idea," Glenn deadpanned, "because as soon as she realized I was really gonna do it, she filed divorce proceedings."

Suddenly there was a new problem hanging over him—divorce, with its crippling alimony payments that would cut into his carefully accumulated stash of cash. Nevertheless, Glenn resolved to carry on alone if need be—and he was busy re-caulking the hull of the *Armorel* one day in the summer of 1963 when who should come visiting but Neely Plumb. Neely had a project in mind; RCA Victor was still interested in Glenn's potential as a solo act. Couldn't Glenn make just one album as a solo act, which he, Neely, would produce, before he sailed off into the Pacific?

Glenn wrestled with the idea for awhile. On one hand, he wanted his long-awaited, hard-earned freedom. On the other hand, deep inside was the burning desire to prove he could make it in show business on his own. All through the Limeliters years, Glenn had been saving material by folk-based writers that either the Limeliters didn't want to do or couldn't do because it was too delicate for their robust sound. This would be a golden opportunity to get some of those songs on records, to try them out for size.

So, with a shrug, Glenn took Neely up on his offer—and they went into RCA's Hollywood studios in October 1963. But it was a courageously different Glenn Yarbrough whose tenor once again filled the room. Not only would Glenn abandon the Limeliters, he also tossed the folk sound itself out the window—and in its place would be the smooth, polished, string and choir-laden sound that has been labeled easy-listening music.

In doing so, Glenn was not necessarily tearing himself away from his roots for the first time. His early work on Tradition and Elektra tried, within the constraints of the shoestring budgets of the Clancy Brothers and Jac Holzman, to reach for a more pop-oriented sound at times. Though he favored a purer approach to folk than Lou and Alex did while they were together, he always wanted to aim for a larger audience than the folk movement, even at high noon in 1963, could provide. It was also a shrewd investment in the future, reaching a once-young audience growing older, more affluent, more settled. They would be more attuned to music that was soothing and reassuring after a hard day at the office than more energetic folk fare.

As hardcore Limeliters fans would discover to their shock, Glenn's commitment to folk music, while ardent, was not particularly deep. "I'd always wanted to get more sophisticated in the chord structures and singing, and I'd always wanted to sing with a large orchestra," he said. "Folk music to me was something that kind of took the place of what I really wanted to do because I was not a writer, never could write a song, and the stuff I wanted to sing was not available at the time. Nobody was writing songs with lyrics that meant anything to me.

"I think folk music's popularity got songwriters to write songs that had lyrical content that meant something to me. When I started singing alone I suddenly discovered, there were songs available for me to sing that I really cared about. Also, I felt that if I was going to be a performer, I'd better make 'em forget about the fact that I had been with the Limeliters. Which I did."

The credit for steering Glenn toward the middle-of-the-road should go primarily to Neely, whose own background as an arranger made him more comfortable with easy-listening music than he ever was with folk. "That decision to put him in a more contemporary setting was mine, along with Glenn's," said Neely. "We felt the real need to get a contemporary feeling to his records, and that was quite deliberate. I don't recall that he objected to it in any way; in fact, he rather liked it. I do believe the folk idiom applied to the Limeliters as a group more than it did to anyone individually."

Glenn insisted he had the final say on the selection of material since he didn't particularly trust Neely's taste. But as far as soliciting arrangements were concerned, he deferred to Neely's expertise. "I was pretty unsophisticated in those days about arrangements," he said. "I usually took Neely's advice."

In any case, Neely knew exactly what to do. He contracted Hollywood chartmeisters like Hank Levine and Perry Botkin, Jr. to whip up some arrangements. Henry Roth, a classical violinist and critic who played on this and many of Glenn's future solo sessions, remembered Glenn as being "very easy to work with," picking things up quickly, a smooth professional.

On the reverse cover of the first album, there isn't even a hint of Glenn's recent past. Nowhere is there a reference to the fact that he had been a Limeliter; even a quote from a review of a Limeliters performance excises all mention of the group. The cover finds Glenn reclining peacefully under a tree, scanning some sheet music like the professional studio singer he was about to become. And the album's title, taken from of all things, an Ernie Sheldon tune, couldn't have been more appropriate—*Time To Move On*.

The album opens on a transitional note—with the powerful strumming of an acoustic guitar and Glenn's confident voice ringing, "You've heard my voice/And you know my name," with a subtle choir backing him up. But, although the lazy, relaxed rhythm guitar dominates the record, soon the strings start coming in—and though the songs are from folk writers, the sound is easy-listening pop, perhaps with a slight Nashville countrypolitan flavor. Glenn is as perfectly at ease with this sound as a Perry Como or an Andy Williams would have been, his honeyed voice mixing easily with the velvety yet not too plush backdrop.

At least two songs—Fred Hellerman's cozy, carefree "The Honey Wind Blows" and an unsweetened version of Jesse Fuller's folk standard "San Francisco Bay Blues"—would remain in Glenn's repertoire for decades. Probably the most ingratiating number, despite the cooing vocal septet in the rear, is a gently swinging Bob Gibson/Hamilton Camp tune, "Stella's Got A New Dress." *Time To Move On* is a pleasant, undemanding, yet undeniably friendly album, one of the better ones in this genre that Glenn would make.

Predictably *Sing Out!* was aghast at Glenn's new direction, listing this record under the ominous category, "Albums to Avoid." "He sings his bag of songs in a voice as sweet as Coca-Cola syrup," wrote Jay Smith. Yet while *Time To Move On* did not make the national charts, it did very well on the West Coast, selling 50,000 copies in the Bay Area alone—and "The Honey Wind Blows" got some airplay as a single.

The promise of *Time To Move On* led to a follow-up album in April of 1964, *One More Round*. While Glenn became even more entrenched in his easy-listening sound, the unvarnished Yarbrough, sans strings and things, was still permitted to emerge now and then, easily swinging and bending notes on "The New Frankie And Johnny Song." And a number like Bud and Travis' trippy near-hit "Cloudy Summer Afternoon" remains pleasantly fresh in Glenn's charming version after so many years. This record actually charted around No. 142, not exactly doing land office business but clearly rebuilding his audience slowly and patiently.

Come Share My Life, recorded mostly in October, relied mostly on the same formula as its two predecessors. But as Glenn's storehouse of folk-influenced material ran down, tunes from Broadway ("More I Cannot Wish You" from *Guys and Dolls*), Don Robertson (whose hand-clapping "The Happy Whistler" was made-to-order for Glenn's superb whistling), and a doleful Charles Aznavour/Oscar Brown Jr. collaboration, "A Young Girl," began to fill the gaps. Also, we begin to hear arranger David Gates give Glenn's music a slightly contemporary boost with the subtle addition of an electric guitar. This album inched up to No. 112 on the charts, pushing Glenn a bit further on his way.

Occasionally Glenn would take a break from Neely and work with other producers during this period. A month after the *Time To Move On* sessions, Glenn made a sole date with the same Herman Diaz who did the Limeliters' first demo, but it produced nothing worthy of release. In 1964, Al Schmitt, who had been the engineer for many of the Limeliters albums, was brought in as a producer to give Glenn's music a slightly more commercial sound. The combination clicked on Mike Settle's intriguing modal tune, "Jenny's Gone And I Don't Care" (which featured Glen Campbell's 12-string guitar) and another track from that session, a driving version of another soon-to-be standard Yarbrough rouser, "That's The Way It's Gonna Be," eventually made it on the *Come Share My Life* album. Tellingly, it was the uptempo, folk-like numbers from this period that remained in Glenn's concert repertoire the longest, not the string-laden ballads.

Meanwhile, Glenn's personal life was still in a state of chaos. He and Peggy were constantly breaking up and getting back together, and Glenn was frequently forced to move out of their Sausalito home down to Los Angeles, only to return shortly after. It led to a frantic comedy of commuter moving runs up and down U.S. 99, driving ever-loyal Jonathan Moore—who loaded and drove the truck—absolutely bonkers.

"I would get a call, 'Jonathan, come and get a truck, we're moving,' he recalled. "So, I move all the shit out of the house in Sausalito down here. Three or four days later, they don't like it, get this truck, load it up again, back up to Sausalito. I get to Sausalito, three days later, 'She's changed her mind.' This happened at least four times. One time, halfway there, I called up to see if I should keep going, and he said, 'No. Bring it back! She's staying.' I turned the truck around.

"The last time it happened, Glenn went back up to the house and we got up there about 2 o'clock in the morning, and someone called the police and thought we were breaking and entering into the house—which we were, because of course, he'd lost the key. I was notorious in Sausalito; I had more tickets out for me and more warrants for my arrest than anyone since Jack the Ripper—and no money to pay them. I remember hiding behind this bush and listening to this stupid police sergeant talking to Glenn, thinking, 'Christ, if he could see me, we'd be nailed, and Glenn would be caught for harboring a fugitive.' But we did get in the house, loaded up the truck again, and drove back. Now Glenn liked to drive back instantly. Never mind sleeping."

Even after his divorce from Peggy became official, Glenn greatly missed his two children, and as a result, he really didn't want his marriage to end. Indeed, Peggy still came down with the children from the Bay Area to stay with Glenn in Los Angeles—and soon, Glenn magnanimously bought a lovely home on Woodstock Road in the Hollywood Hills not far from Laurel Canyon and moved her in. Yet true to form, Peggy was not about to be tied down again. "One day I went out to do a show and when I came back, she disappeared; she just took off with the kids and left," Glenn recalled with an unforced laugh. "And I thought, well that's the end of that."

Glenn stayed on alone in the Woodstock Road home, which has an attached office-guest house and a sweeping view of the tree-shaded canyon below the living room. Naturally he decorated the interior with nautical motifs, preparing himself for the day when he could achieve his dream of sailing around the world.

Meanwhile, he concentrated upon developing his solo career, exploring his new bag of slicked-up, urban folk songs, working again with a touring package containing a jazz group, comedian and himself. He would also be sifting through the abundant catalogue of a hustling 31-year-old ex-drifter who had moved into his guest house-office—a man who within the next five years would become the best-selling poet in the English language.

Rod McKuen had led a rather colorful seat-of-the-pants life up until then. Born out of wedlock in Oakland, California, he claimed to have been shuttled all over the West in his childhood, wherever his mother and stepfather could find work. According to his account, after a few earlier attempts, he ran away from home at 11, working as a firefighter and ranch-hand until the authorities found him.

Three years of the Nevada School of Industry—a reform school— only inflamed his wanderlust, and upon release Rod went on the rodeo circuit, worked as a lumberjack, and eventually ended up at 18 with his own late-night show, "Rendezvous With Rod," back in Oakland. From there, with the interruption of a hitch in the Army, Rod drifted wildly from one bailiwick of show business to another. He was an imitation-Belafonte intermission folksinger at the Purple Onion while the Gateway Singers played the hungry i nearby (for awhile, they shared the same guitar player). He became a Hollywood actor, landing several roles in teenybopper films before having his contract suspended for refusing rather profanely to act in a campus horror flick. He landed in New York, selling pints of his blood and crashing cocktail parties in order to eat. He became a rock 'n' roll singer with a minor 1962 dance hit to his credit, "Oliver Twist," losing his voice as a result of too many nights screaming in front of his rock band.

By 1963, the French had adopted McKuen in his new guise of a rough-hewn yet sensitive American version of the worldly boulevardier. Indeed, McKuen formed alliances with three French chansonniers, Jacques Brel, Charles Aznavour and Gilbert Becaud, translating their songs into English while Brel did the same with McKuen's songs in French. Still, by the time he returned to Hollywood in 1964, he had not really caught on in America except among a tiny cult of insiders who found his foreign records and heard demos of his songs.

But Glenn was one of the few who knew. One of the submissions for his first solo album was a sentimental McKuen tune called "The World I Used To Know," which Glenn immediately liked and included on the record. Not long after the album's release in February of 1964, Glenn picked up the phone one day, and it was Rod McKuen, thanking him for recording one of his songs. He then asked Glenn if he would like to hear some more. Intrigued, Glenn invited McKuen up to Sausalito, and McKuen came prepared with several of his tunes, which even then numbered well in the hundreds.

Glenn was floored by what he heard and what he saw. Here was someone with whom he thought he could identify—a loner, a restless man who always had to be on the move, a man in sneakers and dungarees who was as casual about his clothes as Glenn himself. Here was a fellow who wrote songs about world-weary lone wolves who drifted from town to town, the women they romanced, won, and lost, the inspirational lessons they learned from life, the poignancy of growing old—things that Glenn knew partly from experience, partly from instinct.

McKuen also had a bit of a business problem. "He told me he was in trouble with his publisher because they were holding money from him trying to get him to re-sign his contract," Glenn recalled. "I suggested if he needed any cash to hold him over (so he wouldn't have to do something he didn't want to do) I'd be happy to lend him money. About a week later, he called me up and asked, 'How would you like to be my partner in a publishing firm?' I said I would, and he moved up here where my office is (on Woodstock Road), and he wrote about 100 songs here which we demoed."

A tireless dynamo who claimed to work 16-hour days on only five hours of sleep (to some interviewers, he increased that to 18-hour days), McKuen went into high gear—and Glenn found himself himself carrying the ball for McKuen's songs and poems. They formed a publishing firm that McKuen named Stanyan Music after one of his poem/songs, "Stanyan Street" (an actual street in San Francisco). They turned out demo albums of McKuen songs—occasionally in duets with Glenn's tenor blending with McKuen's unctious, gravelly voice—and began getting action on the tunes from the Kingston Trio, Jimmie Rodgers, and his old mates, the Limeliters. Glenn even taught Rod how to drive, for despite living in the automobile capital of the world, McKuen had never been behind the wheel of a car.

McKuen songs and spoken poems started turning up in greater numbers on Glenn's own albums. "Love's Been Good To Me", "Isle In The Water," and the lengthy poem/song "The Lovers" made the *One More Round* album; three more, including "Stanyan Street," appear on *Come Share My Life*. Over a span of a little over seven years, Glenn would record and release some 79 Rod McKuen songs, an amazing homage to a single writer from a non-writing singer.

Yet while Glenn was rapidly identifying himself with the gospel of life according to Rod, his real breakthrough as a solo star would not come with a McKuen ballad, nor a dressed-up modern folk song. Instead, it would be a movie tune, with music by the prolific film composer Elmer Bernstein and lyrics by none other than Ernie Sheldon.

Moreover, when Glenn was presented with the song, he had no idea it would be a smash. "As a matter of fact," he said, with typical candor, "I didn't want to do it!"

Baby, The Rain Must Fall, a film with Steve McQueen and Lee Remick about a guitar player with a short fuse and his long-suffering wife, is a little-known artifact today. But in late 1964, Columbia Pictures was anxious to break it out, and one way to do that was to get some action on its title tune. Originally the film was called *Traveling Lady,* but when Neely Plumb saw the film and heard a demo of "Baby, The Rain Must Fall," he was so knocked over by the tune he persuaded producer Mike Frankovich to change the name of the film.

While Neely thought the song had the potential of breaking out, he wouldn't have staked his career on the notion. "I wish I could tell you that I had that kind of ken," he said. "I certainly liked it, I felt that it was a new direction, a new projection of Glenn into a market where he could have a hit. But God knows we've been disappointed in the business so many times. I thought I had a lot of hits that didn't turn out to be hits."

"Neely Plumb was trying to talk me into doing it," Glenn recalled. "I don't think he thought it was going to be a smash either, but he had some pressure from the movie company to have me do it because I was beginning to get some reputation and they thought I would be a good person to record it.

"I got a demo of the song, and I didn't like it and I said I wouldn't do it. And he said, 'Why don't you have a screening of the movie, maybe you'll like it better.' I'm kind of a movie buff and I was really excited about the movie; it was the beginning of a new era in moviemaking but it was a little ahead of its time. I thought the movie was going to be a smash and I figured what the hell, just do this song. And it turned out that the movie was a bomb, and the song was a smash, so that shows you how smart I am!"

In fact, the song seems tailor-made for Glenn, for Ernie's lyric comes from the point of view of a restless loner who shuns fame and fortune and lets his instincts lead him through life. David Gates' arrangement was a breakthrough for Glenn, his first embrace of something resembling a medium rock beat, with strings, French horns and vocal quintet cushioning the impact. And the flexible melody line allows Glenn to soar with effortless power, even improvising slightly. It's a well-made pop record, thoroughly contemporary and hip to the times.

While RCA Victor thought they may have had a winner, the single, backed with McKuen's "I've Been To Town," wasn't an instant smash upon its release in January 1965. But Ken Kragen, now Glenn's manager, went straight to work on it with the energy and promotional flair for which he would later become famous. Among other stunts, seizing on the "Rain" theme, he sent umbrellas to the most important disc jockeys in the country. Glenn went on a television show called *Hollywood A Go Go* to lip-synch his new single, dressed in a business suit, looking slimmer than he ever would again, with go-go girls in raincoats gyrating in front of a hungry i-style brick wall.

Finally, after a month or so, Neely was beginning to hear about some action from RCA's men in the field. "I remember one of the first times one of the promotion men called me from some town in New York and said, 'They've sold a hundred records here, that's news,' Neely recalled. "I thought, well, big deal, we've sold a hundred records." But he was right. From that point, it was a wipeout; it just went straight-away from there. That little barometer of a small town in New York State selling a hundred records was what turned the company on, and they really got right behind it. His albums took off after that, and we had a nice run based on that."

Indeed, "Baby, The Rain Must Fall" accomplished for Glenn what the Limeliters never could pull off themselves—a hit single that would be within earshot of anyone with a transistor radio. It debuted on *Billboard*'s April 17, 1965 pop singles chart and quickly rose to the No. 12 spot, staying on for 14 weeks, a respectable total in those days. It reached No. 1 in major radio markets like San Francisco and Chicago. It racked up sales of 500,000 copies, pulling the *Come Share My Life* album (which had just been issued in March) along with it up the album charts. The moment had finally met the material and the artist at the right time.

What the artist lacked at the time, though, was an album that had "Baby, The Rain Must Fall" on it. By now, Glenn was just piling up tracks without a specific album in mind; indeed, even then, RCA Victor was reaching back as far as Glenn's first solo session for filler songs on *Come Share My Life*. Suddenly, "Baby, The Rain Must Fall" had entered the charts, looking like a solid hit, and RCA Victor was caught with only about half an album in the can. They got Glenn into the studio in April to cut four more tunes, including three new ones from McKuen's burgeoning Stanyan catalogue. These were combined with the 1964 tracks and yet another tune from Glenn's first session, and rush-released in June just after the single peaked.

Hence the *Baby, The Rain Must Fall* album, a patchwork that on the whole is no better and no worse than the average RCA Yarbrough package. Nevertheless, it was the album that had the hit—and spurred by that, plus RCA Victor's biggest promotional guns, it became Glenn's best-selling album, peaking at No. 35 and staying on the charts for 24 weeks. The most interesting cuts, other than the hit, are all on side two. Mason Williams' jaunty yet slightly aching "Long Time Blues" is completely different from his inferior rewrite that he recorded later—and Glenn's performance, the arrangement, everything about this track, is captivating. Prior to this, the scuffling multi-talented Texan had been known primarily for a zany, clap-along album called *Them Poems*, though some of his tunes had been taken up by the Kingston Trio. But thanks to Jonathan Moore, who claimed to have turned Glenn on to the song, Williams scored a serious tune on a hit album. Also, there was a driving leftover from 1963, "Billy Goat Hill," with Glen Campbell's 12-string setting the pace, and McKuen's atypical cracker-barrel trifle, "Everybody's Rich But Us," where as a joke, Glenn deliberately sings off-key without his customary vibrato.

As "Baby, The Rain Must Fall" leaped up the charts that April, already there was pressure for a followup, preferably in the same rocking idiom. Again, Columbia Pictures, through its publishing arm Screen Gems/Columbia Music, came up with a tune—"It's Gonna Be Fine," a pounding number by the red-hot husband-and-wife team Barry Mann and Cynthia Weil, whose "You've Lost That Lovin' Feeling" took the Righteous Brothers and their producer Phil Spector to No. 1 only two months earlier. Again, Gates was brought in to do the arrangement. Evidently, he had been listening intently to the radio, for his chart has a booming, reverberant, Spector-like sound—and Glenn soars triumphantly over the grand fog of voices, guitars, drums, violins and harpsichord. It's a powerful, rocking record, even better than "Baby, The Rain Must Fall"—and of course, Glenn didn't want to do that one either.

"I think they probably wanted to make as commercial an attempt as they could," Glenn said. "I didn't want to do that. I wanted to follow

'Baby, The Rain Must Fall' with a ballad because I figured that there were a lot of things I could do well, but ballad singing I do better than most anybody. But they didn't agree. I had no control over what they put out as singles. I had control over what I sang and what went on the albums, but what they took off as a single, they just did it. Unsuccessfully, I might add."

Released right on top of the *Baby, The Rain Must Fall* album in July, "It's Gonna Be Fine" must have been a letdown to RCA Victor, for it only made it as far as No. 56. That would be Glenn's last trip to the Hot 100, although RCA Victor kept on releasing singles in hope of another jackpot. Inevitably, RCA Victor gathered what modest success it had on the "It's Gonna Be Fine" single and issued an album of the same name in October. Glenn's new, soft rocking sound is more in evidence here than ever; with Perry Botkin, Jr. joining Gates in bringing in electric instruments. But while Glenn turns in his usual warm, caressing, professional performances, the material often lets him down; indeed, the title track towers over the rest of the record.

In late 1965, "Ain't No Way," a single written by P.F. Sloan (he of the notorious "Eve Of Destruction") and Steve Barri, went all the way into rock, with double-tracked vocals by Glenn and no strings or choir to muck things up. The backing track sounds like something the Monkees would have been proud to use a year later, and Columbia Pictures submitted another film tune, "You Can't Ever Go Home Again," (from *Ride Beyond Vengeance*) for the flip side. But despite Glenn's ability to assimilate rock material and turn out credible pop singles, RCA Victor was aiming at the wrong audience. Glenn's core audience was older than the baby boomers, and in those days, this older audience bought LPs. His next release, therefore, would be directed right at that market, and the McKuen cult.

The Lonely Things, entirely composed of Rod McKuen and Rod McKuen-translated songs, may be Glenn's greatest solo achievement. Concept albums, of course, were nothing new in the record industry even then. But *The Lonely Things* is more than just an all-McKuen album. Set in romantic, fog-shrouded San Francisco, alternating between spoken poetry and song, it amounts to a complete, self-contained song cycle, one that speaks of a bleak, despairing solitude that follows lost love. Along the way, there is a wonderful love letter to the city ("So Long, San Francisco") that anyone who knows the city will understand. Eventually, the artist's lover comes back but by then, it is too late, the feeling is gone ("People Change"). The last track, "A Kind Of Loving" is an astonishingly fitting epilogue to the cycle; it is as if McKuen himself is speaking, offering a statement of purpose as to why he does what he does.

This album is Glenn's answer to Frank Sinatra's great *Only The Lonely* album, and there are times when he approaches the Chairman in sheer feeling and intensity. Particularly on the title track, Glenn gives a dark and anguished performance, the likes of which we have not heard before in his solo career. Mort Garson's arrangements are uncommonly good, often using just strings against a smooth understated rhythm, and Lincoln Mayorga's subtle piano gets a rare credit on the liner.

Although this album plays as if it had been conceived as a piece, RCA's session files show that several other tracks, including some not by McKuen with different arrangers, were also recorded during these sessions. The day before *The Lonely Things* sessions got underway, Glenn pushed through a double session of material, including several McKuen tunes, that ended up in the reject file. And in the middle of the album's sessions, Glenn cut an Ernie Freeman chart of Alex's "Cold December"—which lyrically, if not musically, would have fit into the album's concept. Even though his song didn't make the final cut, *The Lonely Things* remains Alex's favorite among Glenn's solo albums, citing the unity of its concept. It also found favor with the public, rising to No. 61 on the charts, staying on for nearly half a year. Most importantly, the album launched the sudden rise to fame and fortune of its composer in America.

There is a most interesting addenda to that story. At the bottom of the album, there appeared the message in small print, "The poems included are from the book *Stanyan Street and Other Sorrows* by Rod McKuen, published by Stanyan Music, Box 2783, Hollywood California." Fine, but there was only one problem...there was no book by that title in existence! As the album caught on, letters from fans who bought the album and wanted to order the book started pouring into Glenn's home. While Glenn insisted upon the reference to the book on the liner, it was McKuen who approved the album's proofs in Glenn's absence and inserted the address on the liner. Thus, Glenn had no idea what was going on until he came home from a tour one day and found his living room filled with several tall mailbags. Glenn then marched into his guest house and told Rod, "You gotta start writing this book." McKuen set to work on it with his usual furious enterprise, finishing it, so he claimed, in just two weeks and Glenn himself did the editing. The book came out through Stanyan Music later in 1966, and Glenn and Rod managed to sell 65,000 copies out of Glenn's home until they simply could not handle the tremendous demand by themselves. At this point, Random House stepped in and took over distribution the following year.

McKuen's fortunes skyrocketed from there. By late 1969, two million hardback copies of his books of poetry were in print. By 1976, book sales had reportedly grown to 16 million, and recordings of his 1,500-odd songs by himself and others topped 180 million in sales. *Newsweek* had crowned him the "king of kitsch," and *Time* couldn't decide whether he was "the only American chansonnier" or "the greatest put-on since Tiny Tim." A Jesuit seminarian went so far as to compare Rod with Jesus Christ—which of course, made McKuen more famous than ever.

But his close friendship with Glenn was long over by then. According to Rein Neggo, Jr., McKuen allegedly had sold the rights of the *Stanyan Street* book to Random House before he bought out Glenn's share of the publishing, after which he offered Glenn only a "miniscule amount of money compared to what he got from Random House."

In McKuen's autobiography, *Finding My Father*, though, Rod says that all he wanted and received for the book's rights was a blue Mercedes 250 SL. "He's a fucking liar," Rein angrily retorted when asked about this, claiming that Rod got a lot more money than he was letting on.

Perhaps shockingly in our litigation-happy society, Glenn never filed a lawsuit against McKuen. "Glenn's the type of guy who doesn't do stuff like that," said Rein. "He hates that shit. He'll fight to a point and then instead of fighting any more, he'll say it's over. He got so pissed off at him that he wanted out. He just does that."

In any case, their friendship was ended but not their collaboration, for after a cooling-off period, Glenn would continue to record McKuen material. "Glenn is the type of guy who remembers but doesn't harp on it," said Rein. "If you screw him, he'll remember it, but life is too short to worry about it. He'd rather break off the relationship than to be mad at somebody for the rest of his life."

For McKuen, the critical role Glenn played in launching his career was simply written out of his life. In several interviews McKuen gave to various national magazines in the late '60s and early '70s, not once does he even hint that he and Glenn were in business together. He told *Esquire* that he put out *Stanyan Street and Other Sorrows* with his own money, and if Glenn is mentioned at all—and he rarely is—it is only to acknowledge that, yes, Glenn Yarbrough, among other performers, recorded his songs, and that "Stanyan Street" is on Glenn's album. Glenn's name comes up in McKuen's autobiography just once, and then only in passing with a bunch of other folk performers—including one "Alex Gottlieb" [sic]—who allegedly hung out at the house and apartment he shared with his mom in Hollywood.

Later on, though, McKuen would suffer fits of remorse. "I did meet Rod McKuen one time in the airport in Chicago when I was changing planes," remembered Jonathan Moore. "He said, 'I'm still very upset about Glenn. If it weren't for Glenn, I would have never done anything in my life, probably. But Glenn hates me, and I don't know why.'"

The picture sleeve from the hit single that made
Glenn's solo career take off. Released 1965.

Chapter Fifteen

By 1966, Glenn had arrived at the zenith of his career. Alone, he was probably better-known than the Limeliters ever were—thanks to his hit single, his voice on commercials, and now, the burgeoning demand for anything associated with Rod McKuen. Just as the Limeliters had built a base on the college campuses, so had Glenn, for he would do a lot of campus homecoming concerts during this period. But Glenn's audiences had become completely different from that of the Limeliters' hip intellectual crowd. "Those who were fans of the Limeliters never really continued to remain fans after I started working alone," recalled Glenn. "I never saw many of them."

"The Rod McKuen album on the college campuses was just like an underground hit throughout America," remembered Rein Neggo, Jr. "The girls would just love to play that thing over and over. The reaction we got at the college campuses from the girls was unbelievable. He was like a hero to these girls; these girls would drag their boyfriends to the concerts and boys had no idea what the hell was going on. We did a concert in Denton, Texas at Texas Women's University, and after the show, Glenn was actually mobbed, and all the musicians were even mobbed."

As a souvenir of that period, Glenn made his first live solo album, reserving a block of three days at the faithful, if now struggling hungry i in June 1966, spiriting some L.A. session men to San Francisco, and passing out lyric sheets to the audience. The result is a noisy good time, kind of an antidote to *The Lonely Things* where Glenn finally lays down some tunes he had been unable to successfully record in the studio ("The Mermaid," "What You Gonna Do?"), seven more McKuen songs he had not gotten around to before, and even some out-and-out rock 'n' roll ("Me and My Dog"). Over a decade later, Glenn would profess dissatisfaction with this live album, yet there is an appealingly rollicking spirit afoot as Glenn interacts amiably with his singing fans.

An earlier attempt to record at the hungry i with Glenn's own band on August 9, 1965 was shelved but finally released in 2001 as *The San Francisco Tapes*. This show has a more intimate feel—no horns or added reverb.

He was making more money now than ever before; his income shot up to $350,000 a year in the late '60s. Glenn invested in property all over the globe—houses in New Zealand and Hawaii, a Beverly Hills apartment building, a banana plantation in Jamaica. He set his father Bruce up on a large farm in Hawaii, where he would raise everything he needed there himself, attracting a gaggle of hippies à la Lou who pursued organic farming on land nearby.

Having always loved to drive, Glenn was able to indulge a yen for fast luxury cars for the first time. He bought a white Rolls-Royce, which he took on tour in the fall of 1967 all decorated with plastic flowers apropos the period. He also had a 1958 Speedster, a 1964 Porsche, a Bentley, a Mercedes-Benz and two Ferraris, one of which (a California Speedster) he could have later sold for a million dollars. Neggo remembered that car very fondly, having once driven it himself. "Glenn took it one time from Denver to San Francisco in some ridiculous amount of hours; a plane wouldn't have been any faster," he said. "I'm surprised he didn't kill himself." Glenn would often buy diesel cars, which he thought were the wave of the future—and his friends could always tell when he would be dropping in by the acrid fumes that preceded his arrival. "Glenn loves to pollute," said Jonathan Moore with a wry grin.

Glenn was also buying additional boats such as the *Tiki*, an 85-foot schooner used in the TV series, *Adventures in Paradise*. Actor Sterling Hayden, reportedly an experienced sailor himself, warned Glenn not to buy that boat (actually called the *Pilgrim*) because he watched it being built and noticed how poor a job the carpenters did. Glenn, of course, bought it anyway, and it promptly split in two near Tahiti and had to be towed back to the island by the Coast Guard. Later, Glenn tried to start a charter business in the American and British Virgin Islands using the repaired *Tiki* and a 96-foot ketch called the *Black Swan*, but that project failed, too.

Glenn also owned a commercial fishing boat around this time, another rotting hulk. "Every time we went out, it had to be towed back by the Coast Guard," said Jonathan. "Another time, they decided they would lease it to these people. The boat disappeared with all on board and was never seen again. To this day, we don't know what happened to it."

Moore, who by now was opening Glenn's show as a rather risqué comic, said that he served as Glenn's pimp in those days since the star of the show was still rather shy with women. "That was one of my jobs," he deadpanned. "I used to go out and pick up all these young chicks; I thought he liked very young birds. So, I picked up two of them; one was called Julie and the other was called Delight. Julie was a blonde sort of thing and the other one was a very interesting looking girl. Rod McKuen wrote a song for her called 'Delight.' Glenn and she had this thing going; she was very young at the time and her father was furious about it, but they got along quite well after awhile. I used to have to go down and pick her up at lunchtime at Pierce College because Glenn didn't want to be seen at the college picking up young chicks. Delight should have married Glenn—she was a wonderful girl—but for some reason he never did."

One of the groupies who frequented Glenn's concerts would be more determined than the rest of the pack to snag an ex-Limeliter. Anne Graves was an energetic go-getter, an aspiring actress and run-ner up in a Miss Culver City pageant who worked in a flower shop in that town. There she met Rein Neggo, Jr., a former aeronautical engi-neer who had not yet met Glenn. Rein had an exotic birthright, born in Estonia in the throes of World War II (1944), spirited to relocation camps in Germany and Austria when he was but a week old, coming to America with his family five years later when the visas finally came through, owning nothing but the clothes on their backs. Eventually Rein and Annie became drinking buddies, sharing bottles of Old Crow whiskey, with Annie insisting upon a platonic relationship while Rein longed for something more physical. Later, they found out that they were both Glenn Yarbrough fans, and so they went to Glenn's concerts at the Troubadour together.

Glenn recalls that it was Jonathan Moore, a man with a roving eye for women, who pointed Annie out in the crowd to Glenn. "He started coming back to me and said, 'There's a woman out there you've really gotta see,'" Glenn said. "'She's terrific and she wants your body real bad!' Pretty soon, I started noticing her—and she was everything I hated in a woman. She had platinum blonde-dyed hair, which I can't stand. She would sit in the front row and mouth all the words to the songs, which is something I detest. If I see someone doing that in an audience, it throws me off; can't get the words.

"Finally, I was there at New Year's Eve at the Troubadour one time and Jon said, 'She wants to come up and meet you, just meet ya'. And I said, 'Oh, all right.'"

Jonathan then introduced Annie and Rein to Glenn—and brassy Annie seized the moment. "She came up and said, 'How about a New Year's kiss,'" Glenn continued. "She gave me this kiss and I thought to myself, 'Well…one night wouldn't hurt,' 'cause she was good looking. So, I took her home that night and she passed out. I should have known then; she was an alcoholic. Didn't know it for years. I just left her in the bedroom and slept somewhere else and took her home. She was a very interesting woman, still is, unique."

Glenn not only found a new love, he also found himself a road manager in young Rein Neggo, who had never done this kind of work before in his life. Furthermore, his very first gig with Glenn was a trial by fire. Glenn was asked to substitute for Johnny Rivers at the University of Nevada, Las Vegas, at the last minute in February of 1967. But when they arrived in their rented station wagons, Rein found that there was no sound system in the gymnasium where Glenn was to perform, nor could they rent or buy one. Rein actually had to prowl through the student dorms looking for decent amps and speakers from the kids, and using his high school and college background in setting up shows, rigged up a jerry-built system for the concert. "I had two hours to get this thing together," he recalled. "I was ready to quit that night. But everything settled down after that."

In any case, the romance between Glenn and Annie blossomed to the point where they decided to get married in the classic Yarbrough fashion. Glenn was about to appear in Honolulu's Waikiki Shell anyway, so he decided to sail the *Armorel*, then parked in the Ala Wai Yacht Harbor on Oahu, over to the island of Kauai and have the ceremony there. With Rein and Glenn's father on board, they made the journey—and Glenn and Annie were married June 22, 1967 in Kauai's Fern Grotto.

While the trip to the island was unforgettably idyllic, the trip back to Oahu was a nightmare. Glenn didn't bother to check the weather forecasts and, predictably, they got caught in a storm in the middle of the channel.

"It was the first time I'd ever been on a major boat," recalled Rein, "and we were hitting 40 and 50-foot swells. Glenn was seasick, I had the midnight to 4 a.m. watch, and we had waist-high-deep water inside the boat, and I knew we were going to die. He says, 'Don't worry, everything's fine,' even though he's down below seasick. As soon as we got back to Ala Wai Yacht Harbor, I took my credit card and T-shirt and went to the airport, got on a plane, and went to Los Angeles."

Rein soon found that he had been put in charge of a tireless road warrior at the peak of his earning power. Glenn was determined to ride it as hard as he could, squirreling away cash so he could spend all his time sailing someday, In the fall of 1967, Glenn sang a punishing 68 concerts in 64 days, driving everywhere in his Rolls, with a four-door '67 Chevy for the band and a Dodge van for Rein and the equipment. On that tour, Glenn, just as punctual on his own as he was with the Limeliters, arrived late to only one concert—and only because they scheduled a concert for West Virginia in the afternoon and another in Georgetown University that night, failing to reckon with Sunday traffic going back into Washington D.C. "That's the only concert we've ever been late to in the 23 years I've been with him," said Rein.

Another time, Glenn and most of the musicians were on time to a gig in Ames, Iowa, but Rein's van containing all the instruments blew an engine on Interstate 80 120 miles away. But they still started the gig only about five minutes late.

Jonathan Moore remembered this colorful road story after a Huntington Beach, California gig that indicates just how cool and formidable Glenn could be without even trying. "We were driving along Pacific Coast Highway; these guys are honking at us and giving us the finger," he said. "I gave them the finger back. Next thing I know, they pull over in front of us and make us stop. They want to get out and have a fight.

"They started beating me up, then they dragged the guitar player and started punching this poor guitar player who weighed about 80 pounds and was full of drugs, probably. Then Glenn walked around outside the cars—Glenn's pretty big and these guys are pretty large— and he just looked at them and says, 'I think you'd better just stop this now,' and these bunch of guys suddenly stopped. Then Glenn pointed to me in the car and said, 'THAT'S the asshole you should be hitting. He's the one that did it. But don't bother hitting him 'cause he's an idiot.' And the guys said, 'Oh really, OK,' and they got in their car and drove off. I was called an asshole, but it saved the day."

One thing the people touring with Glenn really looked forward to was the food, for a fellow of Glenn's girth naturally had a gigantic appetite. Jonathan Moore recalled that the apres-concert feasts ranged literally from the sublime to the ridiculous, from all-you-can-eat-for-$3.95 roadhouses to the best, most sumptuous restaurants in town. "They'd see us come in and they'd take a look at the size of Glenn and look at their all-you-can-eat banquet and think, oh shit..." remembered Jonathan. "The nice thing about working with Glenn is that you knew you were going to eat!"

Yet while Glenn thoroughly enjoyed singing and traveling, he absolutely loathed the celebrity trappings that had grown around him since "Baby, The Rain Must Fall." Still a basically shy man by nature, he did just about anything he could to hide from the public when he wasn't performing. For years, his management used the line sketch of Glenn on the *Baby, The Rain Must Fall* album on his publicity with the intent of blurring his features so he wouldn't be recognized easily.

"Glenn was a giant star in those days, and people would come up and mob him in restaurants and stuff," said Jonathan. "He hated that. I loved it, 'cause, I'd pick up the chicks. I was like a bird on the hippo's back."

"He enjoyed coming to a town early and not being recognized," Neggo recalled. "He hated (the period) after the concert, because people would recognize him and he couldn't go get his hamburger, milk shake and French fries, which he loved at the time. He enjoyed driving the bus into the place and asking for directions, and they would tell him where to park the bus, not knowing he was the star of the show. He loved getting into town early and walking around and doing things before the show. After the show, he would lock himself in his room and wouldn't come out.

"He expected a lot from the people around him. The only time he got upset was if somebody did something stupid. He never got upset because of the travel. If he had to do two shows in one day, or if we had to drive 700 miles between dates, he was not going to go to the airport and fly; he would drive with everybody else. He enjoys the road; he's a gypsy at heart."

Indeed, Glenn always insisted upon driving to the gigs whenever possible, which Moore attributed not to a fear of flying but simple cheapness. According to Lou, "Never fear while Yarbrough's here" was his motto behind the wheel.

"Glenn loved to drive," said Moore. "The worst part of Yarbrough jobs was the driving, and he would rather drive 3,000 miles, drive all night, and expect you to be alive at the end and do the thing.

"Glenn liked to drive on empty. As long as the needle said empty, in the middle of the fucking Death Valley, Glenn would be the happiest man in the world. This gave him a challenge, like sailing. And you know, he'd never run out of gas!"

Despite the success with Rod McKuen, Glenn was still musically restless, trying impatiently to move beyond his audience. For the next single in October 1966, Al Schmitt and Neely Plumb brought in arranger Bill Justis, once a hitmaker at Memphis' legendary Sun Records, to try and get Glenn another hit. The result was "Spin Spin," a rocking song by a new singer/songwriter from Toronto named Gordon Lightfoot who had just launched his durable career writing hits for Peter, Paul and Mary and Marty Robbins. With Glen Campbell's 12-string guitar twanging away, Glenn wails with one of his best folk-rock vocals, ear perfectly attuned to the jukebox (though it took at least 18 takes). Backed by Mason Williams' boozy "Love Are Wine," "Spin Spin" deserved to be a smash, but it never appeared above the horizon.

Even though Glenn couldn't even remember recording it, "Spin Spin" is one of the great unknown singles of the mid '60s. It was also the last time Glenn would be in the same recording studio with Plumb, who had recently signed and recorded the Jefferson Airplane—an act of courage and foresight for a major label executive in 1966—and would go on to sign the Monkees for RCA's Colgems label before being abruptly dismissed from RCA Victor.

From the 8th to the 23rd of February, 1967, Glenn was teamed in the studio with producer Rick Jarrard in a crash effort to immerse himself in the writers of the youth movement. Jarrard, who later would break Jose Feliciano and Harry Nilsson into the mainstream, was one of RCA Victor's "hip young producers," in Glenn's words, and apparently, they hit it off well. Together they cut some 20 songs, exploring material by the likes of Stephen Stills, Paul Simon, Ian and Sylvia, Brewer and Shipley, Buffy Sainte-Marie, and Phil Ochs. Though this was their only encounter, Jarrard had a lasting influence on Glenn, for he introduced him to the off-kilter guitar duo of Brian Davies and F. Clark Maffitt— who would work with Glenn well into the '70s. It was also Glenn's first encounter with the new multitrack mores of recording; he cut his vocals in February with just Maffitt and Davies, plus bass and drums, providing the basic arrangements, and either Perry Botkin Jr. or George Tipton would overdub their orchestral arrangements in March. The *For Emily,*

Whenever I May Find Her, album, then, is Glenn's attempt to link arms with the youth movement—or so it seems from Glenn's passionate statement on the liner that expresses regret for only being a "spectator" to the "revolution against hypocrisy and stupidity."

Unfortunately, the package is just too compromised for Glenn to connect with the rock generation. The undistinguished, often intricate orchestral overdubs—known in the business as "sweetening"—get in the way of the songs to a greater degree than ever on Glenn's records; the sound quality is mushy, the voice is often buried. A powerful epic like Ochs' "Crucifixion," which runs for six minutes, is fussed over and diluted by Botkin's trimmings; a simple intense guitar accompaniment would have been far better in this material.

To his credit, Glenn bravely bypassed the obvious standards that every other MOR singer of that time was forced to cover. Yet Glenn seems to back away from the tunes he chose; his delivery is cool, off-hand, uninvolved. Indeed, his earlier unheralded rock singles with Neely and Ai Schmitt sound much more committed than these tracks. Glenn considered it a "very successful album artistically" but the public didn't buy it, for it peaked at a disappointing No. 159, ending a streak of four straight albums that hit the Hot 100. By now, Glenn was openly feuding with RCA Victor, though the main point of dispute was not diminishing sales nor artistic direction. Rather, Glenn was miffed because RCA refused to allow him to participate in a Rod McKuen project on a rival label.

McKuen had concocted the idea of a massive impressionistic union of poetry and music. Now, originally Alex Hassilev had sold the idea of *The Sea* to Jac Holzman at Elektra, with the once and future Limeliter producing and his partner Mort Garson providing the orchestral backgrounds for McKuen's poems. The first volume would be called *The Sea* and later would be joined by *The Earth* and *The Sky* to form a trilogy. "The project actually went quite far along," Alex claims. "Jac Holzman gave us a demo budget and a demo was cut which he heard and approved."

But according to Alex, McKuen suddenly jumped ship, supposedly abandoning the project, only to turn up on Warner Bros' doorstep not long afterwards with the idea. This time, Nashville's Anita Kerr Singers and the San Sebastian Strings would do the backgrounds—and McKuen wanted Glenn, the passionate sailor, to narrate the project.

(In any case, Holzman went ahead with Elektra's *The Sea* project anyway—no contracts apparently had been signed—and Alex went to London to produce the orchestral backgrounds for that and another Garson tone poem called "The City," with *Zodiac* collaborator Jacques Wilson supplying the texts. "I think McKuen felt that Mort was going to overshadow him, and he also felt that Warner Bros. would be a better deal for him," says Alex.)

Innocently, perhaps, Glenn went to the president of RCA Victor and asked permission to do the narration for McKuen's *The Sea*, adding that he would not sing on the record, only recite Rod's poetry. But the record executive turned Glenn down. Glenn retorted, "You're gonna regret this," and stormed out of the office. As a result, a McKuen employee, Jesse Pearson, did the narration for *The Sea*, which went on to sell 500,000 copies for Warner Bros. in 1967 alone.

Cut to later in 1967. It was time for Glenn's contract with RCA Victor to be renewed, and RCA was interested, despite Glenn's declining chart numbers. But Glenn, still fuming from the rejection, instead signed a six-album deal with Warner Bros., despite warnings from Alex, Rein, and others not to do it. "Glenn is stubborn as a mule," said Rein. "They (RCA) wanted to give him a lot of money to renew, and Glenn just basically told them to go to hell. He went to Warner Bros., got less money and probably ruined his career. He was doing this for spite and nothing else."

In effect, the move to Warner Bros. cut Glenn off from one of the critical reasons why he was doing so well on his own. All of those shows that the Limeliters had played for RCA Victor's distributors back in 1960 were continuing to pay off for Glenn when he went solo, for the loyal record men knew how to push his records. Now he had to start from scratch again—and within a short time, Glenn himself realized he had made the worst move of his career, one from which he never recovered.

"It was a very bad mistake I made leaving RCA because although I didn't get along with the brass in New York City, I got along very well with the distributors in the field," Glenn said in a mea culpa. "Consequently, whenever I put an album out, it always hit the charts and went up a certain distance because every distributor would buy X number of copies knowing he would be able to get rid of those copies. But when I moved to Warner Bros., then the distributors essentially didn't know me or what I could sell. And so, they never ordered any records."

Meanwhile, RCA Victor, now bitter over the loss of a steady album seller, systematically began to wreck Glenn's musical reputation. Now, Glenn had already stopped recording for RCA after the Rick Jarrard sessions; indeed, his next album *Honey and Wine* had been assembled from leftovers from the marathon 1966 sessions that produced *The Lonely Things*, plus material from 1965's *It's Gonna Be Fine* and "Ain't No Way" sessions. But despite the unevenness of the material and orchestrations, at least there was an overriding theme; Glenn selecting love songs as a wedding present for his new wife (that's Annie whom Glenn is holding in the air on the back). Indeed, Annie had a major role in programming the album; many of the tunes were Annie's favorites. Also, there are compensations like the Gerry Goffin/Carole King title track in another sharp David Gates arrangement (which flopped as a single), and an attractive Mason Williams tune "They Are Gone" with a good Perry Botkin Jr. bossa nova chart. But perhaps Glenn spoke the truth when his brief liner notes confess, "And you know—we never even got around to listening to the damn thing!"

With *The Bitter and the Sweet*, released in February 1968, RCA started to dig into its refuse pile, ransacking Glenn's outtakes and throwing them together seemingly at random. There are steadily diminishing returns from the "Ain't No Way" sessions ("Face in the Crowd"), five lesser McKuen outtakes, Marvin Hamlisch's insufferably corny "Sunshine, Lollipops and Rainbows," two virtually incoherent arrangements by Mason Williams ("Time and Chance," Hoyt Axton's "I'll Be There") from a disastrous 1966 session.

Having thus undermined Glenn's credibility with record buyers, RCA Victor delivered some really low blows with *Let The World Go By*, released in the summer of 1968 to coincide with Glenn's first Warner Bros. album. Not only did RCA dredge up even worse discards dating all the way back to 1963, they took legitimate singles from Glenn's catalogue, sent producer Sid Feller into a Hollywood studio on April 8, 1968, and ruined them with orchestral overdubs.

Presumably the official rationale was to satisfy the fans who expected lush backdrops on Glenn's albums, particularly those hooked on his McKuen records. But that doesn't explain the inexcusably shoddy quality of these overdubs—with out-of-tune winds and brasses, greasy strings, tangled ensemble. To cite a few examples: a good, loose vocal by Glenn from the hungry i on the title track and two tracks originally recorded with just a lone guitar ("Away," "The Girls in their Summer Dresses") are dragged through the muck and emerge tarnished and glitzy. The worst indignity of all is poured onto the great "Spin Spin," where the brass overdubs are horribly out of sync.

Finally, in November 1968, RCA dumped all the outtakes from the Rick Jarrard sessions, plus another stray from 1963 (Tom Paxton's exquisite "Ev'ry Time"), into the shops on *We Survived The Madness*. Whatever virtues there are here—and Glenn does have some nice moments—are buried with more poor after-the-fact orchestral and organ "sweetening." Once Glenn's fans survived this madness, RCA at last closed the doors of its vaults, mission accomplished.

This sustained campaign of sabotage—which Rein Neggo alleged was the case—took place on several fronts, in the studio and in the shops. "Every time they (Warners) released an album with Glenn, RCA would release another album of stuff they had in the can," Rein claimed. He remembered *The Bitter and the Sweet* and *We Survived the Madness* as "two of the most rotten albums you ever heard because these were all songs that were never supposed to be released.

"Now RCA's field men were very up on Glenn Yarbrough; they had a successful career from the Limeliter days. All the promotion men knew Glenn Yarbrough, all the distributors knew Glenn Yarbrough. So, every time we would go into town and do a concert and expect Warner Bros. promotion men there, no, we saw RCA promotion men.

"We did a record signing in Houston that Warner Bros. had set up. We get to the store and here's a whole thing set up with RCA, with *The Bitter and the Sweet* and the other albums all on a big display. The Warner Bros. guy is sitting there with a very tiny display and just a few albums. The people, they don't know what the hell is on an album when they buy it; they know it's Glenn Yarbrough and they expect a certain level of performance on both albums. And I'm sure they bought the RCA albums and were very unhappy with them."

Warner Bros.—then known as Warner Bros./Seven Arts—at first was very happy to land a star like Glenn; the label's general manager Joe Smith personally presented Rein Neggo with an advance check for $300,000 just before Glenn opened a gig at the hungry i. Immediately, Glenn started working with his old colleague Alex Hassilev, doing a couple of singles en route to an eventual album. One of the tunes, Alex's "Until You Happened To Pass By"—equipped with a nervous beat and ba-baahing foreground vocals—came out in April 1968 and didn't go anywhere.

Smith, mindful that *The Lonely Things* was still a potent seller, went with the tried-and-true, reuniting Glenn and Rod McKuen in the studio around Easter 1968 for another all-McKuen project. Unfortunately, the resulting sequel, *Each Of Us Alone*, lacks almost everything that made *The Lonely Things* so haunting. There is no overriding plot line, just a rewarming of the usual McKuen solitary man persona and sampler-style love philosophy. Glenn doesn't reach down nearly as far into himself, merely applying a routine patina of warmth in the poetry and songs, and the Eddie Karam arrangements are humdrum. McKuen is the producer as well as the composer and, in both capacities, he too seems to be going through the motions. Whatever chemistry they once had is gone; all is mellifluous mood music. (Strangely, the outtakes released by McKuen on his Stanyan label in 1974 are more interesting than the tracks originally chosen for the album.)

"Ea*ch of Us Alone* was rushed through and Warner Bros. wanted to get that thing out and they didn't want to lose the momentum of *The Lonely Things*," recalled Neggo. "That was the whole purpose of signing Glenn in the first place. There was no overdubbing at all. Come in, do it, and get out."

Each of Us Alone received a good-sized promotional buildup, but RCA's simultaneous campaign for its outtake albums may well have confused buyers, for Warners' efforts could only push the album up to the feeble No. 188 slot on the charts. After that, Warners seemed to lose interest in promoting Glenn, and he never charted again with that label.

For his next project, *Somehow, Someway*, Glenn placed his backing in the hands of Jimmy Bowen, trying to move into more contemporary material. But again, the attempt is compromised, a routine session of mild commercial pop/rock with orchestrations that are much too busy. The songs, except for Neil Diamond's "And The Grass Won't Pay No Mind" and Tom Paxton's "The Last Thing On My Mind," are not very interesting, even though Glenn's performances have more sass and vigor than before.

But it wouldn't have mattered much to Glenn's bank account if the albums had become hits. He had already assigned all the royalties to a project that had begun to obsess him even more than sailing. Indeed, Glenn's name isn't even on the front cover—just a white dove and three small boys, one white, one Asian, one Black, all symbols of his new Pilgram SCHOLE foundation.

We have mentioned Glenn's banana plantation in Jamaica in passing but not his purpose for buying it. Glenn wanted to start a school for underprivileged orphaned children there, calling it the School for Children of Happiness, Opportunity, Love and Education—or SCHOLE in shorthand. In Glenn's concert folio around this time, he writes of his motivations for founding the school, borrowing verbatim from the essay that ran on the back liner of *For Emily, Whenever I Have Found Her.* As an earnest example of affluent '60s liberalism casting a longing eye inside the window of the counterculture, this essay is not to be missed.

"I have a firm belief that the future of our nation indeed of the world—is in the hands of the young. A great revolution has begun, led by the youth of this nation, and hopefully will spread around the globe. It is a revolution against hypocrisy and stupidity...against established concepts and precepts that have failed in the past...It is for rebuilding our social structure founded on new premises with more freedom for the individual and his conscience. For mankind, quite possibly close to destruction, salvation seems to be emerging in the young.

"It is my hope that SCHOLE will lead in the establishment of a freer society, and will develop a child to his full potential, with a deeper understanding of himself and those around him."

Rein Neggo, though, recalled that Glenn may have had a less lofty motivation in mind. "The reason the SCHOLE Foundation came about was that he had too much money, didn't know what to do with it," he said. "To save a little bit of money in taxes, he spent a lot of money on this orphanage. But that's Glenn."

In any case, the banana plantation soon became more trouble than it was worth. Jamaica, having been granted independence from Great Britain in 1962, had just gone through its first tumultuous general election campaign of 1967—one marred by considerable violence—and the resulting government proved "impossible" for Glenn to deal with. So he sold the banana plantation and instead purchased 45 acres of wooded land in the San Bernardino Mountains in order to build the school.

The U.S. government obligingly granted it tax-exempt status, and Glenn set to work trying to raise money for it. The original idea was to start small with a student body of about a dozen kids in just one grade, and then add one grade each year afterwards until there was a full slate from nursery school through high school. The kids would live at the school year-round, learning traditional subjects but also with "an emphasis on ecology and the child's personal responsibilities," according to the *Los Angeles Times*.

It opened in the fall of 1970, with a student body of 12, and projections for 60 the following fall. Unfortunately, Glenn ran into the problem that discourages many an idealist from starting charities or running for office—having to ask people to contribute their hard-earned money toward one's dream. And Glenn, always the loner, always one who thought of himself as self-sufficient, couldn't stand that kind of activity for long.

"I had hoped I would find other performers to help finance it, especially Black performers since most of the kids were Black," he recalled. "But I didn't figure on my absolute inability to ask anybody. I hadn't analyzed my own personality enough to realize I am the worst money-raiser there is because I don't ask people for things in my personal life. It was one of the hardest things I ever had to do in my life. And I finally said, that's enough, I'd rather work hard and support it myself."

Once sucked into that situation, Glenn found himself on an exhausting treadmill. He donated his album royalties on *Somehow, Someway*, tour proceeds, all revenue from his concert folios, keeping up his breakneck touring schedule in order to keep his school afloat. Eventually a good deal of his properties—the house in New Zealand, the apartment house in Beverly Hills, the fleet of fast cars—would be thrown into the pot, trying to save his school. He never did teach at the school as he had hoped and planned, for he was much too busy working to support it.

"I did (it) for about three years until it just became impossible to continue because I was working so hard doing things I didn't really want to do in order to support the school," Glenn said. Finally, inevitably, three years after it opened, SCHOLE went out of business, another outpost of idealism done in by the rules of the game it was trying to overturn.

Glenn's career, too, was showing alarming signs of slippage by the turn of the decade. Deserting RCA Victor for Warner Bros. was Mistake No.1, for not only were Warners' distributors unfamiliar with Glenn, the entire company attitude was aiming more and more toward rock and the rise of the singer/songwriter. The mix of Allan Sherman, Bill Cosby, Peter, Paul and Mary and Petula Clark that had built Warners into a major player in the '60s was giving way to the likes of James Taylor, Van Morrison, the Grateful Dead and Alice Cooper. The sister Reprise label was shifting from emphasis on Frank Sinatra, Dean Martin and Trini Lopez to Neil Young, Gordon Lightfoot, Joni Mitchell, and out on the edge, Jimi Hendrix and Frank Zappa. In this new Warner Bros., where the office atmosphere in Burbank was freewheeling and loose, Glenn was probably perceived, unfairly or not, as being a part of the old order, obsolete almost from the moment he signed up.

Mistake No. 2 was the souring of relations with Ken Kragen, who had stayed with Glenn as his manager after the Limeliters broke up. Kragen, now teamed with Ken Fritz in Kragen/Fritz Associates, was making huge strides in the world of entertainment. He was handling the Smothers Brothers, who had landed a major, ultimately path-breaking prime-time variety show on CBS in 1967, and his offices were now in the CBS Television City building at Beverly and Fairfax. Yet he remained in charge of Glenn's career—and one night, when Glenn opened another engagement at the Troubadour, Kragen had flowers sent to the club as a present. Unfortunately, someone at Kragen/Fritz screwed up, and on his monthly statement, Glenn found a bill for the flowers! Steamed by the slight, Glenn demanded and got an appointment to meet with his manager in the penthouse of Television City. Again, there was a slip up; a secretary forgot to tell the security guard that Glenn was coming, and so when Glenn arrived at CBS, the guard refused to let him in, saying he wasn't on the list.

"That typically pissed him off," said Rein Neggo. "That showed how the people at the office didn't know who Glenn Yarbrough was." Glenn's disillusionment with Kragen began at that point, and by 1968, he had cut Kragen off completely by terminating his association with him. That would prove to be a gigantic mistake, given Kragen's managerial triumphs later with Kenny Rogers, whose grey hair and beard and similar laid-back singing style catapulted him to the highest-paid reaches of the music business.

Mistake No.3 was Glenn's refusal to promote himself on television via talk show appearances or variety show guest spots. Glenn had always been a man of candor, never at home with the kissy-kissy, hustling, glad-handing aspects of show business. "If you went on and said what you really thought about serious subjects, it would be more detrimental to you than not going on at all," he told the *Los Angeles Times* in 1971.

"Yarbrough is allergic to TV work," Lou said. "You've got to go on TV in order to sell records, more than he likes to."

One of the few times Glenn made an exception was on a 1969 Chicago TV talk-show, where he promptly got into an argument with another guest about the latter's notion that a tour in Vietnam would straighten out the nation's youth. Not once did he mention his then-current album, to the bafflement of a Warner Bros. promotion man in the studio audience.

Indeed, the Vietnam war greatly disturbed Glenn's artistic equilibrium, leading him further away from his core audience which doted on McKuen love philosophy. The transitions and turmoil of 1968 had affected Glenn so much that he found himself having to abandon for the first time his politically neutral stance on stage. Indeed, in 1971, Glenn worked very hard for Sen. George McGovern in the early stages of his presidential campaign—lecturing on McGovern's abilities after his concerts, trying to organize McGovern chapters on college campuses.

"The war was probably one of the most destructive things to entertainers that ever came up," remembered Glenn. "Most of those I knew who were successful entertainers at the time found it difficult to be entertainers and not to preach. I believe that when you go out on a stage, you just entertain the people and don't hit 'em with your own personal prejudices and beliefs. I always stuck to that principle until after about two or three years of that war, I just couldn't do it anymore. I began to do war protest songs and things I wouldn't have ordinarily done. You can't see what is happening on television and go out and entertain somebody at night without having it spill over."

Moreover, Glenn's moral outrage over the American presence in Vietnam caused him to seek out confrontations; hence the Chicago talk-show imbroglio, hence some other incidents that probably antagonized conservative elements that controlled the music business. "I always much preferred to go in the enemy's camp and hit 'em there," Glenn said. "It doesn't seem to me very profitable for a whole bunch of people with the same idea to get together and pat each other on the back. It always bugged me."

Glenn's next move on records was *Yarbrough Country*, a somewhat cynical Warner Bros. move to capitalize on the country music wave triggered by Johnny Cash's prison albums, Bob Dylan's *Nashville Skyline*, and crossover Top 40 hits by Glen Campbell, Tammy Wynette, Merle Haggard, and others. There isn't very much that is truly countrified about *Yarbrough Country*, other than the cactus, the barbed wire and semi-arid expanses on the cover. Again produced by Jimmy Bowen, at least *Yarbrough Country* isn't nearly as overproduced as their previous collaboration *Somehow, Someway*, allowing plenty of room for the expert, partly-countrified rhythm sections to shine. There is superior material, even some obvious hits to cover—Gordon Lightfoot's "Ribbon of Darkness," the evergreen George Hamilton IV hit "Abilene," Fred Neil's "Everybody's Talkin'," even McKuen's "Jean." Yet again, Glenn doesn't sound terribly involved much of the time; he tosses off the Lightfoot as if he was sight-reading.

Concurrently, Glenn and Alex were slowly patching together Glenn's magnum opus of the Warner Bros. period, *Let Me Choose Life*, which finally came out in 1970. The record is a compilation containing the two singles Glenn made with Alex two years before—now remixed and often greatly improved—five more tracks produced by Alex and his then current single, "Goodbye Girl"/"Every Passing Moment," in which Lenny Waronker and Nick de Caro are listed as producers.

The cover art—a grim, violent collage of America in the late 1960s with the title scrawled in white graffiti—makes its point, an outcry against the dances of death. But the record itself completely avoids any blatant antiwar pitches; if anything, a "you and me against the world" theme often prevails, a deliberately gentle counterpoint to violence and injustice. For his part, Alex was clearly trying to stitch together a unified concept album—and on side one, he succeeds, using pure neo-classical strings as an intimate yet objective connecting thread—as well as tasteful swoops and ghostly white noise from his Moog. Side Two is mostly a patchwork of unrelated singles carefully strung together until the side and album reaches its closing climax with the title track, which contains perhaps Alex's most deeply felt lyrics. Everywhere, Glenn's vocals are strong, committed, punching home the upbeat tunes, soaring to a magnificent peak on the title track. Clearly, he believes in these songs, and he makes even the weakest of them soar.

Glenn considered *Let Me Choose Life* his favorite album, and he pushed it hard. "I put a lot of effort into that record, a lot of beautiful songs went into it, but it wasn't successful," Glenn lamented in 1978. "That's what I wanted to do more of, but I was way ahead of the times."

Rein Neggo, Jr., remembering all the months Alex slaved over it, taking it apart and putting it together again, called it "one of the best overproduced albums ever made. They gave him (Alex) a budget and he started going over budget. Glenn had no idea what the hell was going on until somebody at Warner Bros. finally called Glenn and said, 'We gotta stop this, we're over a hundred grand already. Alex still can't make up his mind.' Finally, Glenn had to step in."

Perhaps as a reaction to the skyrocketing budget for *Let Me Choose Life*, Neggo took over the production tasks himself on Glenn's next record, *Jubilee*. This time, Neggo simply recorded Glenn live at Louisiana State University over three days with just his regular backing group, using a primitive little Shure four-channel mixer. A young fellow named Christian Wilde would be assigned to mix the title track as a single, and as a result, he was given full co-credit for producing the entire album (Rein denied that Wilde had anything more to do with it).

The album was recorded under circumstances that can only be called exhausting. Glenn, his crew, and their families had just come off two consecutive long drives – 400 or-so miles from somewhere in Ohio to Johnson City in eastern Tennessee and then nearly 800 miles from there to Baton Rouge, where they had to perform and record that evening! "The first day of the recording was shit; we were just going through the motions, we were so tired," remembered Rein. "But sometimes you don't think and it comes out fine. The next day we had rehearsals and all, but I think we got most of the takes the first day. As soon as we broke the concert, we were on the road again driving to New Orleans."

Yet despite having never produced so much as a note of music before in his life, Rein intuitively hit upon the best way to present Glenn—just give him solid, minimal, folk-rock backing, good contemporary material he believes in, and let him sing. As a result, of all Glenn's albums in the decade after the Limeliters' breakup, this is the one that sounds the best today, for no cotton candy orchestras nor ambitious production tricks get in Glenn's way.

Jubilee is Glenn's most militant album on his own, for there is no mistaking the pacifistic intent of side one. After Peter Boyd's musings on America circa 1970 in "So Much Comfort in You," we hear a much more effective recording of "The Crucifixion" than the studio version—leaner and meaner in every way—and it segues right into Alex's "A Hundred Men," where the message comes through with unimpeded power. It ironically refutes Glenn's usual credo that entertainers should only be entertainers, for he could be unusually entertaining *and* stimulating when he had politics on his mind.

Norman Greenbaum's goofy, hard-charging ode to a rural weekend, "Jubilee," lightens the mood but Hamilton Camp's "People In A Hurry" is a concise statement of the hippie critique of the American money machine. These subversive thoughts make the three oldies that close the album—"San Francisco Bay Blues," "The Honey Wind Blows" and a hurried "Baby, The Rain Must Fall"—seem like anachronistic append-ages to get some sales mileage.

In fact, the record didn't hit any of its intended targets—be it the coveted youth market, Glenn's old fans, or Limeliters diehards who, hav-ing long given up on Yarbrough, might have connected with this album had they given it a chance. "I never saw *Jubilee* at all in any of the stores," said Neggo. "I don't think they pressed very many of those." But one of those concerts did have an effect upon a young man from Hot Springs, Arkansas who trekked down to LSU for the gig. He was a Rhodes scholar home from Oxford, worried about his draft status, passionately against the war, and a sometime saxophone player himself. Over two decades later, an organizer for the 1993 Kennedy Center Inaugural Gala revealed that Bill Clinton had been at one of the concerts—and after his election, Clinton told CNN that Glenn Yarbrough is one of his favorite singers. It is entirely possible that Glenn's political songs may have had an influ-ence upon the mind of the 42nd President.

Glenn's contract—and desire to keep performing—was winding down, and neither he nor Warner Bros. wanted any more of each other. A rather anemic single, "Friend of Jesus"/"Gentle Hands and Gentle People"—saluting the Jesus fad on one side and the rural hippie move-ment on the other—failed to catch on with either camp. Wearily going back to the old formula, the brass at Warners lured Glenn and Rod McKuen back into the studio one more time in February of 1971, with Rod producing for his own Stanyan label.

Rein Neggo remembered that an ailing Glenn literally came in off his boat to do the album. "If you look at the pictures, Glenn looked awful," he said. "I drove him to the studio, and he was physically ill. Rod was conducting the orchestra, handed Glenn a sheet of paper, and he was out of there as fast as he could. He recorded live in front of the orchestra."

With no real concept in mind, *Bend Down And Touch Me* basically gathers together 14 McKuen tunes Glenn hadn't gotten around to in the past. Yet *Bend Down And Touch Me* is a far better record than *Each Of Us Alone*, thanks mostly to some gorgeous arrangements. Count Basie alumnus Billy Byers handled nine of the songs, including a surprisingly jazzy "Lonesome Cities" (Glenn's vocal proves he could have made a fine jazz singer had he felt like it). Also, there were two charts by Jimmie Haskell and three by one of Frank Sinatra's favorite arrangers, Don Costa, who also arranged Sinatra's McKuen album. Still, one wonders how Glenn could bear to sing the embarrassing tunes from the cartoon feature, "A Boy Named Charlie Brown"—and only Sinatra has made something of the melodramatic "I'm Not Afraid." By now, McKuen's name is as large as Glenn's in every corner of the album from the spine to the jacket to the label. The only image of Glenn is mostly hidden by a sheet of Rod's music on the back of the jacket, and the front has just a provocative photo of an embracing nude hippie couple in the woods (Morningstar?). But even that come-on couldn't lift this final Warner Bros. record into Chartsville.

And Glenn moved on—again. Still in search of a direct connection to youth, whose movement he continued to admire from afar, Glenn hooked up in mid 1970 with a long-haired, hippie rock band known as the Havenstock River Band. This was apparently the real thing, a loud, decibel-crazy group which Glenn thought would put him back in good favor with the college market that had outgrown McKuen.

"Alex saw 'em first and he mentioned them to me and so I went to see them perform," Glenn recalled. "I recognized right away that although they were playing rock, in spirit they were folk musicians. They didn't know it themselves. When I had them, that was the most fun work I'd had in a long time."

Rein Neggo, as ever, thought it another in a long line of quirky things Glenn has done to try and get out of the music business. "It was his way of getting even with the people, the 'normal' people who thought he was normal, who thought he would come out and sing love-moon-spoon-type songs," he said about the Havenstock band. "Their first note they'd do; two of the guys (Archie Johnson and Gordon Curry) would scream as loud as they possibly could into the microphone. Thirty per cent of the audience would leave in the first ten minutes. We were blowing people away in droves."

Glenn was trying to give the young audience what he thought they wanted while repudiating his base, refusing to sing McKuen songs and grudgingly doing "Baby, The Rain Must Fall." Yet while he was interested in the material by young writers, he wasn't interested in performing their hits—the tunes his audiences really wanted to hear. Again, Glenn was adamant about making it on his own; indeed, there were times where Glenn would latch onto new songs with the potential of gold but would perversely drop them just when someone else was scoring with them.

"His motto is, if it's a song people know, I ain't going to sing it," Rein wryly noted. "During that time, we were doing 'Joy To The World' before it was a hit, and it was really done well with this group. Hoyt Axton gave Glenn the song a long time before. We were also doing 'Put Your Hand In The Hand' before it was a hit. Ocean saw the song being done with the Havenstock and that's where they got it from. As soon as a song became a hit, Glenn stopped doing it because then it would be associated with somebody."

Sometime in 1970, Glenn and his new rock band made an album for tiny Custom Fidelity's Im'press label, for whom Alex was vice-president of A&R. Even though Glenn technically still owed Warner Bros. one more album at the time (*Bend Down And Touch Me*), Warners apparently didn't give a damn, for Glenn wasn't selling at all with them anyway. For all the noise and bluster their live appearances may have produced, the Havenstocks come off like pussycats on their album with Glenn, a restrained, tasteful, polished country-folk-rock backup group for a singer eager to vie with the James Taylor-variety troubadours of the day. As produced by Alex, it's a friendly, unassuming, rural contemporary-flavored package, one that would set the pattern for Glenn's live appearances for at least the next decade. It was also poorly distributed (Custom Fi went bankrupt soon thereafter), and subsequently ignored.

But Glenn wasn't too concerned, for he was getting his new luxurious 46-foot sailboat, the *Jubilee*, ready for his long-delayed world cruise. The boat was being built in a shipyard in Vancouver, British Columbia, and Glenn became totally wrapped up in the project—supervising the pouring of the concrete, the carpentry, everything. The boat weighed about 30 tons, and came equipped with bathtubs, gold plumbing fixtures, and a large living room with wood paneling where Glenn kept his 100-volume set of the *Great Books* from St. John's College. A picture of the interior of the boat ran in *People Magazine* in September of 1975, with a quintessential shot of Glenn stretched out on a sofa in shorts, reading something. "It didn't look like a boat; it looked like the Holiday Inn," Jonathan Moore quipped.

Glenn and the Havenstock River Band moved up to Vancouver for three whole months at the turn of 1970-71, playing in a Chinese smorgasbord restaurant by night while Glenn worked on his boat during the day. He spent $250,000 on the *Jubilee*, four times as much as a concrete boat normally costs. "It was real strange," remembered Rein. "We would make a lot of money, he would blow it on his boat, then when he would run out of money, we would work more, pour it into the boat."

Meanwhile Neggo, who was also managing the Havenstock band on its dates without Glenn, was running out of patience with the band, which was developing a reputation for unreliability. "I thought they were going to be the next Three Dog Night," he said. "I didn't know they were going to be druggies. They refused to give in to what the environment demanded. After investing many thousands of dollars, I just gave up."

For his part, Glenn truly enjoyed working with them. By now, he had grown a fashionable beard and let his hair grow a bit longer, trying to feel 18 again. Yet finally, having at last read the writing on the wall, realizing that the Havenstock River Band wasn't going to put him back on the charts, anxious to get on his new boat, Glenn threw in the towel. He left the band in the spring of 1971, then Rein dropped them, and soon after that, the Havenstock River Band was history.

So was Glenn's career—or so he thought. The *Jubilee* at last was ready to go, and Glenn sailed it down from Vancouver to Marina del Rey in Southern California, where he docked it and put some more finishing touches on it. By now, he had liquidated all his property, save the Woodstock Road home, two rental homes and a North Hollywood flower shop he had bought for Annie. He sold off his cars and his luxuries and donated most of his cash reserve to SCHOLE.

In an interview with the *Los Angeles Times* that year, Glenn announced that he was chucking all the trappings of fame and wealth. "I'll have to scrounge for a living again and I'll have fun doing it," he told the *Times*. "Maybe I'll sing in a few bars along the way to pick up expense money. But I just want to get away, to read and think and travel, not as a rich American, but as an ordinary person.

"There just doesn't seem to be any reason to ignore the things that are important to me any longer. I never cared for show business, and I never related money to happiness. I guess what I'm looking for after all these hectic years is a fairly simple life."

With that, he sailed down to Mexico and went off to the South Pacific. He would not perform again for a year-and-a-half, beginning in mid 1971 and continuing through most of 1972, trying to fulfill his fantasy of being a sailor. There would be only one recording during this period, a single (co-produced by Alex) for the MGM-distributed Pride label, called "Back Roads" which amiably celebrates the joys of—what else?—the open road. And when Glenn did return, the strange saga of the Limeliters would take root again in a new, somewhat more hostile decade.

Alex with long hair, Lou, still the middle-aged hippie, and Glenn,
in an early stage of their reunion concerts of the 1970s.

The Limeliters' only single for their unlikely—and short-lived—
association with Memphis' Stax label. Released 1973.

Chapter Sixteen

Nostalgia was big business in 1972, what with Eisenhower's heir, Richard Nixon in the White House gunning for a second term, Marilyn Monroe on the cover of *Newsweek* in the middle of the election campaign, Chuck Berry at the top of the pop charts. People wanted to forget about the dark secrets of the American condition revealed in the 1960s, as well as the economic gloom that in 1970 ended the continuous rise of adjusted per capita income. It was a lull of sorts between the storms of Kent State and Watergate, a national longing for what in the blindness of hindsight was regarded as a Golden Age of Innocence—the '50s and early '60s.

The national tide of nostalgia probably did not escape the attention of Russ Gary—a.k.a. Joseph Bosco—a colorful, irascible operator and onetime big band leader who had taken over the management of seafaring Glenn Yarbrough. Glenn returned to live performing in fits and starts, flying out from wherever the *Jubilee* happened to be anchored, working for a little while, then flying back to his boat to continue his 'round-the-world marathon. Gary, meanwhile, was listening to Glenn's fans and concert promoters, who for the first time in several years, were asking him about Glenn's two former partners, about the possibility of seeing them perform again.

Not one to miss an angle, in the fall of 1972, Gary took the idea of reuniting the Limeliters to Glenn who, in trying to decrease his responsibilities even more, was all-too willing to agree. Gary then called Lou, now living in the Econoline van with his hippie wife and two-year-old son, and Alex, now sitting around his house waiting for lightning to strike, and asked if they wanted to do it again.

"At that point, everybody was ready to go back to work," said Rein Neggo, who left Glenn in 1971 when he really got serious about sailing but who would return into his business life shortly after the first reunions took place. "Lou's burnout was over, Alex needed to get in front of a crowd, and Glenn's had enough time to play with his boats. The problem with the Limeliters initially was burnout."

"I was absolutely tapped out, had nothing," Lou said. "My financial eccentricities had finally brought me to a (halt). So, when the call came, it was a godsend because I had a chance to make a little bread."

"I was getting tired of singing alone," said Glenn. "I felt like I wasn't getting anything new going at the time. Also, I didn't want to work as hard, which was probably the main motivation on my part. When you're working alone, you've gotta maintain the band, you gotta keep changing things all the time. I thought that well, if I got with the Limeliters and just did a few solo numbers myself, once this show was established, I could go away and sail for long periods of time and come back and have everything ready to go. Alex could rehearse the band, Lou could write the songs, and all I'd have to do is come in and sing.

"Unfortunately, it didn't work out that way. It turned out that no matter how much I wanted to be just a member of the group and show up and do my gig and go back on the boat, in fact, I was the leader of the group and in order for it to work, I had to devote my time to it, more of my time than anybody else. In that sense it was disappointing, but it was not disappointing in terms of the show we produced."

In any case, Lou, Alex and Glenn met that fall on the *Jubilee*, now docked in Marina del Rey, and after a jolly reunion, they agreed that the time was right to reactivate the Limeliters. A photograph was taken of the three on the deck of the *Jubilee*, and it reveals three ecstatic old friends, instruments in hand, clearly in an unbuttoned mood. Rehearsals for the resurrected act began promptly around Thanksgiving, preparing for an opening in February of 1973 in the very town that gave them their start—Aspen, Colorado.

Yet while the old personal chemistry was still there, the balance of power within the group had shifted dramatically. While the group may have been Lou's idea at the beginning, and the name Limeliters now legally belonged to Alex, Glenn had become the leader and final arbiter. Lou and Alex were now technically employees of Glenn's, and the act would always be booked as Glenn Yarbrough and the Limeliters Reunion.

"Glenn was the boss," confirmed Neggo. "He decided what went as far as the material goes. Alex and Lou had input, but the decisions were final when Glenn said they were final. Glenn was good at that; he knew how to put a show together and the show Alex does right now is similar to the lessons he learned from Glenn.

"Lou was too intelligent. Lou would put too much thought into the process, and Glenn would come and say, no, no, this, this, and this, and it was done. And Lou would sit and philosophize about it."

During the rehearsals, Lou continued to live in his van, now parked in the driveway of an expensive home his friend Andre Philippe was renting in Benedict Canyon. Unfortunately, Lou's relations with Rena had entered a turbulent period, for she wasn't keen at all on having the middle-aged father of her child going back to work as a touring musician. Ultimately, Rena and Vishnu went to live on the Hawaiian island of Maui with Don McCoy and Sylvia Clarke Hamilton, who had just moved there. Lou went through more paroxysms of jealousy, desperately aching for her body—and soon Rena returned to the mainland, only to flee back to Maui not long afterwards, minus Vishnu, in the company of a fellow known by the picaresque name Tall Tom. So ended what Lou regarded as his Morningstar period, an experiment in leisure and idealism now turned into a countercultural soap-opera.

Back at the rehearsals, Glenn, in his determination to carry less of the load onstage, began to assemble a backup band for the Limeliters, which would become by far the largest they would ever have. Byron Walls, an engaging singer/songwriter from Corvallis, Oregon, became the guitarist and backup vocalist, Harry Robinson was on guitar and banjo, and Lou's own son Tony, now 18, was hired as the bassist.

On piano was Lincoln Mayorga, a longtime friend of Lou's, a master pianist comfortable in classical music, jazz and studio work. Getting Mayorga, who had played on Glenn's *The Lonely Things* album and who could have earned a lot more money in the studios, was quite a coup for the reunited trio. "He is the piano player I always wanted to be, and every sincere singer should have the privilege and thrill of singing at least one song with Lincoln Mayorga at the keyboard," wrote Lou in his autobiography.

Unfortunately, Mayorga didn't work out; he gave in to his recording commitments in Hollywood and perhaps more to the point, he and Glenn didn't see eye-to-eye musically. According to Lou, Glenn thought Mayorga was playing too many notes, taking the spotlight off the singers with his keyboard brilliance. And Glenn had a point; for the relatively simple material the Limeliters were performing, having a polished virtuoso like Mayorga on hand was, in Alex's metaphor, like racing a Ferrari down to the grocery store.

So, when Mayorga quit, Glenn sent for Geoffrey Pike, the Havenstock River Band keyboardist, owner of a simpler, less busy technique. Glenn also found another former sideman of his, Brian Davies of Davies and Maffitt, as a third guitarist—and Davies would stay on with Glenn into the early 1980s.

With a larger, electrified, multifaceted backup band now in tow, the Limeliters' sound and approach was bound to be vastly different than it was in the early '60s. Everyone agreed there would be certain de rigeur numbers from the past—the still-vibrant "John Henry" and "Joy Across the Land," Lou's "Madeira M'Dear" set piece, Alex's foreign specialties like "Gari Gari" and "Curimao," two songs that were as close to signature pieces as anything in their catalogue, "There's A Meetin' Here Tonight" and "Hey Li Lee Li Lee."

Gone, though, were the satirical slants on contemporary American urban life that gave the Limeliters a good deal of their flavor. It could not be helped; the times had changed, the targets had changed. No longer could one deftly lance the comfortable Eisenhower blanket of conformity. The political and cultural atmosphere was poisoned and polarized; it was now fashionable, or even necessary, to go after the Establishment with a bludgeon. One could no longer maintain a position of sardonic, detached distance; one had to choose sides.

The Limeliters found a blunt-edged tool in the form of Randy Newman's totally sarcastic screed, "Political Science," an encyclopedia of xenophobia that concludes with the delicious lines, "They all hate us anyhow/So let's drop the big one NOW." From Morgan Ames came "White House Song," a kind of morose morning-after lament for the sore-losers after the 1972 election. Both pieces were more overtly political than anything the Limeliters had done in the early '60s, clearly lining their sympathies up completely against the Nixon Administration.

As a means of informing their fans as to who they were and where they'd been, Byron Walls, ever-loyal Gene Raskin and Lou came up with perhaps the thousandth variation on the old Washington State folk jam, "Acres Of Clams." The tune that once carried "Charlie, the Midnight Marauder" now became "Acres Of Limeliters" as they turned the humor in on themselves with knowing accuracy ("We're naturally drawn to each other/A naturally unnatural act"). They would also throw in a question-and-answer session in the middle of their concerts, in which all three would field questions about their lives that "Acres Of Limeliters" did not touch upon.

Being the designated star, Glenn would have several solo songs, the inevitable "Baby, the Rain Must Fall" and "The Honey Wind Blows," a grudging token Rod McKuen number or two, personal favorites from the recent past like "Friend of Jesus" and "Easy Now." Glenn thought enough of Walls' songwriting abilities to cover his "Consider It Done" and "One Brief Moment," and give him his own singing spotlight with the silly "Wonderful World of Sex." For the most part, Glenn remained obsessed with the idea of exploring non-hit material from his favorite folk-oriented writers—Bob Gibson, Hoyt Axton, Shel Silverstein—while Lou was trying to get the act to do his own off-kilter material.

Alone among the three, Alex was interested in going out of his way to reach out to new audiences, and he thought the surest way to do it would be to cover tunes they already might have heard on the radio. He introduced Steve Goodman's "City of New Orleans," made famous by Arlo Guthrie, into the act; later he would attempt Paul Simon's "The Boxer." By now, Alex was the only true believer of the Limeliters' potential to make it back to the top of the heap. He had not found himself in the ten-year interval, while Glenn had the sea to make him feel alive, and Lou had the counterculture. All Alex had, for better or worse, was the Limeliters—and until something more compelling would come his way, it would be his primary creative outlet.

The Limeliters made their first comeback appearance at the Aspen Inn in February of 1973—and encouraged by the response, they had Russ Gary set up a six-week spring tour of the Western states and targeted Canadian cities, ending in May. In Los Angeles between Aspen and the first tour, Alex tried to restart the trio's recording career. Having noticed some other artists starting small-scale yet lucrative mail order operations of their own, Alex thought this would be the most direct way to reach the Limeliters' followers.

"I said to Glenn and Lou, 'Let's form our own label,'" Alex recalls. "'Forget about the record companies because I knew all about the record companies. Chances are they're not going to give us a deal. If they do, wonderful, but let's not wait for it. Let's go out and make our own records and we will gather the names of our fans at our shows with little flyers and we'll sell our records in that way. It will be self-sustaining, and we'll make a little profit.' And they didn't want to do it." Or at least Glenn didn't want to, for Lou went so far as to meet with Clinton Roehmer, the brains behind Stan Kenton's Creative World operation, to pick his brain.

But Alex did manage to coax his reluctant partners into his home studio to cut a single which they would sell at their concerts. Glenn was the biggest objector; he hated the idea of hustling merchandise at the gigs, and he still held out hope that a major label would sign them. But he went along with Alex on cutting the single—Walls' "Consider It Done," backed with a tune by Alex and arranger Artie Butler, "A Pound Of Peaches." The best one can say about Walls' slightly pallid folk-rock tune is that it opens with the transparently autobiographical lines, "Considering how we got together/How we get along/Seems only natural/We should make a song." But "A Pound Of Peaches" is an elusive gem, with a lovely, spare backing of organ and acoustic guitars and a wistful lyric gently sung in Alex's new deeper bass voice. Only 500 copies were pressed of this item, the only one in Morningstar Records' "catalogue."

Meanwhile, the first Reunion Tour was proving to be a runaway success on the West Coast. They would play halls from San Diego to Vancouver to a tumultuous response from the faithful, selling out the Civic Auditoriums of Santa Monica and Portland and the Queen Elizabeth Theatre of Vancouver among others. Most of the reviews were ecstatic, marveling at the freshness of their sound and their sharp application of showbiz savvy. But a few of the early reviews noted that the group seemed a bit rusty from the long layoff, particularly in the solo spots.

With flowing long hair and a bushy black beard still intact from the Morningstar days, Lou was wearing an Indian lungi (a wrapped-around skirt) onstage with no underwear—which led to a rather unnerving experience one night in Hawaii at a Hilton hotel. Lou was going through the paces of his "Madeira M'Dear" number, which was rapidly becoming a rather steamy scene of making mad simulated love to his faithful bass fiddle. Well, Lou came to the part where he spins his bass—and lo and behold, the lungi came right off. A lucky thing it was that Lou played the bass, for that was the only thing blocking the audience from a full frontal view of his birthday suit. Ever the professional, he managed to finish the song before carefully slinking offstage while Alex, Glenn and the band were going absolutely bananas. Alex later said that this was one of the biggest laughs the group ever got, rivaled only by the gibberish from the balcony at the Limeliters' London concert.

Lou was certainly the most changed man of the three, no longer interested in playing ego games, more passive and beatific than ever. Glenn, for one, was amazed and delighted by the shift in Lou's personality. "I was not too crazy about Lou from the beginning," he said. "When he went to live on his place, his attitude changed a great deal. Never saw anybody change (like that). Most people kind of remain the way they were when they started, but Lou really did change a tremendous amount. I was more attuned with him after the Santa Rosa experience than I was before. He no longer was interested in material things, he wasn't just in it for the money anymore. He became more humble, he didn't think he was responsible for all the success.

"I remember one time in a hotel during the reunion concerts, I came up the elevator and there was some guy there that was pretty rough-looking (who) got off the elevator. This guy looked like trouble, and in the old days, Lou would just have gone and left me to face whatever. I stopped and talked to this guy for a while in the hallway and as I turned to leave for my room, I noticed Lou was standing there in the door making sure that everything was going to be alright. That was a side of him I'd never seen before, something he never would have done in the old days. He began to be more concerned with other people than he was before."

"In the beginning, Lou was very Mr. Money, always dressed up in suits and could be kind of mean," said Jonathan Moore. "He could be quite cold, was very businesslike and together. He was a doctor of music, Dr. Lou Gottlieb. I was kind of afraid of him, to tell you the truth. Money was Lou's life. Later on, Lou became a very nice person. It changed to where money mattered nothing.

"At Annie's one time, we all came in from Hawaii, Lou and his lady and Vishnu. And the first thing they did was take off every stitch of clothing. The kid stood on Annie's coffee table and pissed on the floor. I was up there with some bird who'd never seen the like of it. They all dived in the pool, swam around, and sat around naked, like nothing is going on. It was quite amusing."

"During the reunion tours, Lou always took a back seat," noted Rein Neggo. "He was like the mellow hippie, just show me the right way and I'll be there. He didn't want to make decisions; he was burned out with decisions from all the stuff he had happening up north."

No doubt touring at this point was also a relief for Lou, who was embroiled in the corrosive closing stages of his relationship with Rena. Rena had returned from Maui the second week of the Aspen gig, and Lou found his straying flower child and attention-starved young son a rented home on an isolated hill in Sunland in the San Fernando Valley. There they would stay while Lou was on tour, for Lou found it too expensive and especially too exhausting to have both of them distracting him on the road. In the meantime, Lou started having excruciating headaches—and again he would interpret them as an allergic reaction to his co-habitant.

Ultimately Lou, possibly by sub-conscious design, confessed to Rena that while on tour in Vancouver, he had a steamy one-night stand with a beautiful red-haired ex-Morningstar resident named Sandy—and to put it mildly, Rena's reaction indicated that even the love generation was susceptible to jealousy like those in the straight life.

Soon thereafter, Lou drove up to Haight-Ashbury in his van, a.k.a. the "boogie-wagon," dropped Rena off, and drove away with Vishnu, breathing a huge sigh of relief. After innumerable breakups and reunions, the "folie a deux" was over at last—and that summer, Lou sought solace with an 18-year-old, blue-eyed, brunette-haired girl named Nancy Ellen Collins, who bore a striking resemblance to singer Judy Collins (to whom she is a third cousin). Solace was hardly the word for it, for upon meeting Nancy, Lou spent a few days with her and two other young girls—none of whom wore any clothes—in an A-frame house on the island of Maui. There, surrounded by papaya trees, a lush lawn, with the ocean a short walk away, one would tend to drown one's sorrows rather quickly.

But Lou's romantic travails were rather placid compared to the sheer hell that Glenn was going through in the early days of the reunion. The problem again was Peggy, who even ten years after their divorce was still very much a player in Glenn's life thanks to the inconvenient fact that they had two children.

According to Glenn, when they broke up, he and Peggy made a deal that Peggy would get custody of Sean and Stephanie until the time they turned about 10 or 11 years old. At that point, custody would revert to Glenn because he felt that Peggy would not be mature or patient enough to deal with a pair of teenagers. "She agreed to that," claimed Glenn, "except, when they got to that age, she reneged because she didn't want to give up the child support."

Storm signals were brewing back in 1971 when Glenn told the *Los Angeles Times* that he had every intention of taking his two children by his first marriage on his sailing trips—and that he would cut off Peggy's child support payments if she refused. Nothing initially became of that threat, but Glenn persisted in trying to negotiate with his ex-wife, who would not be budged.

Finally in 1973, Glenn laid down an ultimatum; he was going to cut off the child support completely unless Peggy turned over their children to him. Which he did—and with impressively vindictive savvy, Peggy retaliated by immediately going on welfare. This meant that now she had the State of California on her side to try and coerce Glenn to make the payments. A warrant was sworn out for Glenn's arrest, and thus began a not-so-merry chase all over the state.

Somehow, even while doing a steady stream of concerts with the Limeliters, Glenn successfully eluded the police for many months. He would develop a set routine in his California concerts which was not too different from his normal post-concert fast getaways. "The police are really not too smart, and I would elude these police all the time," Glenn said, chuckling. "I don't know why they had such a hard time getting me; I was right on stage. I would do things like jump off stage and have an exit where I could get out real fast and have a car waiting and zoom out of the place. I'd have decoys go out as if they were me and then I'd get away."

Peggy unleashed process servers who hounded Glenn day and night, wherever he was, even invading his Woodstock Road home. "They were everywhere," he recalled. "There was a process server that got in the property that is surrounded by a fence. I had a pretty vicious dog here at the time and (the guy) got in the fence, made friends with the dog, got all the way into the house one time. Annie was home; he scared the hell out of my wife because this was during the time of Manson and he looked just like him, thick long hair, and a big beard."

The whole imbroglio inevitably attracted the attention of the press, and one could hear radio news flashes about Glenn Yarbrough eluding the police once again after a Limeliters concert. The amazing thing was that Glenn—who had become extremely heavy in his 40s, with a beard that gave him a Burl Ives-like appearance—was a very conspicuous target, presumably one that could not move terribly fast. And even so, the police couldn't catch him.

One time, when the Limeliters were scheduled to play in the northern California city of Redding, the police thought they finally had a show of force overpowering enough to capture the fox. "I went to case the place and oh my God, there were police cars completely surrounding the auditorium," remembered Glenn. "They had police in the rafters, they had police on both sides of the stage, they were ready. I went and got my car and asked Rein to get someone who looked at lot like me to do the show for me, and if people wanted their money back, just give them their money back."

So Rein immediately found a singer/guitarist from Los Angeles to substitute for Glenn—and believe it or not, the police were completely fooled. "He did the show and when he carne offstage, the police grabbed him and threw him up against the wall," laughed Glenn. "They handcuffed him, started taking him to jail; he's saying, 'Hey, I'm not him!' Finally, they figured out their mistake but in the meantime, I was gone."

Yet Glenn, the free spirit, could not continue to put up with constantly being hunted for much longer. Frustrated, he cancelled some $150,000 of Limeliters gigs and spirited himself across the Mexican border, where he hung out until he was sure that his lawyers and Peggy's lawyers had finally settled the matter of child custody.. Apparently a deal was reached in which Glenn would fork out so much money to Peggy and he would take charge of Sean and Stephanie. A relieved Glenn, thinking the worst was over, came back to the United States and prepared the *Jubilee* for a cruise to the South Pacific with Sean, Stephanie, and his young daughter with Annie, Holly, now nearly four years old.

Glenn picks up the tale from here: "Annie and I were making the final touches on the boat in Marina del Rey. I was really attuned to watching for police because they were after me everywhere. We took Holly to her grandmother's house in Culver City, and we just dropped Holly off and I remarked to Annie, 'Golly, there are a lot of cop cars around here,' not even dreaming they were for me because the deal was set. I drove to the end of Hannum Ave., and five police cars emerged from every direction, and they jumped out of their cars, with guns drawn. The District Attorney had put this huge bail over my head, used only for vicious criminals. These cops didn't know.

"They grabbed me, threw me on the ground, handcuffed me. Annie—she knew everybody in the police department—she said, 'Hey wait a minute.' She's giving the cops the story and these cops are listening, 'Oh my God, this is terrible. Let's let him go.' So just as they were taking my handcuffs off, this plain-clothes-ed car came driving up, and it turned out to be the captain of the district, and the sergeant says, 'Oops, we can't do it now; we gotta take you to jail.'

So, the Culver City S.W.A.T. team snapped the handcuffs back on Glenn—this overweight, harmless pop/folksinger who was so heavy that the cops couldn't get the cuffs on him with his hands behind his back (they had to snap them on in front) and drove him off to the Culver City jail. Stubborn as ever, wondering what happened to the agreement (which evidently had not been signed yet), Glenn was determined to stay in jail indefinitely until Peggy turned over his kids.

Alas, he only lasted a day and a night behind bars. Glenn had been in jail before, but never as a suspected criminal; as a teenager on his hitch-hiking sabbatical, he would occasionally ask the local police if he could sack out in an empty cell for the night. But he did not know what it was like to be locked up—and he did not like that feeling one bit. "I did not realize how claustrophobic I was," he recalled. "Now I realize if that were to ever happen to me, I could not survive it. I couldn't stand the idea of not being able to go and do what I wanted to do."

The next day, when Annie came to visit, Glenn told her to go to the bank and get some bail money. He didn't want to pay a bail bondsman for the service; just get the cash. Annie withdrew something like $15,000 in cash from their incredulous bank, stuffed all of these bills in her jeans and hightailed it back to the police station, where she ceremoniously dumped the bills on the supervisor's desk. The cops were agog, having not seen that kind of cash for bail purposes in a long time.

Meanwhile the press had staked out the station, and Glenn, ever the shy, reluctant public figure, did his best to avoid them. "There were newspaper people and photographers all outside the building, and Annie was trying to get me out of the building without publicity," Glenn remembered. "It was just a mess. The cops were counting all the money and they brought this limousine in front of the jail, all the photographers were there. And this little Volkswagen came in back of the jailhouse, and I zoomed out of there. One Black photographer who was real smart caught me. The police were so bamboozled by all this activity that they failed to get me to sign a paper that signed away my bail money. That left me in complete control again. As long as they had me, my ex-wife was in control."

Once out of jail, Glenn went back into hiding and didn't emerge until all parties had finally signed the agreement and Glenn received custody of his children. Sean and Holly would join Glenn on the road with the Limeliters, as did Alex's son David and Lou's two sons—Tony on bass and Vishnu as an occasional freeform go-go dancer while Stephanie was sent to the Seabury Academy on Maui. Peggy eventually would settle in the small town of Port Angeles, Washington, in the shadow of the Olympic Mountains. "Now she wants me to come back and live with her," said Glenn in 1989. "But it's too late."

Alas, some damage had been done to Glenn's public stature. While many of his tolerant followers shrugged off Glenn's tumultuous battles with his ex-wife as just another weird episode in a rather weird life, it was the biggest piece of hard news that ever came out of the Limeliter Reunion period. "I used to do a section of my show where I just talked to the audience," Glenn recalled, "and there was always a question, 'Why did you fail to support your children?" And for years afterwards, the line in "Acres Of Limeliters," "Now that we're older and wiser/We think that monogamy pays," would always get a laugh following Alex's spoken aside, "And Glenn's sure of it!"

The Limeliters had become a viable concert attraction again, particularly on the West Coast—and nowhere were they more popular than in the Pacific Northwest, which responded to Glenn's hearty, casual outdoorsman persona. On a geographically and culturally opposite plane, they were also a hit in the South, which had not forgotten their numerous college tours that ITA booked in that region in the early '60s. They never did make an impression in the East the second time around, though, and without the promotional muscle of RCA Victor this time, they could not make a national impact.

Indeed, neither strong regional support nor even the national nostalgia craze could entice a major label to sign the Limeliters in the 1970s. As a result, in their first venture into the recording wars of the '70s, the group ended up on one of the least likely rosters imaginable—that of Stax Records of Memphis, Tennessee.

Stax?!

This was the same label that rose to fame in the 1960s on a diet of gritty, bedrock soul stew, the home of rhythm-and-blues stars like Otis Redding, Johnnie Taylor, Carla Thomas and Sam and Dave, all propelled by the solid Memphis grooves of Booker T. and the MGs. Stax had been going through some wrenching changes ever since Redding's tragic death in a plane crash in December of 1967. It wrested its distribution away from Atlantic Records—and consequently lost its entire back catalogue, along with some of its artists. Label head Al Bell rebuilt the catalogue anew, and the initial success of that operation launched an expansion program that was ultimately beyond its means. The label entered a distribution pact with CBS Records in 1972, brought about by the personal diplomacy of CBS kingpin Clive Davis, and had started a new division for white artists, aiming for the country/western field and hopefully the giant bucks of Top 40 pop. But when Davis was fired in 1973 amidst charges of financial shenanigans, the Stax pact was reassessed—and as a result, the now-in-hock

Memphis label began to receive 40% less money per record delivered, thus crippling its ability to pay off its loans.

It was this new "white" division, now saddled with aimless A&R direction, that agreed to take on Glenn Yarbrough and the Limeliters. The catalyst behind that move was Chuck Glaser, a member of the popular country group Tompall and the Glaser Brothers who in 1973 was an independent producer and owner of a recording studio in Nashville. According to Lou, Glaser had always been a Limeliters fan, and at one time, Tompall and the Glaser Brothers had been booked by none other than Russ Gary. One day in 1973, Glaser caught the act in Nashville's Circle Star Theatre, and fired up with enthusiasm, he thought he could persuade Stax into signing and promoting them properly.

Fat chance, for Stax would soon be on the receiving end of a tangle of lawsuits by CBS and the Union Planters National Bank, as well as an IRS investigation that turned up nothing. Gradually, its output dribbled down to zero, and Stax had neither the attention span nor the cash to promote anything, let alone a folk trio from the '60s.

"It was ridiculous," said Lou. "One time we were in Cincinnati, and I wanted to go to Nashville and at least meet the people in the firm. Nobody was in town. They'd just signed an act to a label; they don't even wanna meet ya. So, I knew; that firm was moribund by the time we got there."

Alex offers a devastatingly candid rationale for going with such a doomed outfit. "The reason we signed that deal was twofold," he says. "One, they offered Glenn a separate contract so he could continue his solo career. And two, nobody else asked us!"

In any case, Glaser went right to work with his newly-signed folk trio figuring, as did Neely Plumb, that a live album would be the best way to kick off the act's new contract. The first record to be made was *Reunion*, recorded live in Chicago's Orchestra Hall in the fall of 1973 and packaged in a nightmarish jacket—three murky silhouettes shot from the rear on the front cover, and on the back, a photo of the three seated in the empty hall, looking genial and conspicuously well-fed.

"Three whales stuffed into a little container," said Lou with a rueful laugh about the back cover. "Alex was fatter than a pig at that time, so was I, Glenn of course. The picture should be called 'PIG-OUT.'"

The packaging notwithstanding, *Reunion* is quite good, a condensed but fitting summary of the state of the reunion in its early stages. The first change one notices is the heavier blend of the voices ten years later, largely due to the deepening of Alex's baritone into a resonant basso. Sometimes the blend sounds strained and edgier than before, but one can attribute that to a vocal off-night, for they seem more relaxed in each other's company than ever.

In his professorial comments, Lou now aims his lance mostly at the personal histories and follies of the three, and his countercultural lifestyle is never far from the surface. Even though Lou remains the primary spokesman, Glenn is obviously the star now—and Lou concedes the point in his introduction.

In a solo segment, Glenn punches out "That's The Way It's Gonna Be" with gusto and "Easy Now" with greater dynamic control than ever, and he is gracious enough to introduce the songs' composer Bob Gibson from the audience.

There are only three old songs here—"Joy Across The Land," "Lonesome Traveller," and the best "Curimao" on records, thanks in great part to a subtle Latin arrangement beautifully played by the large backup band. A wildly burlesquing "Political Science" and "White House Song" establish the trio's credentials on the left. But the finale, "Old Fashioned Remedy," would be the thought the Limeliters would register most strongly in the '70s—good times, old times, smiles.

Unfortunately, hardly anyone got a chance to hear it. Within a short time of the record's release in the fall of 1974, Stax filed for bankruptcy and remained inert until it officially went out of business in 1976. With a limited pressing, no airplay, and no promotion other than Alex's announcements onstage, the phantom *Reunion* album reportedly sold only 3,000 copies and that may be a generous estimate, for the record was almost impossible to find. "The only way I was able to get a copy was from a fan," said Alex.

Fortunately, Alex gained possession of the master tapes in the late '80s, and the Stax album became available on a cassette from West Knoll Records. In August of 1991, when preparing a compact disc edition of the Limeliter *Reunion* albums, Alex rummaged through the rest of the Stax tapes and came up with virtually another album's worth of material, some of it unique to the Limeliters' catalogue.

The most substantial find in Alex's archeological dig was a string of antiwar songs which they called their "Peace Medley." Starting with "I Don't Want To Hear The Bugles," gaining in fervor with "A Time Of Peace" and concluding with the blazing "If I Had A Hammer," the "Peace Medley" becomes greater than the sum of its parts as "Hammer" clearly pulls its weak partners along. In comparing the 1973 "Hammer" with the group's earlier versions, one is struck by how much Lou's and especially Alex's voices have mellowed—and that the single most energizing element of the performance occurs when the tambourine kicks in on the last chorus.

Elsewhere, the unreleased tapes blow hot and cold. "The Little Burro," now in a higher key, has lost some of its dynamism in Orchestra Hall, and "John Henry" benefits from some countrified guitar. Only months after the hit movie *Deliverance* lit up the screen, Harry Robinson and Brian Davies trade "Dueling Banjo" licks, leading into an energized "Wabash Cannonball."

Alone, Glenn comes up with an extraordinary "Love's Been Good To Me," holding out each phrase to the limit with impeccable control, almost as if he was in a jazz club. "Baby, The Rain Must Fall" receives another in a series of perfunctory run-throughs, but "I See America," a Mike Settle Watergate-era anthem pleading for a rebirth of the ideals of 1776, is sustained and fervent. Without a doubt, Glenn is the star of the show, relegating Lou and Alex to near-anonymous backup duty on "I See America" and a folk-rock rave-up of "Friend Of Jesus," clearly in charge.

Next up on Glaser's master plan was a studio album, cut not with the Limeliters' road band but with a collection of Nashville's crack session men with the intent of trying to break into the coveted country market. For Alex especially, this was a welcome return, as he still remembered the super-pickers and Chet Atkins' sure, low-key guiding hand from their sessions there in 1963. A preliminary single was cut in November 1973 and rushed out, hoping against hope that they could finally strike a hit.

The A-side was "I See America," with Glenn in the lead and a huge sin-galong production with children's chorus and a folk-rock backing. But the B-side was one of the flakiest and yet most intriguing things the Limeliters ever recorded, a tune written and sung by Lou called "Holy Creation."

Just four days after his 50th birthday, still very much under the sway of Chiranjiva Roy, Lou had what he calls his first "revelation," a sign that in the eyes of "Father" he had reached "super-manhood," a new conscious-ness that came into being when Chiranjiva "found out" he was God in human form. Seized by a form of energy he thought was metaphysical dictation, Lou feverishly wrote down a tract that pointed the way toward "super-manhood"—that is, being chosen by a divinely inspired female to father a child, as a pack of red deer would.

Lou then turned this thought into "Holy Creation," a song with an ominously descending revolving chord pattern and trippy lines like: "

> *"And our joy is fulfilled*
> *For the seed only spills*
> *In the bliss of God's will"*
> *"She's a goddess*
> *She is free*
> *She chose me*
> *To make a baby!"*

That Lou convinced his undoubtedly baffled partners to record this weird, completely non-commercial song is a miracle of holy creation in itself. In any case, it has a great electronic arrangement—and along with the A-side, sank into almost as anonymous a state of oblivion as the *Reunion* album.

Undaunted by the burgeoning chaos of Stax's finances, Glaser and the Limeliters plunged ahead with the studio album in December, with hot instrumental tracks from session men like drummer Kenny Buttrey, guitarists Norbert Putnam and Grady Martin, and other musicians like drummer Kenny Malone, string multi-instrumentalist Norman Blake and guitarist Ray Eddington. The Nashville cats laid down about eleven instrumental tracks, enough for a whole album, and the Limeliters managed to cut several rough vocals. In the meantime, Glenn was cutting a solo album of his own, mixing Nashville and Memphis sidemen.

Ultimately, the money ran out—and given the choice between completing the Limeliters' and Glenn's albums, the decision was made to go ahead with Glenn's. The decision proved to be a moot one, for an exhausted Lou, unable to concentrate on the matter at hand, quit the sessions and moved back to his A-frame harem on Maui with Nancy and company.

Later Alex acquired the unfinished tapes with the intention of completing them someday. He claimed there was a "sensational" instrumental track of "The Boxer" in the stash—and indeed, when the song finally came to light in 1992, it revealed the well-oiled Nashville machine running like a top, with Buttrey cracking the whip. Only in the '90s would the curious get a chance to hear an amusing out-and-out rock 'n' roll rave-up vocal by Lou on "Harbor For My Soul." No "Vikki Dougan" satire this; Lou sounds dead serious.

Glenn's album was pressed in mass quantities and quickly put out in 1974 under the title *My Sweet Lady*—and it would turn up in cutout bins practically upon release. Yet this was one of Glenn's best records, a far superior country album than the ersatz *Yarbrough Country*. Buttrey and his pals lay down a solid country groove at all times, the vocal and orchestral arrangements don't overwhelm the material, and Glenn has a marvelous time tossing his voice over the jeweled-movement rhythm section. Glaser picked some good home-grown material by Mickey Clark, who was contracted to his publishing firm, and Glenn added more contributions from usual favorites Hoyt Axton and Byron Walls, as well as a nice spare rendition of John Denver's title tune. Finally, there is "The Far Side of the Hill," in a beautiful countrified version with bass flute obbligato, the cue for another bout of sailing after the sessions—a months-long odyssey that would take him through the Panama Canal all the way to Florida.

Undaunted by the Stax debacle, the Limeliter Reunion continued to sail forth from 1974 to 1977 for about 15 to 20 weeks out of the year. That was another condition that the three had agreed upon; no more break-neck schedules of 300 days on the road. Now there would be plenty of time to recharge the batteries, plenty of time to engage in sailing (Glenn), pursue the latest countercultural whims (Lou), or just lay fallow until the next tour (Alex).

For Lou, it was something he had dreamed of for years—a permanent part-time job. Probably the only one of the three who relished being in front of an audience, Lou still loved to entertain, and he would be the one who was most appreciative of the support of the old fans.

As Lou would say many times, in one form or another, at almost each and every concert, "It moves me to think that our work has played some part or role in the emotional history of so many people. You know, it's usually a lady that comes up and says, 'Well I haven't seen you since the junior prom at Marquette University in 1962. But the man who was my escort on that occasion is the father of my four children of course we're separated now but we all got together to come and hear you tonight. And we LOVED it.'

"I'm not saying that to pump my bullshit tank or anything," Lou added. "It's a fact. It happens EVERY place."

The part-time nature of the tours was a crucial reason why the reunion performances went as consistently well as they did. Another reason was the sheer professionalism of the trio, which had hardly slackened at all over a ten-year layoff. They always showed up on time, thoroughly rehearsed, giving the illusion of spontaneity even though every detail of the show was frozen, so to speak.

But quite often, Lou's mind was elsewhere when not onstage. He found the work at hand "not very challenging" because of the emphasis on old repertoire. But then, Lou was well past the stage of forcefully trying to steer the trio in directions to his liking. For one thing, Lou's spiritual, sexual and hallucinogenic lives were still in high gear. "Father" had performed a marriage ceremony of sorts for Lou and Nancy at his Foundation of Revelation on Scott Street in San Francisco, not long before Lou's revelation. With the money he made in the 1974 tours, Lou took off for another pilgrimage to India in spring 1975, this time in the company of Chiranjiva, Bombay's prodigal son, whose old Indian friends thought either he had gone crazy or was deliberately hoodwinking a gaggle of rich American innocents. By this time, though, the rational side of Lou's brain, never entirely dormant, was producing doubts about whether the virtues of Indian philosophy has done the people of India any good. His mind had been scarred, indeed numbed, by the visions of desolate poverty in Calcutta, beyond the relief or solutions of anyone.

Dick Rosmini recalled that after one of Lou's journeys in the '70s, a gathering was held in Alex's living room where Lou, in full guru regalia, held court before 25 or so of his countercultural friends, plus Rosmini and Ananda Shankar. Everyone was seated on the floor, expecting to hear about how Lou's latest trip was another cosmic revelation that would lead them further down the road toward everlasting bliss. But the first thing that came out of the prodigal Limeliter quickly doused ice water on the party. "If you ever had any idea that you were your brother's keeper, one trip to Calcutta will disabuse you of that opinion," Lou boomed inimitably.

"I thought it was hysterically funny; it was all I could do to keep from laughing," Rosmini said. "I remember getting up and going downstairs to keep myself from destroying the event. The drug culture was simply not part of the whole India situation, which was a huge disappointment to everybody."

In the Maui A-frame, Lou and Nancy established a Foundation of Revelation West which, from Lou's account, was little more than a setting for hedonistic pleasure, the occasional orgy, and general idleness. He would spend the mornings smoking Maui Wowie and sauntering down to the sparkling beach, whiling away the time. He would spend entire afternoons napping, or perhaps making it with a comely young goddess; he would stay up nights socializing in every degree of intimacy. It was the ultimate hands-on "research" project, part of what Lou would call his "in-depth, broad-spectrum study of leisure," a program of R and R otherwise known as "G and B—goof and ball."

But like Candide in El Dorado, even a confirmed scholar in idleness like Lou eventually tired of the Maui lifestyle. More critically, he hated running into Rena, who had established herself more-or-less permanently on Maui and made sure Lou was fully informed about her continued freewheeling adventures. By the fall of 1975, Lou was gone from Hawaii for good, back on tour with the Limeliters, and later the guest of Ramon Sender in Sonoma County where they collaborated on a screenplay, *Farina*, that never was sold.

In February of 1976, Lou wound up in San Francisco again, in the first of a series of apartments on Scott and Waller Streets down the hill from Haight-Ashbury where he could be in close touch with the burgeoning scene surrounding "Father." By now, an urban village had sprung up in the area around Scott, Lloyd and Waller Streets as the devotees of Shiva Kalpa began renting adjacent and neighboring apartments. Eventually the settlement encompassed some 300 residents from around the world, a community with its own physician, its own school, its own food cooperative, and a village choir which Lou started and rehearsed in his apartment on Saturdays. Lou would host Friday night dinners in which devotees from far-flung places would cook their own national specialties. He had fallen into a contented groove in his off-months from the Limeliters—participating in the spiritual community, playing daddy to Vishnu (soon to be known as Bill) who would visit frequently from Maui for long stretches of time. He and Nancy, though still the best of friends, were drifting apart romantically, so at the end of 1976, Lou had Father grant him a divorce, thus freeing him to pursue and be pursued.

Having retrieved his Bösendorfer from storage, Lou even started playing the piano again—that is, until one of the apartments he moved into had too narrow a stairway for the instrument to be hoisted through. "I love to play the piano," he said in 1978. "That is my favorite activity, neck-and-neck with making love, but it's ultimately the same idea. To me it's literally a tossup whether to make love or play the piano. And I'm a very mediocre pianist, alas."

By this time, Lou had no illusions about becoming a concert pianist. His 50th birthday came and went—and Carnegie Hall was 3,000 miles and a gulf of achievement away. But there was a recital in Lou's plans that day—on a borrowed Wurlitzer electric piano from Alex's studio before a group of friends at his birthday party.

Lou's reaction? "Pathetic," he wrote.

Not long after the aborted Nashville sessions, while Glenn was off puttering around on his boat and Lou was enjoying the hedonistic life in Hawaii, Alex was at home one day when a phone call came from Gerald Purcell in New York. He was busy putting together a show called "The Great Folk Revival," a TV special for ABC-TV's *Wide World Of Entertainment,* and he wondered if Alex would like to appear. But Alex hesitated to go on alone. "I simply had nothing to say for that show that I felt would work for it," he recalled. "I was in a different bag at that time entirely. I said wouldn't it be fun to get some people from other groups and have an ad-hoc group, and he loved the idea."

Alex got right on the phone and rounded up Mike Settle, who had gone on to co-found the group The First Edition, and ex-Kingston Trio member Dave Guard—and the awkwardly-named team of Hassilev, Settle and Guard was born. They sang Lou's arrangement of "Lonesome Traveler" on that show, which was taped at an indoor sports arena on Long Island and shown Feb. 6, 1974, over the ABC network.

The three veterans from the folk revival hit it off so well that decided to work up an act and make a temporary go of it as a unit. They appeared for a week at a dank, funky downstairs club in Mountain View, California called Chuck's Cellar, absolutely packing the joint night after night, and went on to play San Francisco's Great American Music Hall and the ski resort of Steamboat Springs, Colorado.

One of their gigs in Southern California was reviewed in the May 5, 1974 issue of the *San Francisco Sunday Examiner* and *Chronicle* by none other than Lou Gottlieb moonlighting as a music critic again, this time as the ultimate insider to the act. "These three men are masters of that particular blend of patter and song which I have come to think of as the American Folk style of entertaining," wrote Lou. "Working with Dave and Mike has had a miraculously rejuvenatory effect on Alex. His contribution to the work of this unit is evident—a secure sense of form—I mean, a spacing in their arrangements of the presentation of ideas which makes for the greatest possible clarity."

They drew songs from all their repertoires—Alex contributing Limeliters numbers like "The Boxer," "Curimao" and "Those Were The Days," Settle bringing out his First Edition hit "But You Know I Love You," Guard resurrecting "Worried Man" with updated lyrics on the then-current gasoline shortage, and "Coplas" with pokes at Watergate. They covered a Top 40 smash, "Bad, Bad Leroy Brown;" they tried out Shel Silverstein's wild "Freakin' At The Freakers Ball" (which Alex pleaded in vain with Lou to do), and "London Homesick Blues." In working with Dave Guard, onetime rival in the "other" big folk trio, Alex found him to be an amazing entertainer, one with a wonderful comedic attitude. "Dave was a marvelously inventive and original thinker," he recalls. "Fortunately, in our combination, Mike and I were very meat-and-potatoes guys and Settle did all of the vocal arranging. He essentially took over Lou's slot and did an extremely good job."

Alex believed that Dave Guard and Lou Gottlieb were essentially two sides of the same coin, explaining it this way: "They both have the same penchant for tilting at artistic windmills with great panache, with great verve and style, in a non-commercial way, pursuing their artistic star wherever that pursuit might lead. He retuned the guitar in fourths, which gave his playing a very odd quality; the sound was absolutely unique." Alex also might have added that Guard, like Lou, would soon fall under the sway of a spiritual guru, eventually living for a while in an ashram in New York.

Despite its promising start, though, Hassilev, Settle, and Guard had a very short lifespan. Alex believes that Guard wanted to keep going, but Settle made it clear from the outset that this was just a limited gig for him, and he wanted to pursue his pop songwriting career further.

Alex himself was, as usual, ambivalent about the whole experience. "Artistically I loved it; it was a refreshing change from working with Lou and Glenn," he says. "It was a lot more easygoing, from my point of view. But my commercial sense at the time was, where could it go? At that time folk music was at its nadir—at least the perception of it was that. And I was very much into production and Settle was into writing commercial songs for the market. While we felt it was terrific, it probably had very little commercial appeal."

Settle went back to the pop mill, but eventually had to settle for taking charge of the Glenn Yarbrough/Limeliters band. Guard meanwhile continued on his erratic, mercurial artistic odyssey—teaching guitar, writing piles of books on the guitar and other subjects, studying Sanskrit, designing posters, occasionally helping out on John Stewart's solo projects, forming new folk groups that never lasted long. On Nov. 7, 1981, he participated in a memorable reunion at Magic Mountain in Valencia north of Los Angeles with his old colleagues in the Kingston Trio, a unique event where one could see each edition of the Trio in action one after another—and it looked as if there was going to be another such project ten years later. But a long battle with lymphoma finally claimed Guard's life at 56 in March of 1991, a milestone that got only scant attention in the high-tech entertainment world of the '90s.

On the business end of the Limeliters, Alex was still working relentlessly on Glenn, trying to get him to set up a mail order record label. Glenn continued to resist, still hoping that a major label would notice them.

The closest the Limeliters got to any kind of label affiliation after the Stax episode was as part of a live album recorded in September 1974 at the first annual American Song Festival in Saratoga Springs, New York. Modeled after foreign song competitions, this was an ambitious, much-ballyhooed attempt to set up a contest for amateur and professional songwriters in six musical categories—rock, pop, country, folk, gospel/religious and rhythm-and-blues. The organizers claimed that some 60,000 songs were submitted, and the winners would split $128,000 in prize money and have their winning works displayed on television and a record album.

The festival itself would feature star performers like Ray Charles, the Eagles, Waylon Jennings, Sarah Vaughan, Loggins and Messina and several others. The last day, which was recorded, featured the winning songs in each category—and Glenn Yarbrough and the Limeliters were chosen to sing the winner of the Professional Folk Category.

Well, the festival was a financial catastrophe, with skimpy attendance and a poorly planned program that according to Lou, ran until 4 a.m. in the morning. There was a hint of scandal when it became known that Tim Moore—whose "Charmer" won the amateur first prize of the entire festival—was really a professional whose tune "Second Avenue" had been picked up by Art Garfunkel, who subsequently scored a Top 40 hit with it. Worse, the winning songs weren't worth a damn—tuneless, riddled with formulas and cliches. {The Amateur Country winner had the following line as the chorus hook, "No one wants to play rhythm guitar behind Jesus.")

Indeed, the only song that has anything original to offer is the one the Limeliters did, a grim, lengthy tract called "Everybody Wants To Go To Heaven" by Charles L. Larson. In the performance on the album, Lou sounds gravel-voiced and sometimes out of tune but the harmonies improve as the song wears on, and Mike Settle's fine basic arrangement is tarted up by the house brass section. Indeed, the Limeliters thought highly enough of "Everybody Wants To Go To Heaven" to include it in their concert repertoire for years afterwards. For the purposes of generating interest in a record contract, though, the Festival was a useless exercise. The *Winners!* album, released on the Buddah label later in the year, bombed in the stores.

Experiences like this, plus the Stax debacle, plus all the slammed doors of record executives, finally convinced Glenn that Alex was right. At least with their own mail order outfit, they could reach the faithful who still flocked to their concerts and often filled the houses. They could also have complete artistic control of the product, and by putting up the financial risk of manufacturing the albums, they didn't have to turn over the vast majority of the gross proceeds to some entertainment conglomerate.

In 1976, Glenn decided to take action at last. He set up a mail order record outfit and made Annie, his wife, the president of the company. Rein Neggo, Jr., who had returned into the picture in 1974 to take over Glenn's management, claimed that Glenn did this mainly so Annie would have a sort of "retirement plan," something to do to take care of herself. But Annie said the main motivation behind Brass Dolphin was to raise money so Holly could attend the advanced private Buckley School rather than go to the public schools.

Not long before, Annie tried to be Glenn's manager for about six months until it became clear that she was in over her head. "Drove everyone crazy," said Rein. "She got a $2,000 gig and was tickled pink, and then realized it cost $3,500 to do the date."

But Annie took to the mail order business with an energy and dedication that impressed everyone. She ran the whole operation out of the guest house by herself, typing and pasting the labels, licking the envelopes, sending out the orders, writing personal letters to everyone on the mailing list—thousands of individual letters, for she managed to get 30,000 names on the list. Essentially, Glenn acted as if he was just an employee of the company, taking royalties from the recordings and doing little else but going where Annie sent him.

There remained the task of finding a name for the company, and Annie and her lawyer settled upon a strange one that nevertheless reflected Glenn's fanatical passion for the sea. "Annie's in love with dolphins," said Glenn. "When we were sailing three years together, she used to sit and play with the dolphins and she discovered that at night with a strong searchlight, they will play with the light, jump over it. She thought she would like to call it Dolphin Records, but Dolphin Records was already taken, almost everything was taken. The lawyer suggested, 'Well why don't you say something-Dolphin?' He suggested Purple Dolphin or Green Dolphin. He asked, 'What do you like?' She said, 'Brass.' 'Well, why don't you call it Brass Dolphin?'"

Thus christened, Brass Dolphin's first project was to get the Limeliters back on records—and once again, a live album was the most likely, and least expensive, way to go. They started passing out cards at their concerts in 1975 for the fans to fill out—and in about a year, they had enough pre-orders so the cost of recording the concerts was completely amortized. Alex settled back into his old role of producer, and a live remote unit was sent to the Seattle Opera House Sept. 28, 1976 to take down a concert. Two albums worth of material were taped that day—and in an unusual marketing decision for the time, Alex decided to split the concert into two separate LPs entitled *The Limeliters Reunion, Volumes One and Two* rather than package them together in a double-pocket jacket. *Volume One* would concentrate upon newer material the group had worked up while *Volume Two* contains mostly remakes of the old songs from the 1960s.

In this way, unbending nostalgia buffs could get their fix without having to fork over twice as much money for a double album. However, those who still owned record changers could stack the two LPs—beginning with side one of Volume One, changing to Sides One and Two of Volume Two, and concluding with side two, Volume One—and come out with a reasonably good impression of a complete Limeliters concert.

With a rapid-fire bluegrass banjo flourish, we're into the show, with Lou's rousing "Let's Have A Good Time" setting a "wholesome mood"—though not without reference to his leisurely life of "dope and sex." Following the countrified "City Of New Orleans," "Que Viva Espana" revives for a moment the old Limeliters burlesque of international material. "Everybody Wants To Go To Heaven" is now road-tested, much more assured and properly world-weary.

Skipping over into Volume Two, there is a mid-show opening number, "Joy Across The Land" and another "Acres Of Limeliters"—both more relaxed and polished than on the Stax album, followed by a zesty "Funky In The Country." Instead of isolated Irish tunes, the Limeliters would now do a medley of Irish songs from their old albums. Not much has changed save for Alex's swashbuckling vocal on "Gilgarry Mountain" and the electric instruments and piano in the background—and "There's A Meetin' Here Tonight" still has a lot of gusto left.

Though the performance of "The Boxer" is a bit stiff and inhibited, "John Henry" drives hard, still as tremendous a chart as ever, and "Madeira M'Dear" receives, if anything, the most lascivious rendition on records. Another pre-fab medley of "Hard Travelin'/Mount Zion," "Wayfarin' Stranger" and "Lonesome Traveller" closes Volume Two on a surprisingly routine note.

Reverting back to Side Two, Volume One, Byron Walls' "Grandma's Letter" is a rather maudlin piece of material, though well-written and carrying the ring of truth. Glenn introduces Lou's zany takeoff, "Redwood Forest," as "the first intellectual country song"—and it is amazingly sharp stuff, Shel Silverstein with a Ph.D. vocabulary. A controlled "Let Me Choose Life" from Glenn, and then not one but two farewells, Hoyt Axton's gospel-like "Thank You Lord" and "Old Fashioned Remedy," wrap up Volume One—and presumably that night's show.

Yet there would be one more farewell that wouldn't be released until 1991, a wistful Neil Sedaka/Howard Greenfield tune called "Our Last Song Together" where Glenn hurls a gentle barb at the reason why a lot of people were there;

> *"Yesterday is yesterday,*
> *The past is dead and gone…*
> *Nostalgia just gets in the way,*
> *Let's stop hanging on."*

Another tune that didn't make it out of the vault until 1991 is a wry Shel Silverstein number called "Living Legend," in which Glenn pokes fun at himself as an aging folk singer caught outside his time. He would continue to use that song well into the '90s, where its meaning would become ever more pertinent and poignant with each passing year.

Luck was with Alex that September in Seattle, for he caught the Limeliters live on tape on a good enough night to properly preserve the state of the reunion. Though the Limeliters were capable of generating more electricity in those days than they did in Seattle, overall, the group sounds more refined and surer of its direction than on the Stax album. Alex in particular is a looser, more relaxed performer, and his natural warmth comes through probably for the first time on records.

Yet despite Lou's dominating stage presence as the comic laureate spokesman—the hifalutin' professor now turned wacky hippie—his musical influence dwindled to near zero in the '70s. The snap and finger-popping brio of jazz was all but gone from their sound, replaced by elements of country in Brian Davies' banjo/guitar solos and rock in Gary Clontz' hard-edged guitar and Jackie Furman's expert drumming. Mike Settle had taken charge of the musical direction of Glenn's band in 1974, and his orientation was always pop/folk. But Lou simply abdicated his once significant say in musical matters, other than occasionally submitting a few oddball songs. As a result, the Limeliters perhaps were now more in tune with the 1970s, but an important part of their heritage—the jazz leanings picked up from the clubs in San Francisco—was lost.

Nevertheless, the always-optimistic Lou was quite pleased at the time with the way the albums turned out. "I'm delighted with that album," he said. "It was an honest representation of what we did that night in Seattle. It was an average show, it wasn't an on-fire show, but it was a consistent, get-your-money's-worth show, and the album presents that. That's the act."

The act could have gone on indefinitely like that—playing the summer festivals, the Nevada casinos in winter, the solid strongholds in the Pacific Northwest. They could easily carry off an entire show by themselves, as they did at a memorable concert in the Dorothy Chandler Pavilion in Los Angeles on July 28, 1974. And in review after review from this period, one gets the impression that the Limeliters once again were blowing their opening, closing or co-billed acts off the stage—be they Frank Sinatra, Jr., Mary Travers, the New Kingston Trio, or even a seasoned, savvy Andy Williams.

"The rotund minstrel Yarbrough delivered a surprisingly fresh 55-minute set with 13 pleasing songs while Sinatra stiffed his way through an 11-song, 40-minute program," observed *Billboard's* Hanford Searl at a May 27, 1976 Limeliters date at Las Vegas' Aladdin Hotel. "Yarbrough and Co. lift the audience with deft skill. Mary Travers brings it down with a sad, doleful bump," wrote Ian Haysom of the *Ottawa Journal* Sept. 17, 1975, and the *Ottawa Citizen* concurred. "The music sung by Yarbrough and his group...is highly expert and ranges much more widely over the folk spectrum than the Trio's," said *Variety* about a 1976 co-billed date at the Dorothy Chandler Pavilion in Los Angeles. The reviewer also commented on the greater aplomb with which the Limeliters handled the self-deprecatory humor about growing older, while slamming the Kingstons' taste for "frat house humor."

Indeed, a show they performed at Disneyland on Nov. 25, 1977 was another consummate example of how amazingly fresh the Limeliters managed to keep their act, even after more than four years on the road. Even though Glenn later said this was just a condensed, custom-made nostalgia version of their complete show, there wasn't an iota of routine or audible cynicism or boredom in their three gusto-loaded sets. The voices remained ecstatically vibrant, the band was rocking, and Lou's off-the-wall antics were so endearing that Glenn was moved to exclaim in mid-set, "54 years old and whacked out of his mind!" The incandescent Limeliters were so hot they put the co-billed Kingston Trio in the shade, making them seem forlorn and wistful. Alex later acknowledged, "We were on fire that night."

Yet the times seemed to conspire against a major Limeliters revival. Part of it had to do with the nature of the nostalgia revival that supposedly created whatever demand there was for them. Interestingly, and tellingly, the nostalgia industry did not make a bundle on the postwar folk revival in the '70s. One possible reason was that this music played a big role in raising the issues and providing the soundtrack for many of the experiences people wanted to forget. Perhaps there were feelings of guilt, for many people had long since walked away from the commitments that songs like "If I Had A Hammer" would inspire. It was a cynical period in U.S. history, one that had little time for idealism or any musical traditions that didn't spring directly from Elvis Presley.

On another level, Lou Gottlieb—with his long hair, bushy beard, Indian performing getup, hippie lingo, and hedonistic lifestyle of sex, drugs, free land and exotic religion—was the personification of everything middle America was supposed to hate about the '60s. He had decided that the Puritan work ethic was not for him, nor the goals of capitalism beyond making just enough loot to support his lifestyle. Those are dangerous ideas in any period, but they were downright subversive in an increasingly conservative country.

On a more practical plane, some responsibility also lies with Glenn, who doggedly refused to go on television to promote himself or the act. Now it is true that the days of mass-audience variety shows were numbered by the mid-'70s; the demise of the *Ed Sullivan Show* tolled the bell for all concerned. But there were still TV talk shows, national and local, to visit and Glenn, having shot his mouth off more than once on those programs, would have none of them anymore. Without TV exposure, coupled with the lack of a record contract with a label that had clout, the Limeliters' promotional options were limited in the extreme.

Moreover, inevitably, despite the mellowness and understanding that had come with age and the sheer feat of surviving in the music business all these years, the forces of their individual personalities and goals were beginning to pull them apart again.

Though the 20 weeks-maximum work schedule left an abundance of leisure time, Lou was getting very tired of the road. Even in his 30s, Lou's letters give the impression that his stamina was not of herculean proportions—and now in his mid '50s, Lou was feeling the strain even more.

"In March of 1977, I told Neggo, I've got to have a year off," he recalled in 1978. "Even loving to entertain as I do, but man, after three weeks on the road, I am pooped. On March 31, 1977, we came off seven weeks of one-nighters with the Kingston Trio in a bus, and I...was... dead. Dead! I could not move my muscles. My knees hurt. Look, it's just a question of age, man. We can't work any more than we do. I don't think I'll ever be able to work more than 20 weeks a year."

But it was Glenn, again, who was the most restless of the three. He yearned to be out on his boat, out on the sea where he could be free from the demands and peccadillos of the music business. By the fall of 1977, he had come to the point where he simply could not continue with the reunion. "I think it was a fantastic show, far better than the one we did before," he said in 1978, a point upon which Alex and Lou concurred.

"The response has been excellent, but for me, it has not been so good. I am just not a nostalgia type, and it just bothered me to have all of those people coming in expecting to be transported back to the good old days when I wanted to sing new things. It was bad enough when I was working alone and they wanted to hear 'Baby, The Rain Must Fall' and Rod McKuen songs and all that stuff that I had outgrown years ago. But when I got with the Limeliters it became worse because then they wanted Limeliters and Rod McKuen and 'Baby, The Rain Must Fall.' "

According to Glenn, though, another factor besides his longing for the sea and his loathing of nostalgia trips led to the end of the reunion tours. He was put out with Alex because every time the group would reach an agreement on what the Limeliters would be paid, Alex would try to make eleventh-hour changes. "Alex doesn't stick to a bargain," Glenn said bluntly. "You see, I didn't need the reunion but they wanted to work and I felt kind of badly about it. I'd spent four years with them, felt close enough to them so that it isn't going to hurt me to do it and might be fun. I really enjoy working in ensemble music; it's very soul satisfying, much more so than as a single performer.

"But as far as the money was concerned, it was a loss from my point of view. Alex would make a deal and then we'd get tours set, and then he'd come to me and at the last-minute say, 'Oh no, I just can't do this, I gotta have more money.' And I used to just give him more money and finally I got sick of it. I said, 'Alex, you got more money, but this is the last time we'll do this.'" Lou concurred on that point. In his autobiography, Lou wrote, "His [Alex's] attention to detail is laudable, even though he has exasperated not a few of the people who have employed the Limeliters by trying to sweeten the deal in our behalf."

The triumphant Disneyland gig would be one of the trio's last hurrahs as a permanent unit. Only a week later, Dec. 2-4, 1977, at the Circle Star Theatre in San Carlos, California about 20 miles south of San Francisco, the Limeliters Reunion played its final date for nearly three years. Immediately, Glenn started making plans to disappear on his new 35-foot ketch, the *Sea Witch*, which was parked somewhere in Florida. This time, Glenn would be sailing alone, for Annie and the kids had long since had enough of Glenn's adventures out on the untamed seas. Indeed, Annie now had her hands full running Brass Dolphin, which was turning out to be even more successful than Alex had predicted. In the span of only a year, Annie had sold over 15,000 copies of the *Reunion* albums—a mere trickle by corporate standards but pure profit for a small mail-order outfit. The only advertising Brass Dolphin did was passing out leaflets at Limeliters concerts, with the upper-case entrepreneurial message, "We Have Taken Things Into Our Own Hands."

Enthused by the response, Annie now took it upon herself to get some solo material from her husband into the catalogue. Upon the swift demise of Custom Fidelity, the rights to Glenn's album with the Havenstock River Band had reverted back to him, so Annie repackaged the album, changed the title to *Easy Now* and issued it on Brass Dolphin. However, there were some significant differences between the original and the reissue. While Glenn had regained ownership of the album, the master tapes were lost; therefore, the album had to be mastered from a vinyl pressing of the original album. Due to inner-groove distortion, Glenn could not get a clean-sounding tape out of the last tracks on both sides, "Annie's Going to Sing Her Song" and "Epistle." Annie rushed Glenn into a studio with his road band to cut a pair of Mike Settle soft-rock ballads, "Long Lost Feelings" and "She Believes In Me" in order to fill out the album. As ordinary as the two tunes are, at least they don't upset the balance of the tracks recorded seven years earlier.

Also cut around that time by Glenn was a fine new tune by Dave Ellingson called "A Good Woman Likes To Drink With The Boys," a lumberjack's rollicking ode to his fun-loving wife. Thinking this might be her first commercial venture, Annie had a 45 RPM single pressed up and sent it out to several radio stations in the Pacific Northwest, 35 of which added it to their playlists. Unfortunately for Glenn and Annie, Jimmie Rodgers' competing version of the tune caught on and quickly eclipsed Glenn's single in that region. Only 500 copies were pressed anyhow—and it's doubtful that any of them were distributed. Still, it's one of Glenn's best obscure singles.

Glenn also found the time in 1977 to record four songs for the soundtrack of the animated film of J.R.R. Tolkien's novel *The Hobbit*, laying down the vocals in New York (including some doublings) after the backing orchestra was recorded in London. The Maury Laws songs are pleasant, listenable ditties, not condescending in the least, and Laws wraps Glenn in a tasteful blanket of London strings with an alert rhythm section propelling Glenn along.

When the Limeliters were wrapping up their final tour, Annie was already thinking ahead about the absence of income due to Glenn's umpteenth "retirement." The day after the Disneyland gig ended, she sent the Haji Sound recording team out to Doug Weston's Troubadour club in West Hollywood to capture a Glenn Yarbrough solo benefit concert, using the same band that backed the trio.

She also had a surprise up her sleeve for Glenn, for who should barge onto the stage in the middle of the band's intro but an all-too-familiar old face, Rod McKuen. "Wait a minute, I gotta go on," a stunned Glenn pleaded, but the determined Rod pushed his way around Glenn's more-than-ample frame and, after telling the band to shut up, delivered one of the most tasteless impromptu introductions on records. "Had it not been for Glenn Yarbrough, there would be no Rod McKuen," the poet finally admits, later adding "I hope he's still my friend 'cause he's bigger than I am."

"Annie and him (McKuen) get along a lot," said Rein Neggo. "That's why he did the narration on the Troubadour album. It was a surprise to Glenn, and Glenn was pissed off after that. Glenn thought it was 'cute.' She was president of the record company and he let her do anything she wanted."

Just as the "Reunion" albums were an honest reflection of the Limeliters' act, so is *Live at Doug Weston's Troubadour*, a warm, casual appearance before Troubadour loyalists that sprawls over two packed LPs. Like Neggo, in her debut as a producer, Annie strikes exactly the right tone with Glenn—just turn him loose live with his tightly-rehearsed backup band and let him weave a spell.

Inevitably there are old favorites aplenty. "If I'm gonna do old songs," Glenn says, "I thought I might go right back to the very beginning," back to his cruising days at St. John's College. He then rolls out "I'm Goin' Back," fresh as ever, plunking out a minimal accompaniment on his guitar the way he did back in Aspen in the '50s. "That established my innocence," he says, "and then I used to hit 'em with this song"—and out comes "The Far Side of the Hill" with atmospheric guitar and harmonica.

Yet before long, Glenn is mocking his audience with "Sing Us Some of the Old Songs." The loathing of nostalgia is never far from the surface; after an anecdote about Andy Williams' fans not letting him deviate from covering the hits, Glenn tries to praise his audience for permitting him sing new material. The anti-nostalgia tone perhaps takes on a gentler, more ironic touch in Shel Silverstein's "Middle Aged Groupies" and he attempts to put a seal on the whole issue in the concluding "Our

Last Song Together." But Glenn was too canny a showman to break completely with his audience. His silvery tone, now not quite as pure as before, his laid back stage presence, the polished country/rock sound of his band, created a nostalgic mood anyway, no matter what he sang.

These were the days of disco-mania and stadium rock, punk-rock's angry counterattack, and high-tech *Star Wars* extravaganzas on the screen—and in contrast, even Glenn's newer material, however thoughtful or quirky, sounded like a country breeze from the past, aimed at his middle-aged groupies. With the hitmaking days gone, it now made sense to hang on to the audience one had—and however much he professed to loathe it, Glenn hung on to them like a polished pro.

Not for long, though. Once his performing obligations were over, Glenn took off alone for Florida to the *Sea Witch*, sailed around the Caribbean for awhile, and came home in the spring just long enough to review the tapes of his Troubadour album on April 3, 1978. That night, Glenn returned to the *Sea Witch*, now docked in the Bahamas, where he commenced his first solo journey across the Atlantic Ocean, ending up in Ireland. He would not return to the stage until November.

"He loves to get out on the high seas and pit himself against the elements," said Lou around that time. "He says that's when he feels he's living intensely. One of the high points of his life was when he sailed down from Vancouver through the terrible 40s off the Oregon coast. He got caught in a 36-hour sea. He had a broken ankle; he was in a cast. He sat at the tiller for 36 hours.

"He loves that. He said the noise is deafening, you're talking about 40-foot waves coming at you, you know. And when you come out of it, he says there's nothing like that. That's his ultimate thrill."

Lou paused at this point for theatrical effect. "That has about as much appeal to me as a case of spinal meningitis."

To the outside world, Glenn Yarbrough, sailor and part-time singer, seemed content to spend most of 1978 sailing the world—across the Atlantic, down the Dalmatian coast of Yugoslavia, in and out of the scenic bays of the Mediterranean. He was going it alone, pitting himself against the furies of the open sea, fulfilling the fantasies of freedom he had harbored ever since he was a teenager hitchhiking around the country.

And yet...the old thrill was suddenly gone. Being alone on the Atlantic gave Glenn plenty of time to think, to evaluate his direction in life, and he was surprised by what he had learned. He found that the journey itself was the thing that gave him the most satisfaction out of sailing, not reaching the destination. He began to dread every landing, for that meant having to deal with the impatient port captain, the regimented customs and immigration services of the countries he would be visiting. The mere sight of land, or even the anticipation of sighting land began to depress him, a sign that his freedom was about to end. If it were at all possible, he would have preferred to stay at sea indefinitely, like the Flying Dutchman.

And even on the open sea, something was missing. Sailing had become strangely routine, a means of killing time and putting off major decisions. The old restlessness in Glenn began to surface, along with the strong moral streak that had guided his hand in so many of his decisions. "It was like, God, I'm going to be gone for a month at sea, and I don't know if I want to be at sea," Glenn confessed. "I was feeling like I ought to be doing something else."

Inevitably, Glenn's thoughts turned to the one talent of his that was financially responsible for putting him out on the waves—his voice. Brass Dolphin was in full swing in 1978, and Annie's voluminous correspondence had resulted in a lot of fan mail pouring into the Woodstock Road house. In letter after letter, Glenn's fans let him know how his records gave them comfort and solace in times of trouble, soothing the hurt of broken love affairs, preventing suicide attempts, giving them strength to carry on.

Prior to this, Glenn had never taken his voice nor his effect upon his listeners very seriously. The Voice was merely a convenient means of survival, a reassuring gift from the gods that meant he would never have to go hungry. It all came so easily. Up until the mid 1970s, he never had to warm up before a performance. He learned things quickly and fluently, ready to move on to the next tune. He never listened to music for the sheer pleasure of it, only when compiling material for his act.

Nor could Glenn attach himself strongly with what his audiences were feeling when he was singing. Lou recalled that Glenn would be amused that he could reduce his female listeners to tears with his rendition of "Lass From The Low Country" in the early '60s. "Did you see that gal in the third row crying?" Glenn would chuckle at intermission. Glenn's quick get-aways after concerts meant that Lou and Alex would be the ones who would hear Glenn's fans unburden themselves about what his music meant to them. But now, Glenn was getting a full dose—and at last, he was taking heed.

"I was beginning to see that whatever I do is pretty useful," he said. "I never thought of it as useful before. I always thought of it as something to make a few bucks and make enough money to do the other things you want to do. I began to see that whatever I did was healing to a lot of people, and so I began to have a little bit more respect for what I did. I thought, well, there's not that much time left and I ought to be spending that time doing something worthwhile."

Glenn resolved to go back to work full-time, starting in November at Harrah's in Lake Tahoe and Reno. This time, he was going to push hard at getting a major record contract. He would cherry-pick his material, get a contemporary sound, produce a killer album with as lavish a backdrop as he could afford, shop it around and storm the charts. He would go back on the concert circuit to prove a point, that with a bit of effort, Glenn Yarbrough could make it bigger than ever and make everyone forget all about Rod McKuen and "Baby, the Rain Must Fall."

But this time, the vaunted Yarbrough luck ran out. "When I decided to do that is when everything fell apart!" he said.

At first, Glenn had made tentative plans to cut a direct-to-disc recording with Lincoln Mayorga's Sheffield Lab label in April 1979, but that project never materialized. With his ability to learn and retain things quickly, Glenn might have done well under direct-to-disc's demanding conditions, where a single mistake at the end of an entire LP side meant, you would have to start all over again. Ultimately, though, Glenn thought that his vehicle back to the big leagues would be a record of all new love songs and semi-autobiographical sketches, lushly orchestrated, an update of the smooth sound that sustained his solo career in the '60s.

In 1979, he hooked up with a long-flowing-haired, long-bearded producer/songwriter named Dik Darnell who, in the fashion of the '70s, had attracted a fanatically admiring cult of hippies that hung out on the eastern slopes of the Colorado Rockies. Darnell was involved in a number of entertainment projects, some of which were in support of persecuted Indians—and somehow he played up to the side of Glenn that always wanted to be 18 again, convincing him his songs would be the ones that would put Glenn back in the national spotlight.

In the meantime, there were tensions between Glenn and Annie; Glenn said that he was most upset by Annie's drinking, and his long absences at sea certainly didn't help matters either. Yet most of all, they were opposites, stubborn opposites constantly tugging at each other—Annie the outgoing, loquacious go-getter, Glenn the shy, reticent, laid-back wanderer. "It was one of those things that never should have been," reflected Jonathan Moore. "They were so completely different, those people. Annie is a very businesslike, pushing person, and she gets it together. When Holly came along, that held it together a little bit."

Finally, Glenn and Annie agreed to separate, while still keeping the Brass Dolphin operation running. With single-minded concentration, Glenn also wanted to get as far away from the sea as possible, to a landlocked area that would not tempt him to abandon his comeback. He decided to move to Estes Park, Colorado, the gorgeously situated gateway to Rocky Mountain National Park about 65 miles northwest of Denver, and also close to Dik Darnell and his crowd. He sold the *Jubilee* at a tremendous loss ("That's Glenn—buy high, sell low," Rein Neggo would say), leaving him without a boat for the first time in about 17 years, and bought a beautiful two-story mountain home in the woods above Estes Park, near the borderline with the national park.

A local Denver television feature show, *Assignment Colorado*, which profiled Glenn in 1981, shows a contented born-again mountaineer, looking thoughtfully at the majestic Rockies, strumming his guitar and singing "I'm Goin' Back." "If they (sailors) have to live on land, they have to live in the mountains," he told his interviewer, relaxing in his living room with the picture window overlooking the forest.

With a bonafide celebrity in his grasp, Darnell got Glenn into a Denver recording studio, where rates were cheaper than in L.A., to make an album. A large soft-rock backup band was assembled, players from the Denver Symphony were called in for the backgrounds, and a mixed vocal group added more window-dressing touch to the choruses. Entitled *Just A Little Love*, the album was an expensive undertaking—over $50,000, entirely financed by Glenn—and he spent about six months recording and polishing it, a far cry from his RCA Victor period where everything could be done in just a few days.

Yet Glenn's on-again, off-again ability to select good material had mostly deserted him this time. Many of the songs are dull, overlong, plodding, full of predictable melodramatic climaxes that would have even embarrassed Barry Manilow. His voice sounds grainier here, but he still puts everything he has into these songs, spending his gift lavishly on a lot of undeserving material. The only tunes that can withstand more than a couple of plays are "(Trying To Get) Close To You" by Randy Handley, which has a touchingly melancholy lyric about a lounge singer who pushes on despite years of struggle without getting anywhere, and a beguiling, bossa-nova-styled Kostas Lazarides ode to Glenn's favorite pastime, "Sailin'".

With fierce professional determination, Glenn then overhauled his stage act—hiring a mostly new band (Brian Davies and Gary Clontz were the holdovers) with lots of keyboards, two female singers, and a more contemporary rock sound than anything he had since the Havenstock River Band broke up. He sang his new material with more conviction and eloquence than he had displayed in several years, while grudgingly running through a few hits (including "Baby, The Rain Must Fall" with a disco beat) and Rod McKuen tunes so as not to completely alienate his following. "I'll do the songs you want to hear, then I'll do what I want," he would tell a Los Angeles Greek Theatre audience in June of 1980, only to find that the older material went over much better than the new.

Despite the none-too-encouraging public response, Glenn still made the rounds of the major record labels, hoping that someone somewhere might take his new album on. But the most common response that Glenn received was, "I don't hear a hit." Some of the younger executives had no idea who Glenn Yarbrough was; others considered him a has-been who had been away at sea too long. The mailing list at Brass Dolphin was clamoring for its release, but the album cost too much to make for Brass Dolphin to issue it—and of course, Glenn's wife's label couldn't very well give him a hefty advance.

Glenn and Annie hit upon a rabble-rousing idea. Wherever Glenn would perform in the latter half of 1980, he would ask his audiences to write to Bruce Lundvall, then the president of the domestic division of CBS Records and implore him to sign Glenn Yarbrough. Annie made the same request in the annual Brass Dolphin newsletter, listing Lundvall's CBS address. Whatever the response was, it certainly didn't sway anyone at CBS.

Finally, Glenn gave up and thrashed around for a small company—any small company—that would take his luckless album. The only one that stepped forward was First American, a small, precariously financed Seattle outfit which released the record in the early months of 1981 with a heroic promotional mini-blitz. A big press party was given in Denver to launch the album—and hardly anyone bothered to show up. Two singles were released from the album and sent out to many DJs and music critics, almost all of whom tossed them into the circular file. Without airplay or press coverage, the tiny label couldn't do much more for Glenn—and the album sank without a trace. First American did too, bankrupt. It was the Stax and Custom Fidelity debacles all over again, now repeated on a humiliatingly smaller scale.

A&M Records' Canadian branch did pick up the album and, as a result, *Just A Little Love* sold better in Canada than it did in the U.S. But since Canada has only a tenth of the population of the U.S., hardly anyone in the executive suites in New York and Los Angeles was impressed.

In 1978, with Glenn sailing the Atlantic and Lou at home playing the piano and contemplating more G and B research projects, it was left to Alex to try and resuscitate the Limeliters. He alone did not want the reunions to end, and he was determined to make the group count in the business again.

"I think the market is there," he said then. "If we wanted to work that hard, I think we could exceed our past success...if the miracle happens, and my partners—Glenn principally and Lou secondarily—said, 'Let's prove a point.' But when you get to a certain age, you don't want to prove a point anymore. I'm the only one left in our group who wants to prove any points. And the only reason I do is because the game is there to play."

Alex realized that as far as the group's stage persona was concerned, there could be no Limeliters without Lou Gottlieb's uniquely zany humor. But as in 1963, he could see a Limeliters without Glenn Yarbrough. They had made perfectly acceptable, if not spectacular, recordings without him—and he thought that if there could be a really well-matched tenor in place, the Limeliters' sound could conceivably survive.

Glenn, for one, didn't mind a bit. "They want to work and I don't, so I'm kind of holding the thing back," he said.

This time, though, Alex would conduct a real search for the right voice—not just a casual invitation as in the case of Ernie Sheldon. In the winter of 1977-78, he auditioned singers, none of whom he thought could adequately replace Glenn in the blend. Yet Alex finally did find someone who might have worked out, one William Oliver Swofford.

Swofford was a singer/songwriter who simply went by the stage name of Oliver—and he was hardly an unknown in the business. Back in June of 1969, while recording for the small Jubilee label, Oliver scored a huge hit single with a fresh-voiced rendition of "Good Morning Starshine" from the so-called rock musical *Hair*. It soared to the No. 3 slot on the national charts, making Oliver an instant star. Switching to the Crewe label, Oliver followed that up in August with an even bigger smash, a delicately sung version of Rod McKuen's "Jean" that went to No.2.

From those dizzying heights, though, the only direction was down. "Sunday Mornin," released later in the year, only made it to No. 35, and Oliver soon faded from sight. But he had done something the Limeliters never could do—record a Top 10 hit—and that would give them a new built-in audience who remembered those records. Also, Swofford had a sweet, youthful, soaring tenor with a touch of Peter Noone-like nasality and innocence, a total change from the unique timbre of Glenn.

Intrigued by the possibilities, Alex managed to get Lou down from his urban ashram in San Francisco to rehearse with Swofford on March 29, 1978, and Lou came away from the rehearsal encouraged by what he heard. "You know, Bill could give us the first new sound we've had 'cause he is a really good singer and he can sing in octaves with Alex," he said after the rehearsal. "It's a completely different vocal problem to produce maximum resonance with these three than it was with Yarbrough, see."

But then Lou fell back into a reflective mood, uncertain as to whether the whole venture was worth putting his own creative life on the back burner again. "I don't know," he pondered. "I fluctuate between thinking whether I really want to be a Limeliter when I grow up, or whether or not this isn't a tremendous challenge, to see if we can't get the act to mean something again in the record business."

Sure enough, Lou's inertia won out—and he backed out of the act. Later, Alex tried to sort out what had happened. "Bill Swofford, who is a very nice and very talented man, was the most appropriate person I had been able to find," he said. "At the last minute, Lou decided he didn't want to do it—and I can understand why.

"Because when you work with somebody like Glenn, you get spoiled for anybody else. He's one of the great singers of America, and a lot of people don't understand that. He has an extraordinary range. He can sing a low G without any effort at all, with power. There are no tenors who can sing low Gs, except in opera. And he also, in his heyday—he didn't like to use it—he had a high C, a damned good high C."

By the spring of 1979, a visibly depressed Alex seemed to have given up hope, for the time being, that the Limeliters could ever mean anything again in the business. He was disappointed that the *Reunion* albums, of which he was very fond, had received so little exposure—an inevitable problem for a small mail-order firm. He talked darkly about getting out of the music business altogether, perhaps gravitating back towards the theater and films once again.

In this conversation with the author that spring, we clearly see that the gulf between Alex and Lou—always a mismatch of yin and yang even in the closest of times—had become almost unbridgeable. "Lou, God knows, is an incredibly gifted man and certainly one of the more gifted performers I've ever seen," Alex said. "But he's completely in a different world from mine. It's virtually impossible for us to communicate.

"It's possible that we may be able to do some reunions with Glenn. But basically, you know, I really feel it's over. There's nothing more to say. You can go around the first time, then you can go around the second time with nostalgia. But after nostalgia, what is there? The answer is, the only thing left is a synthesis and a move on to something new. I do not believe Lou can move forward. He, of course, is the one who says, 'I don't want to sing the old songs.'"

Don't you all say that?

"I don't say that, not for a second. I believe that any act that has had any notoriety has to sing the old songs. There's no way out of it."

But you all seem to prefer to move on.

"Yeah, but what that means for Lou is something so bizarre I can't comprehend it. What it means for him is essentially singing his own songs, and his own songs I do not unfortunately consider to be viable. That isn't to say all his songs are not viable. He has written some songs I think are useful. But I am incapable of singing material on stage, whether written by myself or by Glenn or by Lou, if I feel they are out of the area of accessibility to our particular audience or even to any audience. Lou and I just don't see eye to eye at all on so many things. That's why it would be so difficult for me to put the group together with him and another singer."

In 1979, Alex speculated that it might be another five years or so before the Limeliters would attempt another reunion, if at all. For Glenn, the figure was more like ten years. As things turned out, it wouldn't take nearly that long.

Meanwhile, the offbeat and the bizarre had become business-as-usual for Lou, and his next career scheme took him perhaps way over the edge. Now that he had a black beard, Lou bore an uncanny resemblance to Fidel Castro—a thought that probably seemed rather romantic to this former member of the Communist party. Lou started to think about putting this resemblance to use, perhaps a comedy in which he would play Fidel after his eventual retirement from power. Then, as the gears continued to turn, Lou thought a mock-press conference, in which he would impersonate Fidel and answer questions from the audience in Spanish, might be the way to go.

A less commercial idea would have been hard to come by, but that had never stopped Lou before. Indeed, when he found out that the Carter Administration had lifted some restrictions for American citizens on travel to Cuba, Lou started packing his bags, thinking it would be a good time to research the act. Having found a ten-day Cuban package courtesy of Mexicana Airlines, Lou took off for Merida, Mexico in March of 1978 to secure a Cuban visa and then it was on to Havana, where he stayed at the Riviera Hotel.

It was like being in a strange time warp from the 1950s, with vintage American cars painstakingly preserved by their owners cruising the streets and hotel signs identical to their onetime cousins in Las Vegas (Lou observed in his autobiography that "Havana in 1978 was like a 1958 Cadillac whose dashboard had been polished to death"). Also, he was quite aware of the unsettling feeling of being constantly watched, by real or imagined undercover police in the hotels. It would be Lou's first immersion into a "socialist" country—and he would come away with the queasy feeling that he could not live in any society that practiced thought control.

Lou didn't get a chance to see Fidel Castro in the flesh, but he did catch one of the caudillo's speeches on Cuban television, a non-stop, two hour-twenty-minute sermon on the subject of the 100th anniversary of the Protest at Barragua. At first. Lou picked up snatches of the speech on a bus radio while on his way back to the Havana airport, and then heard the entire thing on TV while waiting for his return flight home. Thanks to his fluency in Spanish, Lou got a full, undiluted dose of Fidel's act—and in the context of Shakespeare's one-liner, "All the world's a stage," Lou thought he recognized a kindred spirit.

"The greatest entertainer I have ever seen in my life was Fidel Castro," Lou said in 1978. "There's the greatest actor ever. Greatest hypnotist too...It explains how he can educate, delight, and give self-respect to an entire nation. Everybody has self-respect. Everybody has, or thinks he has, a piece of the action."

Lou was so enthralled that he wrote a letter to Fidel in 1978 offering his services as the representative of Cuban music in the United States and Canada as a music publisher! "Nothing has been heard out of Cuba in 20 years." he said, "and there's lots of good music there, lots of it. As I see Cuba today, the most potentially lucrative item of export they have as far as the United States is concerned is music. We don't need the sugar. We don't need the nickel."

Needless to say, Lou never heard from Fidel or anyone in the Cuban government, but he was determined now to put together a Castro impersonation act. With no more reunions in sight and the money from the concerts running low, Lou needed something to do, and he thought that if Hal Holbrook could make a handsome living by impersonating Mark Twain, he, Lou Gottlieb, could do the same with Fidel as his vehicle.

Lou started to put together an act in which he would sing and play the piano in the first half of his set and hold his Fidel Castro press conference in the second half, with actress Zandra Luz Zimmerman-Montilla as an English translator. He even wrote a funny, rambling article about the breakup of the Limeliters and his new solo act for his old paper, the *San Francisco Examiner and Chronicle*. The piece ran on July 29, 1979, featuring a large photo of Lou with a jolly smile, dressed in Fidel's Army fatigues. His reason for going out on his own was admirably succinct. "Bluntly stated," he wrote, "I have tapped out again, need a gig, and feel like working alone."

Lou found himself opening the show the following weekend (August 4-5) for Henny Youngman in San Francisco's Great American Music Hall. The thoroughly baffled audience response soon put an end to his plans to make a career out of Fidel, but Lou was unrepentant. "I think

Fidel Castro is eminently right for satire because he is, curiously enough, almost devoid of humor in his public utterances," Lou said. "So that sets him up perfectly."

Regardless, Lou still had to figure out a way to pay the $400-a-month rent on his Scott St. apartment in San Francisco. He tried writing a novel, got a hundred pages down on paper and then lost interest. He tried getting odd jobs as a pianist, doing lead sheets, teaching piano, tapping some meager sums from his alive but barely breathing Amadeo-Brio publishing business, anything to survive.

In another weird adventure, Lou tried selling electric organs for Sherman-Clay Piano and Organ at the Santa Clara County Fair! Hired for his ability to speak Spanish, Lou would play songs on the organ outdoors until he gathered a small group around him. Then he would stop playing and the group would gradually melt away, leaving a few from whom Lou would find a potential buyer to take into a room where he could sample the organ himself. Then Lou would assume the ruthless role of a "closer," swooping in with a line like, "Shall we deliver this in the morning or afternoon?"

Well, as a high-pressure salesman for the first time in his life, Lou lasted exactly one week. "I never made one sale," Lou shrugged. "It seemed like everybody I got ready to sell to could not afford $3500 for a Kimball organ. I just couldn't see encumbering somebody with a $3500 debt when I knew they didn't have it. I had never sold anything, and I wanted to see what it was like—sort of like a Willy Loman experiment. I'm no good at it.

"But I did learn one thing," he deadpanned. "Nobody in his right mind ever pays retail—for anything."

Eventually Lou doubled back to academia in the fall of 1979, where his Ph.D. and jazz roots got him a job teaching a jazz history class at Cal State University San Francisco. Lou must have been a marvelously entertaining teacher; he hated the grading system but loved to convey his passion for jazz and his often highly original theories. Jazz was the music of insubordination to Lou, invented by a people who had been sold into slavery by their African village chiefs for being independent thinkers—troublemakers, in other words.

Lou's students clearly loved him, judging from the evaluations of the faculty that were passed around after the end of the fall semester, and Lou returned to teach another jazz class in the spring. In the summer he devised yet another class which he was uniquely equipped to teach, that of "Music as Business," a practical survey of non-performance jobs in the music business for those whose dreams don't pan out. But Lou soon got tired of teaching the same thing over and over, and besides, it still wasn't enough to make ends meet.

So, when Lou picked up the phone one day in August 1980 to hear Russ Gary asking whether he would like to join Alex and Glenn again on the road, it was yet another summons he could not refuse. "It's obvious that God intends me to work with the Limeliters," he sighed. "If I could work alone, God knows I would. But I simply cannot do it."

While Lou went back to the Limeliters because he needed the money, and Glenn invited his partners back out of empathy and as part of a general plan to rebuild his career, in Alex's case, Russ Gary's phone call in August 1980 was nothing less than salvation. He had dabbled in this and that ever since the idea of going on without Glenn blew up—going back to the business of making television commercials, dreaming up theatrical projects that never came off.

Alex' bachelor days had finally come to an end, for in 1976 he had married a beautiful, vivacious, nurturing woman from Colombia whom he had met only a short time before. Gladys Rios was a young girl from a farm family outside Bogota, Colombia who had done some work for Alex's father and mother while Leonide was on an engineering job in South America. The Hassilevs brought Gladys home to Florida on a student visa to learn English, and it was there that she met Alex while he was visiting his parents. A whirlwind courtship flared up—and after they were married, friends noticed that Gladys' upbeat, outgoing warmth was a soothing contrast to this reserved, increasingly downcast Russian.

Oddly enough, Alex would be the only ex-Limeliter to receive major-label exposure in the late 1970s. Early in 1977, Quincy Jones was throwing together an impressionistic suite for A&M Records based on the blockbuster TV mini-series *Roots*, to whose opening episode he had contributed some music. In the section depicting the slave ship sailing across the Atlantic to America, Alex was asked to sing the part of one of the white sailors on the record. In the middle of the selection entitled "Middle Passage," you can hear Alex singing the sea shanty "Haul Away, Joe" for nearly 40 seconds in a lusty Irish sailor's dialect. But a determined Limeliters fan most likely would have discovered this chip off the workbench by accident, and it certainly didn't lead to a solo career for Alex. His creative identity, for better or worse, was still wrapped up in the Limeliters—and he jumped at the opportunity to work with Lou and Glenn again, even if it was only for a one-shot fall tour.

Once again, Lou, Alex and Glenn would be hitting the interstates of America, if now as a postscript to Glenn's latest solo adventure. Once again, they would do so in a folk reunion package with the Kingston Trio, whose act had become sharper and tighter over the past few years of non-stop touring, if still agreeably rooted in nostalgia.

It proved to be a grueling tour, from the opening August date at Harrah's in Reno all the way to a Christmas-New Year's Eve stand in Denver. Glenn would do a full set of his solo material and bring the Limeliters on only at the end for a few, mostly predictable recycled numbers from the Reunion days. Glenn's new band was even tighter and more polished than the previous one and all three Limeliters were now in a focused working mode, the pastimes and procrastinations of the '70s banished.

Although Lou's bass now sported a frilly garter belt—a souvenir from a Reno gig—strapped around its belly, Lou was shedding the trappings of his executive hippie days. He had his hair cut short in 1979 (for $14, he recalled) before assuming his teaching post at CSU San Francisco, the Indian wrap-around dresses had long since given way to a comfortable pants suit and by 1981, he would be wearing a business suit onstage. "It just seemed that I was attracting undue attention," he explained. "It never was a really noble head of hair anyway, got kind of lank and waxy at times."

In the battle for survival in the '80s, expediency in dress had finally overtaken the middle-aged hippie. "All of us see that the fooling around days are over," Lou told the *Daily Californian* in San Diego that fall.

Yet there was tension in the air on this tour, more than there had been since the early '60s. Glenn was incensed over Alex's latest attempt to renegotiate his contract with the tour, for Alex threatened to take a hike only three days before it started. Glenn, as was his way, quickly gave in to Alex again but laid down the law; after this tour, that's it—no more reunions.

An unedited video interview for Reno's *P.M. Magazine* television program in October 1980 catches the hostility simmering under the glib, articulate surface of the reunited trio. Lou, his beard now graying, does most of the talking in his ebullient way, while Alex occasionally chimes in with his no-nonsense manner, gesturing with his hands, a cigarette constantly burning.

Meanwhile Glenn, clad carelessly in shorts, looks as if he would rather be anyplace else but here, staring blankly through tinted glasses, bored beyond belief. He rarely says anything—and when he does, there is an edgy tone to his comments. He kids Alex's womanizing at one point—"His main occupation should have been as a gigolo"—he off-handedly dismisses his musical career with the observation, "This is stupid work. I can't imagine anyone liking this kind of work." The differences between the three are never more striking when the interviewer asks them what kind of music they listen to in their spare time. Alex chooses classical music—especially Bach; Lou favors country music; Glenn listens to nothing.

Finally, the atmosphere nearly explodes. The interviewer asks Glenn about how it felt to have a song ("Baby, The Rain Must Fall") played on the radio all over the country. Without missing a beat, Alex immediately cuts in, "I'll tell you how it felt"—and Glenn shoots him a baleful stare that could kill.

The tension showed onstage as well. Their microphones were strategically placed further apart than ever onstage, as if Lou, Alex, and Glenn were on their own individual islands. There was little onstage banter between the three, virtually no eye contact, virtually no physical contact at all except for Lou putting his arms around the three of them in the preamble to "Old Fashioned Remedy." The sound of the three was still gloriously intact, nearly impervious to the passing years, but the frayed nerves now overwhelmed the fun.

Clearly the Limeliters had come to another crossroads.

Alex wanted to continue, Lou financially had no choice but to continue, but Glenn did not. He felt that performing with the Limeliters ultimately was holding him back, generating lots of nostalgia that drew big gates at the box office but keeping his own image stuck squarely in the past. He wanted to succeed or fail on his own, pushing a middle-of-the-road soft-rock sound and material that Alex, for one, could not abide. This would be the end, the last tour, and nothing could dissuade Glenn from his course.

But Lou, Alex, and Glenn did make one last appearance at New York's Copacabana club in January of 1981. This concert, again in tandem with the Kingston Trio, was videotaped and released by Pioneer

Electronics in the then-new laserdisc format—which meant only a tiny handful of fans who owned players saw the show.

Yet this artifact is the clearest record we have of Lou, Alex and Glenn at work, in any era. Not only that, the stiffness and distance between the three one felt in Los Angeles only two months before has been reduced; they sound less tense and more like old friends. The picture quality is razor-sharp in the best laserdisc manner, and Mary Travers sets the nostalgic mood with an introductory speech while walking through wintry Central Park. "There's A Meetin' Here Tonight," the first number and the title of the laserdisc, begins raggedly but the trio soon gets back in shape, accompanied expertly by the band.

There is new material on the disc—"That's The Way It Goes," a Russian-flavored Gene Raskin rewrite of "Those Were The Days" that suave Alex nearly turns into a pop vocal, and an old Pete Seeger sing-along rouser for Glenn, "Precious Friend." And there are the usual oldies—"John Henry," "Madeira," "Acres" and a "Gari Gari" that whirls into hyperdrive. Although there would be further limited reunions down the line, this would be the last time that Alex and Lou would perform an entire 35-minute set with Glenn.

Glenn also gets about 17 minutes on his own, trying again against formidable odds to put over some of the drab new material from *Just A Little Love*. It is a hopeless cause, but Glenn's easygoing charm and excellent pipes make this segment watchable—and he does a convincing job with "(Trying to Get) Close To You." "You're gonna hear a lot of nostalgia tonight," he says, "but not from me!" With a single thrust, Glenn thus undercuts the premise of this laserdisc with gleeful vengeance, and probably made some viewers flip the disc over to the Kingston Trio side.

One of the disc's reviewers was Dave Van Ronk who, after carrying the flag for the folk purists for so long in the Sixties, had begun to mellow. "Back in the early '60s," he wrote, "groups such as the Kingston Trio and the Limeliters caught a lot of flak from the cognoscenti for what they were not. They were not ethnic, they were not authentic, they were not even folk. The purist magazines of the times regularly printed indignant articles with the titles like 'Folk Music Versus Fake Music.' I ought to know. I wrote some of them.

"Well, I think none of us is as pure as we used to be, and in a lot of ways, the Trio and the Limeliters, as well as the Brothers Four, were pinned with a bum rap. In a sense, they were downright more authentic than their critics."

In Lou's words, that was quite an astounding "volte-face."

It would also be an unintentional epitaph to a closed chapter in their history, for the Limeliters, in order to survive, had to cut their links with Glenn Yarbrough.

NIGHT LIFE

Take Henny, too, please

Lou Gottlieb's Reunion With Fidel Castro

By Lou Gottlieb

FREQUENTLY after a "Lime-liter Reunion" performance during the last few years a member of the audience would appear backstage saying something like this:

"I haven't seen you guys since the concert you gave at Marquette University the night of the Senior Prom in 1962. The man who was my escort on that occasion is the father of our four children. We are separated now, but we all got together to catch the show tonight. Even the kids liked it, which is surprising because they are into punk rock. But you didn't sing '———.' "

An entertainer is one who by nature pops into a "peak experience" when confronted by a paying audience and one more opportunity to feel good in public. Encounters such as that with our Marquette alumna constitute my lasting reward, and hearing testimony that my craft has played some role in the emotional history of another human being always gets to me.

However, working together, Glenn Yarbrough, Alex Hassilev and I are, to some extent, prisoners of our repertoire and 20-year association. When the public clearly says, "Sing us some of the old songs," the creative potential of the collaboration tends to wither, and, though we did try to put some new things into the act every year, our Reunions did not produce a new musical direc-

GOTTLIEB AS FIDEL: EVEN KIDS WILL LIKE IT

half of a new show   I got the idea last year while

Lou as Fidel Castro in a self-penned article for the
San Francisco Chronicle, July 29, 1979.

The Limeliters Mk. IV, Alex Hassilev, Lou Gottlieb,
and Rick Dougherty, in concert at the Redondo Beach
Performing Arts Center, May 13, 1995.
(Photo by Richard S. Ginell)

Chapter Seventeen

"I picked a hard way to make an easy living.
Everybody wants to be a star.
I picked a hard way to make an easy living.
Things that look so simple never are."
—Richard Donahue/Peter Derge:
"Hard Way To Make An Easy Living"

Even as the Limeliters were going through the motions of touring with Glenn for the last time, the wheels were turning in Russ Gary's mind about the next step in their evolution. Sometime that fall, at an engagement at Harrah's in Lake Tahoe, Gary took Lou and Alex aside and mused out loud that they ought to go out on their own, with a new tenor to replace Glenn. For Russ, no doubt self-interest was the primary motivation, for instead of having two folk acts to book—the Glenn Yarbrough/Limeliters package and the Kingston Trio—he could now have three—Glenn, the Limeliters on their own, and the Kingston Trio.

For Lou, the moment of truth came sometime on the last tour when he brought out a page of music he had just concocted for three voices. "Glenn's face just seemed to fall because it was something additional he would have to learn, and he has made it clear to me that he does not feel the three of us have any hit potential whatever," Lou said in early 1981. "We have a great nostalgia value in person, and he has utilized that, but the idea of any kind of modern hitmaking potential he feels is very low. He says that with great sadness, of course, 'We need a hit, and I'm closer to it than we are, the three of us.' Which I can't disagree with at all. The only thing I can say is that it leaves me and Alex with absolutely nothing to do but wait for the hit and keep on singing 'Have Some Madeira, M'Dear' and 'Gari Gari.'"

Yet for Alex, Russ' offer—which came with an attractive amount of money attached—revived a dream that had been dormant since the Bill Swofford episode fell through. He had come to believe that the Limeliters' vocal sound was still viable after more than 20 years. More than that, with its unique character, the sound could still be a possible commercial goldmine in the right hands, with the right material. And it didn't necessarily have to be chained to the old folkie repertoire; the sound could be used in other forms of music.

He thought back to the aborted venture with Chuck Glaser, who heard in the Limeliters a striking similarity in blend to his own Tompall and the Glaser Brothers group. He thought back to Lou's hifalutin' satire of country music on "Redwood Forest," which upon straightening out Lou's bent frame of mind, revealed a serious, even spectacular set of country harmonies.

Back in 1980-81, everyone thought the so-called "Urban Cowboy" way of life would sweep all before it—and Alex Hassilev, the urbane, thoughtful, Paris-born son of Russian parents, took a good hard look. If Alabama or the Oak Ridge Boys could make it on their hearty if modest sound, why not the Limeliters—who had a great deal more to offer. Perhaps country radio would be the Limeliters' ticket back to riches, capturing the audience there and from that point, who knows, maybe the vast pop market, too?

Not only that, Lou and Alex were convinced there was a very definite link between country and folk. "Country music is the commercial branch of American folk music," Lou would glibly say, following it with an erudite musical analysis of how country's bass patterns differ from those of rock. On a more concrete level, Alex noted that country music—at least classic country—dealt with real problems that real people had in a down-to-earth manner, often in a story sequence. That recipe, in a different kitchen, would also produce folk music.

Indeed, Alex was encouraged by the success the Kingston Trio was having playing in country bars at the time. Although the Kingston repertoire was still the same old folk-era thing, their raucous, bawdy, crudely funny banter—fueled as always by that authentic, hell-raising party animal Bobby Shane—connected with the good old boys in the crowd, and "Tom Dooley" and "Scotch And Soda" always crossed over all barriers. An old name from the past didn't hurt them, and airplay on oldies radio kept the tunes alive.

First things first, though. Alex had to find a replacement for Glenn, someone who could approximate the old blend and still have the flexibility to roam out of the folk spectrum. Once again, he consulted his contacts in the folk music circles and the recording industry. Once again, he ran through auditions with promising young tenor voices.

Before October was out, Alex's search had ended. Upon the recommendation of his friend Don Lang whom he ran into at McCabe's, a cozy, anachronistic guitar shop and coffee house in Santa Monica, Alex invited a 28-year-old red-headed singer/songwriter from East Orange, New Jersey to submit a tape.

Lang had performed with the ebullient red-headed singer in Chicago, and when Alex asked him if he knew of any tenors, Lang didn't hesitate for a minute. He checked out the young man's reputation with old folk colleague Bob Gibson, who confirmed what his own ears and his friend at McCabe's told him.

Only then did Alex then approach Lou with his find. "When I first heard him," Lou recalled, "Alex very wisely found not one but four tenors and played all four of the tapes of these people for me. The first three left me monumentally unimpressed, and the fourth had me jumping up and saying, 'That's it, that's it, let's go.' It has to be that way. One simply cannot convince oneself of the utility of a person. Either the heart speaks, or you don't have the right person."

Soon the young redhead would come to a Limeliters show at a dinner theater in Lemon Grove, CA, in the company of Dan Seals, where he met Lou and Alex and saw the act for the first time in his life. Another show at the Los Angeles Music Center in November impressed him even more—and he agreed to join the Limeliters at a guaranteed salary of $25,000 a year. By the time the Glenn Yarbrough-led Limeliters were playing their last full gig at the Copacabana the following January, Glenn's replacement was waiting there in the wings, absorbing the act, rehearsing with Alex and Lou in their off-hours.

The young man's name was Robert Grammer, who preferred to be called by his carrot-top-inspired nickname, Red. He was only six years old when the Limeliters made their hungry i debut, only ten when they broke up the first time, a generation or more removed from Lou and Alex. Yet Red was destined to remain a Limeliter for a longer period of time than Glenn Yarbrough, which Alex himself realized with a jolt as the decade came to a close.

Red Grammer, the son of a Congregationalist minister who once had modest ambitions as a singer, was born Nov. 28, 1952 in East Orange, New Jersey, and spent his childhood in Livingston before moving to Red Bank on the coast in the fourth grade. Like a good suburban boy, he had set his mind upon becoming a doctor, but he couldn't help but notice that his high lyric tenor had a strangely beautiful quality that seemed to move people. Even so, when he had a rock band in his teens, the guys in the band wouldn't let him sing (out of envy perhaps?); he merely rattled away on a set of drums in the rear.

Meanwhile, in his spare time, Red taught himself the guitar, learning Beatles tunes, singing along with the records of Johnny Mathis, gravitating to folk music solely through the recordings of Peter, Paul and Mary. He had never heard a Limeliters record before, and he knew Glenn Yarbrough only through "Baby, The Rain Must Fall."

Red was headed on a non-stop course toward pre-med studies at Rutgers when, in a moment of truth during his senior year in high school, the call of music was louder. He switched majors, sticking with Rutgers' music department for two years before transferring to Beloit College in Wisconsin in 1972. He had second, third and fourth thoughts about that decision throughout his college days, right up to his graduation in 1975.

Like many young people in the early '70s, Red also underwent a crisis in faith during this whole period, questioning Christianity as his sole guiding light, investigating other religions and sects. He became attracted by the teachings of Buddha, but his search for religious truth did not end until he came in contact with followers of the B'hai Faith, who revered the wisdom of the Iranian holy man, Bahá'u'lláh. Red believed that Bahá'u'lláh's greatest contribution was in calling for the unification of mankind and the abolition of prejudice. To Bahá'u'lláh, there is only one God, and He is responsible for all the competing religions of the world, which thus are "intrinsically united."

It took just two months in 1972 to convince Red that this was the way to go—and he vowed that his musicmaking would always reflect B'hai's uplifting, positive attitude. "To put it simply," Red told Lou in an intra-group interview, "I don't feel that music, or any music I would want to be involved in, should support and encourage the lower nature of man. Bahá'u'lláh himself, he did say something about music; he said music was created or given to man to uplift the hearts. That music is spiritual food. And with that in mind, I create music or try to create music."

At first, Red tried to live up to those tenets, forming a folk duo in Chicago, hitting the folk clubs, performing in the Ravinia Festival after being chosen as one of Chicago's top five singer/songwriters in 1977. But Red was also a child of his time, attuned to the perhaps less-pure music on Top 40 radio and willing to give it a try. Earlier, his pure legato tenor had nearly landed him a solo record deal with Polydor but the A&R man who spotted him had lost his job before he could sign Red. In the late '70s, he was lured out to San Diego by a fellow B'hai, Joan Bulkin, for whose Silver Nightingale publishing company he made some commercial pop-oriented demos that attracted zero attention. Trying another trendy route, he then formed the three-man Red Grammer Band, a rock 'n' roll group with New Wave-ish tendencies that left him raspy-voiced and exhausted after every gig. Obviously, this wasn't the B'hai conception of music he wanted.

"So when Alex called me on the phone, it was a total shot out of the blue," Red recalls of that October day. "I had never met Alex, I wasn't doing folk music. It took me awhile to orient myself to this opportunity."

But when Red got to know Lou and Alex, absorbed some of their history, and caught the act, he was instantly charmed by his new colleagues. At first, he was loathe to give up the Red Grammer Band, in which he had a strong emotional investment, but Alex and Lou got around that by making Grammer's bass player and drummer the core of the new Limeliters' backup band. That ultimately didn't last, for it soon became clear that Red's old sidemen could not adapt to the Limeliters' folk-grounded sound. Yet when some new players were hired, Red did not back out. He was sold on the positive vibes of his new group.

"The brand of music they do which is so uptempo, so uplifting, so positive, is really where I left off in Chicago," he said just after joining the group. "When you get blatantly commercial, it's much more difficult to be real positive, c'mon let's have a great time. I was missing that a lot in what I was doing.

"I get chills doing 'John Henry.' Of all the songs in the repertoire, if somebody told me you would sing 'John Henry' and get a rush off it, I never would have thought it. It's the arrangement; it's stunning, it's great."

Clearly the chemistry of the Limeliters would undergo a significant change with this bright, eager, straight-arrow B'hai follower in their midst. All traces of the counterculture would vanish. So would a good deal of the old satirical stance, as well as the tension between the members of the trio.

The Limeliters, it seemed, were about to make yet another fresh start.

Yet not long after the January announcement of Glenn's replacement, an unbelievable development on the personal side of the Limeliters would take place. As proof of his determination to go back to work in earnest at last, Lou gave up his San Francisco pad. He donated his prized Bösendorfer grand piano to his son Tony, who would place it in his new recording studio in Nashville. Then on New Year's Day, 1981, Lou packed up what remained of his belongings, headed down Interstate 5 to Los Angeles...and after bouncing around a couple of addresses in Brentwood and West Hollywood, in March he moved in with Alex!

A more mismatched pair—especially given their history of quarreling, second-guessing and apparently irreconcilable musical differences—would be hard to imagine. And yet they stayed under one roof for nearly five-and-a-half years, longer than Lou had lived anywhere since abandoning his home in El Cerrito for the wild life of Sonoma County. Lou took over the back bedroom in which Theo Bikel once lived, saying that he paid a reasonable rent of $200 a month. Gladys Hassilev would do most of the cooking for the two ("Needless to say, with Gladys' cooking, my weight immediately took off," said Lou), and to the surprise of many, Lou and Alex generally got along well together.

"Lou can be a little strange, but usually he is a very cozy person," said Alex's mother, who always liked and got a kick out of Lou. "He would make omelettes in the morning for himself and for Alex, Gladys would go to work, he had his room, and he would mess up that room, and that was it. He had the telephone and laundry done, most of the meals. For Alex, it was not bad to have somebody to talk to. He needs that, too."

Of the two, Lou had clearly changed the most over the years. With the mellowing process that started when he rejected the money culture, Lou came to believe that Alex must have been his brother in a previous life; how else could they have carried on a working relationship for so many years? At one time, the two would constantly, even compulsively, be on opposite sides of an argument over anything. But now, Lou realized that the absence of conflict had an inverse reaction on his happiness level. He was trying to become an expert on avoiding any and all conflicts in his life, and what better training could he have than living with his old sparring partner, who loved to play devil's advocate.

He would learn to deflect Alex's inevitable intellectual parrying by agreeing with him, whether or not he actually did. There was no question as to who was in charge of the Limeliters' destiny. Lou, more passive than ever, made it clear that he would not want to be a part of a reconstituted group unless Alex was the leader. He had had his fill of administration, or command, of any kind. He was prepared, even eager, to be a follower this time—a 180-degree switch from 1959, indeed!—and his moving in with Alex made him even more available to do the legwork for the group, mailing letters, walking to the graphics shop or anywhere his legs could take him, for Lou didn't even have a car then. For a time, Lou ably assumed the role of the Limeliters' publicist, preparing press kits, conducting interviews with Alex, Red and himself, putting Alex's master plan for the Limeliters' future into printed form.

"I'm a pretty good houseguest," said Lou. "I make my bed in the morning and I wash dishes and I don't bring loud and boisterous companions home of either sex. I don't create a lot of trouble. We had very little leisure, we were out of town a lot, Gladys is an easy, easy person to live with, and I'm a housebroken guy, completely defanged.

"And we really did have a common goal; we were working full-time on getting the Limeliters up and running again. So, it was a very close collaboration, and I think, probably the only way in which we could have gotten the thing happening."

As if to drive home the point that they were aiming for Nashville, the new Limeliters made their maiden voyage Feb. 22, 1981 at the Palomino Club, then L.A.'s leading honky-tonk, on Lankershim Blvd. in North Hollywood. The room was packed with invited guests and other Limeliters' aficionados, and they gave Red a tremendous hand when he soared through "Danny Boy" a cappella. The folk medley "Hard Travelin'/Mount Zion" sounded a bit shopworn but not "Acres of Limeliters," now outfitted with a new lyric advertising their new young tenor. New to the act was Willie Nelson's hit "On The Road Again," with another interpolation about Red, as well as a bit of tomfoolery called "Vasectomy," with Lou taking the lead on a Larry Heagle-penned tune about a newly sterilized would-be Lothario.

When the three soared in close harmony, it was difficult to tell the new Limeliters apart from the old, for Lou's old parts were flexible enough so that any number of high-quality tenors could have fit into the blend. Also in the early days, Red tried with some success to simulate Glenn's rapid vibrato. It was when they got off those windswept heights that one noticed how changed the group's timbre was. Red was a much straighter singer than Glenn; he formed his notes in long, seamless legatos almost as if he was crooning while Glenn was far more interested in imaginative phrasings that play with and tease the music in a casual-sounding way. Red was more of a classic Irish tenor than Glenn, who cannot be classified, and the results tended to smoothen the Limeliters' sound a bit without adding excess weight.

On the newer material Lou had revamped his methods of scoring for the Limeliters. Instead of Alex singing the tune, now Lou would assign the melody to himself, taking advantage of Alex's deepened Russian bass timbre by giving him a bass line while Red stayed on top of the blend as Glenn did. "Now we actually resemble a barbershop quartet without the baritone," said Lou at the time. At the same time, however, Red's presence imposed a limitation on how far out the Limeliters could go—particularly on material involving sex. Red was a very straitlaced person whose relentlessly cheery personality was coupled with a strong moral streak. He would not do material he regarded as salacious; he barely tolerated "Vasectomy." He refrained from any vices or any cavorting around on the road, in striking contrast to the still-active libidos of his senior partners.

"Red was a little prudish," admitted Lou. "I've often thought that someday we ought to make a record called *The Slimeliters; The Limeliters Sing Smut*—like Oscar Brand did. They're definitely a part of folk music, for Chrissake. But Red wouldn't hold still for that, ever."

According to Lou, the tenets of B'hai prohibit its followers from engaging in any aggressive evangelical work, so the Limeliters were never in any danger of becoming proselytizers. Nevertheless, once Red got his bearings in the group, he did make a few suggestions. When the Limeliters were appearing with Glenn one time, Red put forth the idea that they ought to do some benefits for the B'hai organization, but Glenn wouldn't put up with that for a minute.

Far from being uncomfortable with Red, Lou—ever the comparative religion dabbler—at last had someone to talk to during the long hours shuttling from one-night-stand to one-night-stand. His spiritual preceptor, Chiranjiva Roy, had passed away peacefully in March of 1981, and while Lou's fervent involvement in Eastern religion declined accordingly, his curiosity about all faiths continued to burn. "I regret Red's absence if for no other reason than on the road, we would have what I call fireside on wheels, where they discuss religion and the scriptures," remembered Lou. "I find the B'hai Faith eminently easy to live with, and

Red never indulges in any 'clangorous proselytization.' In many ways, Red is a model human being, truly."

Following the Palomino tryout, the Limeliters were booked at Harrah's Lounge in Reno, a familiar haunt, for a couple of weeks; made several appearances in small venues like Los Angeles' Playboy Club; and toured extensively through their stronghold, the Pacific Northwest. The response to Red was almost unanimously encouraging from the press, and his crystal-clear rendition of "Danny Boy" never failed to stop the show cold. Yet there would continue to be a few appearances with Glenn as part of some folk reunion packages, usually in the form of walk-ons for a number or two.

Perhaps the most elaborate and historic folk reunion in which the Limeliters were involved was a Showtime telecast that took place on Feb. 24, 1982 at the Wolf and Rissmiller Country Club in Reseda, California. The Kingston Trio, headed and defined as always by Bob Shane, was the focal point as well as the sparkplug of the telecast. The Brothers Four—now based in Seattle, one of the last pockets of resistance for the folk movement of the 1960s—held forth with its smoother, slicker sound.

Mary Travers would hold court in her trailer, chain-smoking, speaking thoughtfully and at length with a Carol Channing-like rasp on folk music and possibilities of its revival in the Reagan era. The prolific spinner of topical songs, Tom Paxton—looking grim and wary of outsiders—spoke relentlessly of the present. John Sebastian—whose solo career never quite achieved the heights to which the brilliance of his music with the eclectic Lovin' Spoonful seemed to point—talked in a gentle singsong about his wrangles with the record industry and his desire to make it back onto the airwaves. Judy Collins had long since moved out of the folk field into a more cabaret-oriented popular song repertoire, but nevertheless seemed right at home and touched by the atmosphere of the folk reunion.

Over in the Green Room, precariously leaning forward on a chair, was Glenn, another self-professed defector from the folk ranks. Typically, he was highly ambivalent about the whole atmosphere surrounding this folk reunion, repeating his by-now-familiar misgivings about nostalgia. But there was little doubt that in spite of himself, he could feel the special vibrations of the occasion. Not much had changed with Glenn; he was still the insider who tried to portray himself as an outsider.

Outside in the Limeliters' trailer, Alex brooded aloud about the obvious raison d'etre for the show. "Economically, of course, it is interpreted as a nostalgia show," he said, his deep resonant bass voice easily filling the rear of the trailer. "That's the point of the exercise, isn't it? Those who want to make money from it see it that way. But as I listen to the people who are here and I see them as people, I see what the years have done to them, both good and bad, and I hear it in the music. It's a warm music; it's a music that wears rather well."

In the Limeliters' portion of the show, a deliberately neat passage of transition took place. First, Glenn sang "Baby, The Rain Must Fall," backed by a thumping rock beat, and then he introduced his now-occasional partners Alex and Lou, sang their old signature tune, "There's A Meetin' Here Tonight"—and instantly, the chemical reaction of these three voices ignited and resounded through the room, the unique profile still gloriously intact. At this point, Glenn gave way to Red, and with their new tenor on lead, the retooled Limeliters performed a country ballad consistent with the direction upon which Alex had his sights set. In hearing the two versions of the group one after another, one was again struck by how comfortably Red's distinctly different voice merged into the blend in its higher flights, at times almost matching the original blend.

Ultimately all the performers formed a single line in front of the stage monitors to sing Harry Chapin's "Circles" as a grand finale. As a group, they were a strikingly diverse, weathered yet handsome lot—survivors all, most of whom knew great material success when they were young and who hoped against hope that fashion would circle around and smile upon their music again. And for a short while, who could resist believing it as they sang Chapin's words, "All my life's a circle..."

But times had changed. True, the dress rehearsal had the audience clapping up a storm, the familiar sounds still amazingly vital and rousing. But in the national marketplace where folk music was pronounced as dead as an Edsel and not nearly as collectible, it meant nothing. To the accountants and lawyers who ran the record industry, folk music meant nothing. Of all the performers who appeared at the Country Club that special day, only one, Judy Collins, still had a contract with a major label (her original home, Elektra) at the time, and that wouldn't last much longer.

No one was more aware of the grim realities of the folk era's endless morning-after than Alex. He looked beyond the oldies shows, which he considered to be a necessary but temporary holding action to maintain their existing audience and resumed his search for a hit studio record. At last he had become the de facto leader of the Limeliters—the only other time, perhaps, had been during the *Time To Gather Seeds* sessions—and he had a point to prove and an agenda to push.

First, Alex made a tape of their act at the Crazy Horse, a country/folk music spot in Santa Ana, with the intention of fashioning a live album out of it. But he was eventually dissatisfied with its sound quality, and the tape only managed to get out as a promotional pressing for the Limeliters' trip to Israel in 1982. The main thrust, however, would be a four-song demo tape, meticulously made in the studio for a hefty $12,000 (put up by Russ Gary) that Alex thought would be his entree into the executive recording suites. Rather than act as producer himself (possibly he had taken heed of his overwhelming need to procrastinate), Alex asked producer/composer Ed Freeman—who had produced Don McLean's epic No.1 hit single "American Pie"—to take charge of the sessions. Believing that Red's voice had the most commercial value, Alex and Ed gave him the lead vocal on each of the four tunes—"She Loves Me Like An Eagle" (later shortened to "She"), Cole Porter's "Begin The Beguine," "Take The L Out Of Lover," and "Different Ways."

How did the Limeliters come to record as out-of-character a song as "Begin The Beguine"? Lou reports that he had been idly sight-reading from a book of Porter songs at the piano in Alex's studio in 1982, and when he came to "Begin The Beguine," Alex's ears perked up and he immediately began to think of an arrangement. Neither of them apparently knew then that Julio Iglesias, the Spanish sex symbol who had not yet caught on in America, had just taken "Beguine" to the No. 1 slot in England in the fall of 1981. Nevertheless, Alex had gleaned onto its possibilities as an international pop hit for his trio.

In any case, the Limeliters' version of "Beguine"—with Red singing the tune absolutely straight in his wide-eyed legato tenor—is a glitzy curio, with a big string synthesized Mantovani-like backdrop and billowing group harmony vocals. Probably the only American audience that would have bought it is the one that goes to Las Vegas regularly for its middle-brow entertainment—and that crowd, it has been scrupulously determined, wasn't really a factor in the record shops anyway.

"Take The L Out Of Lover" and "Different Ways" are conventional country tunes, fine meticulous productions no better and no worse than any other charted country tunes of the time. Byron Walls' "She" sounds like the type of material Kenny Rogers had shot to fame with, the slow pounding beat setting the tempo. None made any impression whatsoever upon recording company executives whom Alex approached, although a Limeliters ex-lawyer who held a lofty position at PolyGram showed some briefly flickering interest—and the tracks were shelved until 1989 when they finally appeared on the *Potpourri* tape and *Singing For The Fun* CD.

While Lou had serious doubts as to whether the Limeliters could pass for a country act, he amiably went along with Alex's plans. He even patched together a medley of well-known country and country/rock tunes for the three to sing live—Alex approximating Jim Reeves' smooth baritone in "He'll Have to Go," Lou bopping along to Jerry Lee Lewis' "Thirty Nine and Holdin," Red doing a soaring job on Roy Orbison's "Crying." "It was a pretty good session; we got all of the A-players like Lee Sklar on bass and Nicky Hopkins on piano, and we sang pretty well on the tunes," said Lou. "But, you know, they were neither fish nor fowl; it wouldn't take any country person three measures to tell this is not a country act."

One of several offbeat things about the Limeliters is that the group had turned the conventional showbiz success story on its head. Generally, a band is supposed to hack it out in the wilderness, paying its dues, scuffling, playing in the foulest of backwater towns and clubs until Lady Luck bestows its favors, if at all. The Limeliters, however, were an instant hit at their first truly professional gig, the hungry i. When Lou claimed that they never scuffled 15 minutes, he wasn't exaggerating. And the Limeliters continued to lead a charmed life after they reunited in the 1970s—on a smaller scale, of course, but there was always as much work as they wanted, and they didn't want much.

But now, without Glenn Yarbrough, the Limeliters were struggling to stay on an even keel. They had the success first, and they ended up paying their dues later—when they could least afford it.

One cannot blame Red Grammer, for he did the best job he could, probably better than almost anyone could, to fill Glenn's shoes. At first, he seemed a bit ill at ease with the Limeliters, awestruck, even stiff, to the point where Alex wondered in despair whether Red could ever turn into a real performer. But the years of work loosened him up, making him gradually reach out to the audience. No one ever doubted his sheer natural vocal gift—and frequently, his long, seamless phrasing would garner the biggest individual ovations of the evening.

Rarely did the Limeliters absorb anything resembling a critical drubbing during the 1980s. Rarely did they walk away from a hall without a standing ovation ringing in their ears. At its best, the act still sounded amazingly fresh and entertaining. The problem was that there were fewer people cheering in the seats now. Management, or a lack thereof, was a major contributor to that—not being with a major concert booker, not making records on a label with promotional muscle.

Neither did it help to be perched right at the beginning of the Reagan years, where the old folkie ideals of sharing and caring were suddenly declared naive and obsolete, and greed and rampant self-interest were considered prudent and realistic. Harry Chapin's sudden death in an auto accident on the Long Island Expressway in July 1981 was a shattering symbolic blow to the communal folk spirit—and though the Limeliters (and others) would add Chapin's "Circles," to their concerts as a memorial, it was clear that the atmosphere of generosity he had tried to sustain had virtually died with him in the '80s.

Moreover, the reconstituted Limeliters, striving as they did to join the country mainstream, never could develop as striking a profile in that area as they once did in folk music. Rather than stand their ground as a unique contemporary folk outfit, they became little more than just another country harmony unit—pleasing to listen to, but only three faces in the crowd.

But even on their folk home ground something else was missing— the intangible yet unmistakable quality, magic. Something special happened when Lou, Alex and Glenn combined their wildly different voices and personalities, something that could not be recaptured even with only one of the ingredients missing.

Red himself would come to realize that as his tenure wore on. At first, he had nothing to fear, for he had never known about the Limeliters before he joined the group. It had only vaguely occurred to him that replacing Glenn might be a formidable task. But it was during the folk package tours, where Glenn would perform on his own and sit in with his old colleagues for a couple of numbers before giving way to Red, that the young red-haired singer realized what he was up against. Lou recalled that Red was not at all thrilled about having to share the show with his predecessor, though he accepted it once he realized that more people were coming to see the act as a result. Rein Neggo Jr. went as far to say that Glenn—who had nothing but praise for Red—felt negative vibes coming from the young tenor. They would stay in separate corners when they were not performing, rarely speaking to each other—and in the occasional joint finales, whenever Red performed a solo, Glenn would leave the stage until he was finished.

Indeed, the buyers around the country complained loudly and long about the format of these shows. They wanted to see Glenn put in more time with his old group onstage, doing more than just a perfunctory few minutes at the top. So did Rein Neggo, who pleaded in vain with his stubborn friend to do some more group singing. "I tried to get them to do a full set with Glenn, but Glenn never wanted to," said Rein. "I wanted Glenn to come in at the end and extend the first part with them. The buyers felt cheated."

"Glenn may not have been the glue that held it all together," said Theo Bikel. "But Glenn, with all his lazy personality, was something that audiences gravitated towards, not necessarily crowning him as the star of the group, but because of that thing he contributed to the group.

"The group was better with Glenn in it than it was after Glenn left. The whole was bigger than the individual parts. Red has a good voice— as a matter of fact, quite reminiscent of that high tenor quality. But what is that little poem, 'You cannot recapture/The first joyous rapture.'" Bikel, as well as the buyers, had a point.

The chemistry that made Lou, Alex and Glenn a much greater whole than the sum of their parts had been blown apart—and the remnants of that split, Lou and Alex on one hand, and Glenn alone on the other, would struggle throughout the '80s.

Nevertheless, as they slogged onward through the bleak decade, the Limeliters would continue to have some interesting adventures. Russ Gary's connection with an Israeli promoter led to a seven-week tour of Israel in 1982, only the Limeliters' second intercontinental engagement. They played all over the embattled little country, everywhere except the southern port of Eilat, always returning to the plush Hotel Diplomat in Tel Aviv which was within commuting distance. They were treated like international superstars by their hosts, staying in that first-class hotel, traveling with a full road crew including a lighting person.

When they weren't performing, they would take in the sights of Biblical country, losing themselves in history. Israel would affect Lou especially deeply, and he would suddenly become more aware of his Jewish roots. "No Jew goes to Israel for the first time and returns the same Jew," said Lou. "Ultimately in Israel, after you go to Jaffa whence Jonah set sail to end up in the belly of the whale, or go to Armageddon, or the hill where David slew Goliath, you begin to get confused as to what century you're in."

Unfortunately, the seven weeks turned into a financial bath for the promoter, who lost at least $10,000 on the whole venture. It didn't help matters that an international incident exploded in the middle of a Limeliters performance in Jerusalem, reminding them of the tinder-box nature of the Middle East. "We were there on Good Friday when that crazy American blew away a couple of Muslims at the Temple of the Dome of the Rock," said Lou. "That seriously affected our gate; we were booked into the Jerusalem Theatre for two shows, and one was cancelled completely."

More bad news hit sometime in 1983, for the hard-working deal-maker Russ Gary dropped out as the Limeliters' manager. He was guaranteeing Red's salary, an enormous drain on the treasury, and he could no longer maintain that because the group wasn't taking enough cash in—far less than Gary expected.

"The act was way overpriced," said Lou. "Russ Gary got something like twenty grand a week for the act, or some unbelievable figure which simply did not materialize in terms of attendance."

So, Alex himself became the manager, taking 15% off the top for expenses and a managing fee, while Gary stayed on as a booking agent. It meant that Alex would be responsible for all the details that other specialists once handled, from getting the gig to making sure they were paid. "That's OK with me because there's nothing drearier than chasing dates," Lou said about Alex's increased share of the take. But others noticed that Lou's involvement with the direction of the group decreased steadily from the day Alex took over completely, as there was little financial incentive for him to put out any more effort.

"They need a manager desperately," Glenn said in 1989. "I think one of the problems they have now is that Lou not only is not head of this thing, but he's not even an equal partner. Alex is getting more money than the rest of them for doing all this extra work so Lou is a minor partner in this arrangement. Alex is saying, 'Oh he's so lethargic, he doesn't care about anything, he just goes through the motions.' And when I found out how they were structured, I said, 'Well, that's the reason. He is going through a five-year pout about not being an equal partner.'

"The only way to solve this problem is to get yourself some management and then divide the money equally so Lou feels at least equal to Alex. For a guy to go from the need to be completely in control to not even having an equal share in the group is not easy to take."

Being a Las Vegas resident, Gary always wanted the Limeliters to play in his current hometown—and there were sound financial reasons for doing so. It meant a long engagement at a time when long engagements were things of the past everywhere else before a built-in captive audience of middle-aged vacationers. Country music had invaded the gambling town long before with striking success, and the Limeliters' new orientation couldn't help but increase their chances of success.

Gary booked them into the Winners Circle lounge at the Sands Hotel for 14 weeks in 1984. "That year I almost went mad," said Lou. "I think 14 weeks in Las Vegas is like 14 weeks in any other minimum security prison farm. But we did have a steady job anytime we came off the road."

Later in 1984, Gary was renting the Copa room from the Sands for his acts, taking the gate and letting the hotel take the bar concession. Glenn Yarbrough and the Limeliters—separately of course, but with the usual handful of reunion numbers—just happened to be playing there when the Musicians Union struck Las Vegas. The story made the national network TV news shows, and when the networks showed the marquee outside the Sands, Glenn's and the Limeliters' names were right on the sign, visible to all.

Way off in Charleston, South Carolina, Ronald P. Byers, the loquaciously colorful owner of a chain of local strip clubs and the self-proclaimed No.1 fan of the Limeliters, saw the clip. Having admired them from his youth, Byers had been looking for the group for 20 years, wondering what had happened to them.

He immediately grabbed a plane for Las Vegas, introduced himself, and offered the trio work at one of his clubs the following year. Byers promptly renamed one of his clubs the Limelite and presented the group there without their backup band for a week in March of 1985. For the first time in many years, Lou went back to playing the bass for that gig, and Alex dusted off his still-formidable skills on guitar and banjo. For Lou, the bass had been a mere prop in the act until he saw a new Clevenger standup electric bass on display at a NAMM convention, a sleek, slender instrument that eliminated in a stroke the immense problems a bass player always has in transporting his axe. Tapped out at the time, Lou went to Dolly for a loan of about $1300 to buy the Clevenger bass—and he used it for the rest of his life.

The "Limelite" club was packed for a solid week—and so successful was the gig that Byers decided to bring them back for six weeks starting in June. This time, though, the trio would not be alone. Somehow Byers got the kinky idea that he had found the perfect showcase for his heroes—the Limeliters, plus the strippers! It would be a smash combination that couldn't miss—folk music and "exotic" dancing.

Obviously the Limeliters had not left behind in the 1970s their magnetic ability to attract the bizarre. They would play their usual set and then the girls would come on, traipsing around in various degrees of undress, then the Limeliters would play another set, then the girls would do their thing again. Predictably, Lou was amused at first, Alex was depressed, Red (who had his family with him on that engagement) was shocked and embarrassed by the whole scene.

It may have been the lowest point in the group's entire performing history—and no, the twin-bill of folkies and strippers did not turn into a bundle of cash for Ron Byers. "As soon as it was known the strippers were there, our fans had already seen us the week we had played there," said Lou. "So, you get the lonely people, and Charleston has a huge naval base, with drunken sailors. No class. I almost went mad at that engagement, too."

Though the Limeliters' dignity may have escaped relatively unscathed from the Charleston follies, their backup band had become a thing of the past. The group wasn't making any headway, stuck in their neither-here-nor-there groove of country/folk, expenses were escalating to the point where they could not maintain the luxury of a band. They could not keep a steady personnel together; musicians were always drifting in and out of the band. Their final Las Vegas dates at the Sands marked the last time they used a band.

Their supporting cast was cut down to just one man, but a versatile musician he was. John David had originally joined the Limeliters backup band in 1983, but when the group was dissolved, Alex asked him to stay on. He could hardly have found a more flexible choice, for this "house orchestra's" expertise ran from electric and acoustic guitars to the banjo, dobro, mandolin, harmonica and fourth-part vocals (John even substituted quite ably for Red when the latter was out sick). In effect, he quietly became the fourth Limeliter, hanging in there through thick and thin into the 1990s.

It also meant a drastic change in the type of music the Limeliters would be able to do. Lou had to take up the bass again, and Alex assumed his old roles with a banjo and guitar strapped on his shoulder while Red strummed on a guitar. No longer could they strive to challenge the Oak Ridge Boys with such a sparse assortment of instruments. They would have to retreat to where they started, back to the folk idiom the pundits had declared "dead in the water," back to what remained of the audiences who sustained them for decades.

But Alex had not yet thrown in the towel on country music.

The Limeliters took one more desperate gamble in 1985, making five more studio sides with Red mostly in the lead, with two Elvis Presley band members—pianist Glen D. Hardin and bassist Jerry Scheff—and Byron Berline on fiddle and mandolin playing on the session trying to make it sound as authentic as possible.

Musically the gamble pays off handsomely, for Lou, Red and Alex have had some time to acclimate themselves to modern country idioms, and they clearly have absorbed a lot—everything except the accents. "Heart Full Of Love" knocks out an uptempo country groove in a professional, meticulous manner while "Beautiful Fantasy" is an attractively harmonized medium tempo number. "Right From The Start" is even more convincing, with the gently whining steel guitar chiming in the background and good use is made of a Nashville-styled female vocal group. "American Tour," with Alex as lead basso, affectionately counts down the cities that a group visits when they tour, and apple-cheeked Red somehow manages to put himself in the position of would-be pursuer of a one-night stand in "Don't Turn Me On (If You're Gonna Turn Me Down)." No one need apologize for these tracks—indeed, "Right From The Start" sounds like a hit from start to finish—they represent the Limeliters' best, most committed shot at country stardom.

Alas, again no one was listening in the executive suites. But this time Alex, who produced the sides rather skillfully and put up his own money to cut them, wouldn't let the tapes gather dust in his studio. He reactivated the idea of a mail order label for the Limeliters, getting a devoted fan from Foster City, California named Althea Smith to run the label. Brass Dolphin had been stopped cold since Glenn and Annie were divorced, and Alex managed to acquire Annie's mailing list and the right to sell the old Brass Dolphin catalogue on his new list until the stock ran out. Alex named the label West Knoll after the street on which he lived, and soon thereafter issued four of the five country tracks on a pair of singles, which the group tried to sell at their concerts (later they turned up on *Singing For The Fun*).

That was a face-saving, cost-amortizing move, though, for Alex knew at this point that the country fling was over. While the audience response was generally good for their country numbers, they could never interest any label into giving them a deal. Moreover, the "Urban Cowboy" fad was dead as a doorknob as mass media pundits turned their attention to such topics as the huge crossover popularity of Michael Jackson, the ribald funk of Prince, and the charismatic stage presence of Bruce Springsteen.

Losing the country gamble was a devastating blow for Alex, and his bouts with depression would only intensify from this point onward. "I would have been perfectly happy to do a nostalgic show when we regrouped with Red," Alex said as a post-mortem. "But I also had in mind an attempt to record. And those two things did not go well together at all. We would have been far better off not trying to make commercial records and sing folkie material, new folkie material, and to put out our records earlier. But I also believe that if we had a proper band, we could make some pretty hot music."

Alex, however, was shrewd enough to go about retrenching his forces. The Limeliters came back to concert life in streamlined form, playing folk clubs again with just the three of them plus John David, reaching back to the distant past for some of the old lost atmosphere. Red continued to improve as a performer, sounding and acting livelier and more personable than ever. There was new, welcome contrapuntal instrumental interplay between the foursome, with David expertly embroidering everything between the cracks, and the rhythms had more drive and point than with the old four-piece backing group.

Buoyed by the response from his fans and friends, Alex set about recording the Limeliters live in Atlanta, Georgia at a club called Banks and Shane in November of 1985. The resulting albums, called *Alive in Concert* would be released on Alex's West Knoll label in June of 1986. In addition, there was a welcome bonus in that Gene Norman, owner of GNP/Crescendo Records (at whose Crescendo club the Limeliters often played in the '60s), was interested in releasing the new live albums himself. Norman and Alex worked out a deal so that the two volumes of *Alive In Concert* appeared on the GNP/Crescendo label in record shops and on West Knoll if one orders from the mailing list.

As in the *Reunion* albums with Glenn, *Volume One* was deliberately programmed to include more commercial—or perhaps more audience-friendly—material. Yet along with the shopworn reprises from the past (a slapdash "Irish Medley," for example) it shows how much the act has changed even from the 1970s. We hear some new tricks that Lou and Alex never attempted with Glenn, like the controlled contrapuntal three-way scatting on Red's showcase "Shine On Me" and "That's Just The Way It Goes." The backing is lean and mean as the skilled John David provides a no-nonsense bluegrass/folk feeling on a variety of fretted instruments and his chugging harmonica. Finally we get a straight version of "Malaguena Salerosa," far superior to the bowdlerized Elektra version, and Red's own "Harmony" is an instructive X-ray of the way the Limeliters would build their three-part (and with David, four-part) harmonies.

Yet *Volume Two* is the more absorbing of the two albums, breaking the good-times, feel-good image to explore darker themes. "That's How I Remember Yesterday" is an evocative, melancholy, how-times-have-changed paean to a partly imagined, partly real past. "South Bound Passenger Train" is something entirely new for the trio, an a cappella steal from a Doc Watson record as suggested by Cary Ginell, and Roy Acuff's "Streamlined Cannonball" makes for a gently driving follow up.

"Hard Way To Make An Easy Living" is a barely-disguised autobiography of the Limeliters' lowered expectations in the '80s, a downbeat sequel to "Acres Of Limeliters." The lyrics are aimed right at Alex—and he sings it with the conviction of a self-aware depressive. "A Million A Day" pokes fun at the attitudes of the '80s, with histrionic anti-Strategic Defense Initiative rantings by Lou. With a Geneva summit conference in mind, Alex comes back with the most powerful performance yet of his finest song, "A Hundred Men," followed by the more hopeful folk anthem, "Last Night I Had The Strangest Dream" and the outright flag-waving of "America The Beautiful" and "This Land Is Your Land."

It's hard to get much of an impression of their live act from these records due to the fadeouts and excision of much of Lou's comedy bits and Alex's gracious introductions (evidently, they were trying to make it easy for radio to single out certain cuts). Nor is the singing quite as polished nor as gleaming as it was in the '60s. Yet the Limeliters clearly returned with affection and distinction to their folk roots, with *Volume Two* going right to the core of the long-forgotten political agenda that gave birth to the movement.

Quality, though, does not guarantee a hit in the record business— and the *Alive In Concert* albums barely made a ripple anywhere except at Limeliters concerts, where they sold briskly from makeshift tables. But since the trio did not have to split the take with some major label and its armies of distributors, jobbers, retailers, etc., the West Knoll albums were making a tidy profit. Althea Smith energetically kept the mailing list humming and started issuing annual newsletter/catalogues featuring "letters from home" by Lou, Alex, Red and John, as well as bundles of new product.

Alex was determined to take advantage of the new compact disc medium, which made its debut on U.S. shelves in 1983. He was floored by the clarity and resolution of digital sound—and rather than merely transfer the analogue *Alive in Concert* albums onto CDs, Alex decided to record an entirely new album for CD buyers. Back the group went to Atlanta in November 1986, this time at a club called Ferlinghetti's which, like innumerable other establishments, placed its performers in front of a hungry i-style brick wall. Folk Era, a small label devoted to the remnants of the folk revival, picked the album up, with copies on the Limeliters' mailing list going under the West Knoll logo.

Ten of the nineteen tracks on the *Harmony* CD duplicate selections on the *Alive in Concert* albums; only four tunes are completely new to the Limeliters discography. Basically, *Harmony* is a recapitulation and expansion of *Alive In Concert* but with a difference, for now more of the between-numbers stage business has been left in to retain more of the live concert ambience.

They found a powerful new opening number at last in Phil Ochs' ironic "The Power And The Glory" and Alex turns in his finest "City Of New Orleans" by far, a thoroughly lived-in performance. Mellower in his

60s, Lou's "Madeira M'Dear" has settled into a tamer mode, while his country contribution is a futuristic whimsical Shel Silverstein lament, "World's Last Truck Drivin' Man." "Oklahoma City Times" is a nearly forgotten remnant of the country experiment while the bouncy "Place In The Choir" would find a place in Red's children's shows. "Zhankoye" has been buffed to a more subdued gloss due to Red's legato, and "Circles" again closes the package with an optimistic yet thoughtful singalong.

With an eye out for almost every available home medium, Alex was able to get extra mileage out of this concert, for he also had it videotaped by WPBA-TV in Atlanta and released on a VHS videocassette as *On Stage At Ferlinghetti's.* Two additional songs that didn't make it onto *Harmony*—the once-ubiquitous "Coca Cola" theme, now added to the act as a nostalgic joke, and another example of Lou feeling his age, "Older Women"—can be seen here, as well as visual versions of several previously released tunes. The audience is a typical Limeliters composite from their latter-day years—mostly middle-aged, loyal, sedate—and the trio looks relaxed, content to lay back and give their following basically what it wants.

And yet while there is instrumental and vocal expertise aplenty, we don't get the feeling of ignition and sharply articulated punch that the best live recordings with Glenn in the 1960s provide; the closest the Ferlinghetti's recordings come is "The Power And The Glory." The Banks and Shane recordings also lack this extra jolt of electricity, though *Volume Two* has deeper moments of truth that were never reached in the 1960s. As warm and friendly and entertaining as these recordings are, a quick flashback to the live albums from the Limeliters' heyday, with their audiences so thoroughly in tune with the Limeliters' contemporary slant and energy, will tell you in seconds what is missing.

On and on the Limeliters trudged throughout the remainder of the 1980s, shuttling by car or RV from stop to stop, from fairgrounds to nightclubs to the occasional high-profile concert gig. They would average about 14 to 17 weeks out on the road, which suited Lou fine but frustrated Alex, who wanted to work more often, to no end. They would be available for corporate conventions, free concerts in parks, even private parties for anyone who came up with their price. Occasionally they would be the featured act on cruise ships, catering mostly to undemanding older fans who mingled with the three travelers who ironically were making their living where their ex-partner Glenn always wanted to be—at sea.

Things started to look up in 1987-88 when the giant Columbia Artists agency signed the Limeliters for the Community Concert circuit in small towns and cities. But when the contract expired, Columbia typically elected not to renew, leaving the Limeliters on their own again. And when Russ Gary died in San Diego of a heart attack on New Year's Day, 1989, Alex had to assume all the business obligations of the group—and despite his efforts to round up more work, the number of gigs continued to fall.

The West Knoll record business continued to flourish, with new self-generated recordings and material from other folk mailing lists taking their places within the smart little booklets Althea Smith issued each December. In 1989, Althea put together what was really the first official Limeliter bootleg, a tape of outtakes, live takes, failed demos, goofs, and other amusing things called *Potpourri*. It is a marvelously informal retrospective of the Red Grammer years caught on the run, often on equipment as primitive as Lou's Aiwa boom box (which he carried everywhere in those days) plugged into the sound board.

The priceless moments are the two hilarious "Oops" episodes, the equivalent of the Limeliters letting us see them with their flies open. Lou completely forgets his verse in "John Henry" as they barely get through the tune, and the three give up altogether on "Fill My Life" when they can't stop laughing. Since the sound quality of most of the *Potpourri* tapes would have been ruthlessly dissected on a compact disc player, Alex patched together a companion album for the more demanding CD medium called *Singing For The Fun*. Another hodgepodge from the '80s, *Singing For The Fun* gathers together almost all the studio country demos, the country medley, tunes from *Alive in Concert* not represented on *Harmony*, and other live cuts with decent sound quality.

Meanwhile Red was beginning to branch out on his own. He had discovered a knack for entertaining children, and he and his wife Kathy became songwriting collaborators, producing a pair of lively children's cassettes *Rolling Along Singing A Song* and *Teaching Peace* and going out as a solo act when the Limeliters lay fallow. Red would raise his high tenor, drawing it out, establishing an instant rapport with the children with his ebullient manner. He would make funny animal noises, twirl around, and snap his fingers, and he would play infectious rhythm guitar, always keeping the beat going for the benefit of young attention spans.

Since Red could perform before children in so natural and uninhibited a manner, it became obvious that his future was in that arena, not with the Limeliters, for he was a far more ingratiating performer on his own. His fans were not the only ones who thought so. National Public Radio picked up on *Rolling Along Singing A Song*, and in 1987, Red was invited to film a concert special for the Disney cable channel. He played at the traditional White House Easter Egg Roll in 1989, his tapes reached the Soviet Union and he began to plan a tour of that vast land. He had moved to a new home on four acres of land in Peekskill, New York, and he continued to work with fevered enthusiasm for various B'hai organizations.

Clearly Red's solo career had burgeoned to the point where a choice between staying with the Limeliters and going out on his own had to be made. The Limeliters were caught in a very familiar predicament, being forced to book the act around Red's availability when it was tough enough finding gigs in the first place.

And so, right in the middle of the Limeliters' 30th Anniversary season in 1989, to the surprise of neither Lou nor Alex, Red gave notice. They played two final gigs in California together, one a free concert at Warner Center's Concerts In The Park series in Woodland Hills August 13 and the last a few days later at a winery in the Napa Valley. There was absolutely no animosity about Red's leaving; indeed, Lou planned to do a book of piano arrangements of children's songs for Red.

This time, however, there wouldn't be an intensive search for a new tenor. Alex and Lou immediately turned to a seasoned 40-year-old Bay Area folksinger whom Lou said he first heard at the San Francisco Folk Club festival in May of 1985. Impressed, Lou proceeded to get his phone number and informed Alex of his find.

Born in Chicago, raised in Pasadena before moving to the Bay Area in 1970, Rick Dougherty caught the folk music bug while still a teenager and was dead set on a career as a folksinger/songwriter. Alas, his timing was a few years too late, and in any case, there didn't seem to be much of a market for a clear Irish tenor in the rock era. Indeed, Rick claims he was once thrown out of a rock 'n' roll group for wearing earplugs to a rehearsal; most rock warriors, then as now, followed Ted Nugent's dangerous credo, "If it's too loud, you're too old!" Nevertheless, Rick plugged away, spending a year in Denver, five years in San Diego, five more in Columbus, Ohio, practicing, playing, writing, trying to get a break.

By 1983, his marriage in ruins, the gigs falling off, Rick gave up and went back to school, checking into Sonoma State University where his tenor got him into the opera program there. He began directing productions for various small companies in the area, even building sets for West Bay Opera, until the urge to return to his folk roots beckoned. Rick would support himself part-time in dry periods by doing routine word processing at the Luther Burbank Theatre in Santa Rosa—and one day in 1985, the phone operator received a call from Alex checking up on the details of an upcoming Limeliters concert there. Red was making noises about taking off on his own at the time—prematurely, it turned out—and taking a leap into the unknown, Alex inquired whether anyone there knew of a good tenor. "Why yes, he's sitting right across the desk from me," Rick remembered the operator saying.

Rick was still in the middle of his B.A. studies at Sonoma State so he couldn't get back into the folk scene again. But he and Alex kept in touch, seeing each other whenever the Limeliters appeared in the Bay Area, and in the fall of 1989, Alex rang Rick up and invited him to become the Limeliters' next tenor.

After a few rehearsals, the Limeliters Mk. IV, clad in tuxedos, made their debut at a spacious Santa Monica club called At My Place Dec. 21, 1989. Rick's tenor was darker and more nasal than Red's—indeed, he sounded a lot like Bill Swofford—yet he sang with Red's legato and thanks to his operatic training, had a generous amount of soaring room up top. The vocal blend wasn't all that different than it was with Red Grammer, yet Rick's voice didn't stand out in the mix as much as Red's did—welding the Limeliters sound more tightly together.

Rick also added another long-missing dimension to the Limeliters that night—irreverence and quick wit from the tenor. In his brief solo spot, Rick produced a wildly hooting, Tiny Tim-like rendition of "Maria" from *The Sound Of Music* that had the audience collapsing over the tables. "Anytime we want to do a Weavers re-creation, we've got the soprano voice," quipped Alex, as Lou rumbled offhandedly with "Some Enchanted Evening."

With the cheers again ringing in their ears, thus did the Limeliters enter the 1990s—with a new tenor and an ever-loyal audience. But that audience was growing older, and new numbers were not being added to their ranks. Having been active in four different decades, these long-running survivors would find the sledding even rougher in their fifth.

For Lou, a decisive turning point in his life occurred in August of 1986 just after a Limeliters summer tour with Glenn, the Kingston Trio and Melanie. After camping out in Alex's horne for five-and-a-half years, Lou finally agreed that he should move out of the south-facing bedroom and live on his own.

There was no real blowup or incident; the two Limeliters still got along generally well despite their diametrically opposed personalities. "It got to be a little too much because the expenses had become higher and higher," explained Alex's mother. "Alex felt that he could not accept the situation where he was bearing most of the cost. And Lou got tired of the arrangement, too. He doesn't mind living a year here, six months there."

"Alex and I have had very few incidents," said Lou later. "Maybe we'd be getting along better if we had more true yell-out sessions but it doesn't pay, you know, because Alex's intentions are uniformly good and whatever he wants to do is alright. It's just that I have become allergic to him. I can predict with almost unerring accuracy his reaction to anything that happens.

"He is a depressive," Lou continued, with considerable compassion. "It is no mood; it is no passing fancy, and saying, 'Snap out of it, think positively!' is not the cure. He's attempted to treat it in his own way, but after a while, you get tired of watching someone trying to kill himself systematically by smoking three packs a day and failing to go less than a hundred yards to a fully equipped gymnasium right across the street."

So the happy-go-lucky Limeliter comic laureate moved out to the beach, sharing a bungalow with old friend Andre Philippe on Buccaneer St. in Marina del Rey. As he did in Hawaii, Lou spent a lot of time on the beach, reading, even studying Hebrew in an attempt to get in touch with his Jewish roots. He would continue to receive his mail at Alex's address until 1987 but they would never cohabitate again.

Lou began to look back at his unusual, incredibly varied life, to take stock and decide what to do next. His thoughts began to turn toward the idea of recording some of those songs he had been sporadically writing, many of an autobiographical nature, that didn't fit into the Limeliters' format. Back in the 1970s, Lou used to muse about making a solo record and giving it away in the true Diggers spirit, yet nothing came of the brainstorm at the time. But now, he would listen to Red Grammer's solo albums, then distributed on the West Knoll mailing list, and he became fired up by the idea of doing a project on his own.

A neighbor of Andre's on the beach, record producer and filmmaker Tim Schumacher, agreed to produce Lou's record—and they worked on and off on the album, entitled *Lucky Lou*, until March 1987. Lou dropped about $10,000 on the eight-session project, using a full complement of session men like John David, Lincoln Mayorga, a full Dixieland wind band, and even his colleagues Alex and Red, who with Hank Linderman formed the one-time-only vocal group, the Lou-ettes. And the results are wonderful, an unblinkingly honest, thoroughly musical, meticulously produced portrait in sound of Louis Gottlieb, Ph.D.

Almost every strain of popular music Lou ever heard pops up on this little tape—from country music to mariachi, from New Orleans jazz to reggae, from the piano bar jazz of his youth to the latest techno-rock. Lou gives the listener vignettes of his life, a country rap on his childhood hero, "Jitney Wright," a blow-by-blow account of his sexual awakening on "Hotel Del Rio" (with bits of "Golden Bell" and "La Llorona" thrown in). He puts forth his strong views on nuclear war and power, adapting folk tunes for his own use; thus "The Jam on Jerry's Rocks" becomes "The Maginot Line," a parable on the folly of Ronald Reagan's Star Wars scheme. The 63-year-old folksinger even rocks out on Schumacher's "I Fly" and he playfully indulges in numerous overdubbed special effects on the zany "Nuclear Dump Site."

Perhaps the most truthful, funniest and most poignant track of all is "The Has Been," where all alone, to the tune of a carefree Irish jig, Lou bemoans the plight of the entertainer who must keep on keeping on:

> *"The has-been spends his time in sellin'*
> *That which has become passé.*
> *Little else he can or will do*
> *He has nothing left to say.*
> *Still the world needs entertainers*
> *Some are treated very well*
> *But if you observe the others*
> *They live in a Gong Show hell."*

But as always, Lou, ever the optimist, finds something to salvage from his bleak situation. "When I think of people starvin' /Out of work and all the rest /Sure, I'm lucky to be workin' /Doin' what I love the best."

Lou really couldn't be bothered with the issue of whether his little project had hit potential, nor did its extremely modest sales—about 500 copies—bring him down. Having made back only $4,000 of his invest-ment, Lou shrugged and cheerfully went back to his original plan; he gave the remaining copies away as gifts to his many friends with the simple bit of advice, "Dig this!"

It may have been inevitable that Lou would someday discover the home computer. These were, after all, the 1980s, the period when the IBM PC, the Apple IIe and Macintosh, the Commodore, the Leading Edge, and the Toshiba laptop exploded into the home market. As a card-carrying member of the intelligentsia, the ever-curious Lou had always managed to keep in touch with the latest newfangled ideas and gadgets. He also might have been aware of Dr. Timothy Leary's interest in computers as the latest mind-exploring tool, a far safer successor to LSD.

In any case, urged on by Ramon Sender, Lou bought a Macintosh SE on May 9, 1987—and his whole life changed overnight. He was dazzled by the capabilities of his new machine, a super-typewriter with extraor-dinary flexibility in writing and editing, able to send and access infor-mation from all over the globe, compose music, print out documents and entire book-length manuscripts. He had suddenly entered the age of technology, and from this point on, Lou became a computer addict. Computer jargon would enter into his conversation and show patter, and Lou would actually suffer withdrawal pains if he was away from his beloved Mac for a couple of weeks on the road. In many ways, the computer was just another manifestation of Lou's obsessiveness when something piqued his interest. Be it jazz, communism, musicology, folk music, raiding the public domain, sex, drugs, Indian religion, or the Macintosh SE, once Lou got into something, he would grapple with it single-mindedly for years.

Once he mastered the word processing program, Lou immediately launched into his autobiography, taking off from the songs on *Lucky Lou* to produce a rambling, uninhibited, freaky, pontificating, unend-ingly fascinating account of his life and beliefs. In the 415-page manu-script, provisionally (and cryptically) titled *Limelite And Wondersound*, Lou curiously skips through the Limeliter years rather quickly and brusquely, preferring to concentrate on his early years leading up to the folk era and his Morningstar Ranch antics. He is unabashedly open about everything, from his very brief experiments with homosexuality on the ranch (which he rejected) to his wide-eyed acceptance of his spiritual preceptor. Despite some occasional matter-of-fact prose, it is an extraordinary document of a life on the cutting edge.

Lou chose to break off his account on Jan. 1, 1981, the day he moved to Los Angeles, hoping that the "demand" for his tome would create a market for a second volume of memoirs. He needn't have planned ahead, though, for when he sent his second draft to a number of publishers, they requested so many stylistic changes and rewrites that Lou simply lost interest in pursuing the project further.

Meanwhile, Lou had a new love in his life. Ellyn Ant Windsor had been a passionate Limeliters buff from her teens, attending their last concert at Red Rocks Amphitheatre in Denver and rejoicing when the group reunited in the '70s. The Limeliter on whom she had a hard crush was Lou—and many years later, she finally would act upon it. One night at the Crazy Horse in Santa Ana, Ellyn mustered up her nerve and gave John David a love note to give to Lou. On it, she wrote her phone number and the message that she would be willing to provide "Champagne For Breakfast" for Lou. Intrigued, Lou rang her up—and before long, the determined Ellyn had snagged herself a Limeliter.

A good thing, too, for Lou's domestic situation was about to give way since Andre Philippe was evicted from his beachfront bungalow a month after Lou bought his Mac. Lou moved in with Ellyn that June and by November, they were living in a modest but comfortable home on Riverside Drive in Sherman Oaks.

Ultimately Lou's live-in relationship with Ellyn didn't last. He had become increasingly tied to his Macintosh, spending almost all his free time in front of his terminal. The Mac had made him more introverted than he had ever been in his life; he would much rather immerse himself in the computer world than converse with most human beings. When he moved into a separate room in Ellyn's place, that was the beginning of the end—and in May of 1989, they separated, while remaining very close friends and confidants until her death following an unsuccessful heart transplant in May 1993.

"You know, I really am no longer able to cohabitate," Lou confessed in 1991. "I think it requires a degree of relating and working things out of which I am no longer capable. For example, I can't sleep with anybody. I don't mind carnal relations needless to say but as far as restful sleep, I just can't. The slightest movement and I'm wide awake."

By now Lou had settled into an avuncular old age. He was far less gregarious than he once was, no longer feeling the need to be "on" all the time, though he could still turn on the life force and charm at will. He didn't require much to live on, had no expensive tastes. With what the Limeliters brought in, along with Social Security, he had enough to travel now and then, to indulge his computer habit, and keep his reliable Honda sedan in good working order.

So after his breakup with Ellyn, Lou moved into the home of his old trumpet-playing friend Jimmy Salko in Canoga Park, camped out in the spacious rear den, surrounded by his Mac, his electronic keyboards and modules, his CD player, books, floppy disks, journals, and other souvenirs which he had managed to hang onto. But inevitably, his thoughts turned to his ace in the hole, his nest egg, Morningstar Ranch. Since giving up the rural life to go back to work, Lou had let the land grow wild, believing that he was restoring the redwood forest to its original virgin condition.

The driveway off Dupont Road was almost impassable, strewn with jagged roots, low-lying branches, and crevices. The buffalo grass, yellowed in the summer sun, had grown waist-high, making passage through the meadow quite difficult, and all the structures—save for the brick-lined concrete foundation of Lou's studio and the old well, whose dry bottom was littered with beer cans—were long gone.

Yet it remained a gorgeous piece of land, with tall redwood trees outlined against the stunning blue sky, and a ravine with a stream whose banks are thickly populated with ferns. It would be an idyllic place to retire to, once the painful memories of Rena were soothed by time—and more concretely, once the injunction against camping on the land was removed.

By 1992, after having moved again for a short time to a high-rise apartment in Marina Del Rey, Lou decided to flee the Los Angeles area for good. He took off for Sonoma County, staying with Stephen Fowler, a friend from the Morningstar days, just a half mile up Dupont from the site of his ranch.

At Fowler's house, he would establish a base of operations, parking his computer and keyboards there, taking meals and receiving his phone calls. He immediately reconnected with the countercultural community that had survived in the narrow strip of coastal redwoods from Marin to Humboldt counties, far away from the money and movie cultures of Los Angeles. Suddenly he found that he had more friends there than he ever had in L.A., many of whom revered the Morningstar experiment and tried to live by its nobler ideals ever since. He felt better, more energetic, more purposeful, making the three-mile round-trip walk every day in the richly scented air to the post office in Occidental to pick up his mail. In a letter to the author that fall, Lou wrote that he felt like he had "returned from exile," that the redwood forest was his "optimum habitat" after all.

The first thing Lou had to do was drive to Santa Rosa and petition the county to lift the injunction for settlement on the land—which was duly granted, a quarter of a century having passed since the heyday of the hippies. At first Lou simply spent the daylight hours hiking and camping on his land, occasionally smoking a bit of weed to enhance the ambience. Then Lou's friends pitched in and built him a splendid little one-room cabin in the eastern shadow of the redwood grove, with a vaulted ceiling, a small kitchen area and a wooden deck extending several feet from the front door. By 1993, the cabin was inhabitable, but it lacked electricity, so Lou continued to rent a room at the Fowler house, which he playfully referred to as "Camp Fowler."

Again, Lou had become a landed squire, and with some hired and volunteered help, he set about clearing and beautifying the property, perhaps with the intent once again of subdividing it and selling off the lower portions bordering Graton Road. He found a new companion in Vivian Gotters, a filmmaker and spiritual seeker who was an alumnus of the original Morningstar commune, and Nancy Collins reentered his life as well.

But another, more consuming and soul gratifying obsession had returned to seize his spirit—the piano. The old dream of becoming a concert pianist had flared up again, and soon after he moved into his new cabin, a small Baldwin Acrosonic spinet piano from the house in El Cerrito moved in with him. Now at last, he could practice every day in splendid solitude with more diligence and persistence than he had ever shown in his life, with only the redwoods as an audience. He also took on some piano students, adamantly refusing to accept a fee, content to pass on his steadily evolving theories of pianoforte practice. Lou would work and work on the English and French Suites and Partitas of J.S. Bach each morning for a minimum of four hours and often five, six or more. Once he became so caught up in musical and spiritual ecstasy at the piano that he didn't even know what day it was.

And at last, his practicing began to pay off. The rhythm, the sense of flow, the subtle characterization of every note that had eluded Lou all his adult life began to bloom from his fingers. On May 13, 1995, during the sound check for a Limeliters concert at the performing arts center in Redondo Beach, California, Lou seated himself at a Yamaha grand piano and played an excerpt from a Bach partita from memory. His playing was good enough to have withstood comparison with a professional concert pianist at that point—and Mary Ekler, the expert keyboardist in Glenn Yarbrough's band, looked on with admiration and envy.

Lou had finally achieved what Nancy Collins remembered as "piano bliss," the point between ecstasy and control where you can do anything you want with the music while hitting the correct notes. "Bach!" Lou once exulted. "It's amazing how it just flows effortlessly when you fix your mind firmly on the Divine! Of course, practicing four hours a day helps a little."

Meanwhile Alex continued to brood and putter in his West Hollywood home, trying to think of some way to break the act through or at least keep it going through the 1990s. He talked distractedly about changing the name of the act so as not to create pre-conceived negative vibrations, confessing that he never liked the name Limeliters anyway. But that thought was never seriously followed up.

The trio continued to rehearse their show in Alex's former studio downstairs, trying out new material, running through the old. Alex was always the major animating force, enthusiastically and tirelessly going over the material, making suggestions, answering the phone, running the show. Rick was also a live wire in selected spots, making wisecracks to lighten the mood, head bent over his guitar during the breaks in an impromptu remembrance of some long-forgotten tune. Yet Lou seemed to be in another world, patiently going through the motions of the rehearsals, amiably agreeing to anything Alex said but without much enthusiasm. Alex would play a demo tape of a song that one of his songwriting friends sent him and ask Lou what he thought, and Lou would inevitably respond with an offhanded, "It's OK." Lou's full attention seemed to kick in only when he was in front of his Mac, making meticulous lead sheets of his arrangements for the group.

There was an attempt to record the Limeliters with Milt Okun producing, a long-standing dream of Alex's, but the project never got beyond the rehearsal stage—and neither Alex nor Milt could pinpoint exactly why the project collapsed. In 1990, Ron Byers came to Alex again with a proposal to cut a charity album on his RTG label (RTG reportedly is shorthand for Ron The Great) to help the victims of Hurricane Hugo, which had battered his home city Charleston pretty badly. Byers wrote some new topical lyrics to the old folk tune "The Galveston Flood" that was used for the folk standard, "A Mighty Day." With Rick Dougherty on lead tenor for the first time, the Limeliters recorded the tune in February, and Byers selected the remaining songs for the album from their West Knoll recordings.

Indeed "A Mighty Day" is a marvelous track—building momentum, driving the message home in the best latter-day Limeliters fashion. It receives a huge boost when Alex kicks in his banjo in the middle, stoking the fires of the locomotive, and Lou's thunderous solo vocal sends the tune into an altogether new energy level.

With the enthusiasm of Ron Byers behind it, "A Mighty Day" triggered a new wave of Limeliters recording activity. In September of 1991, Lou, Alex and Rick returned to Charleston's Soft Rock Cafe to record another album. Originally, the idea was for half the album to be recorded live and the other half to be recorded in the studio. But soon, Alex's fervent desire to produce surfaced again after a long dormant period. Out went the Charleston material—and over a period of a year or so, Alex led the trio into the studio, rehearsing the material until it gleamed, sometimes producing everything himself, sometimes letting John David take over the reins.

The result, *Global Carnival*, was easily the most ambitious Limeliters album since *Time To Gather Seeds*, where their current repertoire is blown up into a big, full, multi-tracked, in-your-face production that keeps punching even when the tempos are languid. The old eclecticism is back in force: Mexico and Peru meet Kentucky bluegrass; Trinidad fuses with Jamaica and Soweto; concern for the environment, the homeless and world peace coexists with satires on Latinos and reincarnation. David may be the real hero of this album; his multi-stringed tapestries have never been put to better use.

Perhaps most gratifying is Alex's reclamation of the aborted 1973 Nashville sessions, where the trio grafts new vocals onto five vintage backing tracks by the session pros. We finally hear Lou's rock 'n' roll rave-up "Harbor For My Soul" with only a handful of barely detectable latter-day vocal overdubs, the superior Kenny Buttrey-driven studio take of "The Boxer," and probably the deepest pile groove of them all, "Heaven Help The Man On The Street."

Alex ruefully referred to the album as "an act of folly," due to the $18,000 it cost him to make it (a paltry sum by music conglomerate standards) and the lack of remaining capital that has kept it from being officially released. However, generically packaged tapes of the album were made available to the public at Limeliters concerts.

The Limeliters Mk. IV did make it onto a CD through the backdoor, as it were, as guest performers on a live Chad Mitchell Trio album, recorded at the Birchmere in Alexandria, Virginia on Jan. 20, 1995. Lou, Alex and Rick were literally called out of the audience by the Mitchells, and without much prompting, they performed a polished mini-set of "Lonesome Traveler," "40-Year Old Waltz," and "Until We Get It Right" before being drafted into the chorus of Christine Lavin's uproariously teasing "Sensitive New Age Guys." The latter number is an amazing moment, miraculously recapturing the warmth and humor of the folk revival in '90s terms—and Lou's monologues fortunately were preserved on the finished disc.

Alone of the three original members, it was Alex who found his identity in the Limeliters, gripping it so tightly that all other career possibilities had gradually fallen away. And it was Alex who was the most discouraged of the three when they found it more difficult to work.

In effect, Alex put his entire range of interests and talents on hold to become the Limeliters' manager. Not only that, he may have also put his self-esteem on the line as well, believing that he could master anything he set his mind toward doing. After all, he could pick up foreign languages with mind-boggling ease, he picked up the guitar and then the banjo to become a virtuoso on both with a speed that astonished everyone. He had tremendous analytical powers, the ability to size up a situation, put it in perspective, figure out what makes it tick. He thought that he could also learn how to manage an act and consequently save a lot of money that could be pumped back into the group.

"What I became was Rein Neggo," Alex said with a mixture of pride and anguish over his role. "I became the guy who took care of all the details. We had no one after Russ left to push the act, and I didn't do a very good job doing that. And I also chased dates and quickly found out that it was very hard to do. But it kept the act alive for a few years because the dates I was able to book made the difference between eating and not eating.

"We do great shows, we get great reviews, and that's it," he added dolefully, matter-of-factly. "Ultimately bookings come from your name value, unless you're a band starting out where you're trying to build a reputation."

Glenn wasn't doing much better himself. Still on the road, Glenn pushed stoically onward in the early 1980s, trying to resuscitate his flagging career on the questionable musical shoulders of Dik Darnell. According to Rein Neggo, Darnell tried to take control of Glenn for two years, even using his drummer as a spy to watch over his singer and report any funny business back to headquarters. Darnell was always pushing for Glenn to become more involved in his "spiritual activities," many of them involving Indian causes.

Eventually Darnell must have pushed too far and Glenn cut off contact with him. "He was trying to control too much, and Glenn doesn't like to be controlled," said Neggo, although one wonders how a lone wolf like Glenn would ever allow himself to be sucked into that situation in the first place.

As a protest against the American way of life under Reagan, Glenn applied for and received landed immigrant status in Canada (a declaration of intent to become a citizen), a move that puzzled his friends since he still lived in Estes Park. He made more albums of consoling yet mundane love songs that didn't sell; he tried a telemarketing package of countrified versions of new and old pop standards with Suffolk Marketing that went nowhere. For a while, it looked as if his career might take off in Europe, thanks to a synth-laden 1987 duet single with aging German chanteuse Hildegard Knef called "Ways Of Love." But when she failed to show up for a joint TV taping in Cologne, German sensibilities were offended; the followup album sessions were stopped dead in their tracks, and Glenn was back to square one, as it were.

He fell in love again, this time with a thrice-divorced, independently wealthy Carmel woman named Laurie Ann Frazier, an apparently gifted amateur artist. That triggered a bitter divorce battle with Annie—things got so bizarre that Neggo said that he himself was listed as community property!—and before long, Glenn simply gave up and said, "Take everything." He gave Annie all his property save the Estes Park home (which he promptly sold) and an unfinished boat, all his record royalties—in all, over a million dollars in property and cash. "He started all over again," Rein said.

When Glenn and Laurie married, they moved first to the Sunshine Coast of British Columbia and then Majorca, where she dumped him for another man—a shock that sent Glenn into the deepest emotional tailspin of his life, one that he said lasted for six months. Yet another divorce followed, with yet another take-everything settlement, and Glenn hit the road on yet another comeback tour to pay the bills.

Eventually all the retirements, comebacks, and mediocre records came back to drain much of the life out of Glenn's career. True, he could still draw some 3,000 fans to a concert in a stronghold like Cupertino's Flint Center in Silicon Valley. But like the Limeliters, he could no longer tour with a large backup group. True, he could still rear back and come up with a fine, passionately sung, folk-oriented record of sailing songs and poems *I Could Have Been A Sailor* in 1991, one-third of which contained tracks from earlier albums. But it only came out on his own tiny CMS imprint, for the big labels were still monumentally uninterested.

He had no home and was living from place to place when he wasn't touring. For a while, he lived in a beautiful Santa Barbara guest house on a larger property overlooking the city. He lived in Marin County; in Beverly Hills; in West Hollywood with a wealthy girlfriend; in Sequim, a small town on Washington State's Olympic Peninsula, with an old flame whom he first met back at Aspen in the '50s, Merle Dulien; and in a small apartment in the back of his mother's home in Desert Hot Springs, California.

On a given day, one could ask Rein Neggo where his client of 26 years was living, and he would answer with an amiable shrug, "I don't know. I don't even know where his mail goes." And in May 1994, Glenn would lose Neggo, too, a victim of stomach cancer at the shockingly young age of 49.

Yet Glenn would still be the same easygoing, shy, completely relaxed person while his career seemed to swoon, and his financial and personal lives tumbled into chaos. His voice remained a soaring, silvery instrument, perhaps not as flexible as it once was, yet even more expressive and imaginative. He remained a captivating showman, an increasingly intimate one, and in the '90s, at last he would often stick around after his show and meet his fans rather than hightail it out the door.

Glenn was in the calm eye of what an outsider would think was a hurricane of troubles. "When Glenn had money, he was much more difficult to deal with," said Glenn's friend Jonathan Moore in 1991. "I think he's a much nicer person now, easier going than he was, because he doesn't have all these worries, all this money and farms and things he was buying, and that stupid school which was perhaps his downfall."

With that, Moore probed the darker realities underneath Glenn's placid surface. "I think he would be happy doing something he liked better," he observed. "The best thing Glenn likes is standing on his boat, looking out over a vast expense of ocean. Or being in the desert running on empty. These things make Glenn happy.

"People get burnt out doing this stuff [performing]. You get to a point where you don't want to do it anymore. Especially with the struggle of working in dumps after he worked in nice concert halls, it's very difficult to take. No, he couldn't be happy. He felt guilty about being rich. Probably feels guilty about being happy."

Though the death of Rein Neggo left a huge void in Glenn Yarbrough's life, he had already found new management in Doug Lyon, a Malibu entrepreneur. Lyon quickly revved up Glenn's recording operations, issuing several CDs on his Calabasas label that found the singer enjoying an artistic rebirth. Among them was a lean, wonderful, salt-sprayed, bedrock folk album of mostly traditional sea shanties, *Chantyman*—one of Glenn's finest solo albums and certainly the closest to the core of his identity. There was an excellent new live double album recorded at Harrah's Reno, and a long stream of reissues reaching back to the RCA Victor days. There were also quirks like an album devoted to the score of Irving Berlin's *Annie Get Your Gun* (Glenn starred in a touring production of it in 1996-97) and a drolly contemptuous country single, "On My Butt," which has to be heard to be believed (was Glenn sticking it to his ex-wives?). Although Glenn broke with Lyon in 1997 and convinced his daughter Holly to take over his management, there would continue to be more Yarbrough product available in the late '90s than at any other time.

Alex also finally decided to loosen his grip and turn the management of the Limeliters over to Lyon as well for awhile and before long, the number of gigs the Limeliters were playing started to increase. In the process, though, he reluctantly had to let go of the reliable John David as the Limeliters' backup musician. Thus, the Limeliters were thrown back to their roots, to a trio of self-sufficient musicians just as they were in Aspen and the hungry i.

At last free of the stigma of being less than pure, they were welcome guests at the steadily burgeoning number of folk festivals that sprouted in the 1990s. Amidst younger, sometimes more traditional-minded, often outright derivative performers, the Limeliters came off as a warm friendly breeze from the past, still vital and polished enough to generate more applause than any of their colleagues.

But there were also signs that the act had largely frozen its ingredients in place. Fewer new songs were being introduced, nor were older ones long since dropped being revived. "You are a prisoner of your repertoire," Lou wearily told the *Los Angeles Times* in June 1996, noting that the fans would be really disappointed whenever they learned a new song and had to leave one of the old standbys out. So, Lou continued to sing "Madeira," Alex continued to perform "Gari Gari" (albeit enhanced in authenticity by his mid-'90s Russian language studies), and Rick still did his humorous falsetto parodies. It was a good show but there was nothing new—and the audiences liked it that way.

Alex remained a trim, strikingly handsome man into his 60s, with his beard and hair graying gracefully; a reporter wrote that he looked like a Russian steamboat captain. He continued to smoke way too much, two or three packs a day, an unceasing stream of one cigarette after another as he talked on the phone or gave interviews. He had tried to quit a number of times, most successfully for many months in 1973 with the result that his weight ballooned up beyond 200 pounds. But he just couldn't see it all the way through, and he routinely resisted his friends' advice to try again until the late '90s when, to Gladys' delight, he finally kicked the habit.

Lou, meanwhile, to all outward appearances appeared to be in his usual robust health after he turned 70, the fresh wood-scented air of Morningstar acting as a tonic. He tried various weight-loss programs with varying degrees of success, visited a local gym three times a week, and told Nancy Collins that he felt healthier than he had since his thirties.

Yet Ramon Sender writes that Lou did feel some discomfort from what was diagnosed as a mild case of diabetes. Alex thought that in the last months of Lou's life, he began to look weaker, older. One wonders if thoughts of mortality occupied his mind in his last months, for old friends like Dick Rosmini, William Malloch, and Ellyn Windsor's daughter Lauren, who was only 35, passed away one after another. For all of Lou's uninhibited ways and "tell all" style, he didn't like to be depressed, so perhaps he kept his darker thoughts to himself. He also didn't trust doctors, so his symptoms perhaps weren't checked thoroughly enough.

Lou continued on his merry way, practicing Bach, occasionally performing with the Limeliters. Lou had taken to the e-mail revolution with relish, and he poured out his thoughts in an ebullient, uninhibited, thoughtful, sometimes kooky rush—always with a positive, life-affirming spin. He continued to travel—stopping off in Nashville in March 1996 to "dandy my grandchildren on me knee," visiting New York City in May just before his son Bill was sworn into the New York State Bar, taking in a baseball game at Yankee Stadium where, in an unguarded moment, the ghosts of Yankee past nearly moved him to tears. His long-sought classical debut was at hand, for when the author invited Lou to play some Bach at a proposed memorial concert for Malloch in Los Angeles in spring 1997, he immediately accepted.

On May 27, 1996, Lou appeared at a free Memorial Day concert with the Limeliters in Thousand Oaks' Conejo Park 40 miles west of Los Angeles. He looked a little tired but performed well and was convivial as usual; when introduced to Sarah DeCovnick, an 89-year-old Ukrainian-Jewish emigre, he broke out into a wild, spontaneous rendition of "Rumania, Rumania." The Limeliters played a concert with Glenn on the bill at the Alex Theatre in Glendale—Lou's former hometown—June 8, and the next day in Riverside, Lou, Alex and Glenn sang together for the last time on one number. Lou continued to perform with Alex and Rick right up to a private party before about 40 guests in Lake Arrowhead—a mountain resort about 60 miles east of L.A.—on July 1.

After that, he took off for Sonoma County and home. No one even gave a thought to the possibility that this modest affair would be Lou's last concert.

So, when the following piece of e-mail, filled with Lou's usual penchant for detail, hit several of his friends' computer screens on Monday July 8 in the early afternoon, it came as an unnerving shock:

From: LUCKY L614
Subj: Weird Happenings
Having achieved my weight goal of 200 lbs. on June 29, 1996 I started experimenting to define a "maintenance" diet. My problem started at a July 4th barbecue when I had three scoops of delicious, spicy salsa dip, then ate a roasted head of garlic drenched in oil and a serving of salad with an oily dressing. I followed that up with yet another large dip into the salsa. When I swallowed that, it was less than a minute before a radioactive tube of cement formed in my upper intestine. Actually, it was just below my left rib cage near the center. One minute later I was on the floor. Not completely passed out but very weak. I lay there for a half hour and then got up and drove home.

I thought it was an attack of hyper-glycemia. Wrong diagnosis, execept (sic) that taking some anti-hyper glycemic pills did make me feel better. Since then I have got (sic) steadily weaker. My stool is black which indicates I am bleeding internally. It could be ulcer or it could be cancer. Doctor is giving me Zantac to stop the bleeding and a whole bunch of blood tests to find out what's wrong.

I feel like I'm not long for this planet, and that's okay with me. I'm gonna stick around to see what happens and I'll keep you informed. One thing I have learned—the intensive care I lavished on my Diabetes made me overlook some other symptoms, like maybe I lost the weight too easily.

Hasta lluego;

Lou

The previous day, Lou had reported his symptoms to Alex over the phone. Lou had dropped his health policy with Kaiser Permanente a few weeks before, and apparently, they had not done any tests. Alex was instantly alarmed and practically shouted over the phone, "Get yourself to a hospital now! Now! Not tomorrow, now!"

But Lou didn't go. Instead, he went to see a private doctor, who put him through a liver scan and blood tests. Indeed, the tone of his letter indicates he was just going through the motions. Just as Lou felt it was the will of God not to ask anyone to leave his Morningstar refuge in the 1960s, he was accepting his mortality passively.

Aware of the general alarm among his friends who wrote or called Tuesday and Wednesday, Lou followed up his ominous letter with phone calls assuring all that he was feeling better. To his e-mail pen pals, he posted the following note on Wednesday in the early evening:

From: LUCKY L614
Subj: Re: Reply to Weird
I'm on the mend.
Lou

The next morning, Thursday July 11—Alex's 64th birthday—Lou was standing on the deck of his cabin at Morningstar with Nancy Collins. Suddenly he felt light-headed and fell off the deck, landing face first on the ground, breaking his nose in the fall. His spleen had ruptured and there was massive internal bleeding. Ironically, the blood tests taken over the weekend would finally come back later that day—and they indicated terminal cancer of the spleen and intestine.

Nancy took off toward Stephen Fowler's house, ran in and implored him to call 911. Fowler, who had wondered why Lou had not shown up that morning as usual, then went back with Nancy to the ranch to find Lou "calmly lying on the ground on his back, blood starting to dry around the edges of his broken nose." Still conscious, Lou typically joked that his face would have "a lot more character" now. Fowler asked where it hurt and Lou replied, "Right here," placing his fingers on Fowler's sweatshirt below his left rib cage. Fowler then rubbed Lou's bare, cold feet, waiting for the paramedics.

The ambulance took Lou to the Palm Drive Hospital in Sebastopol about eight miles away, where en route he reportedly lost two-thirds of his blood. Once they wheeled him into the emergency room, he refused all surgical intervention and extraordinary life-saving measures—and as he lay on a gurney, with only an oxygen mask and intravenous tubes, he went into a deep meditative state, his eyes half-opened. He was ready to die.

At the hospital, Fowler called Ramon Sender, who got on the Internet—and within 15 minutes, the hospital was besieged with calls. Vivian Gotters arrived—and once she explained to the nurse that Lou was conscious and meditating, the room became quiet and peaceful. The staff had trouble trying to move Lou's legs because he was such a large, heavy man, but they managed to get him into the Intensive Care

Unit. There, Lou's son Bill called from New York and talked to the attending doctor. Soon thereafter, the nurse informed Vivian that they were removing the oxygen mask and giving him a shot. She kissed him on the forehead, said "God bless"—and at 11:42 a.m. PDT on a sunny Northern California day, Lou stopped breathing. Vivian reached out to touch his arm twice; the first time it was warm and the second time, cold. She then closed his eyes and left the room.

Alex was at home in West Hollywood that morning when Ron Byers called from Charleston, wishing him a happy birthday. Alex suggested that Ron please call Lou to see how he was feeling. Ten minutes later, Byers called Alex back, informing him that they're notifying next of kin.

On Sunday July 28, about 300 of Lou's friends and family held a Lou Life Celebration at his beloved ranch. Seated in the magnificent redwood grove were people from many walks and persuasions of life, who for all their diversity had been touched by Lou in some way. Nancy Collins was the informal emcee. Alex spoke eloquently, noting that all Lou owned were books, stacks of music containing many unfinished songs, a few utensils, and his piano. Others from the distant and near past remembered and reminisced. Rena came from Hawaii, offering nothing but love to Lou's now-reunited families, "Every one of us here, we are family!" One of Lou's young piano students played some Mozart on Lou's piano—reportedly his first public performance—and Nancy played a tape Lou made of himself playing Bach shortly before his death, which they found on his bed after he was taken to the hospital.

Finally, Delia Moon, one of Morningstar's more uninhibited inhabitants, announced to the crowd that in honor of Lou's teaching that being naked was just another form of dressing, she was going to take off her clothes. And she did!—and a few other brave souls joined her. "It was unbelievable," remembered Alex with a laugh.

Lou playing Bach in his newly-built cabin on Morningstar Ranch, June 1993
(Photos on ths page by Richard S. Ginell)

Lou striding proudly down Gottlieb Lane on his Morningstar Ranch, June 1993

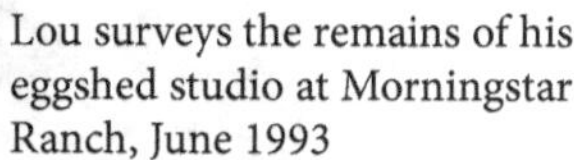

Lou surveys the remains of his eggshed studio at Morningstar Ranch, June 1993

Morningstar Ranch, June 1993

Glenn, Alex, and Lou relaxing
at Glenn's rented Santa Barbara
house, Dec. 1988.
*(Photos on this page
by Richard S. Ginell)*

Lou Gottlieb's one and only solo album,
issued only on a cassette. Released 1987.

Lou finally achieves "piano bliss" playing
a Bach Partita at the sound check in
Redondo Beach, May 13, 1995.
(Photo by Richard S. Ginell

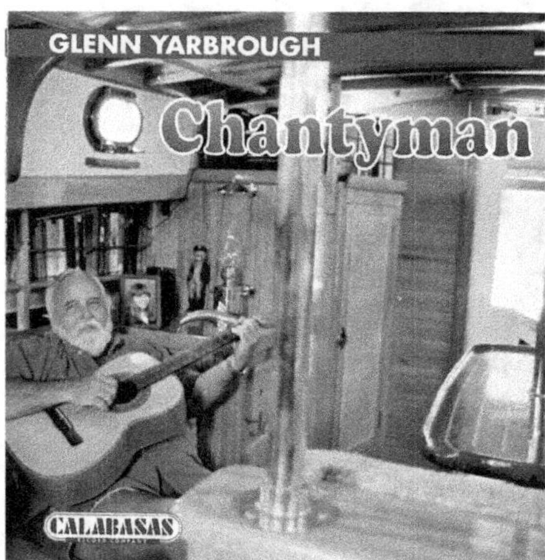

One of Glenn's finest albums,
containing songs about his
favorite pastime – sailing.
Released 2000.

Publicity photo from the 1980s

Lou, Red and Alex in the 1980s.

Alex, Lou and Rick singing and playing at the Redondo Beach
Performing Arts Center, May 13, 1995
(Photo by Richard S. Ginell)

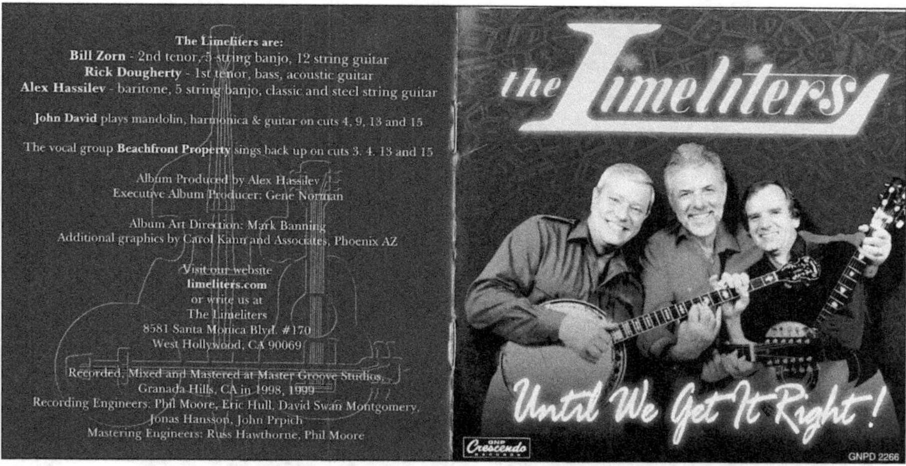

The Limeliters' first post-Lou album, with Bill Zorn, Alex Hassilev
and Rick Dougherty. Released 2000.

The Limeliters circa 2004, Alex, Andy Corwin, and Mack Bailey
(Photo courtesy of Alex Hassilev)

Gladys and Alex with the current lineups of The Limeliters (r) and The Kingston Trio (l) at the Cerritos CA Center for the Performing Arts, Mar. 2023
(Photo by Richard S. Ginell)

Epilogue

In the face of the stark fact that no one can replace Lou Gottlieb, Alex nevertheless decided to shoulder on with the Limeliters after Lou's death. Partly as a way to deal with his grief, as well as to fulfill some future bookings, Alex lost no time in trying to find a replacement. "There was really never any question about that, as I remember," Alex recalled in 2016. "Rick and I were prepared to go on, and we just did, as long as we could get somebody. It just took a little while to see who was available."

By early August, he had decided upon Bill Zorn, a 48-year old veteran folksinger and entertainer who had been living in England since 1977. Zorn was George Grove's predecessor in the New Kingston Trio from 1973 to 1976, and upon joining the Limeliters, he became the first man to have played in both of the top male folk groups of the folk revival. He was also the producer of Glenn's *Chantyman* album, as well as an actor, comic, and voiceover specialist on English and American television.

As heard at his debut with Alex and Rick Sept. 26, 1996, at Pasadena's venerable Ice House, Zorn's high baritone gave the Limeliters a somewhat lighter vocal blend, while his fine twelve-string guitar work added weight and drive to their instrumental sound. To replace Lou's Clevenger bass, Rick learned to play the electric bass guitar and Zorn also filled in quite capably on banjo. But the most astonishing discovery was hearing how durable Lou's vocal arrangements were, for even with this new combination of voices, the Limeliters sound was still robustly present, if shaded differently. In death, it had become clearer than ever that Lou invented the Limeliters sound, and the trio was his most powerful memorial.

This edition of the Limeliters lasted for another six years, crossing into the 21st century. To be sure, the gigs were becoming fewer and fewer in number; they had been ever since Red Grammer left the band ("It was a long day's journey into irrelevance," said Alex ruefully). Yet in 2000, they were finally able to get back on CDs with an official release, *Until We Get It Right*, on GNP Crescendo. Assembled from a series of sessions in 1998 and 1999, with occasional help from the vocal group Beachfront Property and the versatile returning John David, the album is mostly composed of remakes of the group's repertoire, with the energy level varying from track to track. Yet there is one brief curiosity that had been amusing their fans at concerts in recent years. Casting a part-tongue-in-cheek, part-jaundiced eye at what happened to be selling in the mainstream, as well as the cliches of folk itself, the Limeliters perform "Folk Rap," a brief a cappella compendium of snatches of folk lyrics and names with Zorn robustly taking the role of lead rapper (onstage, Dougherty would playfully don a trademark backwards baseball cap, and all would cavort about in mock-clumsy fashion during this number).

In May 2002, the Limeliters participated in a folk reunion concert at Carnegie Mellon University in Pittsburgh, *This Land Is Your Land: The Folk Years*, for PBS along with a galaxy of groups, performers and survivors from the 1960s—including Glenn Yarbrough, who joined Alex, Bill and Rick for one more rousing chorus of "There's A Meetin' Here Tonight." Issued by Rhino as part of a 10-CD Time-Life boxed set and on DVD, it is the last commercially-recorded example we have of Glenn singing with Alex. Elsewhere in the set, the Limeliters without Glenn still make a robust impression with "Generic Uptempo Folk Song," Lonesome Traveler" and "Power And The Glory," and their "Folk Rap" act was preserved on the DVD as a bonus track. In a couple of solo spots, Glenn at 72 is in fine form on "Baby, The Rain Must Fall," even hitting a strong high F at the close, and "I Didn't See The Time Go By" sounds more poignant and wistful than ever. Alex also appeared in an interview segment in which he plugged the virtues of PBS in his usual thoughtful style. Although not strictly limited to the folk revival since it extended its reach into the folk-rock category, the program brought in a gusher of donations to the network from nostalgic folk fans, and it continues to be shown to the present day when PBS holds its pledge drives.

Yet things began to deteriorate in terms of the relationships within the band. "I was not a happy camper in those years," Alex confessed. "After Lou died, a light went out for sure. I mean, Lou entertained me every day that I was around him. Rick is a pretty funny guy sometimes and Zorn has a very good sense of humor. But it wasn't the same at all. Lou and I had a certain intellectual rapport, and we were both Jewish, and now I had two goyem and you know what? It didn't feel so good. Not to be a racist about it in any way, it just didn't have the same vibe. It just wasn't as much fun, traveling in the vans or cars. And that became a big deal." Alex's relationship with Zorn was deteriorating; he thinks that stemmed from a Limeliters/Kingston Trio cruise during which Zorn was forced to forego a family emergency back in England. "During that entire cruise, he hung out with the Trio and their people, and never hung out with Rick and me," Alex recalled.

In October 2002, not long after the PBS concert, disaster struck, for Alex was diagnosed with bladder cancer and as a result, had to cancel his participation in a second cruise the group was scheduled to go on with the Kingston Trio. Alex was out of action for at least six months, but the cruise went ahead, with Gaylan Taylor taking Alex's place while he was undergoing surgery. When he did return, apparently the relationships were no better than before, and when Zorn handed in his resignation, Alex didn't try to stop him. "What I didn't know at the time," Alex goes on, "was the fact that we had been offered this tour called The American Songbook which consisted of the Kingston Trio, the Limeliters, and The Brothers Four that was to tour a bunch of American cities in large venues. Instead of contacting me, the agent sent an e-mail to Rick, who never told me about it and went directly to our so-called manager at the time. This was after the last gig we played together, and I didn't know about this other thing on the horizon."

Instead of the Limeliters lineup as it officially stood in 2003, a different configuration of Glenn Yarbrough, Bill and Rick had been cobbled together to tour under the Limeliter Reunion name that had been used in the 1970s. "When I did find out about it, it seemed clear to me that they had connived to leave me behind and work with Glenn Yarbrough, and substitute Glenn and the Limeliter Reunion—as they wanted to call it—to take over," Alex charged. "You can imagine how that felt."

Beyond hurt feelings about what Alex calls a "bait-and-switch" operation, there was the simple fact that Alex owned the name Limeliters, which Lou had sold to him many years before. "If they wanted to use the name, I would have been very happy to have them use the name—pay me. It never occurred to them that would have been only right.

"I sued them for the misappropriation of a tour that had been offered to my band, the Limeliters, which they had shunted to another entity and tried to use the Limeliter name as a sales pitch. That was a big mistake because I should never have sued all of them; I should have only sued [the manager]. And the second I did that, they dropped the use of the Limeliter name."

After about six months of litigation, both parties settled the case in 2004. "It was the worst event, ever, in my history with the Limeliters by far," Alex says, "because they not only humiliated me, but they stole a tour that was rightfully mine. For Yarbrough to do what he did, that was the worst of it."

Soon thereafter, in another incredulous turn of events, when Bob Shane suffered a heart attack in the middle of the Kingston Trio tour in 2004 and had to leave the road—for good, as things turned out—Zorn stepped right into his role without batting an eye. And when Bob Haworth left the Kingstons the following year, who should take his place but Dougherty! Indeed, the two stayed with George Grove in the Trio until Oct. 2017 when after a new round of legal issues, all three performers were replaced by the new licensees of the Kingston name—including Josh Reynolds, who was the son of Nick Reynolds, Gerald "Mike" Marvin, who was Nick Reynolds' cousin, and Tim Gorelangton. Such are the games of musical chairs in the twilight of the surviving folk groups.

Perhaps the saddest part of the whole tale was the permanent estrangement of Alex and Glenn after an on-again-off-again partnership that had lasted almost half a century. They never spoke to each other again. Only after Glenn was gone for a number of years could Alex again speak objectively and with admiration of his former singing partner.

With all this legal turmoil going on, Alex started scouring around for replacements for the two-thirds of his trio, and the first person he called was Mack Bailey, who had taken over for Dougherty once on a gig in Washington DC. "Mack was a wonderful singer, really a professional, and a really nice man, a good man," said Alex. With a tenor now in hand, Alex then persuaded Andy Corwin, once a member of the clever, hilarious, satirical folk group The Foremen in the 1990s, to join. Alex had been a fan of The Foremen in their day, and when he thought of the tall, bushy-haired Corwin playing standup bass and doing comedy in the act, he thought, *That's Lou!*

"It took me awhile to persuade him," Alex says. In fact, Alex had first approached Andy about replacing Lou just after Lou's death, but the Foremen were still riding high on a Warner Bros. record contract then, so Andy turned down the offer. Eight years later, he was ready to join.

"Lou was an amazing vocal arranger, and that really—perhaps more than anything else—is the signature of the Limeliters," Corwin said when interviewed on Nick Noble's WICN Folk Revival radio show. "And when we bring new material in, one of the first conversations we always have is, what would Lou do with this? Oh no, no, Lou would do it this way, oh yeah, you're right. We're disciples of his, you know? We analyze those arrangements; we're keeping this sound alive."

Alex continued to sing for a while with this new Limeliter configuration, which made an album called *Alive In Paradise*. But the fracas that broke up the Zorn/Dougherty band continued to leave a bitter aftertaste for Alex, both financially and more importantly, psychologically. At last, he seemed to have tired of playing the game of surviving in the music business. "It wasn't any fun anymore," he said. "And when that happens, it's over. I can no longer feel any of that joie de vivre I used to have."

So in 2006, Alex decided to retire to the sidelines from regular performing, and Gaylan Taylor stepped back into the picture as his replacement. Alex would continue to make cameo appearances with the group, and at one point, he stepped in for Gaylan when the latter had injured his leg. But his energies were gradually fading, along with his eyesight and hearing, as he entered his 80s; he confessed that he could barely stand onstage for any length of time, although he could perform seated pretty well. He had to be helped on and off the stage when he made cameo appearances with the Limes and the Honey-Lulus—a perky female trio singing Hawaiian ditties—at Pasadena's Coffee Gallery on Sept. 4, 2015. Yet he sang well, and still had the commanding stage presence and warmth that he had developed over the decades. Much later, at a private party in the Hollywood Hills celebrating Alex's 90th birthday, he reunited for the first time in many years with Red Grammer, who led everyone present in a singalong of "Harmony."

Yet despite his physical ailments, Alex was generally happier toward the middle of the 2010s, especially after he finally sold his often-remodeled house on West Knoll in June 2014 for about $1.9 million and moved to a mostly Latino neighborhood in North Hollywood in the San Fernando Valley. His new home, though modest in size, had been thoroughly modernized before it sold, and it has a big lush backyard for the Hassilevs' five dogs to run free in, almost completely isolated from the working-class neighborhood surrounding it. Since Alex and Gladys spoke fluent Spanish, they got along great with the neighbors who, in

Alex's pointed words, are "the opposite of the uptight snobs who lived around me in West Hollywood." From time to time, Alex was working on putting together a solo album comprised of old Limeliters cuts and new vocals from his home studio—a Best of Hassilev compilation with special emphasis upon his own songs—plus more compilations of vintage Limeliters tracks from all periods.

About the Limeliters' legacy, Alex was less than sanguine in his 80s. "The truth is, when I go back and listen to our work over the years, I think of very few recordings I actually like a lot," he lamented, citing mostly songs closer to the American folk tradition like "Lass of the Low Country," "Jam on Jerry's Rocks," "Lonesome Traveller," "There's A Meetin' Here Tonight," or foreign language material like "Golden Bell," "La Llorona," or "The Lute Player." Alex singled out the latter as an example of "the three of us collaborating in the best way that we did onstage, to make something funny, energetic and hip."

Now without any of the original members on hand for the first time, the Limeliters continued to perform and to record, though with less frequency than before. Mack Bailey decided to leave in 2012 to go back to college and get a new degree, and he was replaced by another tenor, Don Marovich. "Don Marovich, oddly enough, is the perfect voice for the other two," said Alex. "It sounds like Limeliters, or to put it differently, it sounds right. I'm thinking they should rename themselves The New Limeliters" (they didn't).

The latest Limeliters lineup as of this writing consists of Corwin, Gaylan Taylor's successor Steve Brooks—a Texan who used to write songs for liberal Texas radio broadcaster Jim Hightower—and C. Daniel Boling—a veteran folk singer and former park ranger who replaced Marovich after the latter left in 2019 to join the Kingston Trio. In the spirit of letting bygones be bygones, Rick Dougherty "pinch hit" in the tenor slot in the interim period between Marovich and Boling. "Perhaps precise membership is no longer that crucial in a folk group that still retains its signature sound from long ago, despite many changes in 'personnel,'" observed the Limeliters' website.

Under Corwin's leadership (Alex retains ownership of the name Limeliters), the group has established a base in Texas, having been named to the Texas Commission on the Arts Touring Roster. Sporting an inevitably different yet still vibrant blend of voices, they performed at the Cerritos Center for the Performing Arts March 11, 2023 as part of a California tour, mixing some old favorites with numbers by the new members—and as of this writing, they were planning joint appearances with the current lineups of the Kingston Trio and The Brothers Four in a package now called The Trifecta of Folk. The waning of the COVID pandemic of the 2020s had opened up new touring opportunities for the Limeliters as the centennial of Lou Gottlieb's birth loomed in 2023.

In the first decade of the new century, when not on the road or at sea, Glenn Yarbrough had been living on Lake Chapala near Guadalajara, Mexico where according to the *New York Times*, he was growing fruits and vegetables to donate to the poor. This sounds very much in character for Glenn, the son of social workers and the founder of a school for disadvantaged kids.

One amusing anecdote comes from that period in Glenn's life. Now separated from his fourth wife, Kathleen Pommer, he was urged to take out a personals ad. Apparently, he didn't take it very seriously, for according to Jan Holland, his old fan from the Aspen days, the ad read; "Old. Fat. Bald. Broke. Looking for a woman to sail around the world with." On a lark, Jan answered the ad and rang Glenn up, and they talked for hours and hours. "I didn't know he could really talk so dirty," she said.

While the flow of new Glenn Yarbrough recordings slowed to a trickle in the 2000s, he did make a mostly-new, always-absorbing album called *Heaven Help Us!*—"a 21st-century protest by a 20th-century guy." The subtitle is a bit misleading, though. Far from being a strident screed of get-off-my-lawn complaints, it may be the most self-revealing album in the entire Yarbrough corpus, where the 74-year-old troubadour plays the role of a world-wise elder musing unsentimentally and not without humor about matters of love, fate, the plastic computer-driven world of 2004, and what there is to like about America. The majority of songs come from the wicked pen of one of Glenn's favorite sources, Shel Silverstein, who had passed away in 1999. The album contains four recycled items, including the infamous "On My Butt" and another go-round for the Charles Aznavour song of regret that Glenn ultimately claimed was "the story of my life"—"I Didn't See The Time Go By." Whether or not that was the intention, the entire album can serve as a fitting capstone to Glenn's recording career.

Alas, sadly, Glenn's performing career came to a close shortly after his 80th birthday when a minor medical procedure went awry.

According to Glenn's Facebook page, an operation in March 2010 at the Mayo Clinic to bring his vocal cords closer together caused his larynx to swell shut during recovery, bringing on the collapse of his lungs and then, cardiac arrest. The surgeons had to perform an emergency tracheotomy to bring him around, and that robbed him of his ability to sing. His career was over, and it took him a long time to come to terms with the loss of his magnificent instrument.

Glenn retired to Nashville under the devoted care of Holly, spending his time listening to his old recordings, learning how to use an iPad, discovering the endless treasure trove of material available on YouTube, hanging out on the sun deck with old friends like Mike Settle and Tony Gottlieb, enjoying Facebook comments from his still-considerable legion of fans. "I was a 'dead man walking' there for awhile," he wrote in August of 2010, adding with uplifting spirit, "My singing days are probably through, but I'm still here!"

As the years passed, however, advancing dementia and COPD set in, and in October 2015, it was announced that Glenn had entered into hospice care. There is a touching video taken on a hand-held cellphone from April 27, 2016, in which a music therapist came over to the house and sang "This Land Is Your Land" to Glenn, who was bedridden and propped up on a pillow. He looks gentle, virtually impassive, occasionally raising his right hand as if to conduct the music, and according to Holly, he was singing along for one of the few times since his surgery, although his voice is inaudible on the video. By May 2016, Holly wrote on Glenn's Facebook page that he had taken a turn for the worse, and at 9:30 p.m. on the evening of August 11, 2016, with the annual Perseid meteor shower about to reach its peak, Glenn passed away in Holly's home in Nashville of complications from dementia at the age of 86, surrounded by family and friends. Ironically, he was listening to a recording of "Baby, The Rain Must Fall" when his breathing started to falter, and in Holly's words "he drifted up and out during the last chorus." The last words of the chorus, it so happens, are "Baby, I must go"—an uncannily perfect exit line.

"I feel like Dad had a wonderful, lucky life lived on his own terms and filled with adventures of his own choosing," Holly told the *Nashville Tennessean* the next day. "I think he wanted to hitch a ride on a passing meteor," she added poetically. "That would be just like him."

There was a surprise for those in Limeliterland and elsewhere in September 2013 when an obscure track from the deep back catalog suddenly turned up in the mainstream media. On Episode 14 of the wildly popular and acclaimed cable TV series *Breaking Bad*, as the character Walter White rolls a barrel through the desert and the credits roll, the soundtrack suddenly poured out the ballad "Take My True Love By The Hand" (or "Times Are Getting Hard") from the Elektra album. It was such an evocative use of this song that it produced a torrent of hits on social media, probably the biggest response to anything pertaining to the Limeliters in at least 50 years. "Wonderful arrangement vocally," Alex said. "Glenn's rendition of it is perfect, that's as good as pop-folk got with us."

Ultimately, the *Breaking Bad* exposure is small potatoes in the general cultural scheme of things, yet it is proof that there is still a place for Limeliters music in the 21st century. The human element in music, songs with roots, the art of direct communication with an audience, the electric impact of performers who possess genuine charisma, all have become increasingly scarce as the digital revolution took hold in the world. The greatest artists of the 1960s folk revival combined all these qualities—and the sudden success of "Take My True Love By The Hand" proved that there will always be an audience for them.

It is impossible for the author to hear the Limeliters or Glenn Yarbrough without reflecting on their personal histories and the tumultuous times through which they've lived. One can hear their history as a sub-code in their music; one can perceive how the years had changed them, or deepened qualities that were always there.

Alex himself eloquently put it another way in an interview he gave to Glenda Helbert of the *Olympian* in Olympia, Washington in 1986. "To our contemporaries who grew up with us, we offer a long look at themselves," he said. "We are survivors, and so are they. They get a chance to remember the past, to look at the present in the form of what we do and to hear a unique commentary on what it means to do these things. As far as the younger audience is concerned, it's a chance for them to see individuals not made by a cookie cutter, a chance to see some individuals who have followed their own path without compromise. Folk music is about what it is to be alive, to be on the planet."

Survivors. "If you're around long enough, you become an institution," Alex added. "We wouldn't mind that."

BILLBOARD CHART ACTIVITY

Debut date	Peak Position	Weeks on Chart	Title
The Limeliters			
LPs			
9/4/61	40	18	*The Limeliters*
2/27/61	5	74	*Tonight: In Person*
10/2/61	8	36	*The Slightly Fabulous Limeliters*
2/3/62	14	31	*Sing Out!*
6/9/62	25	29	*Through Children's Eyes*
9/29/62	21	12	*Folk Matinee*
2/2/63	37	25	*Our Men in San Francisco*
5/25/63	83	6	*Makin' A Joyful Noise*
9/28/63	73	8	*Fourteen 14K Folk Songs*
5/9/64	118	5	*More of Everything*
45 RPM Singles			
4/24/61	60	3	*A Dollar Down*
Glenn Yarbrough			
LPs			
9/19/64	142	4	*One More Round*
5/8/65	112	8	*Come Share My Life*
6/12/65	35	24	*Baby, The Rain Must Fall*
11/6/65	75	12	*It's Gonna Be Fine*
6/25/66	61	24	*The Lonely Things*
11/5/66	85	9	*Live At The Hungry i*
5/27/67	159	14	*For Emily, Wherever I May Find Her*
9/18/67	141	18	*Honey and Wine*
11/9/68	188	2	*Each of Us Alone*
5/10/69	189	5	*Sings The Rod McKuen Songbook*
45 RPM Singles			
3/13/65	12	14	*Baby, The Rain Must Fall*
7/17/65	54	6	*It's Gonna Be Fine*

Source: Joel Whitburn's *Top Pop Albums* and *Top Pop Singles* books (Record Research Inc.)

DISCOGRAPHY

All dates are dates of release. Reissues are listed only if they have a different title than the original release. A numeral in front of the record label indicates how many discs are in the album.

THE LIMELITERS
with Lou Gottlieb Alex Hassilev and Glenn Yarbrough

LP   *Release Date:*

The Limeliters – Elektra EKL 180/EKS 7180   1960

Tonight: In Person – RCA Victor LPM/LSP-2272   12/16/60

The Slightly Fabulous Limeliters – RCA Victor LPM/LSP-2393   8/25/61

Sing Out – RCA Victor LPM/LSP-2445   12/22/61

Through Children's Eyes – RCA Victor LPM/LSP-2512   4/20/62

Folk Matinee – RCA Victor LPM/LSP-2547   8/13/62

Our Men in San Francisco – RCA Victor LPM/LSP-2609   12/19/62

Makin' A Joyful Noise – RCA Victor LPM/LSP-2588   3/15/63

Fourteen 14K Folk Songs – RCA Victor LPM/LSP-2671   8/12/63

The Best Of The Limeliters – RCA Victor LPM/LSP-2889   6/22/64

London Concert – RCA Victor LPM/LSP-2907   12/21/64

Time To Gather Seeds – Warner Bros. WS 1762   1968

Original "Those Were The Days" – RCA LSP-4100   11/29/68
    (same as LSP 2547, delete Die Gedanken Sind Frei)

Their First Historic Album – Legacy (S) 113   1970
    (same as EKS 7180, delete Gari Gari, Take My True Love By The Hand)

This Train: A Folk Song Festival – RCA Camden ACL1-0602   7/24/74
    (same as LSP 2512)

Reunion – Stax STS-5513   1974

The Limeliters Reunion Volume 1 – Brass Dolphin BDR 2201   1976

The Limeliters Reunion Volume 2 – Brass Dolphin BDR 2202   1976

Pure Gold – RCA ANL1-2336   6/77

The Best Of The Limeliters – TeeVee/RCA DVL1-0442   1980
    (different lineup than LPM/LSP-2889)

The Lost Limeliter Album – West Knoll WK1008CS (cassette only)   6/89
    (same as STS-5513)

CD

Joy Across the Land – West Knoll WK 1012-CD   11/91

36 All-Time Greatest Hits
 – 3-BMG Special Products/GSC Music DRC3-1832   1997

The Chicago Tapes: First Set, August 13, 1976 – Folk Era FE1458CD   2000

The Chicago Tapes: Second Set, August 13, 1976 – Folk Era FE1459CD   2000

The Complete RCA Singles Collection – Tarragon TARCD-1071
 and BMG Special Products DRC-12407 (Tracks 15-18 w. Ernie Sheldon)   2000

45 RPM SINGLE

Charlie, The Midnight Marauder/The Hammer Song
 – Elektra EKSN-45-8   1960

A Dollar Down/When Twice The Moon Has Come And Gone
 – RCA Victor 47-7859 (picture sleeve)   3/7/61

Paco Peco/A Hundred Years Ago – RCA Victor 47-7913   7/3/61

Milk And Honey/Red Roses And White Wine – RCA Victor 47-7942   9/19/61

Jonah/Just An Honest Mistake – RCA Victor 47-7966   11/14/61

I Had A Mule/The Riddle Song – RCA Victor 47-8069   7/24/62

Who Will Buy?/Funk – RCA Victor 47-8094 (picture sleeve)   9/25/62

McLintock's Theme (Love In The Country)/The Midnight Special
 – RCA Victor 47-8255   10/15/63

Cold December (In Your Heart)/A Hundred Men – Warner Bros. 7177   1968

The Importance Of The Rose/Time To Gather Seeds – Warner Bros. 7254   1968

Consider It Done/A Pound Of Peaches (Summer's Here)
 – Morningstar MSR-1 (picture sleeve)   Spring 1973

I See America/Holy Creation – Stax 0185   11/73

COMPACT 33 SINGLE

A Dollar Down/When Twice The Moon Has Come And Gone
 – RCA Victor 37-7859   3/7/61

Paco Peco/A Hundred Years Ago – RCA Victor 37-7913   7/3/61

Milk And Honey/Red Roses And White Wine – RCA Victor 37-7942   9/19/61

Jonah/Just An Honest Mistake – RCA Victor 37-7966   11/14/61

COMPACT 33 DOUBLE

Tonight: In Person – RCA Victor LPC-132 (cardboard picture sleeve)   5/15/61
 (with Hey Li Lee Li Lee; Rumania, Rumania)

VARIOUS ARTIST LP

The Folk Scene (Limeliters on "Greenland Fisheries") – Elektra SMP-6   1962

Cruisin' 1964 (Limeliters on Coca Cola commercial) – INCM 2009   1973

Winners! The American Song Festival – Buddah BDS 5624   1974
 (Limeliters on "Everybody Wants to Go To Heaven")

THE LIMELITERS
with Lou Gottlieb. Alex Hassilev and Ernie Sheldon

LP

More Of Everything – RCA Victor LPM/LSP-2844　　　　　　3/64

Leave It To The Limeliters – RCA Victor LPM/LSP-2906　　　7/20/64

The Limeliters Look At Love … In Depth – RCA Victor LPM/LSP-3385　6/21/65

45 RPM SINGLE

A Casinha Pequenina/No Man Is An Island – RCA Victor 47-8361　　4/8/64

Rose/Seventeen Wives – RCA Victor 47-8535　　　　　　　　3/16/65

THE LIMELITERS
with Lou Gottlieb Alex Hassilev, Red Grammer and John David

LP

Alive! In Concert, Volume 1
　– GNP Crescendo GNPS-2188 or West Knoll WK1001　　　1986

Alive! In Concert, Volume 2
　– GNP Crescendo GNPS-2190 or West Knoll WK1002　　　1986

45 RPM SINGLE

Right From The Start/American Tour – West Knoll WK-1001　　1985

Beautiful Fantasy/Heart Full Of Love – West Knoll WK-1002　　1985

CASSETTE

Potpourri – West Knoll WK1009CS (rec. 1981-89)　　　　　8/89

CD

Harmony! – Folk Era FE2056CD or West Knoll WK 1006　　1987

Singing For The Fun – West Knoll WK1010　　　　　　12/1/89

A Mighty Day! – RTG 1201-2　　　　　　　　　　　　5/90
　(Rick Dougherty on title track, Red Grammer on all others)

THE LIMELITERS
with Lou Gottlieb, Alex Hassilev, Rick Dougherty

CASSETTE

Global Carnival – West Knoll WK 1014CS　　　　　　　1992

CD

An Evening With The Chad Mitchell Trio And Friends
　– Medium Rare Records MR002 (Limeliters on tracks 12-15)　　1996

THE LIMELITERS
with Alex Hassilev, Bill Zorn, Rick Dougherty

CD

Until We Get It Right! – GNP Crescendo GNPD 2266   2000

This Land Is Your Land: The Folk Years – 10-Time-Life M18903-B   2002
(with Glenn Yarbrough and many other performers)

THE LIMELITERS
with Alex Hassilev, Andy Corwin, Mack Bailey

CD

Live In Paradise – Limeliter Music   2004

THE LIMELITERS
with Andy Corwin, Mack Bailey, Gaylan Taylor

CD

Right From The Start – Limeliter Music   2007
(with Alex Hassilev on tracks 11-14)

THE LIMELITERS
with Andy Corwin, Gaylan Taylor, Don Marovich

CD

Pass The Music On – Limeliter Music   2013

THE LIMELITERS
with Andy Corwin, Don Marovich, Steve Brooks

CD

Turnin' 60 – Limeliter Music   2018

THE LIMELITERS
with Andy Corwin, Steve Brooks, Daniel Bolling

CD

Live Tracks – Limeliter Music   2020

The Cutting Edge Of Passé – Limeliter Music   2022

LOU GOTTLIEB

CASSETTE

Lucky Lou – West Knoll WK 1005   1987

LOU GOTTLIEB
with The Gateway Singers

LP

Puttin' On The Style – Decca DL 8413	1/4/57
Live At The hungry i – Decca DL 8671	2/10/58

CD

Live At Stanford 1957 – 2-Folk Era FE1480CD	2009

45 RPM SINGLE

Puttin' On The Style/The Midnight Special – Decca 9-29972	8/13/56
Bury Me In My Overalls/Monaco – Decca 9-30088	10/22/56
Roving Gambler/This Little Light Of Mine – Decca 9-30510	1957

78 RPM SINGLE

Puttin' On The Style/The Midnight Special – Decca 29972	8/13/56

ALEX HASSILEV

LP

Man Of The World – RCA Victor LPM/LSP-2911	11/23/64
Affairs Of The Heart – RCA Victor LPM/LSP–3434	9/20/65
Lieder der Völker (Songs Of The People) (with Theodore Bikel) – Bayerischer Rundfunk	1968
…Roots (Quincy Jones) (Alex on "Middle Passage") – A&M SP-4626	1/77

45 RPM SINGLE

Young Man/Dear Love – RCA Victor 47-8630	7/6/65

CD

Hassilev, Settle and Guard (with Mike Settle and Dave Guard) – (rec. 1974)	to be released

GLENN YARBROUGH

LP

Come Sit By My Side – Tradition TLP 1019	Summer 1957
Glenn Yarbrough (aka Here We Go, Baby) – Elektra EKL 135	Fall 1957
Marilyn Child And Glenn Yarbrough Sing Folk Songs – Elektra EKL 143	Winter 1958
Time To Move On – RCA Victor LPM/LSP-2836	1/20/64
One More Round – RCA Victor LPM/LSP- 2905	6/25/64

Come Share My Life – RCA Victor LPM/LSP-3301   2/22/65

Baby, The Rain Must Fall – RCA Victor LPM/LSP-3422   5/17/65

It's Gonna Be Fine – RCA Victor LPM/LSP-3472   9/20/65

The Lonely Things – RCA Victor LPM/LSP-3539   4/25/66

Live At The hungry i – RCA Victor LPM/LSP-3661   9/19/66

For Emily, Wherever I May Find Her – RCA Victor LPM/LSP-3801   4/10/67

Best – Tradition 2054 *(presumably same as TLP 1019)*   1967

Honey And Wine – RCA Victor LPM/LSP-3860   7/24/67

The Bitter And The Sweet – RCA Victor LPM/LSP-3951   1/22/68

Let The World Go By – RCA Victor LPM/LSP-3983   5/20/68

Each Of Us Alone – Warner Bros. WS 1736   9/68

We Survived The Madness – RCA Victor LSP-4047   10/25/68

Glenn Yarbrough Sings The Rod McKuen Songbook – 2-RCA VPS-6018   4/69

Somehow, Someway – Warner Bros. WS 1782   5/69

Yarbrough Country – Warner Bros. WS 1817   11/69

Let Me Choose Life – Warner Bros. WS 1832   1970

Jubilee – Warner Bros. WS 1876   1970

The Best Of Glenn Yarbrough – RCA LSP-4349   5/70

Looking Back – Tradition 2095 (same as TLP 1019)   1970

Bend Down And Touch Me – Warner Bros. WS 1911   1971

Glenn Yarbrough And The Havenstock River Band – Impress IMPS 1612   1971

Kaleidoscope: Glenn Yarbrough Sings Rod McKuen
    – 2-Stanyan 2 SR 10098   1974

My Sweet Lady – Stax STS 5506   1974

The Hobbit: Original Soundtrack – Buena Vista 5007   1977

Easy Now – Brass Dolphin BDR 2203   1977

Live At Doug Weston's Troubadour – 2-Brass Dolphin BDR 2204   1978

Just A Little Love – First American FA 7766   1981

Stay With Me – A&M SP 9084 (Canada)   1983

Most Loved Songs – 2-Suffolk Marketing SMI 1-434   1983

Sentimental Favorites And Treasury Of Love Songs – 2-Suffolk Marketing 63   1985

Love For Life – CMS C1700 *(cassette only)*   1987

Divine Love – CMS 1701   1987

CD

I Could Have Been A Sailor – CMS 1702	1991
Glenn Yarbrough Live – CMS 1704	1991
Michael McLean's The Forgotten Carols – 2-Calabasas CL 62181-2	1991
Christmas With Glenn Yarbrough – CMS 1705	1992
Dreamland – Kids USA Music KUSA 012	1993
Family Portrait (with Holly Yarbrough) – Folk Era FE1416CD	1994
Chantyman – Calabasas CL 62184	1995
Live At Harrah's Reno – 2-Calabasas CL 62185-2	1995
All-Time Favorites, Volume 1 – Calabasas CL 16287-2	1996
All-Time Favorites, Volume 2 – Calabasas CL 16288-2	1996
Glenn And Holly Yarbrough Sing Annie Get Your Gun – Folk Era FE1706CD	7/9/97
36 All-Time Greatest Hits – 3-BMG Special Products/GSC Music DRC3-2061-1	1998
The Day The Tall Ships Came (with The Shaw Brothers) – Folk Era FE1455CD	2000
The San Francisco Tapes – First Set – Folk Era FE1462CD	2001
The San Francisco Tapes - Second Set – Folk Era FE1463CD	2001
Heaven Help Us! – Folk Era FE1716CD	2004
No One Is Alone (with Holly Yarbrough) – Realtrue/Folk Era RT1475CD	2005
Ain't You Glad You're Still Livin' – 4-Folk Era	2014

78 RPM SINGLE

Follow The Drinking Gourd/The Reaper's Ghost – Stratford ST-3	1951

45 RPM SINGLE

Here We Go, Baby/All My Sorrows – Elektra EKSN 45-2	1957
The Honey Wind Blows/San Francisco Bay Blues – RCA Victor 47-8366	6/3/64
Jenny's Gone And I Don't Care/An Acre Of Gal To A Foot Of Ground – RCA Victor 47-8447	10/6/64
Baby, The Rain Must Fall/I've Been To Town – RCA Victor 47-8498 (picture sleeve)	1/9/65
It's Gonna Be Fine/She – RCA Victor 47-8619	6/22/65
Baby, The Rain Must Fall/The Honey Wind Blows – RCA Victor Gold Standard 447-0740	10/19/65
A Hand To Hold At Christmas/Simple Gifts (Rod McKuen) – Stanyan Music Co. ST34-1	1965
Ain't No Way/You Can't Ever Go Home Again – RCA Victor 47-8745	1/4/66
The Lonely Things/Channing Way – RCA Victor 47-8796 (picture sleeve)	3/22/66

Spin Spin/Love Are Wine – RCA Victor 47-9019 — 11/15/66

Gently Here Beside Me/Golden Under the Sun – RCA Victor 47-9187 — 4/18/67

Honey And Wine/Ain't You Glad You're Livin.' Joe
 – RCA Victor 47-9309 — 8/29/67

Face In The Crowd/Times Gone By – RCA Victor 47- 9452 — 1/30/68

Until You Happened To Pass By/Downtown L.A – Warner Bros. 7196 — 6/68

Charlie And Me (both sides) (from the film "Travels With Charley")
 – Warner Bros. PRO 275 (promo only) — 1968

Let Me Choose Life/I'll Catch The Sun – Warner Bros. 7247 — 12/68

Somehow, Someway (I'm Gonna Get To You)/Child Of The Night Time
 – Warner Bros. 7269 — 2/69

(Don't Let The Sun Set On You) In Tulsa/Wisconsin – Warner Bros. 7335 — 9/69

Goodbye Girl/Sunshine Fields Of Love – Warner Bros. 7382 — 2/70

Jubilee/I Wish I Knew How It Would Feel To Be Free – Warner Bros. 7427 — 9/70

Gentle Hands And Gentle People/Friend Of Jesus – Warner Bros. 7448 — 11/70

The Ivy That Clings To The Wall/Lonesome Cities – Warner Bros. 7478 — 4/71

Friend Of Jesus/Colorado Exile – Impress IMP-710 — 1971

Annie's Going To Sing Her Song/Easy Now – Impress IMP-714 — 1971

Back Roads/Back Roads (instrumental) – Pride PR 1020 — 12/72

Everyone's Reaching Out For Someone//Freedom To Stay – Stax 0204 — 3/74

Mary Makes Magic/Ride This Road – Stax 0225 — 8/74

A Good Woman Likes To Drink With The Boys/She Believes In Me
 – Brass Dolphin BDR 0022 — 1977

She Touched Me (mono and stereo) – First American FA-122 — 1981

Sailin'/(Tryin' To Get) Close To You – First American FA-125 — 1981

If You're Gonna Leave (Why Don't You Get Going)/Just A Matter Of Time
 – A&M 548 (Canada) — 1981

Fools Make Dreams Come True/Stay With Me – A&M 640 (Canada) — 1983

Ways Of Love (with Hildegard Knef)/Ways Of Love (instrumental)
 – Jupiter 887-171-2 (West Germany) (picture sleeve) — 1987

Baby. The Rain Must Fall/It's Gonna Be Fine
 – Collectables 4563 (from RCA Victor originals) — 1987

CASSETTE SINGLE

Rock Me Grandpa/Grandma's Last Letter – CMS 1703CD — 1991

CD SINGLE

On My Butt/Rock Me Grandpa/Southern Pine – Calabasas CAL 62180-2 — 1993

America-America (with The Kingston Trio) - Folk Era FE1776CD — 2005

INDEX

About the Author

Music critic, lecturer, and program annotator Richard S. Ginell is a frequent contributor to the *Los Angeles Times, San Francisco Classical Voice, Musical America,* and *Classical Voice North America*, the latter for which he is currently West Coast regional editor.

Ginell was chief music critic of the *Los Angeles Daily News* for 12 years, where his beat included classical music, jazz, folk, and home audio. He wrote over 1,600 reviews, essays and bios for the *All-Music Guide*, and his work has appeared in many publications, including *The Gramophone, Variety, Chicago Tribune, Montreal Gazette, Emmy magazine,* and *The Strad*.

He has written program notes for the Metropolitan Opera, Lincoln Center, and Los Angeles Opera; liner notes for Verve, Telarc, Naxos and Fantasy; and contributed a dozen discographical essays to *The Essential Listening Companion: Classical Music* (Backbeat Books). He also plays keyboards and drums, and curates an extensive collection of recordings in all genres.

He currently lives in Frazier Park, California.

Photo: Richard S. Ginell standing behind Alex Hassilev, 2019
Photo by Gladys Hassilev

* 9 7 9 8 2 1 8 2 8 6 6 8 2 *